REQUIREMENTS ANALYSIS

From Business Views to Architecture

David C. Hay

ISBN 0-13-028228-6

9 780130 282286

90000

PRENTICE HALL PTR
UPPER SADDLE RIVER, NJ 07458
WWW.PHPTR.COM

Library of Congress Cataloging-in-Publication Data

A catalog record for this book can be obtained from the Library of Congress

Editorial/Production Supervision: *Donna Cullen-Dolce*
Cover Design Director: *Jerry Votta*
Cover Design: *Anthony Gemmellaro*
Manufacturing Manager: *Alexis R. Heydt-Long*
Executive Editor: *Greg Doench*
Editorial Assistant: *Brandt Kenna*
Marketing Manager: *Debby van Dijk*

© 2003 by David C. Hay
Published by Pearson Education, Inc., Publishing as Prentice Hall PTR
Upper Saddle River, New Jersey 07458

Prentice Hall books are widely used by corporations and government agencies for training, marketing, and resale.

For information regarding corporate and government bulk discounts please contact:
Corporate and Government Sales (800) 382-3419 or corpsales@pearsontechgroup.com

Or write: Prentice Hall PTR, Corporate Sales Dept., One Lake Street, Upper Saddle River, NJ 07458

Printed in the United States of America
10 9 8 7 6 5 4 3

ISBN 0-13-028228-6

Pearson Education LTD.
Pearson Education Australia PTY, Limited
Pearson Education Singapore, Pte. Ltd.
Pearson Education North Asia Ltd.
Pearson Education Canada, Ltd.
Pearson Educación de Mexico, S.A. de C.V.
Pearson Education—Japan
Pearson Education Malaysia, Pte. Ltd.

To my dear Jola, the fabric of my life

Contents

CHAPTER   3

Column One: Data   57

CHAPTER 5

Column Four: People and Organizations   199

APPENDIX   A

APPENDIX   B

APPENDIX   C

APPENDIX   D

Foreword

Once upon a time, my son was five years old. Like most five-year-old children, he was very curious about the world around him. As I was reading Dave's book, one of my son's curious moments came to mind. While our family was cruising in a small boat, he questioned how it was possible for the boat to float in the water, instead of sinking to the bottom of the bay.

To put this moment of childhood curiosity into proper context, it is important to know that my husband is a civil engineer by background. I am a mathematician by training. So, this is exactly the kind of question we enjoy pursuing with our children. In fact, our enthusiasm for my son's question led to our brilliantly delivered revelation of Archimedes Principle, complete with an explanation of its input and output parameters.

Now, those of you who are familiar with five-year-old children already know how this turned out. Not only did my son begin to squirm immediately, but also he was quite unimpressed with Archimedes. Rather, he was interested only in knowing whether something about the boat made it float in the water, or whether it was something about the water that pushed on the boat.

This was one of those puzzling parenting moments. We were speechless. What kind of question is this? Indeed, what kind of answer does it deserve?

Of course, John Zachman's Framework provides insight into the source of our confusion. John's framework teaches us that there are as many as six different perspectives of the same phenomenon. The business expert sees the world differently from the information architect, who in turn sees things differently from the system designer. More importantly, each perspective is legitimate in its own right.

Typically, a spectator views the boat's behavior in terms of the perspective that is most intuitive to that spectator. It was painfully obvious that my son felt most comfortable with an immediate, concrete perspective, where he perceived that the objects are in control. My husband and I simply felt more comfortable with the perspective concerned with the underlying laws of science (or business policies and parental rules!) that are running the show.

But, both perspectives (and others) were at play in floating the boat, even if we weren't explicitly aware of them.

The confusion over these perspectives has tormented information professionals for decades. Today, with the Zachman Framework as a foundation, we now know better. That is, we now know that if two people discussing a prospective system cannot understand each other, it is probably because they are each operating in a different cell of the Framework. Neither professional is necessarily incorrect or incomplete, but simply viewing the same problem space from a different perspective.

But, the total architecture is the holistic view of how individually organized deliverables relate to each other in a blueprint (not unlike a musical score, as Dave writes in his introduction) and how they interact with each other in the working world.

It is no easy task to create such a blueprint. The Zachman Framework is elegant in pointing out the breadth and depth of the challenge. But, as a practitioner, how do you navigate through it? Until now, you were on your own, but Dave's book is an excellent directory for this journey. Specifically, Dave provides a comprehensive survey of techniques for the Framework cells that defines the path from vision to architecture.

The value of this book is three-fold. First, the book is appropriate for both newcomers and old timers because it is historical and tutorial in nature. Second, the book has something of value for every reader, whatever a reader's emotional attachment to a particular systems development paradigm. That's because the book graciously incorporates techniques from well-known to the lesser known disciplines. It includes proven insights from structured systems analysis to information engineering to object-orientation and to the most recent, a business rules approach. It is destined to become the authoritative source for defining roadmaps from vision to architecture. The book is articulate (a natural strength of Dave's) and to the point. We can be grateful for Dave's opinions on this subject and his generosity in sharing them in a serious, but entertaining way.

Third, and most important of all, this book elevates (necessarily again, thank goodness!) the importance of the requirements analysis process. Why is this so important?

Dave points out that in our business, painfully, we operate most often without a score to follow. We are the epitome of improvisation. Bob Giordano of Knowledge Partners Inc indicates that this is not new. He states, "We have always employed iterative approaches to development. It is just that in the 70s and 80s, each iteration took years and cost millions because monolithic systems morphologically coupled everything to everything else."

Today, the iterative phenomenon is more obvious, prevalent and perhaps exaggerated, with the recent trend toward iterative development methods and extreme everything. Without a doubt, these trends are useful for specific aspects of systems development, for those pieces that are uncertain or that are discretionary. But, is there a hidden cost to sacrificing the fundamental elements of analysis? Perhaps so.

Dave points out that analysis is needed in order to see simplicity, and to avoid the development of unnecessarily complex systems. Analysis is also needed to understand the elements of change. We live in a world of accelerating change and uncertainty. Therefore, change should not stop when the system goes into production. The ability to change should be designed into the system so that incremental change is the name of the game forever, at a reasonable price. Otherwise the business will march in place and possibly go backwards.

You are setting the pace and direction of business change through information technology. You ought to have a score by which an uncertain future can unfold in an orderly way. Use this book as a roadmap for creating that score.

Time has passed. It has been many years since my son's question about floating boats. Supposedly, he has long forgotten the question. Hopefully, he is old enough to have a greater appreciation for Archimedes' role in the boat's behavior.

What is the answer to my son's question? I still don't know because I don't understand the whole picture, only parts of it.

But, if I wanted to know the answer to my son's question, I could find the answer in the score or blueprint.

It would all be so elegant. It would also seem simple because someone took the time to make it so. As you can see, the score or blueprint is a valuable investment because it represents solid analytical thinking. This thinking has one eye focused on simplicity and another looking to enable change. When these two properties are present (simplicity and agility), the blueprint (or score) should stand the test of time. If you skip Requirements Analysis, you miss this thinking. Dave helps you rediscover it.

Barbara von Halle

Preface

The Inspiration for This Book: Object-Oriented Analysis

Object-oriented programming has, in recent years, radically reduced the amount of time and effort required to build systems. A technology derived from real-time systems, it has been successfully applied to interactive, windows-based user interfaces and the systems they support. One of its appeals is that it is highly modular, allowing pieces to be built and repaired easily without major surgery on an entire system. Moreover, modules can be reused.

In recent years the object-oriented community has ventured into the world of requirements analysis. Numerous books on "object-oriented analysis" have appeared, and the UML has come on the scene as a technique for supporting this.

There are three attendant problems: First, object-oriented programmers, like all programmers, tend to focus on the technology of producing programs, and they find it less interesting to go out and analyze the nature of a business. The skills required to do that are different, so they may be less likely to have them. The idea seems to have arisen that object-oriented designers are natural systems analysts, although this does not necessarily follow.

A second problem is that some authors consider requirements analysis an object-oriented phenomenon. Ideas developed from information engineering and other sources are ignored as though they were irrelevant to the object-oriented world. This has meant, among other things, that disciplines which have been important and valuable to the field for several decades have been simply ignored.

In 1991, for example, James Rumbaugh, Michael Blaha, William Premerlani, Frederick Eddy, and William Lorensen published *Object-Oriented Modeling and Design*.[1] This book presented an object-modeling notation along with a methodology called the "Object Modeling Technique", or OMT. The notation consisted of symbols for the same concepts that Clive Finkelstein and James Martin had presented ten years earlier in

---

1. All of the works cited in this book are listed in the Bibliography. For this reason, and to minimuze clutter, annotations will be given only for direct quotations, listing the page number of the quotation.

their work on information engineering. OMT is concerned with object classes (entity types), associations (relationships), and attributes.

The methodology, while it purported to be a significant departure from "traditional software development approaches" [Rumbaugh et al. 1991, p. 146], was very similar to information engineering. Like information engineering, it was based on the principles of "shifting of development effort into analysis", "emphasis on data structure before function", and a "seamless development process". These are precisely the principles that had already been articulated by Messrs. Finkelstein and Martin. One significant difference is that OMT is much more oriented toward an iterative approach.

Deep in Chapter 12 the book does give credit to Peter Chen as the inventor of entity/relationship modeling, and it recognizes that object-modeling's techniques are descended directly from entity/relationship modeling [Rumbaugh et al. 1991, p. 271]. But this is not obvious from the language in the rest of the book.

Modern requirements analysis is in fact the combined work of many people who have been contributing to the industry for over 30 years. The role of requirements analysis in the system-development life cycle is more important than ever, even with the advent of object-oriented technologies. Contrary to what some say, it has not changed fundamentally with the advent of these techniques.

Object orientation has indeed contributed to requirements analysis, but it has less to do with it than some perceive. The requirements analysis process is intended to identify business requirements for information technology, not to determine the technology used to solve those requirements. A properly done requirements specification should be able to guide designers using any technology.

The third problem comes from authors who insist on including "object-oriented features" in the requirements process. "Control objects" and "interface objects" are artifacts from object-oriented *design*, but they are often (inappropriately) described as part of the requirements analysis process.

The fact of the matter is that the process of identifying requirements is fundamentally different from the process of applying technology to address those requirements. It should be possible to identify requirements without necessarily knowing (except in the most general terms) what technology will be applied to address them. The same set of requirements might be satisfied by an object-oriented application, by an application implemented with Oracle Corporation's relational tools, or by a set of COBOL programs.

About the Book

Rather than viewing requirements analysis from the perspective of a particular implementation technology, this book views it as fundamentally an architectural process.

Specifically, it sets out to answer the question: How do we identify and understand the architecture of an enterprise, so that whatever systems we build for it can truly support that architecture? To do this, it attempts to bring together as many as possible of the best techniques and approaches from the entire history of systems development (including some that originated in the object-oriented world), and it will argue the relevance of all of these in developing object-oriented and other kinds of systems.

Merriam Webster defines "architecture" as "a unifying or coherent form or structure" [*Merriam Webster*, 2001]. When the present book describes an architecture for requirements analysis, it is describing the structure of the entire requirements process. The book is informed by the work of John Zachman, who has described the architecture of systems development as a matrix, with the perspectives of the players in the development process as rows, and the things to be seen from each perspective as columns. The various techniques presented are organized in terms of the cells in such a matrix.

This book's premise is that requirements analysis is the translation of a set of business owners' views of the enterprise to a single, comprehensive architectural view of that enterprise. After some introductory chapters, there is a chapter on each of the dimensions (what, how, where, who, when and why) of the two perspectives.

While the book's focus is on these two rows, attention must be paid to the "scope" perspective that puts all our efforts in perspective. Also, where it is useful to our understanding (notwithstanding the remarks above), reference is occasionally made to the implications for technology designers of what we learn.

While, in one sense, this book will cover ground explored by others, it is unique because it describes in one place the full range of artifacts that can be delivered in an analysis project. This should give the book a completeness not found in most. It addresses not only analysis of data and process, but also the analysis of data networks, people and organizations, events, and motivation.

This is not the kind of book that you can read through like a mystery novel. The Introduction and Chapters 1 and 2 provide an overview of the field and should be read first. The remaining six chapters provide both a roadmap and a reference guide. The roadmap describes 12 of the 36 cells in the Architecture Framework and how they relate to each other. The reference guide is to the myriad of techniques that are available for each cell. If there is a technique you've heard of and you would like to know both more about it and how it fits into the general scheme of things, you should be able to find it here.

Note that Mr. Zachman's great insight was to provide a framework for organizing what we know. That we don't know everything equally well becomes quickly apparent when we try to populate the matrix. You will observe as you go through the book that the various chapters do not describe each area of knowledge equally well or equally completely. Indeed, the chapters are of very different lengths. Moreover, each is written in a somewhat different style, depending on the kinds of information available for that column.

We've had a lot more experience modeling data, for example, than we have in modeling locations or even people and organizations. Mr. Codd gave us a mathematical basis for modeling data that does not exist for any of the other columns. For the others, we are trying to establish discipline, but it doesn't come easy.

A colleague of mine once remarked that he would like a book "to assist people like me who don't have time to learn anything that's not new". I would like this to be such a book. It will show you what's already been invented and point you in the direction of things that have not.

It is the joy and aggravation of our times to have the opportunity to be in on an industry that is building itself before our very eyes. At its best, this book is no more than a snapshot of what we know in the year 2002 of the modern era. With luck, future editions will have a great deal to add. The homework assignment for every reader of this book is to be diligent in expanding this body of knowledge.

The Important Stuff

Arguments about which technique is better are not what this book is about. It attempts to present a wide range of techniques and asks you to choose the best ones for your particular situation. So far in our history, the most models are available for modeling data and modeling activities. The most important chapter here, however, is not about modeling either of those. Chapter 6 is about understanding people and organizations, the roles they play in the success of an enterprise, and the importance of communications channels in making that success happen. This, alas, is something that has not been very well or very systematically addressed in our industry.

For this reason, the chapter digs back twenty years to the field of cybernetics, and it uses insights from this field to discuss the communications channels that constitute the lifeblood of an organization. Specifically, it describes the way we use "amplifiers" and "attenuators" (filters) to manage the proliferation of "variety" (complexity) that confronts every business. Managing variety, after all, turns out to be what everyone's job is all about. Buried in the middle of that chapter is an expression of the true purpose of the requirements analysis process:

Requirements analysis is the examination of an organization to determine the most effective amplifiers and attenuators to build. What are needed? How are those now in place ineffective or counter productive? What should they look like, given the purpose and organization of the enterprise?

Amplifiers and filters? What are those? I hear you ask. To learn more about them, you are just going to have to read Chapter 6.

Acknowledgments

This book is more a compendium of other people's work than it is an original work itself. Some of the people quoted have personally been very helpful in assembling these materials. Foremost among these is John Zachman himself, developer of the original Architecture Framework. I appreciate his being willing to discuss the issues I have with some of his names. This also includes Terry Halpin, Mr. Object Role Modeling, Clarence Feldmann, the authority on IDEF0, John Sharp, who developed the clever method for validating data models described in Chapter 4, John Hall, one of the original authorities on entity life histories, and the Queen of Business Rules, Barbara von Halle. Please be aware, however, that any errors remaining in this book are mine and not theirs.

I am also grateful to Edwin Landale, who reviewed the entire book in detail. He and I agree on many things, which made it particularly useful when he observed, uh, short-comings. Mike Gorman and Pauline Hannemann also reviewed the entire book in detail and made helpful suggestions. Beau Cain graciously spent time reviewing the language for clarity.

Spencer Roberts and Scott Ambler helped me address the object-oriented arena. We *don't* agree on many things, which was also extremely useful in forcing me to be rigorous in my thinking.[2]

The Business Rules Group has, over the years, helped me come to grips with corporate motivation and business rules. In addition, Keri Anderson-Healy, Michael Eulenberg, and Dennis Strunk from that group graciously read and commented on various chapters.

My thanks to the people at Aera Energy of Bakersfield, California, for their contributions to the specifics of the project plan in Chapter 3. This is a company that is actually doing things right: They conducted a complete Enterprise Architecture Strategy, followed by a carefully laid out set of specific requirements analysis projects. They understand the techniques being employed and have been enthusiastic in employing them.

Other people who reviewed various parts of the book include Mike Lynott, Anne Marie Smith, Paul Dorsey, Lwange Yonke, Edwin Landale, Marc Danziger, Cheri Howe, Scott Warren, Bob Schmidt, Diane Blaum, Kathi Bean, Roger Gough, and Alan Nitikman.

---

2. "We find comfort among those who agree with us; growth among those who don't."—Frank A. Clark

Thanks to Greg Doench, Donna Cullen-Dolce, and Bob Lentz of Prentice Hall for shepherding the process of getting this book published.

My mother, Henrietta Hay, in her eighties, still writes a weekly column for the Grand Junction, Colorado *Daily Sentinel*. She's a liberal in a conservative town and she takes great delight in stirring things up. Early in my life, she taught me the importance of discipline and clarity in writing, and her lessons have been with me to this day. Thanks, Mom! (Oh, and she did work for the Mesa County Public Library for many years—the source of the fictional Dinosaur Public Library that appears in many of the examples in this book.)

And thanks of course to my dear wife, Jolanta, for her support—and for her editing. Thanks too to my children, Pamela and Bob, for their ongoing contributions to my education.

Special thanks go to Bob for being the toughest editor of all. For some reason, he didn't find it at all difficult to be critical of his father's writing—and I am proud of the results.

David C. Hay
Houston, Texas, USA
dch@essentialstrategies.com

Introduction

A few years back your author attended a dress rehearsal of the Houston Grand Opera's production of Richard Wagner's *Lohengrin*. I was part of an audience of maybe five people in Houston's great opera theater, the Wortham, and it was as though the entire production were being put on for me personally. It was wonderfully impressive.

During one of the more spectacular scene changes, where it takes about thirty minutes for our hero to arrive on stage in a boat pulled by swans (figuratively speaking, at least—the swans weren't real), I started thinking about what I was seeing. In addition to the dozen or so leads, there were seventy-five choristers. The orchestra in the pit had over one hundred players. There had to be close to fifty technicians about—stage crew, lighting engineers, the guy who ran the sur-title machine, etc.—not counting the set designers and builders, the makeup people, the costumers, and so forth. And then there was the Houston Grand Opera administration. Altogether, nearly three hundred people were working together to produce one of the most spectacular pieces of stage work I had ever seen.

In our industry, we're lucky if we can get three people to cooperate. Why is that?

The secret to *Lohengrin* is, of course, Richard Wagner. Some 150 years ago he conceived this opera and documented it to a high degree of detail. Most significantly, he produced the score and the libretto. Every actor, every chorister, and every musician has a script to follow. The set designer, to be sure, has some latitude. In this case Adrianne Lobel based the sets on the surrealist works of René Magritte. This certainly gave the stage a distinctive appearance. But even the stage crew, who have less direct guidance from Wagner, have tasks that follow both from the set designs and the actions on stage.

What we so often are missing in our business is the score.

Requirements analysis is the process of creating a score for a systems effort. What is the objective of the effort? What are its components? Who should do what? Absent the score, each person does what seems appropriate, given a particular view of things. The result is neither coordinated nor integrated and often simply does not work. It certainly does not last 150 years.

Back in the old days, programmers simply wrote programs to perform specific tasks. If you knew what the task was, you could write the program. Improvisation was fine back then. Programming was more like a jazz concert than an opera. Now, however, we are building systems to become part of the infrastructure of an organization. We cannot build them without understanding the nature of that infrastructure and what role the systems will play in it. You cannot construct an opera without a score.

There is an unfortunate tendency in our industry to respond to the various pressures of system development by short-circuiting the analysis process. We don't sit down before creating a system to decide what it will look like and, by implication, how we will get there. It's not that we don't know how. It's just that multiple, conflicting demands often force us to take shortcuts and skip the specification step.

This invariably costs us more later. We clearly do not produce the systems equivalent of great opera.

One main problem with short-circuiting the analysis process is that it leads to unnecessarily complex systems. It is important to understand that, while simple systems are much *easier to build* than complex ones, simple systems are *much harder to design*.

You have to be able to *see* the underlying simplicity of the problem. This is not easy.

Analysis of requirements should be done by people who are able to focus on the *nature* of a business and what the business needs by way of information. It should *not* be done by people immersed in the technology they assume will be used for solving whatever problems are discovered.

Consider, for example, the following poem:

> *Un petit d'un petit*
> *S'etonne aux Halles*
> *Un petit d'un petit*
> *Ah! desgrés te fallent*
> *Indolent qui ne sort cesse*
> *Indolent qui ne se mène*
> *Qu'importe un petit d'un petit*
> *Tout Gai de Reguennes.*

—Luis d'Antin van Rooten
Mots d'Heures: Gousse, Rames [Beer, 1979, p. 301]

If you know French, you will find this impossible to read. It looks like French. It has all the structures of French. But it is completely wrong! It makes no sense. ("A little of a little astonishes itself at Halles"?) On the other hand, if you don't know French but have a friend who does, ask that person to read it aloud. If you listen very carefully with a non-French ear, you will figure out what it really is.[1]

---

1. . . . and if you can't, there's a hint at the end of this Introduction.

The point is, your ability to see the problem depends entirely on your perspective. No matter how hard you study it, if you come at it from the wrong direction, you simply will not see what is in front of you.

The techniques described in this book will show you how to look at problems from a different direction in order to see the true nature of an enterprise and, with that, its requirements for new systems. Then you can design systems that, as part of the infrastructure of that enterprise, truly support it rather than adding yet another burden to its operation.

About Requirements Analysis

How do we capture what is required of a new software product? How do we do so completely enough that the requirement will last at least until the product is completed, if not longer?

In 1993, after spending over half a billion dollars on it, the London Stock Exchange scrapped its "Taurus" project (intended to control the "Transfer and AUtomated Registration of Uncertified Stock"). It had been Europe's biggest new software undertaking. What went wrong?

The problem was failure to do an adequate analysis of requirements. Requirements for the project were not clearly defined, and they were changed constantly by the myriad of players in the project. "Share registrars, anxious to protect their jobs, demanded a redesign of the system to mimic today's paper-shuffling. Scrapping share certificates called for 200 pages of new regulations. Computer security, with all messages encrypted, went over the top. Companies' insistence on the 'name on register' principle, which allows them to identify their shareholders instantly, made design harder. And so on." [*Economist*, "When the bull turned", 1993, p. 81]

The Economist, in an essay accompanying the story of the crash, discusses the reasons projects fail. "Software's intangibility makes it easy to think that the stuff has a Protean adaptability to changing needs. This brings with it a temptation to make things up as you go along, rather than starting with a proper design. [Even] if a proper design is there to begin with, it often gets changed for the worse half-way through. . . . Engineers in metal or plastic know better than to keep fiddling – and so should software engineers.

"The fact that software 'devices' can have flexibility designed into them should not mislead anyone into the belief that the design process itself can be one of endless revision . . . .

"Successful software projects require two things: customers who can explain what sort of job needs doing, and engineers who can deliver a device that will do the job at a price that makes doing the job worthwhile. Lacking either, engineers must be honest enough to say that they are stymied." [*Economist*, "All fall down", 1993, p. 89]

This book is about understanding an organization well enough to determine "what sort of job needs doing". This requires several things:

- A close relationship with the project's customers—ideally via a project champion
- Effective project management
- A known and understood set of steps

Our first requirement is for development of a special sort of relationship with our customers, as well as skill in knowing how to capture and represent what we are told.

The second requirement, effective project management, means nothing other than assuring that you have chosen the most capable project manager available.

The third requirement is a clearly defined set of steps. This is where this book is especially helpful. Chapter 2 describes the steps required for success, and the remaining chapters describe the work to be done during those steps.

What is this company (or government agency)?[2] What is it about? How does it work? If we are to create a system significant enough to affect its infrastructure, we'd better know something about that infrastructure. This means that defining requirements for an enterprise begins by describing the enterprise itself. This book is primarily a compendium of techniques to do just that.

History

There are numerous ways to describe an enterprise: data models, data flow diagrams, state/transition diagrams, and so forth. Many people have been working for many years to develop the techniques we use today.

Structured Techniques

In the mid-1970s Ed Yourdon and Larry Constantine wrote their seminal book, *Structured Design*, which for the first time laid out coherent criteria for the modular construction of programs. It presented the *structure chart*[3] and described what makes one modular structure effective and another not so effective.

---

2. Everything said about requirements analysis in this book applies equally to the public and the private sector. For this reason the word most commonly used will be "enterprise", meaning either a company or a government agency.
3. All specialized terms introduced in this book are shown in boldfaced italic and are defined again in the Glossary.

Mr. Yourdon next collected around himself a number of other talented people who themselves contributed greatly to the body of system development knowledge. Among others, these included Tom DeMarco, Chris Gane, and Trish Sarson. In 1978, Mr. DeMarco wrote *Structured Analysis and System Specification*, and a year later, Ms. Sarson and Mr. Gane wrote *Structured Systems Analysis: Tools and Techniques*. Both books described the **data flow diagram** (albeit with different notations) as a technique for representing the flow of data through an organization. Later, in their book *Essential Systems Analysis,* Stephen McMenamin and John Palmer refined the data flow diagram technique with a formal way of arriving at the essential activities in a business.

Together with structured design these techniques became the industry standard for describing information systems, although their use was limited by lack of tools for producing the diagrams. Only those souls deeply dedicated to the principle of disciplined system development were willing to prepare the diagrams by hand. And once they were complete, these diagrams couldn't be changed. They had to be re-drawn if circumstances changed.

The first CASE (computer-aided systems engineering) tools appeared in about 1980, making the diagramming much easier to carry out and therefore more accessible to more people. Even so, it was clear that by organizing our efforts around the activities of a business, we were vulnerable to the fact that business processes often change. While the use of good structured design techniques made programs more *adaptive* to change, it was clear that it would be nice for them to *accommodate* change better in the first place.

Information Engineering

In 1970 Dr. E. H. Codd published "A Relational Model of Data for Large Shared Data Banks", defining the relational model for organizing data. While the technology for taking advantage of his ideas would not be practical for another fifteen years, he planted the seed that there was a way to understand and organize data which was far superior to any that had gone before. The process of **normalization** is a profound way to understand the true nature of a body of data. It provides a set of rules for assuring that each piece of information is understood once and only once, in terms of the one thing that it describes. Databases organized around this principle can now keep data redundancy to an absolute minimum. In such databases, moreover, it is now possible easily to determine where each datum belongs.

From this came Peter Chen's work in 1976, "The Entity-Relationship Model: Towards a Unified View of Data", in which he was the first to describe the **entity/relationship model** (a kind of **data model**). Here you had a drawing that represented not the *flow* of information through an organization, but its *structure*.

Inspired by his work, Clive Finkelstein created a notation derived from Mr. Chen's and went on to create what he called **information engineering**, which recognized that data structure was much more stable than data flows when it came to forming the foundation for computer systems.[4] He also recognized that the process of building systems had to begin with the strategic plans of the enterprise and had to include detailed analysis of the requirements for information. Only after taking these two steps was it appropriate for a system designer to bring specific technologies into play.

Mr. Finkelstein collaborated with James Martin to create the first publication about information engineering in 1981. This was the Savant Institute's *Technical Report*, "Information Engineering". Mr. Martin then popularized information engineering throughout the 1980s. With the appearance of viable relational database management systems and better CASE tools, information engineering, with its orientation toward data in systems analysis and design, became the standard for the industry by the end of the decade.

Object orientation

As these things were going on in the methodology field, object-oriented programming was developing. Whereas programs originally tended to be organized around the processes they performed, the real-time systems and simulation languages developed in the 1960s revealed that organizing these programs instead around the data they manipulated made them more efficient and easier to develop.

All data described "objects", so identifying objects and defining the data describing those objects provided a more robust program structure. In the late 1970s Messrs. Yourdon's and Constantine's ideas about modularization also contributed to this approach to program architecture.

As business programs became more and more oriented toward "windows" or screen displays, it became clear that they shared many characteristics with real-time systems, so the object-oriented approach fit there as well.

In 1988 Sally Shlaer and Stephen J. Mellor brought the concepts underlying object-oriented programming together with information engineering and its data-centric approach to system architecture. In their 1988 book, *Object-oriented Systems Analysis: Modeling the World in Data*, they renamed entity/relationship diagrams "object models" and created their own notation for them. Thus, for the first time, a ***data model*** could be either an ***entity/relationship model*** or an ***object model.*** Then in 1991 James Rumbaugh and his colleagues followed with *Object-oriented Modeling and Design*, again referring to object modeling but adding their own notation. In 1990 Ed Yourdon and Peter Coad added their object-modeling notation in *Object-oriented Analysis*. Other books added yet more notation schemes.

---

4. Indeed, in the years that followed, "computer systems" were gradually replaced by "information systems"—in the popular language at least.

Then, in 1997, the first version of the **Unified Modeling Language (the UML)** was published by the Object Management Group. It was intended to replace all of the object modeling notation schemes with a single technique for entity/object modeling. This was brought about through the collaboration of James Rumbaugh, Grady Booch, and Ivar Jacobson, but it was in fact based on the work of David Embley, Barry Kurtz, and Scott Woodfield (*Object-oriented Systems Analysis: A Model-Driven Approach*, first published in 1992). The UML has since been the basis for yet more books on the subject of object-oriented modeling.

Note that this "object-oriented analysis" is not significantly different from information engineering. Both are concerned with entities and entity types that are "things of significance to the enterprise" (called "objects" and "object classes" by the object-oriented community). That is, both view systems development from a data-centric point of view.

What is new in object-oriented modeling is the combination of entity/relationship models and behavioral models. In the object-oriented world, each object class (entity type) has defined for it a set of activities that it can "do". This made more sense, however, in the world of object-oriented programming, where the object and the behavior were both bits of program code. The activities of an enterprise are often far more complex than can be described on an entity-type by entity-type basis. The idea is not unreasonable, but it cannot readily be done with a kind of pseudocode typically associated with object classes. Behavior of entities in analysis is better described with a technique called "entity life histories". (See Chapter 7.)

From Analysis to Design

It is important not to confuse requirements analysis with system design. Analysis is concerned solely with what some call the **problem space** or the **universe of discourse**: What is the nature of the enterprise and how does it use information? Design, in the **solution space**, is the specific application of particular technology to address that enterprise.

In other words, analysis is concerned with *what* is to be done, not *how* to do it.

The models developed during analysis must be technologically neutral—models that describe the business without regard for the technology that may be used to address them. This allows the designers to come up with solutions that otherwise might not have occurred to them when the project started.

There is a common tendency for designers, when they are analyzing requirements, to construct the analysis results in terms of a particular technology that they wanted to apply before they started. They go into the effort with preconceptions of what the solution space is going to look like, so they seek out problems they already know how to solve.[5]

The "object-oriented analysis" referred to above is an example of this. The idea here is that analysis should be conducted with the understanding that the solution will probably be a set of object-oriented programs, so the models should be biased to reflect that.

In my view this is wrong. I take this position, you should understand, in the face of considerable opposition. Martin Fowler, for example, in the October 1999 issue of *Distributed Computing* [Fowler, 1999, pp. 40–41] argues for merging analysis and design. He begins by asserting that, however it is done, an analysis model is an artifact constructed by the modeler. "We try to abstract, and thus simplify our analysis models, yet such abstractions are *constructed*—you can't really say they are *in the world*. Can we, should we, be passive describers when we analyze? And if we are not, are we really doing design rather than analysis?"

Of course it is true that analysis is all about constructing artifacts. The whole point of this book is to describe the artifacts analysts create as they move from the business experts' views of things to what will here be called "the architect's view". That is, the analyst will indeed construct artifacts, but the purpose of these artifacts is to describe the fundamental structures and concepts behind the world that the business people see. This is not the business owner's view, and it is not the designer's view, either. The architect's view is of structures and concepts without regard for technology. To move from the architect's view to the designer's view will require a second translation.

Mr. Fowler recognizes this and points out that there is then a cost associated with transforming a technologically neutral analysis description of the business "to the technology we eventually build with, and if we want to keep the analysis picture up to date we will pay an ongoing cost". This is true, just as there was a cost to translating the business owners' views into the architects' views in the first place. But the benefit of making the steps *explicit* is that the process can be better monitored and controlled.The position taken in this book is that the translations are well worth their costs.

If a programmer speaks to a business expert and then turns around and produces a system, he or she has just done those two translations—unconsciously. The problem is that no one is in a position to evaluate the quality of either translation. There has been no publication of either the business owners' views or the architect's views. If (dare it be said?) errors were made in either or both translations, they will not be evident until the final product is created.

Imagine, for example, an analyst who looked at an airline with the assumption that any new system would be concerned with issuing paper tickets. That analyst would completely miss the opportunity to issue electronic tickets instead. (Indeed that ana-

---

5. This is an example of the old maxim, "When all you have is a hammer, every problem looks like a nail."

lyst's client would be left in the dust when its competitors did just that.) The analyst, however, who recognized that the problem was getting passengers on the plane—not the issuance of tickets—would be in a much better position to help the client lead the way into the new marketplace.

What is the cost of the wrong system? What is the cost of a system that is built of technology that becomes obsolete quickly? What is the cost of myriad systems that don't communicate with each other very well? These costs should be considered when evaluating the costs of analyzing requirements first.

Mr. Fowler goes on: "My view is that the key to the usefulness of an analysis model is that it's a communication medium between the software experts and the business experts. The software experts need to understand what the model means in terms of building software, and the business experts need to understand that the business process is properly described so the software experts are understanding the right thing."

In this he is absolutely correct. But that is precisely the point of organizing our efforts around a framework that recognizes differences among the perspectives of the various players. These perspectives must be addressed, and the two translations to get from the business experts' views to the designer's view must be made explicit. For the translations to reside only in the heads of programmers is very dangerous indeed.

The models used during analysis, then, are different from the models that will be used in design. On the data side, for example, entity/relationship models or business-object models must be translated into table designs or computer-object classes. In processing, a business data flow diagram or function hierarchy chart must be translated into one or more program structure charts—and so forth. In both cases, the translation may be straightforward, but even if it is not, there must be a translation. The points of view are very different.

About This Book

This book addresses requirements analysis in terms of two different conceptual structures:

- *The System Development Life Cycle*: the set of steps required to build and implement a system
- *The Architecture Framework*: the perspectives of the players in the development process, and the things they will see from those perspectives

System Development Life Cycle

Many methodologies are organized around the "system development life cycle"—the set of steps required to develop systems. The names vary, but in principle the steps are these:

- *Strategy*: The view of the enterprise as a whole. What is the overall systems-development effort going to look like? What are the overall things of significance to a business? What parts of the business should be addressed with new information systems? What priorities apply to those things?

- *Requirements Analysis*: The detailed examination of a particular area of the business. In that area, what are the fundamental, underlying structures, what are the information-processing gaps, and what kinds of information technology might address these? What data are required, when, and where, for each function to be performed? What roles perform each function, and why? What constraints are in effect?

- *Design*: The application of technology to address the gaps identified during the requirements analysis phase. Here, for example, the data structures become database designs or object classes and the function definitions become program specifications. At this point, in the interest of defining the behavior of a prospective system, attention is also paid to the human interface.

- *Construction*: The actual building of the system.

- *Transition*: The implementation of the system to make it part of the new infra-structure of the organization. This involves education, training, definition of new organizational structures and roles, and the conversion of existing data.

- *Production*: The ongoing monitoring of the system to make sure that it continues to meet the needs of the organization.

In terms of the system development life cycle, then, this book is concerned with the *analysis* phase of this process, along with descriptions of that phase's relationship with strategy on one side and design on the other.

Architecture Framework

In 1987 John Zachman published his ideas about the structure of the body of information that constitutes the systems development effort. In his "Framework for an Information Systems Architecture", he made two important observations about the system development life cycle:

- First, rather than the "phases" or "steps" in the effort, he is interested in the *perspective* of each set of players in the development process. It is as important, he asserts, to recognize that systems are developed by distinct groups with different points of view as it is to see the movement of systems from one step to another. These views correspond approximately, but not exactly, to system-development life-cycle phases.

- Second, he addresses more than data and functions. He establishes a matrix that encompasses, for each perspective, not only data and function but also location, people, time, and motivation.

The framework for system architecture, then, is a matrix of rows and columns, where the rows are the different perspectives and the columns are the things to be viewed from each perspective.

The framework is described in more detail in Chapter 1. Briefly, the perspectives are the following:

- The first is the *planner's view*, which is of the enterprise as a whole. This also defines the boundaries of specific projects to be undertaken as well as the relationships among them.
- The *business owner's view* is that held by the people who run the business, with their particular jargon and technology.
- Row Three is the *architect's view*.[6] The architect attempts to understand the fundamental underlying structures of the business. These structures will be the basis for any new systems-development effort.
- The *designer's view* is the first one concerned with the technology of new systems. The designer looks at the structures the architect describes and the information requirements they imply, and he applies his knowledge of technology to design new systems.
- The *builder's view* is the perspective of the person actually dealing with the nuts and bolts of designing the system.
- The final view is that of the *production system*—that is, the view of the new world created by the system analysts, designers, and builders.

The columns in the matrix represent what is seen from each perspective. Mr. Zachman began with *data, activities,* and *locations*. Then, with John Sowa in 1992, the frustrated journalism student in him recognized that he had addressed only three of the journalistic interrogatives: what, how, and where. There were three more: *people and organizations* (who), *timing* (when), and *motivation* (including *business rules*) (why).

It turns out that the entire body of knowledge currently available in the information-processing world fits into the cells of this matrix. It also turns out that the most passionate arguments occur because different people are viewing things from different perspectives. In the data column, the designer is interested in the design of a database, while the architect is trying to build a conceptual model of the business data. The busi-

---

6. As will be discussed in Chapter 1, the terminology used here varies somewhat from that used by Mr. Zachman. For example, he calls the third row "the information system designer's view".

ness owner, on the other hand, is concerned with the tangible things that come up every day. If they all understand the differences in perspective, they can translate. The people who argue most violently are those who do not recognize these differences in perspective.

The Framework and Requirements Analysis

In terms of this framework, then, requirements analysis can be seen as the process of translating the business owners' views of an enterprise into an architect's view that can be the basis for future systems development. That is, the models and techniques in this book will be concerned with describing what actually happens in a business and with the inherent structures that underlie what happens.

The book will cover all the columns of the framework. Many methodologies address only activities, data, and sometimes timing, but most do not address network locations, people and organizations, or business rules. All of those will be covered here.

By the way, "Un petit . . ." when read in French, sounds a lot like "Humpty . . ."

A Framework for Architecture

The Zachman Framework

As described in the Introduction, in 1987 John Zachman published his ideas about the body of information that constitutes the system development effort. In his "Framework for information systems development" he made several observations about the system development life cycle:

- First, he doesn't look at the "phases" or "steps" in the effort. Instead, he is interested in the *perspective* of each set of players in the development process. It is, he asserts, as important to recognize that systems are developed by distinct groups with different points of view as it is to see the movement of systems from one step to another.

- Second, he addresses more than data and functions. In his original article he established a matrix that encompasses, for each perspective, not only data and function but also location. Then, in 1992, he and John Sowa extended it to include people, timing, and motivation.

The framework architecture is a matrix, where the rows represent the different perspectives and the columns the things viewed from each perspective. Mr. Zachman's original "Framework" is shown in Appendix A. For reasons explained below, a modified version of this Framework is diagramed in Figure 1.1.

The Rows

The rows represent the points of view of different players in the systems development process, while columns represent different aspects of the process. The perspectives are:

1. *Scope (planner's view)*: This defines the enterprise's direction and business purpose. This is necessary in order to establish the context for any system development effort. It includes definitions of the boundaries of system development or other development projects.

2. *Enterprise model (business owner's view)*: This defines—in business terms—the nature of the business, including its structure, processes, organization, and so forth.

3. *Model of fundamental concepts (architect's view)*: This row, called the "information-system designer's view" in Mr. Zachman's version, defines the business described in Row Two, but in more rigorous terms. Where Row Two describes business processes, as perceived by the people performing them, Row Three describes the underlying functions each process addresses. For example, where Row Two saw "Issue purchase order", Row Three sees this as "Place order". These functions are then expressed specifically as transformations of data.

    Similarly, where Row Two described all the things of interest to the enterprise, Row Three describes the fundamental things about which the organization wishes to collect and maintain information. The Row Three "things" are those of which the Row Two things may be but examples.

    Note that, to arrive at this view, it is necessary to examine the fundamental structures that lie below the business owners' views of the enterprise.

4. *Technology model (designer's view):* This describes how technology may be used to address the information-processing needs identified in the previous rows above. Here object-oriented databases are chosen over relational ones (or vice versa), kinds of languages are selected and program structures are defined, user interfaces are described, and so forth.

5. *Detailed representations (builder's view):* The builder sees the details of the particular language, database storage specifications, networks, and so forth.

6. *Functioning system:* Finally, a new view is presented to the organization in the form of a new system.

	Data (What)	Activities (How)	Locations (Where)	People (Who)	Time (When)	Motivation (Why)
Objectives / Scope (Planner's view)	List of things important to the enterprise - Term 1 - Term 2 - Term 3	List of processes the enterprise performs - Function 1 - Function 2 - Function 3	List of enterprise locations	Organization approaches	Business master schedule	Business vision and mission - Vision ... - Mission ...
Enterprise model (Business Owners' Views)	Language, divergent data model	Business process model	Logistics network	Organization chart	State / transition diagram	Business strategies, tactics, policies, rules
Model of Fundamental Concepts (Architect's View)	Convergent e/r model	Essential data flow diagram	Locations of roles	The viable system, use cases	Entity Life History	Business rule model
Technology Model (Designer's View)	Data base design	System design, program structure	Hardware, software distribution	User interface, security design	Control structure	Business rule design
Detailed Representation (Builder's View)	Physical storage design	Detailed program design	Network architecture, protocols	Screens, security coding	Timing definitions	Rule specification program logic
Functioning System	_(Working System)_					
	Converted data	Executable programs	Communications facilities	Trained people	Business events	Enforced rules

FIGURE 1.1 The Architecture Framework.

The Columns

The columns in the architecture framework represent different areas of interest for each perspective. The columns describe the dimensions of the systems development effort. These are:

1. *Data*: Each row in this column addresses understanding and dealing with the things of significance to an enterprise, about which information is to be held. In Row One this is about the most significant objects dealt with by the enterprise. In Row Two it is about the language used, and in Row Three it is about specifically defined entity types and their relationships to each other. In Row Four this concerns the representation of data by computer software and database management systems. This may be in terms of tables and columns, object classes, and the like. In Row Five it is about the way data are physically stored on the computer, in terms of tablespaces, disk drive cylinders, and so forth.

2. *Activities* ("Function" in Mr. Zachman's original Framework): The rows in the second column are concerned with what the enterprise *does* to support itself. This is the enterprise's mission in Row One, the strategies, tactics, and business processes used to carry out that mission in Row Two, and the underlying functions the strategies and tactics implement in Row Three. Row Four concerns program functions, and the Row Five perspective is of the specifics of programming languages implementing the program functions.

3. *Locations* ("Network" in Mr. Zachman's original Framework): This column is concerned with the geographical distribution of the enterprise's activities. In Row One it is concerned with the parts of the world where the enterprise operates. In Row Two it is concerned specifically with the enterprise's various offices and how they are related to each other. In Row Three it is concerned specifically with the roles played in each location, and how they relate to those in other locations. Row Four is about the network of computers and communications, while Row Five is about the protocols and particular components of a communications network.

4. *People and organizations*: This column describes who is involved in the business and in the introduction of new technology. Row One addresses the enterprise's attitudes and philosophy concerning the management of human resources. Row Two is concerned specifically with the positions people hold and how they are related to each other. The architect's row addresses the fundamental nature of human organizations. This includes the actual and potential interactions between people and functions. Row Four is concerned with the design of man-machine interfaces, while Row Five, in conjunction with the activities column, is concerned with the programming of those interfaces and security steps.

5. *Timing*: This column describes the effects of time on the enterprise. This includes annual planning at Row One, business events at Row Two, and data-related events

at Row Three. Row Four translates the data-related events into system triggers. Row Five is concerned with the implementation of those triggers.

6. *Motivation*: As Mr. Zachman originally described this column, it concerned the translation of business goals and strategies into specific ends and means. This description has since been expanded to include the entire set of constraints (business rules) that apply to an enterprise's efforts. Row One is concerned with the enterprise's vision and mission; Row Two addresses its goals, objectives, strategy, and tactics, as they are translated into business policies and business rules. Row Three addresses the specific articulation of business rules in terms of their effects on data and activities. Row Four is about the design of the programs that will implement those effects, and Row Five is about the construction of those programs.

The Architecture Framework

Mr. Zachman's original paper described Row Three as the "designer's view", also known as the "model of the information system", meaning that this row had the first seeds of system design. Row Four then was called the "builder's view", which introduced the technology model, and Row Five was the "subcontractor's view", where the subcontractor was the one actually carrying out the work.

While agreeing in general with the meaning of each row, your author respectfully takes a different view of the names of the rows and attempts to refine their definitions.

"Design" is the set of decisions that determine what a new product is going to look like. Specifically, these decisions take into account the technology that will be used to create it and the relative economics of the technical alternatives. "Architecture", on the other hand, is the set of decisions that determine the shape and characteristics of the desired product. In his original article, Mr. Zachman's analogy is to the field of architecture itself, with the architect creating both the Row Two and the Row Three artifacts.

In Mr. Zachman's view, the Row Two artifacts for an architect are the "architect's drawings", representing "a transcription of the owner's perceptual requirements" [Zachman, 1987, p. 278]. This is clearly analogous to the "business owners' views" of the Framework. The Row Three artifacts are "the translation of the owner's perceptions/requirements into a product"—except that they aren't. They do not take into account the contractor's concerns with "technology constraints". Either the tool technology or the process technology may constrain his ability to produce precisely what the architect has designed. In either case, the contractor will have to design a reasonable facsimile which can be produced and yet satisfies these requirements.

Commonly called an "elevation", the architect's Row Three drawings describe *characteristics* of the building, rather than the building itself. They show the appearance of the structure from the outside, as well as its floor plan in detail. In Mr. Zachman's example, the architect describes the building from 16 different points of view—site plans, electrical system, and so on. Each one of these is describing not the technology to use but rather *what is to be accomplished* by such technology.

The architect is clearly an important player in this process and has a particular point of view. For this reason, Row Three will be described here as the "architect's view".

We can still call it a "model of the information system", although this limits the view of the framework to information systems. In other articles, Mr. Zachman points out that the framework is really describing the enterprise as a whole, not just an information system. It is the "logical (automated or nonautomated, systematic) *representation* of the enterprise" [Zachman, 1999].

A more general term, then, would be to say that the Row Three artifact is a "model of the fundamental characteristics of the business" or, more briefly, a "model of fundamental concepts".

In this view, then, Row Four is the "designer's view" and Row Five is the "builder's view". The designer merges technology with the requirements. The builder then actually produces the product.

One last issue: In later versions of his Framework (including the one included here as Appendix A), Mr. Zachman calls the business model "conceptual", the "system model "logical", and the technology model "physical". As is described in Chapter 3, these terms were originally used by a committee in the Computer and Business Equipment Manufactures Association (commonly known as ANSI/SPARC), in their description of the "three-schema architecture". This book takes their position that the view held by each person in the business is according to an *external schema*, the distillation of all these views into an enterprise view is according to a *conceptual schema*, and the actual way data are stored in the computer is according to an *internal schema.* Later, people began to refer to the structures of data recognized by specific database management systems as the *logical schema.* This seems very reasonable, and would suggest that the Business Model is external, the Architect's model is conceptual, the Designer's model is logical, and the Builder's model is physical.

None of these discussions of terminology in any way changes the fundamental message of Mr. Zachman's Framework, or even its underlying structure. Because Mr. Zachman is disinclined to change his terminology, however, and modesty prevents your author from referring to what is still 98% Mr. Zachman's work as the "Hay Framework", it will henceforth be referred to here simply as the "Architecture Framework".

The Analysis Process

Given the Architecture Framework, then, requirements analysis can be seen as the process of translating business owners' views of an enterprise into an architect's view. This is always done for a specific project, whose scope was defined by those with the planner's view.

A business owner's view is usually expressed in terms of industry jargon and is about the mechanisms involved in running the enterprise today. Requirements analysis must analyze this to determine the fundamental structures and functions of the business, in order to suggest new ways that these might be addressed.

In this book, the models will be organized by column as much as possible, although several of them have implications for more than one column.

Data

Requirements analysis of data involves translating the owner's views of the things encountered every day into a model of the fundamental things of the enterprise. That is, where an owner in one division is concerned with "clients" and "suppliers" and an owner in another division is concerned with "customers" and "vendors", the architect's model will address "people" and "organizations" and the various roles they may play in the course of the entire company's business.

An important part of the process is to capture the business owner's language. What terms are used to describe the business, and what do they mean? What facts of the business are expressed in those terms? This includes dealing with the fact that different people will use different terms for the same thing and one term to mean different things. Such discrepancies should be resolved—or, if that is not possible, at least clearly documented.

The business owners' views of data are here referred to as *divergent*, because there are many of them, and because they encompass many not necessarily related things. The architect's view, on the other hand, is called *convergent*, because it brings together all these views in what is supposed to be a coherent whole.

To the extent that the architect's model may be more abstract than the business owner's view, each one of the architect's artifacts (entities, functions, etc.) must be translatable into the business owner's language.

In addition, where the business owner sees objects in many-way relationships, which are often "many-to-many", the analyst must translate these to the architect's view of one-to-many binary relationships.

Activities

Business owners' views of enterprise activities are inevitably biased toward the mechanisms currently in use. For example, the procedures an interview will reveal may describe entry of data into the current system, transmission of faxes, and the like. The analyst's job is to determine the underlying functions being performed, without regard for the technology performing them. "Cut a purchase order, sending the white copy to the vendor, the yellow copy to accounting, the blue copy to the warehouse, and the green copy to the requester" becomes "Place an order", accompanied by descriptions of the contents of the communications to the vendor, accountant, warehouse, and requester.

Locations

The business owner sees geography as a set of offices and communications points with physical addresses. The analyst examines the roles of each of these locations and describes a functional network of those roles. More than for any other column, analysis of this column is highly dependent on analysis of the other columns at the same time. Where are the data? Where are the activities? And so forth.

People and Organizations

Traditionally, the businesses viewed their employees in terms of the people reported to and the people doing the reporting. In modern times those relationships, along with relationships to colleagues, customers, vendors, and even others in the industry, are all changing. The analyst sets the stage for business process re-engineering by determining exactly what roles are being played and what kinds of communications are required to play those roles.

Timing

The impetus for business is the set of business events in the world and the reactions required to respond to them. The analyst examines these events and translates them into criteria for better understanding data relationships, functions, and business rules.

Motivation

The mission of the organization is its motivation as expressed from the scope perspective. The business owners translate this mission into sets of objectives, goals, policies, and business rules. The analysis process is concerned with examining business policies and business rules to determine precisely how they affect data and activities.

Implications

There are many books on the market about requirements analysis. For the most part, each describes a particular set of methods or techniques. This book instead presents the broad scope of the requirements analysis field, and the Architecture Framework provides an excellent vehicle for doing this. Any particular technique (whether covered in this book or not) can be placed somewhere in the Framework matrix. Indeed, many controversies in our industry arise from the fact that the role a technique plays is misunderstood, because its position in the Architecture Framework is misunderstood. This book should allow each technique to be intelligently compared with others in the same or different cells.

Managing Projects

2

Introduction

The bulk of this book describes approaches to understanding the true nature of an enterprise. The Architecture Framework provides a way to organize the techniques intellectually in terms of the kinds of things being described. Something besides these techniques, however, is needed to carry out a requirements analysis project. We must know what should be done and when. This chapter describes that process. It lays out the kinds of tasks to be performed, including those that must be done and those that may be skipped.

In many ways, the set of steps described in this chapter is the heart of the book. All the techniques, approaches, and perspectives in the world won't help you with requirements analysis unless you organize the effort correctly. Over the years, this has proved to be the single most difficult aspect of carrying out systems projects. There are no technical problems: there are only "people problems".

A successful project—in any area of endeavor—has the following characteristics:

- It is completed within the allotted time.

- It is completed within the allotted cost.
- It is completed at a predefined performance and technological level.
- It utilizes assigned resources effectively and efficiently.

This requires careful planning. Project planning takes time, so it is often viewed as a significant cost—and thus as something to be avoided. The cost of avoiding it, however, is invariably far higher than the cost of doing it.

The task of project management is described in Harold Kersner's 2001 book, *Project Management: A Systems Approach to Planning, Scheduling, and Controlling*. This book describes the topic much more extensively than can be covered in the few pages of this chapter. Here, however, the key elements that are required specifically for a system development project can be described.

As described in the Introduction, effective management of a systems project requires several things:

- A close relationship with the project's customers—ideally via a project champion
- Effective project management
- A known and understood set of steps, based on the premise that we must first understand the nature of the company before determining what kinds of computer systems might help it

The first requirement is for a special sort of relationship with the development customers that shows skill in knowing how to capture and represent what they have to say.

Karl Wiegers, in his 1996 book, *Creating a Software Engineering Culture*, advocates identification of a "project champion" for each project.

> Project champions serve as the primary interface between the customer community and the software developers. They are the focal point for collecting requirements from the potential users of a new application. We also expect the champions themselves to provide substantial input to the requirements for the proposed system. The champions also help to define the acceptance criteria that will be used to determine when a product is ready for delivery. The requirements analysis portion of development is now a shared responsibility of the software engineers and the project champions [Wiegers, 1996, p. 66].

Indeed, the project champion should be part of the project management team—which leads us to the second requirement: effective project management.

Before going any further, it is important to observe that this book is largely concerned with techniques and technologies. The secret of a successful systems project, however, is not the technology or the techniques used but the skill of the people using them. In the area of project management, some people are very good at getting projects completed. Others are less effective.

The managing of projects is best done as a joint effort between people able to manage the technology and people representing a business with a vested interest in the project. Developing a major computer system involves changing the way an enterprise does its business. For such a project to be successful, it must be driven by the business people who will live with it—specifically, among others, the project champion mentioned above.

The third requirement is a clearly defined set of steps for understanding both the nature of the enterprise and what the enterprise requires from new systems. Here is where the contents of this book come into play. This chapter describes the steps required for success, and the remaining chapters describe the nature of the work to be done during those steps.

Defining steps involves the following:

- Definition of phases and tasks
- Specification of the deliverables expected from each one
- Description of the resources to be used

The first two items are very pertinent to the topic of this book and thus are the primary subject of this chapter. The last item is very specific to your particular organization, so, for the most part, it cannot be discussed in detail here.

One comment about allocating resources is in order, however. In establishing the amount of time and resources to apply to a project, it is important to remember the triangle shown in Figure 2.1. In any project, you can maximize at best two out of three. If you want short development time and high quality, it will cost a lot. If you want short development time and low cost, the quality of the resulting product will suffer. If you want low cost and high quality, it may take a long time to achieve it.

If unpleasant surprises are to be avoided, it is important to clarify the project's priorities at the beginning.

FIGURE 2.1 The Trade-off Triangle.

Summary of Development Phases

So, what must we do to build a system? Many projects follow the system development life cycle portrayed in Figure 2.2. The project begins by programming something that looks interesting. Then it turns out that the program doesn't do something else that's important. So we modify the program, expanding it and introducing errors. We then discover that this isn't satisfactory and go around again. This continues until we run out of money or patience or both and the project is given up.[1]

FIGURE 2.2 The Usual System Development Life Cycle.

This approach has been common in our industry for most of its history. It has been given formal recognition more recently under the name the *prototype approach*.

In some circumstances, indeed, the prototype approach can be used successfully. When new technology is being used, and it is not exactly clear what the final product will or should look like, experimentation is very appropriate. But it is important to recognize that experimentation is what is going on. When presenting a prototype to users, be sure to communicate one very specific message:

> This is *not* the final system. That could still take a very long time to build.

---

1. ... or the program is accepted as the "beta" version.

At the other end of the innovation scale, the planning time can also be minimized if a project being built is small and very similar to others that have been built by the same people, using familiar technology.

For projects of significant size, however, the prototype approach is not satisfactory. It tends to yield multiple, relatively small systems that don't communicate with each other very well. In other words, as Edwin Landale wrote in a 2001 letter to your author, "If you have only a few weeks to do the job, if the system doesn't have to talk to any other system, and if the system won't exist for long, then quick and dirty is the right approach."

The important point here is that this approach will not reflect any sort of underlying corporate architecture. A more methodical approach is to start at the beginning of a well-defined system development life cycle and conscientiously work from one step to the next.

A *system development life cycle* is a predefined approach to developing systems, beginning with strategic planning and carrying through analysis, design, construction, and implementation. The specific phases vary from methodology to methodology, but the overall concept is the same: Plan carefully before executing the plan.

Figure 2.3 shows a sample system development life cycle. There are many variations on this theme, but most have approximately these six phases:

- *Strategic Planning*

  Lay out the vision, mission, priorities, and constraints of the enterprise. From this, define a set of projects, carefully setting the boundaries among them so as to make the whole coherent. These boundaries then define the scope of each project. This phase is carried out from the perspective of the planner's view (Row One) of the Architecture Framework.

- *Requirements Analysis*

  For each project, determine the nature of the portion of the enterprise that it affects. From that derive a statement of what is required from a new system. This phase arises from the translation of the business owner's view (Row Two) to the architect's view (Row Three) of the specified part of the business. From analysis of the differences between these views come the requirements for what prospective systems might do. This phase, of course, is the primary subject of this book.

  Note that the first two phases have nothing to do with selecting or making decisions about computers or software.

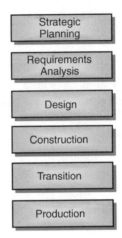

FIGURE 2.3 System Development Life Cycle.

- *Design*

  For each application area defined during the analysis phase, determine the technologies to address the requirements derived above, and define the specific configurations of those technologies. This is done from the designer's (Row Four) point of view. Design will be in terms of a set of system components, each of which will be addressed during construction.

- *Construction*

  Build each component of the new system. The builder's view (Row Five) is operative here.

- *Transition*

  Make the new system part of the enterprise's infrastructure, replacing one or more older systems in the process. This is the translation of the business owner's previous view (Row Two) to a new business owner's view.

- *Production*

  Maintain the system, ensuring that it continues to meet requirements. This involves fixing bugs and adding enhancements.[2] This is a view of the production system (Row Six).

This approach is often called the "waterfall method", since you start at the top and progressively "fall down" the phases.[3] The underlying idea is that you should com-

---

2. Note, of course, that anything more than trivial corrections actually fires up the system development life cycle once again. Again it will be necessary to analyze requirements, design any corrections, and so forth.
3. Presumably one does not actually fall down during the process.

pletely finish strategy before moving into analysis; you should completely finish analysis before starting design, and so forth.

Of course, no one really approaches it this way. At each phase, there is often review of previous phases and discovery of things that were left out. After an iteration of Design, for example, it is often appropriate to revisit Analysis.

As Edwin Landale points out, this makes the process more like a river than like a waterfall. A river twists and turns, occasionally bumping into rocks that produce eddies swirling backward.

As previously stated, this book is concerned with the second phase of the system development life cycle—requirements analysis. Subsequent chapters describe the models required to address various facets of the problem, and this one addresses the specific processes that will be required to carry it out.

Much of this chapter is derived from Oracle Corporation's 1996 "Custom Development Method" and from work with Aera Energy, LLC of Bakersfield, California, but some of it comes from other sources as well.

About Strategy

It is extremely difficult to do an effective requirements analysis project if the company has not done a proper job of strategic planning. The first step in building systems of any significant size is for all involved (from the CEO on down) to understand exactly why they are being built. Ultimately, a system's success must be measured in terms of its contribution to the vision and mission of the enterprise, but this can't happen if no one really knows what those are.

A proper strategic study should address most or all of the following components:

Articulation

The strategy study should articulate what the company is about—to wit:

- *Motivation:* Why does the company exist? What are its identity and its purpose? What are its vision, mission, priorities, and constraints? What is it trying to achieve? What obstacles does it face?

- *Data:* What key performance indicators are used to determine success in carrying out the company's mission? What overall categories of things does the enterprise need data about?

- *Activities:* What does the company do? What does it make, or what services does it offer?

- *Locations:* Where does the enterprise operate? What are the overall functions of each location? Why are they located here (e.g., close to raw material)?
- *People and organizational units:* What is the company's philosophy of organization? Hierarchical? Matrix? What values drive its human-resource activities?
- *Timing (planning cycle):* Is the company driven by its annual budget cycle? What events in the world require it to take action?

Definition

The strategy study should also provide clear definitions for the projects to follow. The *system development plan* itemizes projects and their purposes, addressing the questions: Which projects come first and why? In what order do others follow? This sequence should be based on the inherent dependencies among the projects. Specifically, for each project, the plan should include:

- *Scope and purpose:* What is the project about? What information-processing capabilities is it to create? What part of the enterprise is it to address?
- *Personnel:* Who is assigned to the project? Who is ultimately responsible for it? Who owns the data and functions involved?
- *Performance criteria, key performance factors:* How do we know if the project is done? How do we know if it was a success?

Fundamentally, a strategy study must describe the strategy of the organization, the information-systems components of that strategy, and the scope of the resulting efforts.

An excellent guide to conducting strategy projects is Stephen Spewak's 1992 *Enterprise Architecture Planning.*

About Requirements Analysis

Once a strategy has defined projects and articulated the vision and mission of the overall effort, requirements analysis performs the following processes for each project:

- *Process One: Define Scope:* Re-examine the scope given to the project by the strategy phase. Does it still make sense? Determine how big the project is. Confirm what data categories will be covered, and what functions. Confirm what part of the organization will be addressed.
- *Process Two: Plan the Analysis:* Lay out the steps specifically, identifying who will do each and defining how you will know if each is done successfully.
- *Process Three: Gather Information:* Meet with the people who will own the system. They are the ultimate source of all your information about the company and what it should do.

- *Process Four: Describe the Enterprise:* Use the modeling techniques described elsewhere in this book to portray the six dimensions of the enterprise: *what* data, *how* it is processed, *where* things are done, *who* plays what roles in the enterprise, *when* events take place that trigger activities, and *why* the enterprise is constrained the way it is.

- *Process Five: Take Inventory of Current Systems:* While requirements analysis, for the most part, is not concerned with technology or current systems, it is useful to know what exists, and what roles technology plays in the current operation of the enterprise. While the other analysis steps are being done, this is a good time to take stock of current systems and what they are used for.

- *Process Six: Define What is Required of a New System:* This is the "requirements" part of requirements analysis. What motivated this project? What specifically would make people's lives and work easier? What kinds of technology look promising?

- *Process Seven: Plan for Transition:* If a system that is built based on this analysis is at all significant, it *will* change the infrastructure of the organization. In addition to the mechanics of installing a new system, transition will entail extensive education and training, and it will probably involve organizational changes as well. Planning for this should begin during the requirements analysis phase.

These processes are described in more detail in the following sections.

Process One: Define Scope

The scope of the strategy study should have been the whole enterprise, with definitions also of the scope of each project ("Replace the general ledger system", "Create an e-business", etc.). The definition of that scope, however, may be further refined at the beginning of the requirements analysis project. What is needed now, then, before the requirements analysis process can begin in earnest, is to specify that scope in terms of the Information Architecture's columns:

- *Data*: What things of significance define the scope of the project?
- *Activities:* What activities are to be included in the project?
- *Organizations:* Who will be involved in the activities?
- *Locations:* Where will the activities be addressed?
- *Timing:* Which events are in scope?
- *Motivation*: Which corporate goals and objectives are being addressed.

The strategy study should have listed the basic things of significance to the business—people, organizations, products, and so on. The scope should now be defined in terms of which of those broad categories are to be addressed. The strategy study should also have listed, at least in global terms, the functions of the business. The scope statement for a project should at least be articulated in terms of those functions.

Note that figuring out which entity types and functions are included in the project is not as important as defining which are *not* included. It's better to argue this out now, rather than have some people assuming that things will be part of the project that others believe will not be. This way, if later someone tries to assert that something should be in the scope of the project, it can be pointed out that it was specifically excluded. If you can make a case for including it now, recognize that it will cost the project something.

Be careful to constrain the scope to something that can be done well by relatively few people. If the scope is larger than that, divide it into smaller projects such that each can still be done by a small group. In doing that, however, be sure that the overall architecture is addressed first. Perhaps a data model must be done for a relatively large part of the business, but the detailed analysis will address only portions of it.

There are no rules for drawing these boundaries. You have to rely on experience and common sense.

This process produces a detailed statement of the project's scope.

Process Two: Plan the Process

This chapter, as well as other books on the subject, can give you templates for developing your own project plan. There are many good sources for the definition of required tasks.

Oracle Corporation, for example, sells a product called the "Custom Development Method", which is a collection of manuals, MS Project templates, and MS Word templates. The set of steps described in this chapter was informed by that product, although it is not identical. In addition, Suzanne and James Robertson in their 1999 book, *Mastering the Requirements Process,* have created a very good template for Process Six, defining requirements. Other companies have similar products. Project management tools can be helpful, and there exist commercial templates for these as well.

Your project is your own, however, and fundamentally you must define the exact steps, resources, and timing that will be your project. Among other things, the planning process includes identification of the key users and others who will be the source of the analysis information. These are often referred to in the industry as **subject matter experts**. These are the people who will be interviewed, attend modeling sessions, and so forth. These will be the final arbiters of whether the resulting system performs its intended functions. Ideally, a subject-matter expert should be high enough in the organization to provide perspective, but not so high as to be ignorant of the detailed business processes.

Try to include people who will take a more strategic approach as well as those who are more concerned with the day-to-day running of the operation.

Don't rule out, by the way, selected individuals whose title might appear to be outside the area of interest, but who in fact have deep, specialized knowledge about the business. These people often turn out to be your best sources of information. For example, an engineer who knows a lot about oil refining, or a former technician who knows about clinical research, may be an excellent source of information. Sometimes you can include experienced information technology personnel, although be careful that prejudices in favor of older systems don't corrupt the data-gathering process.

Interestingly enough, a good measure of the size of the project is the number of subject-matter experts identified. If there are more than about 12 to 15, it is likely that the project scope is too big to be practical. It may be worth revisiting Process One to cut it down to manageable size.

The length of the project will be in direct proportion to the number of people involved. Estimate one day per interview, plus a multiple of that for modeling. (This multiplier depends on the skill and experience of the modelers.) Add, also, fixed amounts of time to prepare for and conduct modeling feedback sessions and to prepare the final report.

The deliverable from this process is the first draft of the project plan or project charter.

Process Three: Gather Information

So, how do we go about learning about the enterprise and its requirements? The steps are:

- *Step 1: Conduct briefing.* Introduce yourselves to the people you will be relying on for information.
- *Step 2A: Conduct interviews.* Speak to subject-matter experts individually to learn the nature of their work.
- *Step 2B: Conduct "joint application development" (JAD) sessions.* Alternatively, speak to people in small groups, developing models with their assistance.
- *Step 3: Obtain industry information and patterns.* Seek out information about how other companies in this industry work. A similar project is very likely to have been done before in another company. Take advantage of that, if possible.
- *Step 4: Review the range of available software.* At all costs you should avoid having the characteristics of available software lead your analysis, but it is sometimes possible to learn important things about the nature of the business from the design of software that has served similar functions.

The primary deliverable from this process is a set of notes and sketches, along with a log of who was seen. It also includes any supplemental industry and current systems information that might be available as well as samples of as many reports and forms as can be collected.

These steps are described further in the following sections:

Step 1: Conduct Briefing

Before imposing on the subject-matter experts' time for interviews and modeling sessions, it is polite to introduce the project to them. A one- to two-hour briefing session is an excellent way to do this. Gather together the key users identified in Process Two who will be the targets of interviews and modeling sessions. In this session, introduce:

- Yourselves
- The purpose and scope of the project
- Your requirements on these people for time, and so on
- The modeling process, with enough samples of the technique to get across what you are trying to do

The project sponsor should lead the meeting, and it is useful if one or more executives are present as well, in order to communicate the importance of the whole effort.

Step 2A: Conduct Interviews

Talk to people. Arrange to meet with each of the subject-matter experts that you have identified. Ask them what they do for a living. Do *not* ask them what they want from new systems—at least until the end of the interview. The idea is to get a clear picture of their activities and needs, uncorrupted by their preconceptions as to how a system would help. Have a second person present to take notes. Plan to devote a full day to each interview: the first half to conduct the interview itself, and the second half to review your notes and make them readable.

There are actually two kinds of interviews that you will conduct: A survey interview, typically with a top executive, covers general ideas and perspectives. This usually takes no more than an hour or so. You are trying to get a sense of the company's priorities, objectives, and constraints. A detailed interview with someone in the organization's operations will then take you into the nitty-gritty of exactly how a department works. Here you ask what forms and other information the person receives, what is done with them, what is produced, and to whom it is sent. This could take many hours.

Step 2B: Joint Application Development (JAD) and Feedback Sessions

A *joint application development session* is a meeting of a small group of subject-matter experts to examine an application area in detail. Often this involves creating one or more models of the organization in front of the experts and getting their agreement at that time. These sessions can be used either to get information initially or to get confirmation of models developed from interview notes.

Begin by choosing a subject and discussing the things of significance in that area. Follow the logic of the relationships among them to arrive at a model. If it is truly prepared jointly, all involved will take it as their own.

Note that the entity types first identified may not be the ones finally arrived at. Be alert to patterns in the model, and try to recognize cases where several entity types are really simply examples of a more general concept. Once the concept has been identified, see if there are other examples that were not initially identified.

In each case, identify the relationships between pairs of entity types and verify that they are correct: Is the name meaningful? Is the cardinality ("one and only one" or "one or more") correct? Is the optionality correct? (Must at least one occurrence of the second entity type be related to each occurrence of the first entity type?)

If you are leading a session to develop a model from scratch, construct it on a whiteboard or flip chart as the meeting goes along, based on the comments of the participants. If the session is based on a previously developed model, present it on transparencies and eagerly mark them up. Understand that the objective of the session is not only to create (or update) the model, but to do so with the maximum involvement possible by participants.

Step 3: Obtain Industry Information and Patterns

This is about two kinds of information. First there is the basic information about the industry. If you are dealing with oil exploration, you will have to learn something about geology. If you are addressing pharmaceutical clinical research, you will have to learn the vocabulary of FDA New Drug Application submissions. For cable television, you will have to learn about spots and program segments. Some of this will come from your interviews, but, where possible, it is also valuable to seek out background texts, journals, and other publications.

A more specific kind of information is about how others in the same industry are addressing the problem you are attacking. Are patterns of data or function models available? Check out industry organizations for additional information.

Your author, for example, has published a collection of generic patterns that apply to all industries [Hay, 1995]. IBM has developed specialized data models for insurance, banking, and so forth. The Petrotechnical Open Software Corporation (POSC) has developed a model of the "upstream" oil exploration and production business [POSC, 2000]. Undoubtedly others are available as well.

Step 4: Examine Current Systems

It is *not* a good idea to obtain requirements for new systems from existing systems. Consider that, when the existing system was built:

- Someone from the business community had a set of requirements.
- The analyst interpreted those requirements and transmitted that interpretation to the designer.
- The designer interpreted the analyst's interpretation and passed the result to the programmer.
- The programmer interpreted what the designer said and created program code accordingly.

How close to the original business community's requirements do you suppose the resulting system is? Now it's five or ten years later and you are going to try to infer *current* business requirements from the programmer's interpretation of the designer's interpretation of the analyst's interpretation of what was heard from the business community that long ago?

This doesn't seem like a good source of requirements.

It is, however, an excellent source of information about how the business currently operates. There are data elements captured that are probably still important. The processes may not now be the same (or be desired to be the same), but you can infer essential functions (and important business rules) from the existing processes. In these systems, you also have a lot of information about the data actually being used by the enterprise.

Most significantly, if a system is to be replaced, it is important to know all of the things it does and to know that each of these things is being replaced or is being discontinued intentionally. It is especially important to know how any replacement system will communicate with adjacent systems.

Step 5: The Deliverable

The primary result of this process is not a formal deliverable. It is a set of notes and sketches, along with a log of who was seen, plus any supplemental industry and current systems information that might be available.

Process Four: Describe the Enterprise

The enterprise is described by a series of graphic and textual models. Each of the 36 cells in the Architecture Framework contains models of some aspect of the enterprise. In requirements analysis we are concerned only with the second and third rows: We need models that describe the business the way the business owners see it and models that describe it in more architectural terms.

This book presents alternative models that lie in those two rows. Not all of them are appropriate for all situations. A primary purpose of this book is to present enough information about the techniques to allow you to make informed choices.

Clarence Feldmann, in his 1998 book about the activity modeling technique, IDEF0, described seven basic principles of modeling that drive that technique. Of those, the following apply to all the models described in this book.

- The method must accurately represent the problem area.
- The model must separate function from design.
- The model must reflect all the important factors in an enterprise.
- The model must be the product of disciplined, coordinated teamwork.
- The model must present all information in writing.

Overall, this is a good list of characteristics to help us judge the quality of modeling approaches.

In addition to these principles, Mr. Feldmann said that all IDEF0 models must be graphic. Making all models graphical is desirable, of course, but we don't know how to do so for all cells yet. Indeed, many aspects of the typical enterprise that must be captured cannot be represented graphically. Pictures are good for displaying the overall structure of something, but they are very poor for describing details. Text remains a vital part of each deliverable.

Mr. Feldmann also said that all IDEF0 models must be hierarchical, but not all models in all cells are that, either. (See Chapter 4 for more information on IDEF0.)

Briefly, in terms of the columns of the Architecture Framework, the categories of modeling effort to be done are the following:

- *Step 1: Create data (object class) models*—Identify things of significance about which the organization intends to collect information.
- *Step 2: Create activity models*—Identify both the current processes and the underlying functions of the organization.
- *Step 3: Create location models*—Identify where the business is conducted.
- *Step 4: Create people and organization models*— Identify who plays what roles in the operation of the business.

- *Step 5: Create event and timing models*—Identify how time affects the operation, in terms both of corporate schedules and of the events that cause things to happen in the company.
- *Step 6: Create motivation models*—Identify the business policies of the enterprise, as well as the strategies and tactics they support and the business policies and rules derived from them that constrain the way the business works.
- *Step 7: Present models*—Show the models to as many business-area experts as possible, obtaining corrections and enhancements, along with agreement on the final product.

The deliverable from this process is a set of models, fully documented. The models are described in detail in the remainder of the book, but it is worthwhile to understand the significance of each as we establish a project plan.

The above are described further in the following sections:

Step 1: Define Data Models (See Chapter 3)

These describe the things of significance to the business and the relationships between them. A data model may be either an entity/relationship model or an object model. In Row Two, this describes the concrete things seen by the people running the business, defined in terms of business jargon, possibly with anomalies. In Row Three, the model captures the underlying structures of the business, of which the things seen by business people may be only examples. The Row Three models must be consistent and coherent. This implies two main tasks that make up this step:

Task 1: Create Business Data Model

The first data model describes the objects seen by the people who carry out the business. This tends to consist of tangible entity types or object classes representing the things people see. Relationships may be multivariate, involving more than two entity types, and they may be "many-to-many". There is no requirement for the models to be "normalized".[4]

This task may be skipped, if it is possible to create the conceptual model directly from interviews or session notes from one or more "joint application development" (JAD) modeling sessions. Realize that doing so, however, will put an additional burden on the subject-matter experts to understand and validate the conceptual model. In some companies this is not a problem, but in others it is. At the very least, when the conceptual model is presented, each generic entity type should be described in terms of the concrete entity types it replaces.

---

4. "Normalization" is a technique for organizing data to minimize redundancy. It is described in detail in Chapter 3.

Task 2: Create Conceptual Data Model

The second data model in this phase is the model of the *fundamental* things the business is concerned with. First, this means that certain modeling constraints are applied. If entity/relationship modeling is used, for example, all relationships are binary and all relationships are "one-to-many", following the rules of normalization. It also means that the entity types themselves may be redefined to be a bit more abstract, so that they represent the more generic things, of which, as stated above, the things viewed by the business are often examples. For example, where the business sees CUSTOMER, VENDOR, AGENT, EMPLOYEE, and so forth, the conceptual model sees simply PARTY or BUSINESS ENTITY, encompassing the two subtypes of PERSON and ORGANIZATION. The other terms ("customer", etc.) are actually descriptions of roles played by people and organizations, to be modeled explicitly.

Step 2: Define Activity Models (See Chapter 4)

These models describe what the enterprise *does*. In Row Two, they describe the current physical business processes understood by the people in the company. This will be in terms of the forms, computer systems, and other mechanisms by which people carry out their work. All activities carried out are represented, whether they contribute to the company's objectives or not. Indeed, this may include many activities done in a typical company only to make up for shortcomings in existing systems.

In Row Three, the model describes the underlying functions being performed: the content of the data being processed and the activities required to meet the firm's objectives. Mechanisms are not portrayed, nor are activities that don't add value to the company's products and services.

Chapter 4 contains more detailed descriptions of each of these techniques. Step Two consists of the following tasks:

Task 1: Identify Current Business Processes

The process of identifying the activities of a business begins with analysis of the way things are done now. Ideally, you should begin with a global view of the organization as a whole, describing the players or external entity types that feed information to and use information from it. Once the context has been established, examine each process that comprises this global view, carefully documenting each step, the data received by it, and the data produced by it.

In fact, it may only be possible to work "bottom up", tracing processes from their triggering events, through the activities performed, to some kind of conclusion. It may be that only after these atomic activities are identified will it be possible to group them into meaningful larger processes.

Several techniques are available for doing this. The oldest, the *physical data flow diagram*, uses one box or circle for each activity, indicating within each the agent performing the activity. Each activity may then be "exploded" to describe its component activities and flows. A *context data flow diagram* is used at the highest level, with a single box or circle representing the entire company's operation, along with all the external entity types (customers, suppliers, etc.) with which it interacts.

More recently, *business process diagrams* also show processes as boxes (although some tools permit replacement of these with graphic icons). They line up the processes on the diagram, however, so that each agent is shown with its processes in a row. Process diagrams in the UML take a similar approach.

As part of this task, in anticipation of Step 5, begin to identify the principal external events that the company must respond to in order to carry out its mission.

Task 2: If Appropriate, Create Essential Data Flow Diagrams

Physical data flow diagrams and process models are usually intimately tied to the mechanisms that carry out each activity. To complete the analysis process, it is necessary to separate the underlying functions of an organization from the mechanisms that carry them out. The idea is to create models that are *technologically neutral*.

The physical data flow diagram or the business process model can be converted to what Steven McMenamin and John Palmer call an *essential data flow diagram* [McMenamin and Palmer, 1984]. This differs from the more physical models in three important ways:

First, the activities are described not as physical processes, but in terms of the underlying functions being performed. For example, instead of "Fill out purchase order", you have "Order products".

Second, activities that are simply there to accommodate inadequate systems but do not support the goals and objectives of the organization are not included. In other words, the only activities presented are those which add value to the enterprise's efforts, plus those that directly support these functions.

Third, an "essential activity" is defined in terms of the external events that affect the enterprise. These might include such things as "Receive order", "Receive job application", "Receive shipment", etc. The activities are grouped according to these events, and then the parent activity of each group (which represents the complete response to an event) is considered an "essential" activity. (Internal events, where one activity triggers another, are not of concern here.)

See page 32, as well as Chapter 4, for more information about creating an essential data flow diagram.

Task 3: If Appropriate, Create IDEF0 Diagram

IDEF0 diagrams are similar to data flow diagrams, except that they merge the elements represented on both physical and essential data flow diagrams. In addition to the data flowing into or out of an activity, an IDEF0 diagram also shows which activities control it, and what mechanisms may be used to perform it. It doesn't show external entities or data stores explicitly, but it does provide a much more sophisticated approach to "exploding" an activity into its component activities. Some companies may prefer to use this technique over the data flow diagram version.

Task 4: If Appropriate, Create Function Hierarchy

A simpler way of representing the underlying functions of an enterprise is the *function hierarchy,* also called the *functional decomposition diagram.* This is simply a hierarchical representation of the functions of the enterprise. At the top of the hierarchy is the company's mission, broken into the six, seven, or eight primary functions that contribute to that mission. Each of these is broken out in turn.

Even without the procedures associated with creating essential data flow diagrams, the developer of a function hierarchy should identify the underlying functions of the business, without regard for the technology used to carry them out. A proper function hierarchy contains only those functions that are directly concerned with meeting the objectives of the enterprise, not those required to support these functions because of current technology.

At the bottom of the hierarchy, one level should be clearly identified as the "essential" level, according to the criteria for essential activities described above.

Task 5: Create Function/Data Map

Once the data entity types have been defined and functions have been modeled, it is necessary to relate them to each other. Each function transforms some data into other data. Using the language of the data model, specify the entity types (and attributes) that are *used* by each function. Then specify the entity types and attributes whose occurrences are *created* by the function.

This can be arranged in matrix form, with the entity types representing the columns and the functions representing the rows. Each intersection represents the relationship between a particular entity type and a particular function. The function may create, retrieve, update, or delete occurrences of the entity type. (People typically call this the *"CRUD" matrix*"[5] from the first letters of these four actions.)

Among other things, this is a good cross check of the models. If a function has no data associated with it, look carefully to see if it is really a function. Or see what data are missing from the data model. If an entity type does not have at least one function to

---

5. Note that this is not an editorial comment as to the quality and nature of these interactions.

create occurrences and one to retrieve occurrences, then either you are missing one or more functions, or that entity type doesn't really define anything of significance to the enterprise.

Step 3: Define Location Models (See Chapter 6)

These describe *where* the company operates. In Row One this is simply a list the cities where the enterprise operates. At Row Two this is a detailed list of company offices by location, which may or may not be represented graphically on a map. It also includes major communications lines between locations. At Row Three, this is a description of, among other things, where functions are carried out, where data are kept and used, where people work, etc. Indeed, Location, more than any other column, is intimately connected to *all* the other columns. These models may or may not be in graphic form.

Task 1: Describe Location Network

Where does the company operate? What kinds of things are done at each location? How are they related to each other? One location may be headquarters and others may be manufacturing plants. In one pharmaceutical company, its headquarters is in the American Midwest, where research is planned and ultimately the results are processed. But primary research locations are in several European cities as well, and other, smaller, locations are in other cities around the world.

Task 2: Define Roles, Data-Distribution Requirements

Specifically, what tasks are done at each location, what roles are being performed, and what communications must happen between the various offices?

Be careful here to distinguish between communications required to carry out the business and communications which take place simply because it is more economical to process data in one place instead of another. There was great confusion in the early 1980s when corporate divisions discovered that they could afford mini-computers to do their local processing and did not have to rely on a central mainframe. The problem was that some data were still required in headquarters, but this requirement hadn't been articulated before. This genuine business requirement tended to get lost in the power struggles to gain control over the computing processes. A great deal of jockeying went on as that was sorted out.

Step 4: Define People and Organization Models (See Chapter 5)

At Row Two, these are often organization charts, although even there, organization charts are rarely adequate to describe the complexities of human interactions in an enterprise. More creative representations may be required. The advent of knowledge management has made it even more important to deal with the intricacies of the real organization.

Row Three models of people and organizations are not very well developed in the industry, so Chapter 5 has reached into the field of cybernetics to find a good model of the nature of organizations. Whether the approach behind that model is followed or not, an important step in the requirements analysis process is to recognize and articulate the operating principles that both now and in the future guide how people work together.

Note that only part of the enterprise is involved in any one project. In principle, only the part of the organization that is of concern to the project need be addressed.

Task 1: Articulate Organizational Philosophy

In the last part of the twentieth century, companies' attitudes and approaches to the way they organized themselves changed radically. The military model, based on generals and enlisted men in a rigid hierarchy, isn't adequate to describe the running of modern corporate organizations. This is because people's work now is concerned more with knowledge than with physical labor. People (and the knowledge they hold) have in fact become the most important asset in any company. In the twenty-first century it has become important, to an unprecedented degree, that people feel satisfied with their jobs and that their work is respected. This has required significant changes in the way companies are organized.

As part of the definition of requirements for new systems, it is important to articulate a company's approach and attitude toward its people. What philosophical premises are guiding the way the company is organized?

Task 2: Create Organization Chart, Including Descriptions of Lateral Communications and Roles

Based on this philosophy, what organizational structures are in place, and how successful are they? Who reports to whom?

An important part of the requirements analysis project is to identify and articulate the nature of this organization.

Task 3: Map Organization to Viable Systems 1–5

Chapter 5 presents a model of what Stafford Beer calls, in his 1979 book, *The Heart of Enterprise*, "The Viable System". This is the structure that any self-sufficient system (company, government, biological organism, etc.) must have. Mr. Beer's view of an organization is, to say the least, unusual, and it is impossible to summarize it here. Suffice it to say that his model provides insights into the true nature of an organization's operation. With these insights, it is possible then to understand the real roles played by each part of an organization in a new light. Chapter 6 maps these organizational parts to components of Mr. Beer's model.

Task 4: Define Information Requirements, by Role

Specifically, for each role in the organization, what information is required in order to perform that role? Give an answer not only in the concrete terms of an entity/relationship diagram, for example, but also philosophically, in terms of the roles being played in the viable system. Use cases can be used to articulate in detail how each role is played.

Step 5: Define Event and Timing Models (See Chapter 7)

These models describe the role of time in the enterprise's operations.

At Row Two, these are characterized by annual and other periodic planning cycles, as well as descriptions of the business events that cause the company to do what it does: receipt of an order, resignation of an employee, and so on. At Row Three, these are translated into data-oriented events: recording an order, recognizing the resignation, and the like.

Events and timing play a role in various kinds of models, as described in detail in Chapter 7. The extent to which this is important will depend on the nature of the systems development effort. Some applications are strongly concerned with timing and events, while others are less so.

Task 1: If Appropriate, Create Essential Data Flow Diagram

As described previously (see page 28), Steve McMenamin's and John Palmer's *essential data flow diagram* is fundamentally connected to the events that determine an enterprise's activities. It is the external events impinging on an enterprise that determine the nature of its activities. For this reason, the technique affects both Columns Two and Five, and it is described in both Chapters 4 and 7.

Even if you don't actually create an essential data flow diagram, this thought process can still inform your building of a function hierarchy. Look for the level in the hierarchy where all the functions are responding to the same external event. When you find such a level, the next level up is an essential function.

The significance of the essential functions in the function hierarchy is that they and everything above them are inherent in the nature of the company. That set of functions is fundamentally how the company works—and will continue to work regardless of how the technology changes. Below each essential function the component activities represent the particular way the company has *chosen to implement* that function. That means that these activities can be changed. It may prove useful to perform that essential function in a completely different way from the way it has been performed. This is the secret of business process re-engineering.

Task 2: If Appropriate, Create State/Transition Diagrams

The interplay of events and data can also be represented in *state/transition diagrams*. These diagrams, described in more detail in Chapter 7, represent how an entity type changes state in response to events.

A state/transition diagram describes the set of states that a particular entity type (or part of the business, for that matter) can assume. It consists of a set of circles or round-cornered rectangles, each representing one state of the entity type. Arrows then describe the transition from one state to another. Each arrow is labeled with the event that causes the transition.

Task 3: If Appropriate, Create Entity Life Histories

An alternative to the state/transition diagram that is more closely connected to the entity/relationship diagram is the *entity life history*. This was originally described in detail by Michael Jackson in his 1983 book, *System Development*. It was further described in a 1991 paper by John Hall and Ken Robinson, *Logical Data Modeling and Process Specification*. This diagram, presented in detail in Chapter 7, is specifically organized by entity type. For each entity type, identify the stages an occurrence of it goes through in the course of its life. What causes the creation of an occurrence, its use in various contexts, and its destruction? The diagram looks a bit like a Yourdon structure diagram [Yourdon and Constantine, 1975] and, unlike a state/transition diagram, includes notations to indicate loops and repetitions. Once the structure of events has been defined, it is possible to identify the specific operations that are invoked for each transition.[6]

Step 6: Define Motivation Models (See Chapter 8)

The "why" column of the Information Architecture is about what motivates and what constrains the enterprise. The Row One scope project should have given us the mission of the organization and the specific contribution any particular project may make to that mission, as well as to the enterprise's other goals and objectives.

At Row Two, Column Two, activity models describe how business strategies and tactics are carried out in an organization. In Column Six we see how those strategies and tactics are derived from the organization's goals and objectives. Business Goals include such things as "become the leading renter of used cars", while objectives cover such things as "increase market share this year by at least 5%". Moreover, the goals and objectives also result in business policies and business rules. Business policies and rules are derived from the company's goals and objectives. These specify exactly (well, OK, approximately) how the enterprise is going to operate to accomplish the goals and objectives.

---

6. For object-oriented fans, the entity life history is the way to document the *behavior* of an entity. Pseudocode in an entity box is not adequate to express the complex behavior of business objects.

At Row Three the business rules are translated into constraints on the data and function models, determining when and under what circumstances specified data may or must be updated.

The first four tasks shown here concern Row Two, the Business Owners' views. The remaining two tasks are concerned with Row Three.[7]

Task 1: Describe Background

The heart of the motivation model is derived directly from the strategy study described above. The first task is to restate the *vision* and *mission* of the company, as revealed in that study. This should largely have been done in Process One, described above, but these statements should be reviewed as part of this task as well.

A *vision* is the ultimate, possibly unattainable, state the enterprise would like to achieve. A vision is often compound, rather than focused toward one particular aspect of the business problem. It is a statement about the future state of the enterprise, without regard to how it is to be achieved. The vision should have been already defined in the strategy study and is usually not addressed during requirements analysis.

A *mission* is a statement of the approach to be taken to achieve the vision. Like vision, a mission indicates a long-term approach—one that is focused on achieving the vision. Like vision, mission is broadly stated in terms of the overall functioning of the enterprise. Also like vision, the enterprise's mission should have been defined during the strategy study and is usually not addressed during requirements analysis. It simply provides a context for requirements analysis.

Evaluate the vision and mission statements from the strategy study, and elaborate as necessary.

Task 2: Define Ends and Means

From the vision and mission statements it should be possible to define the ends and means that will be used to achieve the vision and mission. An *end* is a statement about *what* the business seeks to accomplish. It does not include any indication of how it will be achieved. Examples include:

- *Goal*—a statement about a state or condition of the enterprise to be brought about or sustained through appropriate means.
- *Objective*—a statement of a specific time-targeted, measurable, attainable target that the enterprise seeks to meet in order to achieve its goals. Unlike a goal, an objective must be time-targeted, measurable, and attainable.

---

7. The definitions which follow—and which are described in more detail in Chapter 8—are derived from two reports by The Business Rules Group: *Business Rules: What Are They Really?* [Business Rules Group, 1995] and *Organizing Business Plans: The Standard Model for Business Rule Motivation* [Business Rules Group, 2000].

The enterprise's means, on the other hand, are described here to provide a context for Column Two activities. A *means* is any device, capability, regime, technique, restriction, agency, instrument, or method that may be called upon, activated, or enforced to achieve ends. Remember that a means does not indicate either the steps (workflow) necessary to exploit it, nor responsibility for such tasks, but rather only the capabilities that can be exploited to achieve the desired *ends*. Means include a mission (described above) as well as:

- *Strategy*—one component of the plan for a mission. A strategy represents one means to achieve a set of goals.
- *Tactic*—a course of action that represents part of the detailing of a strategy. Tactics are formulated to achieve set of objectives.

Thus, it is important in the requirements analysis to articulate and clarify the enterprise's overall goals and objectives, based on the vision from the strategy study. Among other things, these will inform the effort to understand the functions of the business in terms of its strategy and tactics. These will likely determine the direction any system development project may take.

Task 3: Articulate Business Policies

All objectives, goals, strategy, and tactics are constrained in an organization by *elements of guidance*. An element of guidance is a declarative statement (or set of such statements) that defines or constrains some aspect of an enterprise. It is intended to assert business structure or to control or influence business behavior. An element of guidance may be either a business policy or a business rule.

One kind of element of guidance is a *business policy*. This is a statement (or set of statements) that describes the desired operating environment of the enterprise. This could include anything from "Always treat the customer with respect and courtesy" to "Ensure that complaints are always resolved quickly".

These business policies are the basis for business rules, and they will provide a context for any system development project.

Task 4: Define Business Expression of Business Rules

A more specific element of guidance is the *business rule*. From the business owner's point of view, a business rule is a specific constraint upon the operation of the business. It could affect overall operations, as in "All employees must arrive by 8:00 a.m. each morning", or specific handling of a particular situation, as in "A credit order may not be accepted if the prospective customer has exceeded his or her credit limit".

It is important to identify the business rules in effect in an enterprise, since these will significantly constrain what a prospective system may do.

Task 5: Map Business Rules to Data Model

All of the above are architecture Row Two issues. They describe the motivation of an enterprise in terms of the business owners' perspectives. To translate these into Row Three architectural terms, it is necessary to understand the data implications of each business rule. In a manufacturing plant business rules are seen to constrain shop floor actions. In an information system, however, they ultimately constrain data. The rule to prohibit creation of an order when the prospective customer's credit rating is bad becomes a constraint on the ability to create order data when examination of credit rating data shows a bad value.

For Row Three, the Business Rules Group in 1995 defined four kinds of business rules:

- *Definitions of terms*—These define the nature of a business and how communication is performed within it.
- *Facts*—Collections of terms that assert something about the nature of the enterprise.
- *Action assertions*—Other constraints on how data may be added to or updated in a system.
- *Derivations*—The fact that a particular fact is derived in a defined way from one or more other facts.

Barbara von Halle, in her 2002 book, *Business Rules Applied*, called "action assertion" simply "constraint" and asserted that this could be either a *mandatory constraint* (rigorously enforced) or a *guideline*. She also asserted that a *derivation* had to be either a *computation* (derived from a mathematical formula) or an *inference* (based on a logical expression).

In addition, she recognized *action enabler rules*, which are assertions that if a condition arises, certain actions must be performed (or may not be performed).

The first two categories—definition of terms and facts—are actually in the domain of the Column One data model. That is, the data model is about the terms which refer to things of significance, and about the relationships, attribute assignments, and supertype structures which are facts about those things. Data models can also be extended to include representation of derivations, with the documentation of each captured behind the scenes. Action assertions, however, for the most part cannot be represented in the data model [Hay, 1996]. It is the constraints represented by action assertions that are the domain of Column Six. The tools for representing them, alas, remain primitive.

Ron Ross has developed a notation for adding business rules to a data model [Ross, 1997], but this is fairly intricate. The modeling technique *object role modeling* [Halpin, 2001] can also describe many rules directly. (See Chapter 8 for descriptions of the Ross and ORM approaches.) At the very least, action assertions should be described in natural language as part of the documentation that accompanies an entity/relationship model. Even when natural language is used, identifying patterns of business rules can be useful in organizing them [Brenner, *et al*, 2002].

Note that when we describe the domain of Column One as being facts and definitions, we are characterizing it as a representation of the *structure* of the organization. These definitions and facts are fundamental truths about the enterprise. The action assertions, on the other hand, are in response to conditions on the business. As such, they may change over time. For this reason, they should *not* be part of the data model that will form the basis for the underlying architecture of a new system.

So, action assertion business rules should be documented (by whatever means) independently of the description of the company's data structure. Indeed, it would be desirable if they could be implemented independently by means of a tool that would make them easy to change. In 2002, such tools are only beginning to be built.

Task 6: Map business rules to function model

As stated above, business rules are fundamentally constraints on *data*. A particular row may not be created if the rule is violated, regardless of the process that is trying to do it. Still, using the rules specified for each entity type (or group of entity types) and the matrix relating entity types to functions (the "CRUD" matrix, described above[8]), we can determine which functions or processes will be affected by a business rule. This may well affect the way the function is implemented in a future system.

Step 7: Present Models

In Process Three, above, one way to get modeling information was with a group of subject matter experts in a "JAD" modeling session. Whether or not this process was followed to get the initial information, a session is at least required to present the final model back to them.

The models should be presented not only back to the subject matter experts but also to the company's management, to verify that they are correct and consistent with the organization's strategies. In a modeling feedback session, unlike other kinds of presentations, the job of the person presenting models is *to be wrong*. However skillful the modeler, there will still be errors and omissions. After all, what is being presented is a series of assertions about the nature of the enterprise. These assertions were created based on conscientious effort, but probably with missing or erroneous information.

It is much cheaper to have the modeler be wrong at this stage of the system development life cycle than it would be to use the models as the basis for developing a system and then to discover, as the system was being implemented, that there was a serious

---

8. See Process 4, Step 2, Task 5 (page 29), for more information about the function entity matrix.

misunderstanding about the nature of things. Figure 2.4 shows the relative cost of discovering an error during various stages of the system development life cycle. An error in understanding an application area that cost a dollar to discover during strategic planning could cost a thousand dollars or more to fix if discovered only after a system was implemented.

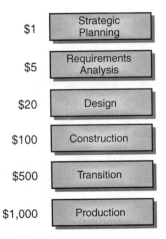

FIGURE 2.4 The Cost of an Error.

The modeling feedback session presents various models for validation. Typically the models are shown via overhead transparencies, so that they can be marked up and corrected as necessary. This means that the subject-matter experts and managers should be encouraged to participate actively. There are two secrets to achieving this:

First, the model itself should be as clear and easy to read as possible. In 1998, your author wrote an article on "Making Data Models Readable" for the Auerbach publication, *Information Systems Management*. In it, he asserted that a data model should be uncluttered, with a minimum of different symbols. The only things that should be obvious on an entity/relationship diagram, for example, are entity types and relationships. Representing other things on the diagram merely clutters it. The entity types should be stretched so that it is not necessary to bend relationship lines. (An "elbow" in a relationship is another symbol on the page—albeit one with no meaning. This is a distraction.) Functions, for the most part, should be presented in hierarchical form. Data flow and process flow diagrams should be presented only to the people who can verify their specific truths. These diagrams are too detailed for most people.

The second secret to getting subject-matter experts involved is in the way the model is presented. First of all, diagrams should be presented piecemeal. Begin the entity/relationship presentation with a slide containing only one entity type. Discuss that entity type—its definition, attributes, and relationships to other things in the business.

Add a second entity type and a relationship. Is the relationship correct? Is it really only one? Can it ever be more than one? Must it be one? Little by little, you will have built up the entire model and your audience will have followed every step.

Similarly, begin the function hierarchy with the root function. Then add one level. Pick a branch and add another level. Proceed until the entire hierarchy has been presented. Then, if appropriate, go back and discuss any data flows or other dependencies among functions.

Third, your presentation style must be one of making assertions about the business in your native language and seeking validation of those assertions. The natural language structure of the relationships used in the Barker approach to data modeling makes this easy: For example, "Each AGREEMENT must be *composed of* one or more LINE ITEMS, each of which must be *for* one and only one PRODUCT TYPE." Forget the model. It is only there for taking notes. The important question is, is this sentence true? May an AGREEMENT exist without LINE ITEMS? Can a LINE ITEM be for more than one PRODUCT TYPE? For each entity type, ask for definitions and **predicates** (which may be either attributes or relationships to other entity types).

Step 8: Deliverables: Model Descriptions

The deliverable from Process Four, then, ultimately is a set of validated and accepted Row Three (and, as necessary, Row Two) models with associated definitions, one for each of the Architecture Columns. These are described briefly above and in detail in the other chapters of this book. The entity/relationship model, the function hierarchy, data flow diagrams, and state/transition diagrams can often be produced by CASE (computer-aided systems engineering) tools. It is equally important, however, to provide, behind the diagrams, extensive documentation as to what each symbol on the diagram means. In the case of entity/relationship models, this means definitions of entity types, attributes, and business rules. In the case of function models, this includes not only a detailed description of the function itself, but also who or what (system) currently carries it out, the events which trigger it, and the result of each.

It is also useful to estimate, for each entity type, how many occurrences are expected—both initially and over the coming five years or so. In addition, estimate how frequently each function occurs in a typical week, month, or year.

In addition, it is often useful to provide a text narrative, explaining the model, one step at a time. This is organized around the corrected slides from the modeling feedback session, with the model drawings accompanied by a description of each. In the case of entity type models, this means describing each entity type and relationship in a conversational style. Business-rule descriptions can be included in the narrative as additional information about the entity types, attributes, and relationships constrained.

Publish this report as an attractive book. It should be possible for anyone to read it and understand it, even those who cannot read the models themselves.

Process Five: Define What Is Required of a New System

The "requirements" of requirements analysis are the specification of what is to be done with a new system. This does not mean that a new system itself is to be described in detail. Rather, what is produced is a statement that includes:

- The purpose of a proposed system
- Key players
- Required capabilities
- Requirement constraints
- Non-functional requirements
- The level of technology to be employed
- Capacity requirements
- The decision to make or buy the new system

Step 1: Restate Project Purpose

In the beginning, there was a reason why this requirements analysis project was initiated. There was a perceived need for information or processing that was clearly not being met by current systems. The pharmaceutical company wanted to shorten the time required to gain FDA acceptance of a new drug. The oil refinery wanted to improve control over its processes. The cable television network wanted to have more control over where commercials were placed, and, similarly, to provide more control to its sponsors.

In all cases, there is an overriding business need, expressed in the strategy report, that created the project in the first place. Write that down, and publish it as the frontispiece to all other project documents.

Step 2: Identify Key Players

The ultimate success of any project will be its acceptance by the people who will depend on it for their jobs. These people are the ultimate source of all requirements definitions.

Suzanne and James Robertson, in their 1999 book, *Mastering the Requirements Process,* describe these key players as:

- *Clients* and *customers:* A *client* of a project is one who pays for the development of the product. This person has financial responsibility for it until it is delivered. A *customer* is a person who will pay for the final product. You must understand these people well enough to build a product they will buy and use.
- *Users:* A *user* is a person who will ultimately work with the product. Satisfying a user comes from designing a product that can be operated effectively. This requires you to have considerable understanding of the work to be done.
- *Stakeholders* and *consultants:* The Robertsons describe *stakeholders* as "people who have an interest in the product. They will manage it, they will use it, or they will in some way be affected by its use. Stakeholders are people who have some demands on the product, and hence must be consulted in the requirement gathering activity" [Robertson and Robertson, 1999, p. 35]. These include management, business subject-matter experts, safety inspectors, the Legal Department, and others. They may also include outside groups, such as the marketplace, professional bodies, special interests, and cultural interests.

    A consultant (internal) typically does not have a vested interest in the project but may know useful things about the enterprise or about this application.
- *Information-technology workers:* These people typically should not be the source of requirements information, but they should be active participants in the analysis process, so that they know whence the requirements came.

Step 3: Identify Required Capabilities

The Robertsons describe *functional requirements* as "the things the product [new system] must do—an action that the product must take if it is to provide useful functionality for its user. Functional requirements arise from the fundamental reason for the product's existence" [Robertson & Robertson, 1999, p. 104].

In addition, *non-functional requirements* are "properties, or qualities, that the product must have. In some cases the non-functional requirements are critical to the product's success" [Robertson & Robertson, 1999, p. 112].

To arrive at these required capabilities, then, it is necessary *not* to ask the users what they want, but to look at the models, examining the difference between the business owners' views of their current systems and the architect's view. What data that are in the enterprise model are missing from the current world? What processes could be rendered more rational?

Task 1: Identify Missing Data

A conceptual data model will describe all (or nearly all) the things of interest to an organization. It is a theoretical artifact, in that it was created without concern for what data may actually exist. At this stage of the project, however, you have to address that question. For each entity type, does that information exist? How easy is it to get at? How easy is it to present it in conjunction with other information that is required?

Categories of information that either do not exist or are inaccessible to the people who need them represent an important dimension of what is required from any new system.

For example, a new system may be needed to make sales projections available alongside actual sales. A new system may be needed to provide information about plant efficiencies to the plant manager within a day or so. A new system may be needed because the company is becoming customer oriented instead of product oriented, and current systems cannot present data that way.

Task 2: Identify Missing Functions

In producing both current physical data flow diagrams and essential ones, we should have revealed what processes are being carried out that do not contribute (either directly or indirectly) to the income of the enterprise. Typically these functions are required to make up for shortcomings in some current[9] physical systems, or they exist because things have always been done that way, and no one challenged that before. This includes things like re-entering data for analyses that cannot be performed by current systems, or re-entering data for the second part of a process that cannot get data from the first part.

Even if all you have is the function hierarchy, you can examine each function and ask: How is this being done? Is it being done as well as it could be?

For example, the order-processing function may suffer from lack of access to important product data, hindering its ability to respond to a received request for products. That function and event, plus the currently used and currently unavailable data, constitute a functional requirement. Activities involved in the maintenance of those data, if not directly part of the order-taking process, are non-functional requirements, as are requirements for such things as backups, security, and so forth.

Task 3: Propose Systems and Define Use Cases for Them

From the above two tasks you can begin to define the parameters of new systems. Can automation eliminate that convoluted process in the Accounting Department? Can automation improve the company's interactions with customers? Define the scope of the system in terms of the functions to be performed and the data to be handled.

As mentioned above, you can use external business events and the essential activities that respond to them to define the scope of the application development project. An essential activity may be a very appropriate target for automation (or new automation).

---

9. . . . or long discontinued!

Once you have postulated a system, you can use use cases to describe exactly how the system will behave. Who are its prospective users and how will they interact with it? As defined originally by Ivar Jacobson in his 1992 book, *Object-Oriented Software Engineering: A use case Driven Approach*, "A use case model uses actors and use cases. These concepts are simply an aid to defining what exists outside the system (actors) and what should be performed by the system" [Jacobson, 1992]. The graphic for a use case is simply one or more stick figures, representing the actors, plus an ellipse representing a system being interacted with. Subsequent authors have elaborated on this definition to include considerable text documentation. Alistair Cockburn, for example, in his 2000 book, *Writing Effective Use Cases*, presents a set of detailed templates for documenting a set of actors' interactions with a prospective system.

A use case does not document in detail the data flowing into and out of the system, but it does represent in its underlying documentation the interactions between the actors and the potential system. A use case is typically documented in terms of its purpose, plus the set of triggers issued by the actors and its responses to each. The set of responses is often documented in terms both of the normal responses if all goes well, and of alternative responses if something does not [Cockburn, 2000].

Step 4: Identify Requirement Constraints

A *requirement constraint* limits the design choices available to meet one or more required capabilities. That is, you may want to manage inventory, but there are requirement constraints that limit how you can go about doing so. These include hardware platforms available, budgetary limits, and architectural decisions previously made.

Specifically, these may include *input and output constraints* having to do with restrictions in the environment about how data can be entered. In a manufacturing environment, for example, terminals may have to be hardened and made immune to dust and chemicals.

Also included are other *design constraints*, which derive from economics, existing systems, and training constraints. For example, certain technologies may be prohibitively expensive, there may be restrictions as to what data are available from feeding systems, or there may be specific requirements for the user interface.

Step 5: Identify Non-functional Requirements

A *non-functional* requirement is a property or quality that the proposed system must have to support the functional requirements. These include such things as:

- Quality
- Response time
- Look and feel

- Security
- Cultural
- Legal

. . . and so forth. Identifying non-functional requirements involves the tasks described below:

Task 1: Identify Quality Requirements

It is not sufficient to say simply that a new system will calculate an account balance. How accurate must it be? It may be that not all information required is available. How is it to deal with that? What are the *quality* dimensions of the required function?

Data quality may be measured on the following dimensions, among others:

- Accuracy
- Completeness
- Precision
- Timeliness
- Accessibility
- Clarity

Business rules ultimately control the process of entering data into systems. These address the issues of *accuracy* and *completeness*. They provide the validation tests to be applied to any data that are entered. Clearly a system's data are not of high quality unless they comply with the company's business rules. This means the business rules must be stated explicitly and then enforced appropriately.

The nature of the functions being performed will determine the *precision* required. This is related to the accuracy issue, in that if the data are not to be very accurate, they ought not be stated to the fourth decimal place. A reasonableness test should be applied here.

The expected operational procedures will determine the *timeliness* and *accessibility* of the data. Here it is necessary to articulate just how current the data are required to be (instantaneous, within a week, etc.), and how available they must be to how many people.

Clarity refers to the ease with which people will understand the meaning of data. The requirement is a function of the amount of knowledge and the sophistication of the expected users of the data. Clarity will be delivered through both the reasonableness of the data structures (that is, the quality of the data models produced during analysis), and the user interface (whose quality is determined during design).

Task 2: Define Response-Time Requirements

System requirements may also include requirements for the response time of interactive systems. There are two components to this:

First of all, a *behavioral response-time requirement* concerns the interaction of the system with a user. In general, no matter what they are doing, users expect the computer to respond to an input within a few seconds. That response may not be delivery of an output, but it is at least an acknowledgement of the input. It is essential that, no matter what the application is, entry into the computer be immediately responded to in one way or another.

The trickier one is an *operational response-time requirement*. If this system is replacing a manual one that required a week to produce results, and if it now takes an hour to do the same thing, this is a net benefit. It is important, in evaluating response time, that the response time required to perform a function be honestly evaluated. How soon are results required in order to achieve the function being addressed?

Note that even if the data are not required immediately, behavioral response-time requirements still apply. If it is acceptable for the analysis to take longer than the second or two permitted by the behavioral response-time requirement described above, then the job should be done on a batch basis. In this case, the user's interaction should consist of submitting the batch job. It should not be necessary for the user to be imprisoned at a terminal, awaiting results, when something else could be going on at the same time.

Task 3: Define Look and Feel Requirements

Ultimately the look and feel of a system is determined by the designer. There may be requirements defining the boundaries of that look and feel, however. This includes specifying standards and determining the overall aesthetic for the system. Microsoft Corporation, for example, has published an excellent set of standards in its 1999 *Microsoft Windows User Experience*.

Task 4: Define Security Requirements

Security may be examined in terms of three factors:

- *Confidentiality*—Data are each owned by and legitimately viewed by specific people. Any new system must accommodate this. What security is required to prevent unauthorized use of data? How important is it to keep the data out of the hands of unauthorized users? This will determine the amount of money and effort that must be spent as the system is developed.

- *Availability*—Data must be made easily accessible to the people who need them. Define clearly who they are (or at least their roles) and what they need. This is subject to requirements for procedures to prevent the loss of data, as well as design of security procedures so that authorized users are not prohibited from using the data.

- *Integrity*—This is directly related to the data quality requirement described above, but it specifically addresses the correct translation of input data into output data. All data received from an adjacent system are expected to be recorded accurately. It should not be possible to change data except under controlled circumstances. It should not be possible to misuse data (the toughest requirement of all).[10] If there is a major disruption, such as a power failure, it must be possible to determine whether any data were corrupted, and to recover from the failure.

Task 5: Define Cultural and Political Requirements

If the proposed system is to be used outside the immediate organization developing it, be sure to understand the culture of any other organizations that may be using it. This includes professional cultures (accountants may want their screens to look different from those for advertising executives) as well as geographic ones. (The English and the Americans spell "flavo(u)r" differently.) If cultural factors are going to be a problem, this should be identified early.

Political considerations include everything from what constitutes acceptable and unacceptable practices in a company to concerns about religion or political correctness. Be alert to these factors. They affect requirements.

Task 6: Define Legal Requirements

To the extent that laws apply to the environment in which your proposed system will be installed, you must be aware of them when you are defining your requirements. This may include laws about disabled access, privacy, consumer protection, and the like.

Step 6: Determine Level of Technology

The requirements analysis phase should be carried out independent of technology. The assignment here is to determine what data and processing a business requires to carry out its objectives. Once these requirements have been stated, then the design phase can apply technology to these requirements.

It is appropriate, however, at the end of the requirements analysis phase to indicate desirable technological directions to take. Steps 6, 7, and 8 of Process Five, as well as Process Six, below, begin the process of addressing the technology that ultimately will be used to implement any new system. These steps could as easily be considered at the beginning of design as at the end of analysis. The point here is that they constitute the transition from one to the other.

---

10. It is desirable to make a system "fool resistant". It is not possible to make it "foolproof", since they are always improving the quality of fools.

It may be clear from the requirements exercise that the time has come for the workers each to have a personal computer. Perhaps the World Wide Web is an appropriate medium. Requirements may suggest moving from a batch-oriented mainframe to a client server network. These kinds of global decisions may be made at this point.

The statements at this point, however, should be no more than general decisions recommending broad categories of technology.

Step 7: Identify Capacity Requirements

As mentioned above, the activity and data models should include measures of the "size" of each. In the case of the data model, this means, for each entity type, the number of occurrences expected. This includes the number expected initially as well as the number expected over (for example) the next five years, with a projected growth rate. In the case of the function and process models, this means a measure of how often the activity is carried out, along with some measure of its relative complexity. This information can then be used by the designer to estimate disk space and processing requirements.

In this step, these statistics can be collected and summarized to get a picture of just how big the problem ahead is. (Some CASE tools, for example, have utilities that calculate the estimated required disk space from the expected size of each entity type.)

Step 8: Decide Whether to Make or Buy

Requirements analysis is just as important if you buy software as it is if you build it yourself. You cannot adequately evaluate software unless you have a clear idea of what it should do and what the underlying structure of its data is. Only at this later phase of the requirements analysis process can you ask whether to build the system yourself or to buy a *commercial off-the-shelf* [11] package from someone else. This question makes sense only after you have exhaustively analyzed the data and the processing that the new system will be required to address.

Note that if the functions to be automated are routine maintenance functions, like accounting, which are not central to your business, it is perfectly appropriate to use standard, commercial software to address them. On the other hand, if you are automating a part of the business which is central to your operation—which is at the heart of what makes you stand out from your competition—then you can assume that commercial software has not addressed the points that are unique to your company. In this case, you are better off developing the application yourself.

---

11. It is currently fashionable to refer to this option as "COTS".

Step 9: Deliverable: Requirements Statement

The deliverable from Process Six, then, is a report itemizing

- The project goals
- Key players
- Functionally required capabilities
- Non-functional requirements
- Required constraints
- Level of technology
- Capacity requirements
- A discussion of the decision whether to build a new system or to buy one

Process Six: Determine the Existing Systems Environment

As stated above, the set of current systems should not define the requirements for systems in an organization. The requirements analysis phase should be carried out independent of technology. The assignment here is to determine what data and processing a business requires to carry out its objectives. Once these requirements have been stated, then the design phase can apply technology to these requirements.

Still, to the extent that systems usually constitute an important part of the business owners' views of their current environment, it is useful to know just what exists presently and the roles of various systems in the way the enterprise's business is carried out. Moreover, it is important to document the existing systems environment. This knowledge can provide useful insights in preparing the models described above, and it is important during transition when the time comes to move from the existing systems environment to a new one.

Because the skills required for conducting this kind of research are different from those used to model the business, this Process can be done by a separate team in parallel with and at the same time as other Processes in the requirements analysis project.

This process is one of making sure we understand not just what systems exist and what they do, but also the operating environment,

- The physical architecture,
- The technical architecture,
- Operating procedures, and
- Capacity.

Specifically, it involves the following steps:

Step 1: Define Operating Environment

What is the overall environment? A centralized mainframe? The World Wide Web? Hundreds of independent personal computers? A "client/server" network? This environment provides a context for the entire system development project. And of course there is the accompanying question, "How would this environment change with the advent of new systems"?

Step 2: Identify Software Environment

What software (purchased or developed inhouse) is currently in place? Specifically this step consists of identifying the following:

- *Database management systems:* Does the company have a single database management system or several? How compatible are they? How many people are conversant with each?

- *Applications software:* This is the big one. An inventory of all systems developed within the company may well be beyond the resources of any particular project. With luck, the Y2K project back in 1999 produced some sort of inventory that can be drawn upon.

  At the very least, however, it is important to know the principal systems that are used in the area of interest to this particular requirements project. A good source of information is the set of current physical data flow or process flow diagrams. These present the information used by each process and should also indicate the source (human or technological) of that information.

  In general, this research should also include determining who uses the software, although this may not be easy for something disseminated via the World Wide Web.

  What packages has the company purchased? Which departments maintain and use each? What functional areas and what parts of the data model are addressed?

  What systems have been developed inhouse? Because of the informal nature of many inhouse projects, the boundaries may not be as clear for these systems as for those purchased from an outside vendor. Still, it is important to at least document them and their purposes and to describe their scope as best you can.

Task 1: Identify Development Tools

What sort of CASE and other development tools will be used to support this effort? What kinds of query tools, data-transportation software, and fourth-generation languages are available? These are not the applications that will do the work to meet the objectives of the project. Rather they are tools to be used by developers to create such applications.

- *System data structures:* What are the actual files that exist to hold the company's information? What systems are they part of? How valid are the data contained in them? What will be required to clean up the data and move them into the structures envisioned by the data model?
- *Current software standards:* Does the enterprise already have in place standards for data definition, program structure, documentation, and so forth? What are they? To what extent are they currently enforced? Should they be re-evaluated?

Step 3: Define Technological Architecture

This is all about describing the kinds of technology that now exist and how they are connected to each other.

- *Hardware, including processors and networks* (including current hardware standards): This includes everything from mainframes and other servers to personal computers on employees' desks. It also includes the web servers and other computers that run various networks and perform less visible tasks.
- *Network protocols and the like:* What is the nature of the enterprise's networks? This includes local area and wide area networks, intranets, and so forth. Document the existence of each, along with its protocols, extent, and other technological characteristics.
- *Systems software:* What operating systems are in use? What kinds of applications are run under each? How are they interconnected? There may be more now than in the 1970s but, with luck, fewer than were in use in the 1990s.

Step 4: Define Operational Procedures

What is the operating environment of the systems? This involves:

- *System processes:* For batch jobs, how are the various program runs organized? For interactive systems, how are the various users linked together? What preconditions exist for each? That is, in order for Samantha to enter a transaction, must Charlie have done something first? Much of this will be revealed by the process flow and/or data flow diagrams, but here we are looking for more specific information about what components of various systems are involved.
- *System data communications (interfaces):* Data pass from one software application to another. In what form? How frequently?

Step 5: Identify Existing Capacity

How much processing capacity and disk space is available (or can be made available) for this project? Below we discuss determining capacity requirements. What capacity can be drawn upon, and what approaches are available for acquiring more?

Step 6: Deliverable: System Inventory

The steps in this process will result in reports and lists of various kinds. These will provide the basis for planning further development phases.

Process Seven: Plan for Transition

Looking at the system development life cycle, the most problematic of all the phases is transition. *Transition* is the establishment of a new system as part of the infrastructure of the enterprise. It involves education, training, implementation of software, and conversion of data. It addresses the conversion of a set of existing business owners' views to a new set. This recognizes that, if this system is at all innovative, it *will* require the enterprise to change the way it does business. If this project does not provide a new tool that will be different from previous tools, you have to ask whether it is worth doing. To do it means that many in the enterprise will have to change the way they do their jobs. Indeed, many may have different jobs altogether.

The people developing a system can give the enterprise all manner of new tools. It is for the enterprise itself to accept them, however, and make them part of its new infrastructure. This is the one phase of the system development life cycle that the system developers do not control. The system will be implemented only if the people who run the business assume responsibility for implementing it.

What the people developing a system can do is provide insights into the meaning and implications of the system, education and training, and assistance with the various tasks required to implement the system.

Because transition can be the largest and most expensive of the phases in the system development life cycle,[12] it is necessary to begin planning for it early—specifically, during the requirements analysis phase.

Transition will involve:

- Reorganization
- Education
- Training
- Data conversion
- Installation of hardware and implementation of software

Preparing for these is described in the following steps:

---

12. Your author has had experience with manufacturing planning and control systems where the software required cost about half a million dollars, but the implementation cost on the order of two million dollars.

Step 1: Begin Reorganization

Examination of the current physical process flow diagram in the context of a logical data flow diagram or a function hierarchy reveals where systems could improve processing. But adding systems undoubtedly will entail changing the organization of the processes and changing the nature of the jobs involved.[13] It is important during requirements analysis to understand the implications of these organizational changes and to prepare for the upheaval they might bring. To do this, you must completely understand what the new organization structure will look like. Will the philosophy of organization change? How will reporting relationships change? What new kinds of links between workers will be established?

Once you have done that, you can begin education and training.

Training is explaining to specific people how a new system will work. Which button do you push to do a specific action? This should not happen until the system has been built and tested and is ready to be implemented. *Education*, on the other hand, is explaining to an entire organization what we are doing and why we are doing it. Of the two, education is the more important, and it should begin as early as possible.

Step 2: Begin Education

As stated above, any new system that is worth doing *will* change the way a company operates. It will cause disruption in various areas of the organization. In order to mitigate the effects of this, it is important that all affected people have the opportunity to understand *why* it is happening. It is education that provides this understanding. The people who feel part of a larger effort, with contributions being recognized and events fully communicated, will be the heart of the project. Those who do not will be its greatest obstacle to success.

What is the company trying to accomplish? How will this effort contribute to that accomplishment? What is each department's role in it? Education begins with the strategy study. As many people as possible should participate, at least to some degree. At the very least the strategy study's results should be disseminated throughout the enterprise. Then, during requirements analysis, the process of gathering information is also the process of both communicating direction and assuring all concerned of the importance of their contributions.

Model feedback sessions are an important part of the education process.

---

13. Indeed, it may be more appropriate to change (or eliminate) processes than to develop new systems.

Step 3: Prepare for Training

Training is the process of instructing the users of a system on its operation. Which button do you push to accomplish a particular task? Unlike education, which should start early, the particulars of training have to await the completion of the system. But if the requirements analysis project is successful in using existing and proposed process flow models to direct design, the same models can frame the training effort. They will reveal where training will have to take place and the nature of that training.

The amount of training will depend on the design of the new system's user interface. The better the design, the less training will be required. For this reason, not very much about the specifics of training requirements can be known during analysis. Some planning can begin, however, during the last steps in requirements analysis, when use cases and proposed process flow diagrams reveal the nature of the work to be performed. The extent of training required may be determined by the extent to which the new interface is similar to the one to which users of the old system were accustomed. Alternatively, the extent of training requirements may be determined by the simplicity of its steps. Ideally, the new system is not exactly like the old one but is, in fact, much simpler to use.

Step 4: Prepare for Data Conversion

Now comes the big job—getting all those data from legacy systems into the new world. Once the data model is complete, you have an idea of the domain of proposed systems. You don't know it completely, of course, until the final scope decisions of this phase have been made. Moreover, you don't know the actual design of any new database until well into the design phase. But it is not too early to begin examining current systems to determine how their data will be organized in the new world.

It is extremely valuable to create a map linking each column in each legacy system to be replaced to corresponding attributes in the entity/relationship model. If this were a simple one-to-one mapping, it would be simple, but of course it is not. Several situations make it complicated:

First of all, columns in older systems often encode more than one piece of information. The "product code", for example, may include everything from where the product was manufactured to its membership in various product categories. In this case, the code must be parsed to reveal the bits of information contained in its components, and it may therefore be linked to multiple attributes.

Similarly, one attribute may show up as several columns (inevitably with slightly different definitions).

There are other mapping configurations that can cause problems. [See English, 1999, pp. 266–274.] It may not be practical to address all of these in detail during the requirements analysis project, but plans should certainly be made to do so before the conversion must take place.

In recent years, a number of software products have come on the market to ease the mechanical task of copying data from one file to another. These are called *extraction, transformation, and load* (ETL) *programs*. You specify to the software the format of the source, the format of the target, and the transformations to be done in between. This will greatly ease the process, but it still means that a particular package (among several competitors) must be chosen, and people must be trained in its use. This can begin during the requirements analysis phase.

Step 5: Prepare for Implementation of Hardware and Software

The requirements analysis phase is not too early to begin consideration of the hardware and software implementation process. Included in many of the modeling techniques, but especially in entity/relationship modeling, is provision for estimating how many things there will be. How many products? How many contracts? As described above in Process Four, Step 6, these numbers should be specified for the time of the initiation of the application, with a growth rate and an estimate of the limits to growth, if any. This can be used to estimate disk space requirements.

If these requirements are significantly greater than what is currently available, the time is ripe for beginning the process of acquiring the additional capacity. This may mean buying new computers or simply expanding the amount of disk space available. Or, if the architecture is changing (as in the move from a client/server architecture to the World Wide Web), major capital expenditures may be required.

Your company may already have procedures for implementing new software, but if not, consideration must be given to testing and the migration of software from "test mode" to "production mode". What will be the exact steps, and how will they be controlled?

Step 6: Deliverable: Transition Plan

The transition plan is the blueprint for the transition process. It will, of course, be refined as the design and construction phases progress, but its basic shape should be determined during the requirements analysis phase, at the same time that the basic shapes of the proposed systems are being determined.

The transition plan will lay out the basic elements of:

- Reorganization
- Education

- Training
- Data conversion
- Installation of hardware and implementation of software

Its structure will form the basis for implementation when that time arrives.

Summary

A project's success depends on many factors all coming together correctly. This includes, to be sure, the use of appropriate techniques, but more significantly success depends on the proper organization of the efforts. This means doing first things first, insuring that resources (analysts as well as people for them to talk to) are available, and applying skill both in organization and in the techniques involved.

Column One: Data

## 3

The first column of the Architecture Framework is about data. Data are all of those numbers and letters (and now pictures and sounds) that computers manipulate. The history of our industry is one of an evolution of our attitude toward data.

This chapter begins by linking the Architecture Framework with an understanding of perspectives on data that preceded it by twelve years. It then provides a brief history of data architecture and an exposition of different modeling techniques, before elaborating on where the techniques fit in the Framework. After that is a discussion of the "normalization" process and a few words about data modeling conventions.

Views of Data

As shown in Figure 3.1, the Architecture Framework shows the six different views of data: Planner's (scope) view, business owner's view, architect's view, designer's view, builder's view, and production view. As it happens, the second through the fifth views map directly to views of data that have been recognized since long before John Zachman published his Framework. In 1975, a committee in the Computer and Business

Equipment Manufactures Association (commonly known as ANSI/SPARC) identified and defined a complete set of schemas characterizing the structure of data. A draft of this report was published and the 42 schemas were short-handed down to just three. This then became known as "Three Schema Architecture" [Tsichritzis and Klug, 1978].

The *business owner's view* is not one but many ways of looking at a body of data—each one by a particular user or provider of the data. In each case, the data are organized according to terms appropriate for the job being done by the person. Each is shown in Figure 3.2 as an *external schema.* Note that each is different, but of course they may overlap, often using the same terms of reference, although even these terms may be defined differently.

Note that the users whose views are reflected here may be either creators or consumers of data or both.

The information *architect's view* combines these different external views into a single, coherent definition of the enterprise's data. In this view, each data element is defined only once for the organization, and its relationship to all other data elements is clearly defined as well. Each external schema may consist of a selection of these elements, but the underlying definitions are consistent across them all. This unified version of the company's data is called the conceptual schema. A *conceptual schema* is an organization of data where each datum is defined only once for the organization, and it relationship to all other data are clearly and uniquely defined as well. Each external schema may consist of a selection of these data, but the underlying definitions from the conceptual schema apply to all external schemata as well, and they are consistent across them all. The architect's view of data is of the conceptual schema. This is often maintained by someone with the title, *Data Administrator* or, more recently, *Data Architect*.

An *internal schema* is an organization of data according to the technology being used to record it. This includes—for a particular database management system—the external terms of reference ("tables", "segments", "object classes", etc.) and the internal components ("tablespaces", etc.). It also includes terms for the physical storage of data on the computer ("cylinder", "track", etc.)

Note that the internal schema combines the *designer's view* with the *builder's view*. That is, it covers the full range of things required to convert a conceptual schema into a database. This includes selecting a particular database management system, modifying the model to accommodate problems of system performance, and determining the actual layout of files on a disk.

The organization of the conceptual schema is intentionally independent of both how people see the data and how the data are arranged in a particular database management system. More than that, the conceptual schema certainly does not reflect how the data are physically arranged on a storage device. The database management system and physical perspectives represent additional views of the data.

	Data (What)	Activities (How)	Locations (Where)	People (Who)	Time (When)	Motivation (Why)
Objectives / Scope **(Planner's view)**	List of things important to the enterprise - Term 1 - Term 2 - Term 3 ...	List of processes the enterprise performs - Function 1 - Function 2 - Function 3 ...	List of enterprise locations	Organization approaches	Business master schedule	Business vision and mission - Vision ... - Mission ...
Enterprise model **(Business Owners' Views)**	Language, divergent data model	Business process model	Logistics network	Organi-zation chart	State / transition diagram	Business strategies, tactics, policies, rules
Model of Funda-mental Concepts **(Architect's View)**	Convergent e/r model	Essential data flow diagram	Locations of roles	The viable system, use cases	Entity Life History	Business rule model
Technology Model **(Designer's View)**	Data base design	System design, program structure	Hardware, software distribution	User interface, security design	Control structure	Business rule design
Detailed Represen-tation **(Builder's View)**	Physical storage design	Detailed program design	Network architecture, protocols	Screens, security coding	Timing definitions	Rule specification program logic
Functioning System	*(Working System)*					
	Converted data	Executable programs	Communi-cations facilities	Trained people	Business events	Enforced rules

FIGURE 3.1 The Architecture Framework—Data.

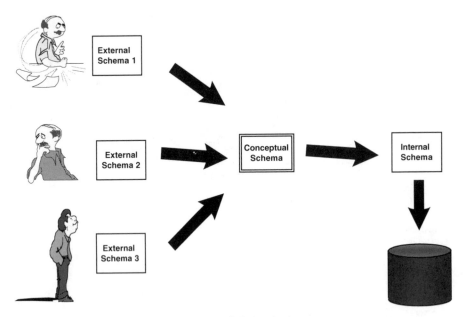

FIGURE 3.2 Three Schema Architecture.

This independence means that the external schemata (business owners' views) can change, without changing the conceptual schema (information architect's view). The physical designer and builder can rearrange the data in a database or on a disk, without affecting the conceptual or external schemata.

In the past, one of the elements of the internal schema was called the *logical schema*, which originally simply represented the conceptual schema in terms of a particular kind of database management system. In more recent years, however, the term "logical schema" has been used interchangeably with "conceptual schema", thereby generating considerable confusion. This book will be interested only in the conceptual schema and its derivation from a set of external schemata. Since it is concerned with technology, the logical schema (in the original sense of the word) is the domain of the designer.

A Brief History of Data Architecture

While this multifaceted view of data is not universally practiced, it is generally accepted as a reasonable way to look at the world. How we got here turns out to be an interesting story.

The "Application Approach" to Systems . . .

Originally, we wrote programs to address particular problems. From the beginning of the computer industry in the 1940s, and through the early 1970s, data processing professionals focused on program processing. From machine language, through assembler, Fortran, and COBOL, programmers were concerned primarily with what a program was supposed to *do*. Presumably that was in support of some activity in an enterprise. Any data referred to were defined as needed by the program and then promptly forgotten. For example, we might write a program for a client that would take Whiz-bang input data and produce a Framis report of some kind. (See Figure 3.3.)

(Whiz-bang data)   *(program)*   *(Framis Report)*

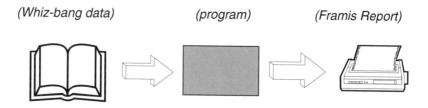

FIGURE 3.3 One Program.

As it happens, the fellow sitting next to our client sees the report and likes it. He'd like one, too. But could you add this little dollop of Knart data, and maybe summarize things a little differently? This gives us the configuration in Figure 3.4.

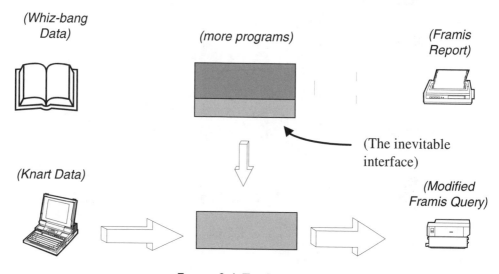

FIGURE 3.4 Two Programs.

Now, our popularity grows. Lots of people want variations on the report, using not only the data originally provided but various other kinds of data as well. This gives us Figure 3.5.

In fact it usually gives us a picture even messier than is shown in Figure 3.5. There could be hundreds of these programs, all copying data from one place to another—often requiring re-entry of the same data—with no particular organization or cohesion.

The problem is compounded by the fact that the business is dynamic. Our clients are always changing the way they want things to work. By the time the configuration has matured to this complexity, the situation is all but hopeless. Errors cannot be fixed and enhancements cannot be added without generating yet more errors.

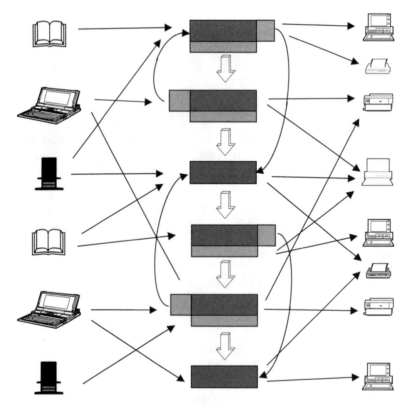

FIGURE 3.5 Until . . . .

What Went Wrong?

It is easy to bemoan the mess we have found ourselves in. It is easy to imagine that things simply got out of control by virtue of general incompetence. The fact of the matter, however, is that this approach was based on *three* very specific *mistaken assumptions*.

1. Input's Connections to Output

First, we assumed that input and output were closely related. (See Figure 3.6.) Each project was a matched pair of inputs and outputs. Take some data, process it, and generate a report.

The problem with that assumption is that it's false.

The dynamics of input are in fact radically different from those of output. Input data tend to come from the operations of the company. The mechanisms for collecting them are difficult to set up, but once in place they are relatively stable and often are difficult to change. Output requirements, on the other hand, are usually highly dynamic. "I want a report that looks like this. I have never asked for this kind of report before, and I never will again, but this is what I want today."

When somebody wants a new report and is told that it can't be produced because the structures for collecting the data are too inflexible, you have an unhappy client.

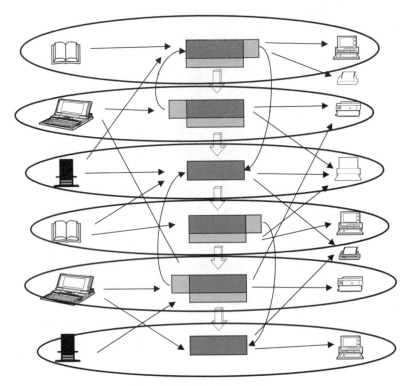

FIGURE 3.6 The Assumptions.

2. Overlapping Applications

A second, related, assumption was that each of the applications was a ***separate entity***. By assuming that applications could be addressed in isolation, we wound up duplicating:

- Data definition
- Data entry
- Program code

. . . with the effect that we couldn't:

- Guarantee consistency
- Find errors easily

The fact of the matter is that much of the data that any one department requires is often required by other departments as well. For each and every department to pursue collection and massaging of the same data is not very productive.

3. Encoding Business in the Programs

A third assumption we made was that programs should represent the workings of the enterprise. This meant:

- The structure of the company's business was encoded in the programs.
- Changes in the business meant changes to programs (by programmers).
- "Ease of maintenance" (for programmers) was an issue.

But processes are inherently subject to change. To encode the business in the programs was to condemn the Information Technology Department to be forever trying to keep up with business changes. The advent of structured design techniques was intended to address this problem, and it did make programs easier to change—but the fundamental problem remained. Programs could *adapt* to change, but they could not *accommodate* it.

It is these three assumptions, not a general undifferentiated incompetence, that left us in this sad position.

The Solution—Version 1

So, how should we address this problem and these fallacies?

In 1970, Dr. E. F. Codd introduced the **relational** approach to organizing data [Codd, 1970]. Dr. Codd's theory included specific criteria to ensure that data structures remained simple and non-redundant ("normalization"[1]). This approach produced much simpler database structures than had been seen before. Before that, COBOL programs arranged data hierarchically, as did many early versions of database management systems. This meant that to find a piece of data, it was necessary to start with general categories and search through progressively narrower ones.

Dr. Codd's insight was that you could do everything you needed to store data coherently with two-dimensional tables, or **relations**, as he called them. He based his theory on the mathematics of set theory, and from that he derived a set of rules to ensure that data were stored with the least possible redundancy. Moreover, relationships between data were defined by the data themselves, not by internal (and invisible) pointers.

Thus, four years before publication of the three-schema architecture, Dr. Codd had already described the nature of the conceptual schema.

Shortly after Dr. Codd's paper was published, the IBM San Jose Laboratory began work on System R as a database management system based on his relational theory. At about the same time, a group of students at the University of California at Berkeley

---

1. See a complete description of normalization below, starting on p. 91.

built the Interactive Graphics and Retrieval System (INGRES), and Relation Software, Inc. was developing the Oracle Database.[2]

Six years later, in 1976, Peter Chen introduced "entity/relationship modeling" or "data modeling" as a way of representing data structures graphically [Chen, 1976]. Two years after that, Oracle Corporation introduced the first commercial relational database management system.

These insights and techniques drew our attention to the structure of the data our programs were manipulating. And the more we looked at things, the more we realized that these data structures were more stable than our program structures could ever be. The things an enterprise is concerned with don't change very much. The processes they carry out change all the time.

Thus, our orientation changed from the programs we wrote to the data they used. The advent of this data orientation made it clear that we had been looking at the problem all wrong. Instead of addressing the problem of a company's systems horizontally, why not address them vertically, as shown in Figure 3.7?

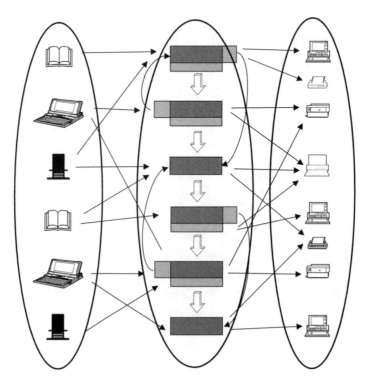

FIGURE 3.7 Cut a Different Way.

---

2. Thanks to Simon Williams and his 2000 book, *The Associative Model of Data*, for this history.

This means addressing the entire problem of *collecting data* in the organization as a single project, utilizing all the best technology available. This might include time clocks, process-control equipment, and bar code readers.

A second project can then address *reporting* overall. There are excellent tools for retrieving data in many different ways and forms. These include query languages, online analytical processing tools, and other fourth-generation programming tools.

The idea is to isolate these processes from each other. This is done by redesigning the middle. The secret of this redesign is the addition of a buffer *database*, as shown in Figure 3.8.

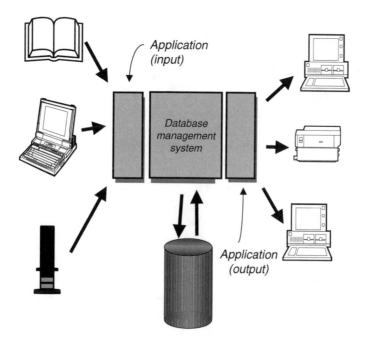

FIGURE 3.8 The Database Approach.

Included with this buffer is a standard piece of software called a *database management system*. Traditional programs tended to have a lot of code concerned with reading from and writing to files. A database management system is specifically equipped to read from and write to the database. Because the mechanics of reading and writing have been standardized, the only programming required now is that to:

- define the structure of the input transactions, and the translation of input data into a form for storage
- define the structure of the data as stored
- define the nature of each query, in terms of the data as stored

An "application" is now just that required to enter or retrieve (and manipulate) data. (See Figure 3.8.)

Note that with this arrangement, the definition of the nature of the enterprise is no longer just encoded in programs. It is now reflected in the structure of the data. The task of designing the database is nothing other than the task of defining the structure of the enterprise itself.

The database management system is then charged with distinguishing the external views of data from the conceptual and physical views. Indeed, relational database management systems, via the standard language SQL, have the ability to represent "views" of data that are different from the physical tables and columns that constitute the database.

All this, then, constitutes "the database approach" to designing systems.

Data Management

A significant effect of this change in orientation is the appearance of "data management" as a function. Companies and government agencies have come to recognize that information itself constitutes an important asset to the company, and throughout the nineties the functions "database administrator" and "data administrator" began to appear.

The meanings of these two terms have varied widely but appear to be converging on the following: the *database administrator* is the person responsible for maintenance of the database management software, while the *data administrator* (also called the *information resource manager*, or IRM) is the person responsible for the integrity of the data themselves. The data administrator is responsible for data models as well as for the quality of the data captured.

Professional societies such as the Data Administration Management Association (DAMA)[3] have been formed to further the body of knowledge concerning data administration, and numerous books have been written on the subject.

The Solution—Version 2

The database approach to developing systems has been undertaken in various forms since the late 1970s. Relational database management systems in particular now make it possible to design a database along the lines of a conceptual schema and then provide different "views" of the database to both the creators and consumers of its data. In addition each database management system has the ability to tune physical storage parameters independently of the table and column structure. The principles of data "normalization" (described below) provide guidance for the design of the central database, while SQL views are used to construct specific external schemas.

---

3. Information about DAMA can be found at http://www.dama.org.

In spite of these advances, however, different companies have had varying degrees of success in trying to carry out this approach, and few have been able to do so completely. It turns out that there are other problems besides the ones we first identified.

The first problem relates to the first assumption the database approach was supposed to deal with previously. The way creators and consumers look at data is very different. (See Figure 3.9.)

Creators of data tend to deal with it one transaction at a time. It is not impractical to analyze a transaction and figure out where each of its components fits into the database based on the conceptual schema.

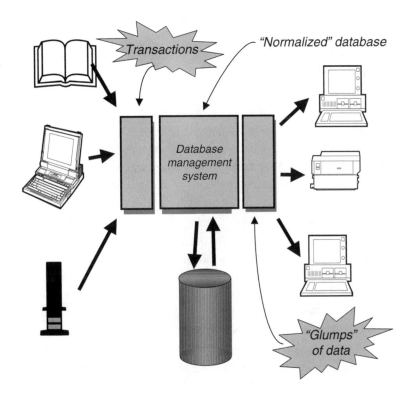

FIGURE 3.9 Inputs vs. Outputs.

Consumers of data, on the other hand, tend to want to see large sets of data, with many records taken from various parts of the underlying database. As powerful and fast as computers have become in recent years, they still are not up to the task of retrieving data as complicated as those typically requested, in the time required.

The response to these problems has been development of the central database into what has come to be called the *data warehouse*. This term has two meanings: First, it is a configuration consisting of a central database that reflects an enterprise's conceptual schema, plus one or more *data marts*, each of which represents a particular external schema—summarizing data in particular ways that will be useful to a particular data customer. The second meaning is that a data warehouse is the central database itself. It is an integrated, enterprisewide database that serves as a central point of reference. It's purpose is to store data for retrieval, not to support operations, so it will not be quite as current, and some data in it may be stored in summarized form.

It is this second meaning of the term that will be used here. A data warehouse is analogous to a discount warehouse of the sort run by Costco or Sam's Club. Here, the pretzels are stored in one part of the store, the beer is in a second part, and the video tapes are in a third part altogether. At the local convenience store, however (the mart), the pretzels, beer, and video tapes tend to be displayed close together, to encourage customers buying one to buy them all. This configuration means that most queries will not have to examine the entire data warehouse at all.

Mapping software extracts data from the central database to create these *data marts*. (See Figure 3.10.)

The data marts each tend to be organized in terms of a central *fact*, such as "sales", with various *dimensions* for collecting groups of facts. A dimension could be identification of the fact's product and product group, its point in time, or geographical location. A collection of facts, then, is expressed in terms of the product group, time, and geography to which they apply. ("Give me all the sales for green vegetables in the Eastern Region last quarter.") This organization of data is also called a *multidimensional database.*

For example, while a data warehouse (in the sense of the central database) might keep the complete structure of customer information and contracts, one multidimensional data mart might just concern the fact "sale", accessible through the dimensions of time (day, week, month, or quarter), geography (region, state, city), customer (customer group or individual customer), and product (product group or product). In such a data mart, it would be easy to report on sales at any level of detail along any dimension.

One problem with early incarnations of the database approach was that a typical company's management was not prepared to replace all its existing systems and base the entire company's operations on a single database. Older systems are not replaced if there seems no need to do so.

The data warehouse architecture, then, often involves feeding the central database from existing systems (*legacy systems*). This means additional mapping software to translate data from the terms in which they were stored there into terms appropriate for the data warehouse. These are shown on the left side of Figure 3.10.

The result of all this is a configuration that may include a set of older systems, a "mapping" from those systems to a central data warehouse, and then another "mapping" to the data marts used for user queries.

One or more of the systems which support the organization's daily operations may also be based on the conceptual schema. To the extent that this is done and the operational system comes to resemble a data warehouse, the database becomes what is called an *operational data store*, or ODS. The dynamics of a data warehouse and an operational data store remain very different, however. To the extent that a database is an ODS used to support applications, it will be more dynamic, with potentially less room for history. To the extent that it is used only as a warehouse to support retrievals and analysis, it may have more history and be updated less frequently. In either case, however, the underlying structure will be basically the same.

Since the data warehouse is used only for retrievals, it does not require the structures and mechanisms for enforcing business rules that are to be found in the operational data store and in other operational legacy systems.

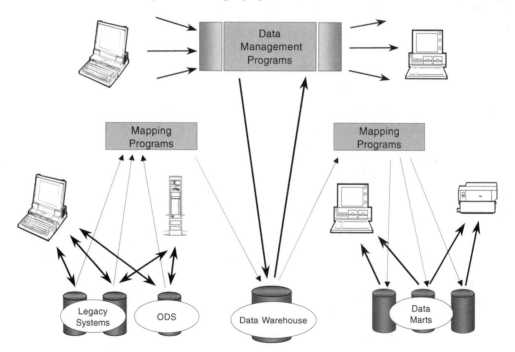

FIGURE 3.10 The Data Warehouse.

Advanced Data Management—Meta-data

From the beginning, the organization of fields in a computer record has been documented in a kind of database called a data dictionary. A *data dictionary* is a compilation of file layouts, including definitions of each field in each kind of record in a file. As the database industry has matured, it has become clear that the data required to keep track of data are much more complex than simple record layouts.

Meta-data are data that describe the entity types, attributes, tables, columns and all other elements that constitute a modern information system. As users become more sophisticated in using data warehouses, they need access to the definitions of what they are trying to retrieve. It is meta-data that a data administrator administers.

A *meta-data repository* is a database for holding, maintaining, and using meta-data.

Graphics—Data Modeling

A Short History

Computer programs are fundamentally abstract products. In the mid-1970s people began to realize that these abstractions could benefit from more graphic representations. Flow charts led to data flow diagrams on the process side. And in 1976, *entity/relationship modeling* was invented to represent data structures graphically.

Entity/Relational Modeling

Peter Chen first introduced a graphic approach to relational design with *entity/relationship modeling* (a kind of *data modeling*) in 1976 [Chen 1976–1977]. Based on Mr. Codd's idea of associating simple groups of data, entity/relationship modeling used a box to represent a relation, and a diamond and lines to represent a *relationship* between relations. This simple idea has revolutionized the way we represent data structures. It began essentially as a graphic technique for modeling relational data, but it subsequently evolved to representation of a particular nonrelational structure as well ("super-type" and "sub-types", described below).

While originally data modeling was supposed to depict relations, it quickly became clear that the boxes really represented the things in a business about which it wished to hold information. They represented entity types. An *entity type* is the definition of something of significance to an organization, such as "person", "product", or "activity". An entity type has attributes and relationships with other entity types.

Indeed, data modeling describes the structure of a business itself.

Thus, a data model reflects the structure of an enterprise as well as the potential design of a database that would similarly reflect that structure of the enterprise. And it turns out that while a company's processes may change, its fundamental (data) structure rarely does. Base a system design on the structure of a company's data and you have a system that promises to last more than a few months.

Mr. Chen's approach to entity/relationship modeling was only a first version, however, and many people since then have tried to improve upon it. A veritable plethora of data modeling notations have emerged.

Clive Finkelstein invented a different data modeling notation to use as the basis for his idea of information engineering. Not just a new modeling technique, *information engineering* is a comprehensive approach to the whole process of system development. It is based both on a data-centric approach to analysis and on the *system development life cycle* (described in Chapter 2 of this book). It portrays the development process as progressing from strategic planning and requirements analysis through design, construction, and implementation. Mr. Finkelstein and James Martin first published this in 1981 in the article "Information Engineering" in the Savant Institute's *Technical Report*. Later Mr. Martin popularized this approach through various books, and Mr. Finkelstein finally published his version in 1989 as *An Introduction to Information Engineering: From Strategic Planning to Information Systems*.

Messrs. Finkelstein and Martin added to the relationally oriented data model the concept of *sub-type* and *super-type*. This concept is derived from the idea of inheritance, first identified for object-oriented programming in the 1960s. It is a representation of the fact that occurrences of a thing of significance may themselves be categorized. An ORDER, for example, may be either a SALES ORDER, a PURCHASE ORDER, or a WORK ORDER. This is not a structure that can be directly represented in a relational database without serious translation. But it is a powerful data modeling concept for representing things in the business.

Subsequently, several other data modeling notations were developed. Among these were IDEF1X, primarily used by the United States Defense Department [Bruce, 1992], and one developed by the British consulting firm CACI. The latter was further developed by Richard Barker and the Oracle Corporation and is also used in Europe as part of the Structured Systems Analysis and Design Method (SSADM). Among other things, this modeling method introduced a discipline for naming relationships—a discipline that makes it possible to read relationship names as simple natural language sentences.

Object Modeling

While all this was going on in the world of business requirements analysis, programmers also discovered that organizing their programs around data had great advantages. Since the mid 1960s, *object-oriented programming* has been taking over the world of writing programs. Where programs were originally organized around what they did, with data being attached where necessary, the object-oriented programmers organized their work around the data—or rather, they organized it in terms of the objects the data described. This turned out to be a particularly powerful way to look at the problem—especially in the realm of real-time systems. It burst upon the general data processing scene in a big way in the 1980s, when the advent of graphic user interfaces introduced object-oriented programmers to the world of commercial applications. They realized that the problem of defining requirements in this world could benefit from their insights into the world of objects. Without appreciating that commercial systems analysts themselves had already discovered the modeling of "things of significance to the business", they introduced the idea of *object models.*

Thus, while the systems analysts were becoming data oriented through information engineering, the programmers were becoming data oriented through object-oriented programming.

In 1988 Sally Shlaer and Stephen Mellor wrote *Object-Oriented Systems Analysis: Modeling the World in Data,* and thus introduced *object-oriented analysis* to the world at large. They acknowledged that information engineering had developed a modeling technique that was singularly compatible with the object-oriented view of things. They invented their own notation for it, however (adding to the four or five that already existed), thus introducing the notion of "object modeling" to the world of commercial applications.

In fact, the symbols in Ms. Shlaer's and Mr. Mellor's books corresponded exactly to those in information engineering. There were entity types (now called *object classes*) and relationships (called *associations*). The relationships had a single arrow when referring to a single occurrence of a class and a double arrow when referring to multiple occurrences of a class. Each relationship was assumed to be mandatory, unless marked with a "C" for "conditional".

Then, in 1991, James Rumbaugh, Michael Blaha, William Premerlani, Frederick Eddy, and William Lorensen published *Object-Oriented Modeling and Design.* This book presented another object modeling notation, along with a methodology called the "Object Modeling Technique", or OMT. The methodology included variations on the information engineering concepts of analysis, system design, "object design", and implementation. It modified the information engineering approach to the extent that it was much more tolerant of iteration in the system development life cycle.

After 1991, several other authors tried their hands at developing object-modeling techniques. Ed Yourdon and Peter Coad wrote *Object-Oriented Analysis* in 1990. David Embley, Barry Kurtz, and Scott N. Woodfield wrote *Object-Oriented Systems Analysis: A Model-Driven Approach* in 1992. So now, in addition to the various entity/relationship modeling notations available, there were as many or more under the rubric of object modeling.

In 1997 the experts of the object world got together and devised the Unified Modeling Language (the UML), to replace at least all of the object-modeling notations [OMG, 1998].

Where it was concerned only with *business objects* (tangible things seen by people in the enterprise or intangible things commonly understood by people in the enterprise), object modeling essentially represented the same things as the data modeling techniques available at the time. It had the advantage, however, of being from the "object" world, which made object-oriented developers more comfortable with its ideas. As it happened, the ERD concept of inheritance from super-type to sub-types had been developed in the context of object-oriented programming in the 1960s.

This doesn't mean that object modeling is not useful to support object-oriented design specifically. By portraying *computer objects* an object model can be very helpful in clarifying the implications of particular designs. And the model of an object oriented design may be very different from the corresponding model of relational design.

For example, object-oriented associations are treated differently from relational relationships in design. Where a relationship implemented in a relational database remains structural, consisting of a foreign key, in an object-oriented program it is part of a class's behavior. A piece of program code is required to implement the navigation from each class to each other class. Separate pieces of code are required for the two directions of a relationship.

Object-oriented programming does combine objects with their behavior, bringing together data and process in a very effective way. In the context of object-oriented programming, *behavior* describes the program which implements the behavior of an object along with the description of the object itself. Mr. Rumbaugh et al. extended this to allow for describing the behavior of business object classes as well. This did not, however, affect the structural aspects of the technique.

While the idea of incorporating behavior in analysis data models is appealing, it turns out to be problematic. Where, in a program, behavior is always described by program code, the behavior of real-world objects is much more complex. Since the objects in object-oriented programming are themselves pieces of code, it is reasonable to package with them the code that describes their behavior. Objects in the world, however, that are the subject of requirements analysis behave in ways that are far more varied and complex than can be described by a bit of pseudocode. Describing the complete behavior of a person, for example, has taxed the skills of novelists for generations.

The best way to describe business object behavior appears to be *entity life histories*, a technique described in Chapter 7.

The net effect of all this, even with the consolidation under the UML, is that there are still many ways to model the structure of data. Appendix B presents the most significant notations in detail and compares them.

Regardless of the symbols used, data modeling during analysis (whether of the object or entity/relationship kind) is intended to do one thing: describe the things about which an organization wishes to collect data, along with the relationships among them. For this reason, all of the commonly used systems of notation fundamentally are convertible from one to another. The major differences among them are aesthetic, although some make distinctions that others do not, and some lack symbols to represent all situations.

Object-Role Modeling (ORM)

Another approach to modeling data was developed by G. M. Nijssen in the 1980s. This is significantly different in its approach from either entity/relationship or object modeling. It was originally called NIAM, an acronym for "Nijssen's Information Analysis Methodology". More recently, since G. M. Nijssen was only one of many people involved in the full development of the method, it has been renamed "object-role modeling", or ORM. ORM takes a different approach from the other methods described here. Rather than representing entity types as analogs of relational tables, it shows *relationships* ("roles" in ORM parlance) to be such analogs. Like Mr. Barker's notation, it makes extensive use of language in making the models accessible to the public, but unlike any of the other modeling techniques, it has much greater capacity to describe business rules and constraints.

With ORM, it is difficult to describe entity types independently from relationships. The philosophy behind the language is that it describes "facts," where a fact is a combination of ORM objects: entity types, value types, and roles.

In ORM, an *entity type* is portrayed by an ellipse (often a circle, actually) containing its name. An ellipse can also represent a *value type*, which is effectively a *domain*. A value type describes a kind of data, like "date" or "amount", and can be related to entity types just like other entity types.

Relationships between pairs of objects are shown as pairs of roles. A *role* is the half of a relationship reading in one direction. In other words, entity type 1 plays a role with respect to entity type 2. Entity type 2 plays a complementary role with respect to entity type 1. A *fact* is the playing of a role by an entity type. Figure 3.11 shows that each relationship between entity types represents two facts. For example, each Event must be *an example of* one and only one Event Type, and each Event Type must be *embodied in* one or more Events.

In fact what would be an "attribute" of an entity type in an entity/relationship diagram, in ORM is simply a role played in a relationship. It is intentionally not clear initially whether the attribute is pointing to a value type or another entity type.

The dot where a relationship is attached to an entity type means that for each occurrence of the entity type, there must be at least one occurrence of the role involved. The double-headed arrow over one or more roles means that there can be no more than one occurrence of the roles so marked; they are *unique*. For each occurrence of the entity type, there can be no more than one occurrence of the role.

Object role modeling is described both in Appendix B and in Chapter 8 of this book. Chapter 8 describes ORM's approach to business rules. ORM is fully documented in Terry Halpin's 2000 book, *Information Modeling and Relational Databases.*

For example, the dot on Event makes it mandatory that each Event must be an example of at least one Event Type. The double-headed arrow over "an example of" means that there can be no more than one occurrence of this role for each Event. Absence of a dot next to Event Type makes it optional whether there are any events for that Event Type, and the absence of a double-headed arrow over "embodied in" means that the role can occur any number of times for an Event Type.

When it is related to another entity type, the role it takes is an attribute of the first entity type. Figure 3.11 shows an example: Event and event type are entity types. "Event description" and "event type description" appear to be attributes, but this is left intentionally ambiguous. Indeed, an attribute is treated as an object, just like an entity type. Event Type Description appears here to be a value type (domain). It is conceivable—albeit unlikely—that "Event Type Description" could turn out to have attributes of its own, thereby becoming an entity type. If this were an entity/relationship diagram, and "event type description" were initially shown as an attribute of Event, later, when it turned out that it had an attribute of its own, the model would have to be restructured to make Event Type an entity type. Here, it doesn't matter. The relationship between Event Type and Event Type Description is independent of whether or not there are attributes of Event Type Description.

An entity type *label* (an attribute which is a sole identifier) may be shown with a dashed ellipses around a value type, although as a shorthand, it also may be shown within the entity type ellipse in parentheses, below the entity type name. In the example, "(ID)" is the identifying attribute for event, and "(Code)" is the identifying attribute of event type.

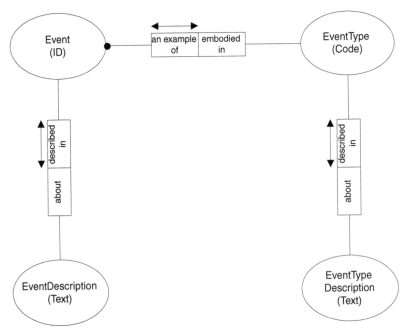

FIGURE 3.11 An ORM Model.

Relationships not only connect entity types to each other but also connect value types to entity types. ORM is unique in being able to graphically show the optionality and cardinality of attributes. That is, is the attribute mandatory? Can it take more than one value?

Where most methods portray *entity types* in terms that allow them to be translated into relational tables, ORM portrays the *relationships* so that they can be converted to tables. That is, the two parts (or more) of the relationship become columns in a "relation" (table). In effect, these are the foreign keys to the two entity types. Attributes of one or more of the related entity types also then become part of a generated table.

In Figure 3.11, for example, a table would be created from the *an example of / embodied in* relationship, with columns for "Event (code)" and "Event Type (code)". Another table would have the columns "Event Code" and "Event Description", and yet another would have "Event Type Code" and "Event Type Description". This is shown in Tables 3.1.

TABLES 3.1 Relationship Tables

Event Code	Event Description	Event Type Code	Event Type Description
A	Mary's wedding reception	X	Wedding party
B	Sam's retirement bash	Y	Retirement party
C	Sally's rehearsal dinner		

Event (Code)	EventType (Code)
A	X
B	Y
C	X

ORM represents a unique way to create conceptual data models for Row Three of the Architecture Framework.

How to Draw a Data Model

As stated above, Appendix B contains a comparison of the various data and object modeling techniques currently available. It compares their syntax, aesthetics, and appropriateness to each of the audiences described here.

Because this book is concerned with requirements analysis—the translation of a business owner's view to an architect's view—the data modeling technique used here will be the one that seems most suitable for presenting to an audience of business owners. It is graphically the simplest, with the fewest different kinds of symbols to learn.

The technique was developed by the British consulting company CACI and then made part of Oracle Corporation's approach to modeling. It was brought into its final form and publicized by Richard Barker in his 1990 book, *CASE Method: Entity Relationship Modelling*. It has since been made part of the European methodology, "Structured Systems Analysis and Design Method" (SSADM). (More information about SSADM can be found in Malcolm Eva's 1994 book, *SSADM Version 4: A User's Guide Second Edition*.)

In this notation, two major types of symbols are used in an entity/relationship diagram:

- A *rectangular box* with rounded corners, which represents an *entity type*
- A *line*, each half of which may be dashed or solid, which represents a *relationship* between two entity types

Other elements of the diagram may add additional information.

Entity Types

An entity type is a person, place, event, thing, or concept that has characteristics of interest to the business and is uniquely identifiable. It is something about which data are kept.

Examples of four entity types are shown in Figure 3.12.

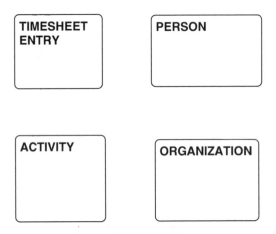

FIGURE 3.12 Entity Types.

Note that, as originally defined, what you see here are really *entity types* or *entity classes*. Each is the definition of a TIMESHEET ENTRY, a PERSON, an ORGANIZATION, or an ACTIVITY. In the original terminology, a *particular* person, organization, timesheet entry, or activity is an *entity*. That is, originally, the definition was called an "entity type", and the occurrence was called an "entity", but the language has since been corrupted. Now *entity* often refers to the definition, and an instance of the thing is called an *occurrence*. This book will retain the original definitions of "entity type" for the definition and "entity" for the occurrence. In the object-oriented world, the occurrence is called an *object*, while the entity is called an *object class* (or simply *class*.)

Sub-types and Super-types

When the occurrences of an entity type fall into two or more subcategories, the subcategories can themselves become entity types which are then called *sub-types* of the first entity type. The first entity type is called a *super-type*. For example, in Figure 3.13, PERSON and ORGANIZATION are examples of the larger class called "PARTY" (as in "party" to a contract). That is, each PARTY (a super-type) must be either a PERSON or an ORGANIZATION (a sub-type), each PERSON must be a PARTY, and each ORGANIZATION must be a PARTY.

Note that there is a rule with this notation that each occurrence of the super-type may be an occurrence of only one sub-type, and it must be an occurrence of one of them.

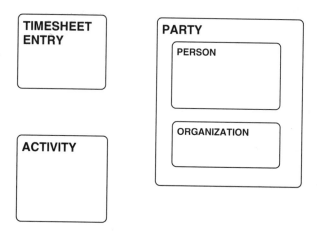

FIGURE 3.13 Sub-types and Super-types.

Relationships

A relationship is a pair of named associations between entity types. In an entity/relationship diagram, a relationship is represented by drawing a line between two entity types.

The *cardinality constraint*—the assertion that an occurrences of an entity type may be related to no more than a specified number of occurrences of another entity type—is represented on a diagram by the presence or absence of a "crow's foot" symbol next to the second entity type. If there is no crow's foot, an occurrence of the far entity type may be related to no more than one occurrence of the adjacent entity type. If there is a crow's foot, there is no limit to the number of occurrences to which the occurrence of the far entity type may be related.

The *optionality constraint*—the assertion that an occurrence of one entity type must be related to at least one occurrence of another entity type—is represented by the half-line next to the first entity type being solid or dashed.

In most notations, there are no real rules about the naming of relationships. People generally use verbs, but with no particular system regarding the way they use them. Cardinality and optionality are not expressed in the resulting sentences, except by saying such things as, for example, "A PERSON has zero, one, or many ASSIGNMENTS". The Barker notation, however, uses a convention that both adds additional discipline to the names and makes them more readable as normal English sentences.

Relationship sentences may be constructed from the symbols in the Barker technique as follows:

Each

<first entity type name>

must be (solid line from first entity type)
(or)
may be (dashed line from first entity type)

<relationship name>

one and only one (single line into second entity type)
(or)
one or more ("crows foot" into second entity type)

<second entity type name>,

    Examples of two relationships are shown in Figure 3.14.

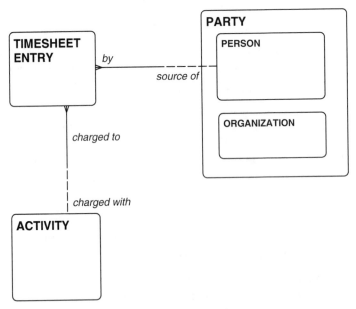

FIGURE 3.14 Relationships.

The top relationship in Figure 3.14 is represented by the following two sentences:

- Each TIMESHEET ENTRY <u>must be</u> *by* <u>one and only</u> one PERSON.
- Each PERSON <u>may be</u> *the source of* <u>one or more</u> TIMESHEETS.

The lower relationship in Figure 3.14 is represented by the following two sentences:

- Each TIMESHEET ENTRY <u>must be</u> *for* <u>one and only one</u> ACTIVITY.
- Each ACTIVITY <u>may be</u> *charged with* <u>one or more</u> TIMESHEET ENTRIES.

Attributes

An ***attribute*** is the definition of a characteristic, quality, or property of an entity type. It describes an entity type. In an entity/relationship diagram, an attribute of an entity type names and defines a characteristic, while an occurrence of an entity type provides a discrete value for the attribute.

Examples of attributes may be shown as text in the entity type boxes in Figure 3.15. Note that any attribute of (or relationship to) a super-type is ***inherited*** by each of the sub-types. In the example, "Party ID", an attribute of PARTY, is also an attribute of PERSON and of ORGANIZATION. This does not go the other way, however. "Family Name" is an attribute of PERSON only and therefore is *not* an attribute of either PARTY or ORGANIZATION. Similarly, TIMESHEET ENTRY is related to PERSON only, and not to ORGANIZATION.

When presenting data models, you may chose not to show the attributes. They tend to clutter the diagram unnecessarily if you are presenting a model for purposes of discussing structure only. On the other hand, some would like to see attributes to clarify the meaning of each entity type.

Note that on this diagram, attributes are preceded by different symbols.

- The open circle (O) means the attribute is optional—it may or may not be given a value for a particular instance of the entity type.
- The asterisk (*) means that it is mandatory.
- The pound sign (#) means that it is part of the "unique identifier" of the entity type. That is, the value of that attribute at least partially identifies different occurrences of the entity type—distinguishing them from each other.

The entity types PARTY and ACTIVITY are examples of ***reference entity types*** or ***independent entity types***. Occurrences of them do not require occurrences of any other entity type. The entity type TIMESHEET ENTRY is an example of a ***dependent entity type***, because an occurrence of it can only exist if it is related to occurrences of PERSON and ACTIVITY. The entity type TIMESHEET ENTRY is also an example of an ***intersect entity type***, sometimes called an ***associative entity type***. This is because its sole purpose for existing is to relate other entity types to one another.

PARTY is also an example of a reference entity type. A ***reference entity type*** is an entity type that usually refers to something tangible in the enterprise (in this case, a PERSON or an ORGANIZATION). It may also refer to a quality (like COLOR) that is used to describe another entity type, or to a classification for other entity types, such as ACTIVITY TYPE or CONTRACT TYPE. Usually, a reference entity type is also an independent entity type. By contrast, a ***transaction entity type*** (always a dependent entity type and usually an associative entity type) refers to something that occurred at a particular time.

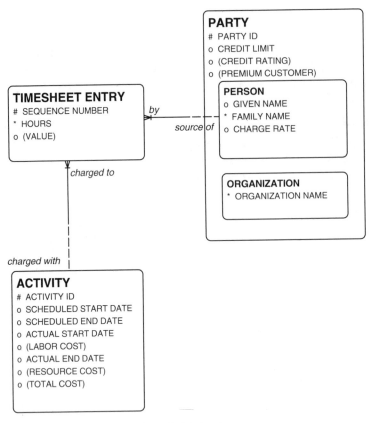

FIGURE 3.15 Attributes.

All independent entity types are reference entity types, while nearly all reference entity types are independent. All dependent entity types are transaction entity types, and all transaction entity types are dependent on reference entity types. It is possible for a reference entity type to be dependent on another reference entity type.

Some of the attributes in Figure 3.15 are in parentheses. This means that the value for that attribute is computed from other attributes. For example, "(Value)" in TIMESHEET ENTRY is computed as "Hours" in TIMESHEET ENTRY, times the "Charge Rate" in PERSON. "(Labor Cost)" in ACTIVITY is the sum of "(Value)" across all the TIMESHEET ENTRIES that an ACTIVITY is *charged with*.

Note that any notation may be used for derived attributes, but it is constrained by the process that will be used to convert attributes in entity types to columns in tables. Parentheses are not usually permitted in table names. If this conversion will be done automatically, the convention used here will not work. In that case, simply precede the attribute name with a "c".

Note also that the definition of the calculation does not show on the model. This must be documented behind the scenes.

Unique Identifiers

The first rule for specifying an entity type is that each of its occurrences must be unique. Duplicates are not permitted. An occurrence is made unique through some combination of attributes and relationships. By the end of the requirements analysis project, each entity type in the model must be assigned at least one unique identifier.

In the sample model in Figure 3.16, each occurrence of PERSON is made unique by a value for "ID". This is shown by the octothorpe (#)[4] in front of "ID" Similarly, COURSES are uniquely identified by values for "Course number".

A COURSE OFFERING, on the other hand, requires a value for "Offering date" plus identification of the COURSE that the COURSE OFFERING is an *occurrence of*. This is shown by the octothorpe in front of "Offering date" and the short line across the occurrence of relationship. A CLASS ENROLLMENT, meanwhile, can only be identified by identifying the PERSON enrolling and the COURSE OFFERING enrolled in. This is shown by lines across both relationships.

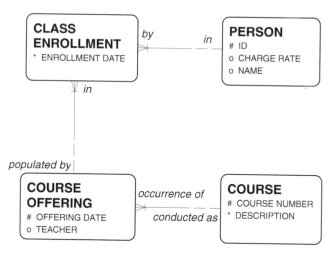

FIGURE 3.16 Unique Identifiers.

In the original relational theory, each entity type's unique identifier should be a combination of natural attributes. In practice, however, it is difficult to assert that any

---

4. This symbol (commonly known in the United States as the "pound sign") was given this name by the American Telephone and Telegraph Company in the 1960s when the Touch-Tone keypad was developed.

attribute is absolutely immutable—a requirement if it is to be part of a primary key. For this reason, it is common to assign a *surrogate key* at least for reference entity types. This is a sequence number that has no intrinsic meaning. It is simply incremented for each new occurrence to ensure that that occurrence is unique. In Figure 3.16, "ID" is a surrogate key to PERSON.

If all reference entity types (those that have no mandatory relationships to any other entity type) have surrogate keys, it is still reasonable to let natural keys serve as identifiers of the relationships to such reference entity types. It is not necessary to have a surrogate key, *unless* it is important to allow multiple occurrences of each combination the entity type describes. In Figure 3.16, for example, using the two relationships to identify occurrences of CLASS ENROLLMENT means that no PERSON may be enrolled in the same COURSE OFFERING more than once. If you want to allow such duplication, it is necessary to add a "Sequence number" as part of the identifier.

Using Entity/Relationship and Object Models

The definition of a data model says only that boxes represent things and lines represent relationship between pairs of things. The definition doesn't say anything about how a data model is to be *used*. In fact, the meaning of the boxes and lines can be very different in three of the Architecture rows we've been talking about.

Figure 3.1 shows the Architecture Framework with the Data column highlighted. Three perspectives have a particular interest in data or object models:

- *Business owners* are interested in seeing representations of the tangible things of their business. They see things as being related to each other in complex ways. They view the data's external schema.
- *Architects* are interested in the underlying structure of data. For them all relationships are binary and one-to-many. The principles of normalization have been applied. They are concerned with the conceptual schema.
- *Designers* are interested in representations of the implications of data structure on the physical design of databases, whether they be relational, object oriented, or something else. They are interested in the logical schema that is appropriate to the technology they are using.

The graphic structure of data modeling is the same in all three rows, although, as described in Appendix B, different notations are better for the different views. Chen's notation is suitable for Row Two models, for example, since it can describe multi-way relationships. Oracle's notation works well for Row Three models, since it has minimal extra symbols for things not needed there. Object-role modeling can also be used for both Row Two and Row Three. In a relational environment, IDEF1X works well as a design technique, while object-oriented designers favor the UML. The following sections discuss this issue in more detail.

Business Owners' Views (Row Two)

The most important element of the business owners' views to capture is *language*. The first artifact to be created in any analysis project should be a *glossary*. This captures every technical, industry, and other specialized term and its definitions. If the same word is used in multiple ways, work with people to come up with a single definition, or, if that isn't possible, document the disagreement.

Once the terms have been captured, capture the *facts* of the enterprise. These are constructed from the terms in the glossary, and for the most part they can be represented in data models. However they are represented, the models prepared for *business owners* must be clear to them, in their language. In principle, any of the modeling notations could be used here, but since these models will be discussed with nontechnical people, it is desirable to use a technique whose aesthetic qualities make it attractive and easy to understand. In Row Two, the business owner's view, the entity types (classes), attributes, and relationships (associations) represent external schemata—*business objects*. The notation for such a model may allow multiway relationships, many-to-many relationships, and multivalued attributes. The important thing about this model is that it represents exactly the things the people in the business see. There is no diagrammatic rigor to the model, but it is important to use language precisely and clearly.

The business owners' models are also called *divergent data models*, because they constitute a diverse set of entity types.

An entity type could be a PURCHASE ORDER or a VENDOR, each of which is actually a combination of entity types and relationships. Multivalued attributes are permitted, such as the "line items" contained in a PURCHASE ORDER. Many of the relationships will be "many-to-many", and relationships may be portrayed that are not binary. (A PROFESSOR teaches a COURSE in a CLASSROOM, for example.)

The aesthetics of the diagrams are important, since such people will have little patience for learning arcane diagraming conventions.

Architect's View (Row Three)

Models prepared for information *architects* (information system designers) are more disciplined. In Row Three, the architect attempts to identify underlying structures. At the syntactic level, all multiway relationships are transformed into sets of *binary relationships*. All many-to-many relationships between entity types are transformed into *intersect entity types* that represent occurrences of associations between the two entity types. All *multi-valued attributes* are converted into additional entity types, according to the rules of "normalization" (described below). Following these disciplines insures that the true natures of the data are really understood. In addition, at the semantic level, this model is expressed in terms of the most fundamental things of the business. What the business owners see may be but examples of these fundamental things. For example, business owners are usually conscious of VENDORS, CUSTOMERS, EMPLOYEES, and the like. In the architectural model, these are replaced with PERSON, and ORGANIZATION with a super-type called PARTY, where a PARTY is defined as either a person or an organization of interest to the enterprise. These are then related to each other, contracts, and other things, in order to show their roles as customers, vendors, employees, and so forth.

This means that entity types in architects' models may well be combinations of entity types in business owners' models. This is called a *convergent data model*, because the diverse entity types of the divergent models have been consolidated ("converged") into a smaller number of more fundamental entity types.

Again, in principle, any of the modeling notations could be used for this kind of model, but, since these models also will be discussed with non-technical people, they should be as aesthetically clean and easy to understand as possible. Remember, it is the clients who ultimately must ensure that any assumptions made while creating either model were in fact true.

In addition to the simple resolution of anomalies in the context of a particular area, the architect also reaches out to other spheres of interest, to create a model that extends beyond the immediate environment. This means, for example, that what may appear to be a one-to-many relationship in the context of one department is really a many-to-many relationship when all departments are considered.

Designer's View (Row Four)

The set of boxes and lines that constitutes a data model's notation may also be used to represent the things in the *designer's view*. A designer sees a data model as an expression of computer artifacts. Specifically, what you see in Row Four depends on the technology you will be using: A relational designer sees tables, columns, and foreign keys; an object-oriented designer sees classes, attributes, and associations to be navigated. What is represented here are no longer things in the business but things in the computer.

Aesthetics are not as important to the designer as they are to the architect or the business owner. The designer likes to see more details in the diagram than do audiences of either of the other two kinds of models. Hence, these models may be more cluttered and complex.

It is here that the data model and the object model are used quite differently. The logical schema the designer uses depends on the database management system and development technology being used. If the implementation is to use relational technology, the boxes in the diagram represent tables, with variations on the technique representing foreign keys and other relational structures. IDEF1X is particularly suited for this.

Alternatively, the boxes can represent an object-oriented programmer's object classes, with additions to the notation for certain object-oriented constructs, such as composition and association navigation. The UML does this well.

Note, for example, that relational developers and object-oriented programmers view relationships quite differently in the design model. A relational database relates tables by *associating* matching columns. That is, a relationship represents a structure that is, by definition, mutual. If A is related to B, then by definition B is related to A.

In object-oriented programming, however, a relationship represents the two *navigation paths* from each class to the other. Where in a relational database a relationship simply asserts that two tables could be joined together in an SQL statement. In an object-oriented environment, a relationship means that program code implementing the behavior of each class will be used to implement one or both interactions between them.

Scott Ambler, for example, in a 1999 white paper, "Mapping Objects To Relational Databases" (http://www.ambysoft.com/mappingObjects.html), describes a model of ADDRESS and POSTAL AREA.[5] In the world, and therefore in an analysis model, each ADDRESS must be *in* one POSTAL AREA, while each POSTAL AREA may be *the location of* one or more ADDRESSES, as shown in Figure 3.17.

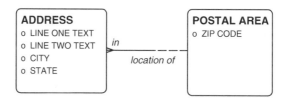

FIGURE 3.17 Analyst's ERD.

Note that the relationship's roles are named in both directions. The relationship from POSTAL AREA to ADDRESS is optional, since it is possible that a POSTAL AREA may have no addresses in it. For purposes of this exercise, we have stipulated that each ADDRESS *must be* in one POSTAL AREA, even though in the real world it may be the case that some addresses are specified without the POSTAL AREA, especially outside the United States.

This model, then, presupposes that any ZIP code specified for an ADDRESS will be validated by comparison with the ZIP codes for POSTAL AREAS in the reference entity type. It also envisions both a query as to the POSTAL AREA of an ADDRESS and of the ADDRESSES in a POSTAL AREA.

---

5. Actually, in Mr. Ambler's model this entity type was "ZIP Code", which is the name in the United States for a postal area code. It has been renamed here both in the interest of internationalism and because ZIP code is an attribute of POSTAL AREA. It is not a thing in its own right.

In Mr. Ambler's version of the model, however, there is not a "requirement" for the relationship to be documented in both directions. In his view, POSTAL AREA only exists to provide the behavior for validating a ZIP code attached to an ADDRESS. This validation, however, is limited to what can be inferred from a format and from the "City" the ADDRESS is in. It does not extend to examination of a master list of ZIP codes, and there certainly isn't any requirement to be able to go from a POSTAL AREA to the ADDRESSES in that POSTAL AREA. For these reasons, his model is much more constrained than the analysis entity/relationship diagram. Figure 3.18 shows the entity/relationship diagram of this design version of the problem. (The arrow is an annotation only. It is not an official part of the model.)

In Mr. Ambler's version, the model will only be navigated from ADDRESS to POSTAL AREA, so there is no need to specify the relationship from POSTAL AREA to ADDRESS. Since graphically there is no way *not* to specify the relationship in that direction, it is shown here as a "must be one and only one" relationship, without a meaningful name. Indeed, if the ZIP code is specified uniquely every time an ADDRESS is added, the relationship is in fact one-to-one, and it is mandatory. (Note that this means the same ZIP code can appear more than once in POSTAL AREA.)

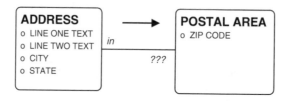

FIGURE 3.18 OO Modeler's ER Model.

In Mr. Ambler's example, the entity/relationship diagram in Figure 3.18 is not adequate to represent what is needed for design. UML is much more suited for this. Figure 3.19 shows the UML version of this model. Here we can see the arrow showing the only navigation direction. We can also see the names of the programs that implement each entity type's behavior. (OK, cardinality from POSTAL AREA to ADDRESS is shown, but your author doesn't know why.) The key program for this discussion is "validate" in POSTAL AREA. This is a program that will check the format of the code and check for consistency between the code and the state specified. (In the U.S. the first two digits of a ZIP code determine the state where the POSTAL AREA is located.)

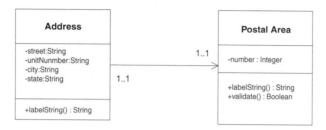

FIGURE 3.19 OO Modeler's UML Model.

This is clearly a design model. The notation has details (attribute formats, for example, and symbols qualifying attributes and behaviors) that are of interest to designers, but that are not of interest during analysis. It does not have relationship role names. In addition, as we have seen, its content differs from the original analysis model because of economic evaluations that were performed to constrain the design. The company cannot afford to buy a ZIP code master file (either from a financial or a logistical point of view), and it currently has no interest in locating addresses by ZIP code, so the design is modified to recognize that. Mr. Ambler says that this constrained approach is what is "required" by the business, but in fact it is only required because circumstances forced design to be something less than what is envisioned by the conceptual model. After all, applying economics to the conceptual model is what design is all about. The validation in this design is weaker than might be possible, but the company can decide to accept that. This is the sort of economic trade-off that designers do all the time.

Note, however, that circumstances may change in the future, and the ZIP code file may be deemed a good idea. The company may decide at that time that it wants to see all the addresses in a particular POSTAL AREA. Then it would be valuable to have constructed the conceptual model correctly, so you can see how the design model varied from it, and what now must be changed.

Normalization

Dr. Codd's relational theory includes a specific set of rules for organizing data, if they are to be considered relational. These rules are expressed in terms of *relations* (two dimensional arrays of values), *tuples* (rows) and *attributes* (the definitions of columns in a relation). Databases supporting the relational theory express relations as tables, attributes as columns, and tuples as rows in those tables. These rules for organizing data are observed in the architect's version of data modeling, although modeling can reveal things not evident from relational theory alone. (See discussion on page 104.)

Dr. Codd expressed the rules as a series of progressively more restrictive constraints on the structure of data. The idea is that if all of the constraints are applied, the data will have the least redundancy. Every element (unless it was used as a key) would appear once and only once in the structure.

The constraints are described in terms of *functional dependence*. C. J. Date gives a mathematical definition of this [Date, 1986, p. 365], which amounts to the fact that a column is "functionally dependent" on another column, if, given a value of the second column, you will always have the same value for the first column. The column the others are dependent upon is called the *primary key.*

The process of normalization goes through a succession of "normal forms". [6] In each case, for data to be in that normal form, they must be in the preceding one and then meet at least one additional constraint. The first four forms (first through third, and Boyce Codd) apply structural constraints that allow one to assert compliance absolutely. Fourth and fifth normal form, on the other hand, assert that if the *meanings* of the data are of a certain kind, *and* you draw the model in a way appropriate to that meaning, then the constraints are satisfied.

Two points should be made about normalization:

First, its purpose is to create the simplest, least redundant organization of data possible. For this reason, it is a Row Three process. Designers in Row Four often depart from the normalized structure.

Second, the process looks at actual sets of values. It must assume that the sample data shown completely represent the relationships that exist in the things the data describe. In the real world, alas, you cannot assume that there is anything to prevent someone from introducing a new row that invalidates the whole analysis. This means that it is critical for any relationships identified to be verified by a subject matter expert.

Before Normal Forms

For a set of data to be a relation at all requires certain things:

1. It must be arranged in tuples of uniform length—that is, where every tuple has the same number of attributes.
2. There may be no meaning attributed to either the sequence of tuples or the sequence of attributes.
3. Each tuple must be uniquely identifiable by one or more attributes, called the **primary key.**

6. While the term "normalization" is derived from the mathematics that Dr. Codd used to derive the technique, he was amused to observe that, in 1970 while he was normalizing relations in data, President Nixon was "normalizing" relations with China.

In other words, the data must be arranged in simple, two-dimensional forms. For example, see Table 3.2. The data describe various environmental chemical tests conducted on samples taken in someone's back yard. Each tuple represents the set of tests conducted on a particular sample. In this case, the primary key is a combination of the "Sample Date" and the "Mat'l Code" describing the material sampled. This example assumes that the same kind of material will not be sampled twice on the same day.

TABLE 3.2 Before Normal Forms

(primary   key)

Sample Date	Mat'l Code	Mat'l Description	<----------- Test 1 ----------->				<----------- Test 2 ----------->				<--------
			Date	Type	Desc	pH	Date	Type	Desc	pH	Date
1/15/95	3256	Pool water	1/19/02	A	strips	5.2	1/25/02	B	chem	5.2	2/2/02
1/15/95	4287	Soil	2/25/02	B	chem	3.2	2/30/02	B	chem	3.9	3/1/02
3/2/95	3256	Pool watter	3/5/02	A	strips	5.8	3/6/02	A	strips	5.9	3/15/02

First Normal Form

First normal form adds an additional constraint:

---

4. Every attribute may have only one value for a tuple in a relation.

Note that in Table 3.2, the "Date", "#", "Test" (type and description), and "pH" for each test are repeated for as many tests as exist. This has several effects:

First, it is impossible to specify a uniform record length for the tuples. Ten percent of the tuples might have eight tests, while 90 percent might have two only.

Second, to find out the number of times a particular kind of test was run, it is necessary to examine not only every tuple, but also all the attributes in that tuple.

First normal form essentially eliminates the phenomenon of repeating groups. A *repeating group* is a set of attributes that can take multiple values for a given occurrence of an entity type. This is not permitted for a relation. There will be only one value for "Test Date" in any tuple of the relation. This produces a relation that looks like Table 3.3.

In this relation, notice that there is one tuple for each occurrence of a test. Hence we have named the relation "TEST". This means that the primary key is now a combination of not only the "Sample Date" and "Mat'l Code" that we saw before, but also includes the "Test #".

TABLE 3.3 First Normal Form

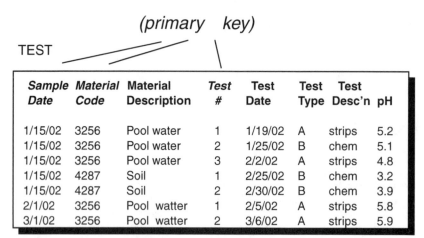

Sample Date	Material Code	Material Description	Test #	Test Date	Test Type	Test Desc'n	pH
1/15/02	3256	Pool water	1	1/19/02	A	strips	5.2
1/15/02	3256	Pool water	2	1/25/02	B	chem	5.1
1/15/02	3256	Pool water	3	2/2/02	A	strips	4.8
1/15/02	4287	Soil	1	2/25/02	B	chem	3.2
1/15/02	4287	Soil	2	2/30/02	B	chem	3.9
2/1/02	3256	Pool watter	1	2/5/02	A	strips	5.8
3/1/02	3256	Pool watter	2	3/6/02	A	strips	5.9

Second Normal Form

In Table 3.3 the "Material Description" value repeats every time the same material is sampled. This has several effects:

First, the repeated description uses unnecessary space.

Second, multiple entry of the same fact permit errors and inconsistencies to creep in. Note the two occurrences of the misspelling "watter".

Third, if the description is changed for any reason, it must be changed for all tests of that material.

Fourth, you cannot assert that a material exists until it has been the subject of a test.

Note that all of these problems are derived from the fact that "Material Description" is functionally dependent on only part of the primary key, "Material Code".

To address this, another constraint is added, constituting Second Normal Form:

---

5. Each attribute must be dependent on the **entire** primary key.

Addressing this issue yields the structure shown in Table 3.4. In this, a separate relation was created to correlate "Material Code" and "Material Description". Since the value of "Material Description" is dependent only on the value of "Material Code", it should not be in the TEST relation but in a relation by itself, here called MATERIAL. Note that "Material Code" is still in TEST, since the test data are still dependent on the material being tested. But data about each material need not be. That's what the MATERIAL relation is for.

TABLE 3.4 Second Normal Form

Sample Date	Material Code	Test #	Test Date	Test Type	Test Desc'n	pH
1/15/02	3256	1	1/19/02	A	strips	5.2
1/15/02	3256	2	1/25/02	B	chem	5.1
1/15/02	3256	3	2/2/02	A	strips	4.8
1/15/02	4287	1	2/25/02	B	chem	3.2
1/15/02	4287	2	2/30/02	B	chem	3.9
2/1/02	3256	1	3/5/02	A	strips	5.8
3/1/02	3256	2	3/6/02	A	strips	5.9

MATERIAL

Material Code	Material Description
3256	Pool water
4287	Soil

IMPORTANT NOTE: As stated previously, this analysis presumes that the sample data exhaustively define the relationships. Unless someone who knows the business can verify it, you have no assurance that a new tuple will not invalidate the whole analysis. In the above example, if material code 3256 could also describe "Radiator water" (or if "watter" is in fact a special kind of material), the second normal form step shown here wouldn't work.

Third Normal Form

In Table 3.4, the primary key of TEST is still "Sample Date", "Material Code", and "Test #". All of the attributes are functionally dependent on those attributes for their values. But notice something. Every time "Test Type" has the value "A", "Test Desc'n" has the value "strips". Every time "Test Type" has the value "B", "Test Desc'n" has the value "chem". In other words, in addition to being dependent on the primary key, "Test Desc'n" is dependent on another *non-key* attribute.

This means that the value "strips" must be entered every time a "Test Type" has the value "A". This causes many of the same problems described above for first normal form: Space is wasted; every entry must be spelled identically, and it may well not be; if the description of a test type is changed, it must be changed for every occurrence of the type; a test type may not be defined until it is used in a test. In other words, "Test Description" is dependent on "Test Type", which is not part of the primary key.

This leads to specification of an additional constraint, to bring us to Third Normal Form:

---

6. Each attribute must be dependent **only** on the primary key.

This leads to the structure shown in Table 3.5. Since "Test Description" is dependent on "Test Type", regardless of the actual tests conducted, these attributes are pulled out to a separate relation, TEST TYPE.

The "Test type" code still appears in TEST, since the type of test conducted is still an important part of the information about a test.

TABLE 3.5 Third Normal Form

(primary key)

TEST

Sample Date	Material Code	Test #	Test Date	Test Type	pH
1/15/02	3256	1	1/19/02	A	5.2
1/15/02	3256	2	1/25/02	B	5.1
1/15/02	3256	3	2/2/02	A	4.8
1/15/02	4287	1	2/25/02	B	3.2
1/15/02	4287	2	2/30/02	B	3.9
3/1/02	3256	1	3/5/02	A	5.8
3/1/02	3256	2	3/6/02	A	5.9

MATERIAL

Material Code	Material Description
3256	Pool water
4287	Soil

TESTTYPE

Test Type	Description
A	strips
B	chem

Boyce/Codd Normal Form

To get to this point we've established that each attribute/attribute must be a function of "the key, the whole key, and nothing but the key, so help me Codd."[7] All of the forms so far have been about relationships between the key and non-key attributes.

But it may be the case that there are dependencies within parts of a compound key. Table 3.6 is a variation on our previous example that concerns where testing is to take place. Instead of using "Test Type" as in the previous examples, the primary key here is composed of four attributes: "Material Type", "Test Type", (Test) "Location", and "Date".

(As a simplification for this example, "Sample Date" and "Test Date" can be collapsed into "Date" by assuming that the same "Test Date" does not occur for two "Sample Dates".)

The value of the test information ("pH") is determined by what is being tested, what kind of test is conducted, where it is conducted, and when it is conducted.

Closer examination, however, suggests that every time "Location" is "yard", the "Test Type" conducted there is "A". Similarly, each time "Location" is "Lab", the "Test Type is "B", and each time "Location" is "Office", the "Test Type" is "C". That is, the test type is determined by the location where the test is conducted. This means that if the Location name changed, it would have to be changed for every occurrence of the corresponding "Test Type", or, alternatively, if a Test Type Code changed, it would have to be changed for every occurrence of the corresponding Location.

In other words, "Location" and "Test Type", two parts of the primary key, are dependent on each other.

TABLE 3.6 Another Example

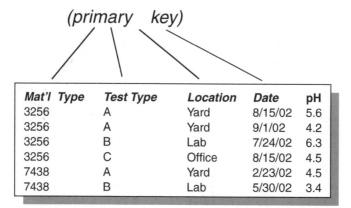

Mat'l Type	Test Type	Location	Date	pH
3256	A	Yard	8/15/02	5.6
3256	A	Yard	9/1/02	4.2
3256	B	Lab	7/24/02	6.3
3256	C	Office	8/15/02	4.5
7438	A	Yard	2/23/02	4.5
7438	B	Lab	5/30/02	3.4

---

7. This quotation is part of industry lore. Your author has been unable to determine its source.

If the relationships indicated by the data are true, there is an additional relation required: one that shows the relationships between "Test Type" and "Location". This in turn implies that there are in fact two different candidate primary keys for TEST: "Material Type"/ "Test Type"/ "Date" and "Material Type"/ "Location"/ "Date" (see Table 3.7). Use of either of these, plus creation of the LOCATION relation, puts the configuration in "Boyce-Codd Normal Form".

This is embodied in the following constraint:

7. No part of the primary key may be dependent on another part of the primary key.

TABLE 3.7 Boyce-Codd Normal Form

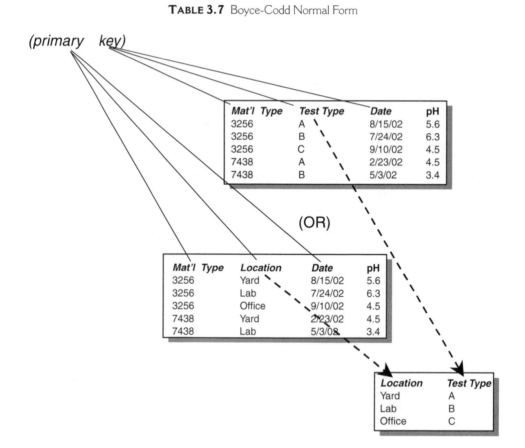

Fourth Normal Form

The next two kinds of normal form are more subtle, since, instead of having a single solution, they are each satisfied in one of two ways, depending on the nature of the data being described.

Table 3.8 shows a different variation on our problem. This relation describes the possible combinations of material type, test type, tester, and location of test. Each tuple requires all four attributes to be identified. Here we see that each material can be given a test type by someone ("Conducted By") at a particular location ("Conducted At"). (We are not speaking here of actual tests, but simply of provision for who can conduct them and where.)

In the example Sam can conduct test type A at the Lab, in the Office, and in the Yard. Shirley can do so as well. In addition, Sam can conduct test type B in each location. Notice that if a new tester is added, a tuple must be created for each of the locations where the tester is qualified.

It appears, though, that each tester for a given test type is qualified for *all* possible locations. If that is the case, it is an unnecessary amount of extra work to itemize these.

TABLE 3.8 Yet Another Example

POTENTIAL TEST

Material Code	Test Type	Conducted By	Conducted At
3256	A	Sam	Lab
3256	A	Sam	Office
3256	A	Sam	Yard
3256	A	Shirley	Lab
3256	A	Shirley	Office
3256	A	Shirley	Yard
3256	B	Sam	Lab
3256	B	Sam	Office
3256	B	Sam	Yard

(primary key)

What this reveals is that there are independent sets of dependencies within the primary key. Each "Material Code"/ "Test Type" combination can be conducted at one of the three "conducted at" locations shown, and independently of this, each "Material Code"/"Test Type" combination can be "conducted by Sam or Shirley." This calls for two relations instead of one.

The Fourth Normal Form constraint is:

---

8. There may be no independent sets of dependencies within a primary key.

If this is required and it is done, the result is in *Fourth Normal Form*, as shown in Table 3.9.

Note, by the way, that if Shirley is *not* permitted to conduct test A on Material 3256 in the yard, or Sam is not permitted to test Material 3256 in the office, then the "Conducted By" and "Conducted At" attributes are not independent. In that case, to be in Fourth Normal Form, the data must be left arranged as in Table 3.8.

TABLE 3.9 Fourth Normal Form

(primary key)

CONDUCTORS

Material Code	Test Type	Conducted By
3256	A	Sam
3256	A	Shirley
3256	B	Sam

TEST LOCATIONS

Material Code	Test Type	Conducted At
3256	A	Lab
3256	A	Office
3256	A	Yard
3256	B	Lab
3256	B	Office
3256	B	Yard

Fifth Normal Form

Our next example examines the relationships among Material Code, Test Code, and Location. Tables 3.10 include basic reference relations for MATERIAL, TEST TYPE, and LOCATION. Tables are also included for the intersections of each pair of these reference relations: MATERIAL TO BE TESTED, LOCATION OF TEST, and LOCATION OF MATERIAL. It is also possible to create a relation that contains permutations of all three reference relations—MATERIAL TO BE TESTED IN A LOCATION.

A structure is in Fifth Normal Form if these relations are properly configured.

TABLE 3.10 Still Another Example

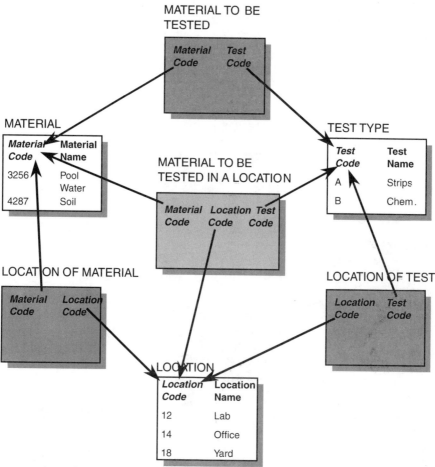

Specifically, if the set of tuples in MATERIAL TO BE TESTED IN A LOCATION represents all possible permutations of the tuples in MATERIAL TO BE TESTED, LOCATION OF TEST, and LOCATION OF MATERIAL, then that relation is not needed.

In the example in Table 3.11:

- Material Type 3256 can only be subject to Test Types C and A, while Material Type 4287 can be subject to Test Type B.

- Material Type 3256 can only be collected at Location Types 12 and 14. Furthermore, Material Type 4287 can only be conducted at Location Type 18.
- Test Type A can be conducted at Locations 12 and 14, but not 18, while Test Type B can only be conducted at Location 18.

If the three associative relations (Location of Material, Material to be Tested, and Location of Test) determine what can be in MATERIAL TO BE TESTED IN A LOCATION, then only the tuples "C 3256 14", "A 3256 12", and "B 4287 18" are permitted. Indeed, these are the tuples contained in MATERIAL TO BE TESTED IN A LOCATION, so that relation is redundant and must be eliminated to put the configuration in Fifth Normal Form.

TABLE 3.11 Fifth Normal Form—Case 1

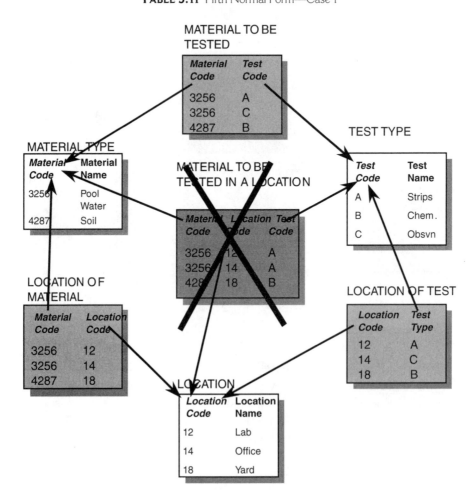

On the other hand, if there are combinations in MATERIAL TO BE TESTED IN A LOCATION that are not reflected in one or more of the other intersect relations, or vice versa, then MATERIAL TO BE TESTED IN A LOCATION is required, as shown in Table 3.12.

Here MATERIAL 4287 can be subject to TEST TYPE B *if* it is in LOCATION TYPE 14, even though LOCATION OF TEST does not show Test Type B/"Location type" 14 as a legitimate combination by itself. Alternatively, Test Type B/"Location type" 18 is legal in LOCATION OF TEST, even though there are no examples of it in MATERIAL TO BE TESTED IN A LOCATION.

In other words, Fifth Normal Form adds the (informally worded here) constraint:

---

9. A three-way (or more) relationship is redundant if all its occurrences may be derived from combinations of two-way occurrences.

TABLE 3.12 Fifth Normal Form—Case 2

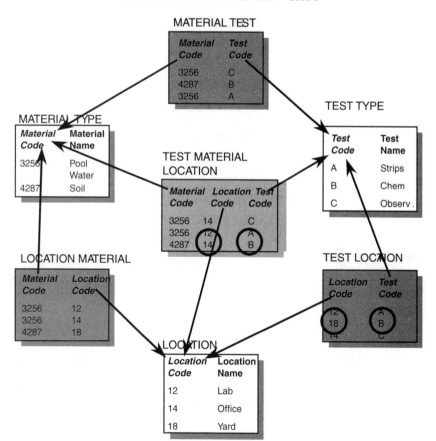

Data Modeling and Normalization

Dr. Codd's techniques for defining data structures rigorously apply specifically to relations and attributes. They are expressed in terms of the relationships between attributes, and particularly in terms of dependencies between attributes.

Thus, they represent a conceptual model of data. Relational database management systems can implement relational structure as is, but they also permit "de-normalization" (violations of the normalization rules) for performance and other reasons. Also, different database management systems implement aspects of the relational model in different ways. Hence, once a particular database management system and a particular table design is involved, you are in the designer's world, not the architect's.

Because relational theory yields a conceptual view of data, it should obtain the same view of data as is yielded from data modeling. Because it is an inductive (bottom up) process, however, rather than a deductive (top down) one, the results can be different.

For example, in Table 3.3, reproduced here as Table 3.13, we conclude that "Material Description" is dependent upon "Material Code", based on the example tuples shown. There is no guarantee, however, that another tuple will not appear—in data that we have not yet seen—that shows a Material Code of "3256" but a Material Description of "soil". In that case, Material Description would *not* be dependent upon Material Code, and the reconfiguration for Second Normal Form would not be appropriate. (And, as mentioned above, we shouldn't automatically rule out the possibility that "Pool water" is a different substance of interest.)

Yes, we can usually apply inductive reasoning to real data and come up with good results, but there is no guarantee.

TABLE 3.13 Induction about Data

(primary key)

TEST

Sample Date	Material Code	Material Description	Test #	Test Date	Test Type	Test Desc'n	pH
1/15/02	3256	Pool water	1	1/19/02	A	strips	5.2
1/15/02	3256	Pool water	2	1/25/02	B	chem	5.1
1/15/02	3256	Pool water	3	2/2/02	A	strips	4.8
1/15/02	4287	Soil	1	2/25/02	B	chem	3.2
1/15/02	4287	Soil	2	2/30/02	B	chem	3.9
3/1/02	3256	Pool watter	1	3/5/02	A	strips	5.8
3/1/02	3256	Pool watter	2	3/6/02	A	strips	5.9

Modeling of the conceptual data schema at Row Three of the Architecture Framework approaches the problem from a different direction. The thought process here is not "what can we infer from this pot of real data" but "what are the things that this entity type is about?" In Figure 3.20 we start with the idea of TEST, but simple examination of the attributes suggests that it is about more than that. Based on the *meaning* of the attributes, the model seems to be about sampling and materials, as well as tests. That would suggest the existence of entity types SAMPLE, MATERIAL, and TEST.

Moreover, it would seem that there are both a reference to test types and actual occurrences of tests. That is, instead of simple TEST, what we really have seems to be TEST and TEST TYPE.

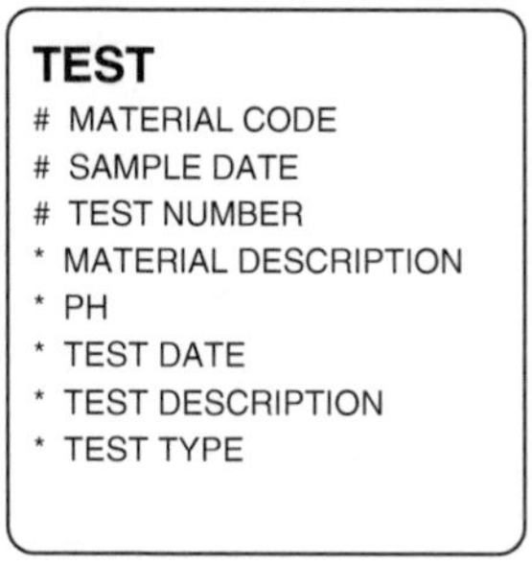

```
TEST
# MATERIAL CODE
# SAMPLE DATE
# TEST NUMBER
* MATERIAL DESCRIPTION
* PH
* TEST DATE
* TEST DESCRIPTION
* TEST TYPE
```

FIGURE 3.20 The TEST Entity Type.

This examination, presented in entity/relationship model form, gives the picture in Figure 3.21. This did call for us to come up with relationship names, but that helps as well in our understanding of what is presented. The model, then, asserts that each SAMPLE must be *of* one MATERIAL, and that the SAMPLE may be *tested in* one or more TEST OCCURRENCES. Each TEST OCCURRENCE in turn must be *on* one SAMPLE and *an example of* one TEST TYPE. Note that we are now describing aspects of the business in English, not simply immersing ourselves in a lot of data.

The question, then, is not whether, for example, "Material description" is dependent on "Material code". Rather it should be "What thing in the world does material description (and material code, for that matter) describe?" Logically those turn out to be the same question, but the latter version gives a much clearer view of the *nature* of the data.

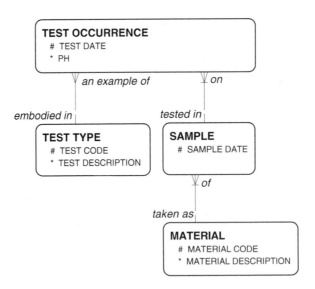

FIGURE 3.21 Test Occurrences.

Tables 3.14 are derived from this model. Note that they are almost the same as the Third Normal Form example in Tables 3.5, reproduced below as Tables 3.15.

There are minor differences between these two relation designs: The TEST relation has become the TEST OCCURRENCE relation. This is not terribly important. It simply clarifies the distinction between the definition of a test (its TEST TYPE) and examples of it (its TEST OCCURRENCES).

A more significant difference is the addition of the SAMPLE relation. Clearly, examination of the model has shown us (as normalization did not) that *samples* are one subject of this model. Since each test is for one sample only, however, the sample has no non-key attributes. Moreover, since the key to TEST (OCCURRENCE) already includes "Sample date" and "Material code", the normalization process did not identify any need for a separate relation. In a relational *design*, this omission may well be appropriate.

In the future, however, if it becomes desirable to have attributes for SAMPLE (such as "Sample location", for example), it will be convenient to have already at least postulated the entity type, even if it was not implemented as a relation. If the only "model" of these data is the normalized relation structure, the sudden addition of a new attribute will require a complete revisiting of the normalization process.

TABLE 3.14 Test Occurrence Tables

TEST OCCURRENCE

Sample Date	Material Code	Test #	Test Date	Test Type	pH
1/15/02	3256	1	1/19/02	A	5.2
1/15/02	3256	2	1/25/02	B	5.1
1/15/02	3256	3	2/2/02	A	4.8
1/15/02	4287	1	2/25/02	B	3.2
1/15/02	4287	2	2/30/02	B	3.9
3/1/02	3256	1	3/5/02	A	5.8
3/1/02	3256	2	3/6/02	A	5.9

SAMPLE

Sample Date	Material Code
1/15/02	3256
1/15/02	4287
3/1/02	3256

MATERIAL

Material Code	Material Description
3256	Pool water
4287	Soil

TEST TYPE

Test Type	Description
A	strips
B	chem

TABLE 3.15 Normalized Test Tables

TEST

Sample Date	Material Code	Test #	Test Date	Test Type	pH
1/15/02	3256	1	1/19/02	A	5.2
1/15/02	3256	2	1/25/02	B	5.1
1/15/02	3256	3	2/2/02	A	4.8
1/15/02	4287	1	2/25/02	B	3.2
1/15/02	4287	2	2/30/02	B	3.9
3/1/02	3256	1	3/5/02	A	5.8
3/1/02	3256	2	3/6/02	A	5.9

MATERIAL

Material Code	Material Description
3256	Pool water
4287	Soil

TEST TYPE

Test Type	Description
A	strips
B	chem

Data modeling is particularly helpful when it comes to understanding the higher orders of normalization.

Table 3.16 shows the example from Tables 3.9. Here we had two attributes that may be independently a function of the rest of the primary key—"Material Code" and "Test Type". By creating two data models of the alternative solutions, it is easy to ask which is true.

TABLE 3.16 The Fourth Normal Form Problem

POTENTIAL TEST

Material Code	Test Type	Conducted By	Conducted At
3256	A	Sam	Lab
3256	A	Sam	Office
3256	A	Sam	Yard
3256	A	Shirley	Lab
3256	A	Shirley	Office
3256	A	Shirley	Yard
3256	B	Sam	Lab
3256	B	Sam	Office
3256	B	Sam	Yard

(primary key)

In the first example (Figure 3.22), the conductor and place of testing are determined to be independent. Each POTENTIAL TEST may be independently *conducted by* one or more CONDUCTORS and/or *conducted at* one or more LOCATION OF TESTS. By drawing these assertions in a data model, their shape is much more clear. Note that in this examination we realized that CONDUCTOR itself is a reference to a different entity type, PERSON, and LOCATION OF TEST is a reference to a SITE. While this is the model that represents Table 3.9's solution, these entity types were not evident in the normalization exercise.

In the second example, (Figure 3.23) each POTENTIAL TEST is a unique combination of PERSON who is the *conductor of* it and the SITE which is the *location of* it. This means that only combinations of MATERIAL, TEST TYPE, SITE, and PERSON that are explicitly specified for the POTENTIAL TEST are permitted. You cannot infer combinations from combinations of less than the whole set.

The point is, you can *see* the implications of each solution much more clearly in the data model than you could in the tables of sample data.

Thus, while data modeling properly done provides a model in fifth normal form inherently, it can also provide additional insights that are not seen in the normalization process alone.

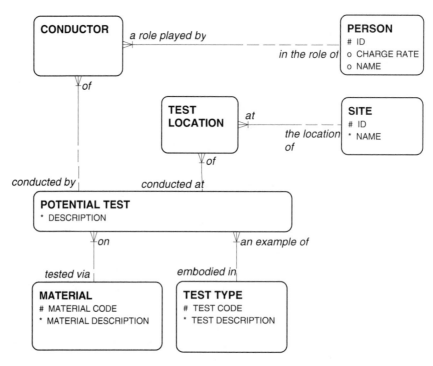

FIGURE 3.22 The First Fourth Normal Form Solution.

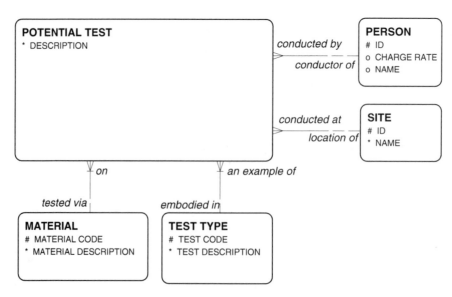

FIGURE 3.23 The Second Fourth Normal Form Solution.

Object-Oriented Design

Object-oriented design does not have to follow the normalization guidelines. Object-oriented technology can readily handle multi-valued attributes, object classes "within" other object classes, and so forth. As such, object-oriented designers often implement the business owners' views directly, with all their complex, un-normalized views of data. Moreover, it can more directly accommodate the inheritance presented in the sub-types and super-types of an entity/relationship or object model.

A system so designed, however, is vulnerable to future changes in the business. An object-oriented designer can take a normalized architectural model and combine entity types in all kinds of ways that appear to match the business owners' views, but when those views change, it is very nice to have the model of the *fundamental* nature of the data to refer to. If you go directly from the business owners' views to design, you are likely to be in trouble if the business owners change their minds as to what they want.

The disciplines used to ensure that an architect's entity/relationship model is consistent with normalized principles are critical to understanding the true nature of the data. To bypass this step is to create a system that can be devastated by changes in the business environment. Once the architectural understanding has been obtained, then the flexibility object-oriented designers have in representing data can be very useful.

Referential Integrity

Relational theory includes an algebra for describing the combination of relations to arrive at clusters of data in any form. Specifically, a *view* is a relation that is assembled from others. The rules of normalization do not have to apply to a view. Hence the sample tables above that were not in fifth normal form could be constructed from the normalized tables for display to a user.

This is accomplished by *joining* tables together. The tables in Tables 3.4, for example could be joined together on the "Material Code" column to produce the "view" of the data that is Table 3.3.

Implicit in this join is the assertion that the "Material Code" column in each table in fact mean the same thing.

The idea behind relational theory is that all relationships are explicit, through the meaning of the columns, not implemented in some way behind the scenes. Everything you must know is contained in the data in the relations.

In the world, however, there is a category of business rules that are not evident in the data. Specifically, for a set of relations to be properly used, they must address the question of *referential integrity*. Tables 3.5 (page 96) show three relations, TEST, MATERIAL, and TEST TYPE. What is not evident from these tables is what would happen if you delete MATERIAL 3256, "pool water". A business rule must be applied:

- *Cascade delete* – deletion of parent also deletes all of that parent's children. For example, deleting an occurrence of MATERIAL 3256 automatically means deleting all tuples in TEST with "Material Code" 3256.

- *Restricted* – deletion of parent is prohibited if that parent has children. For example, MATERIAL 3256 may not be deleted if there are any tuples in TEST with "Material Code" 3256

- *Nullify* – deletion of parent causes the value of the join column for all children to be set to "null". (Allowed only if that column is optional.) For example, deleting MATERIAL 3256 is permitted, leaving tuples in TEST pointing to a non-existent MATERIAL 3256 (or if the value of "Material Code" in TEST is simply set to "null".)

Data Modeling Conventions

Data modeling is a relatively new field, and standards have not yet fully been laid out. There are actually three levels of conventions to be defined in the data modeling arena:

- The first is *syntactic*, about the symbols to be used. Barker's technique, the UML, and IDEF1X are all examples of syntactic conventions.

- *Positional* conventions dictate how entity types are laid out. These guide the shape of the model. Often they are not followed, resulting in models that are chaotic, confusing, and very difficult to read.

- *Semantic* conventions describe standard ways for representing common business situations. Semantic conventions are relatively new in the industry. They were first described in 1995 book by David Hay, *Data Model Patterns: Conventions of Thought,* and then in the 1997 book, *Analysis Patterns*, by Martin Fowler. Other books on the subject have been published since then.

These three sets of conventions are, in principle, completely independent of each other. Given any of the syntactic conventions described here, you can follow any of the available positional or semantic conventions. In practice, however, promoters of each syntactic convention typically also promote at least particular positional conventions.

Syntactic—Symbols

Different sets of syntactic conventions are presented in Appendix B of this book. The appendix is organized in terms of the appropriate audience for each. The basic elements are the same across all the techniques, but each approach is concerned with different kinds of details, as was deemed appropriate for its particular audience.

All notations have symbols for entity types (or object classes), relationships (or associations), and attributes. The Barker notation has an additional symbol to represent the case where an entity type may be related to one or another different entity types, but not both. IDEF1X has special symbols to represent foreign key implementations. The UML has room for describing the behavior of entity types, and the ability to describe business rules between relationships.

Positional—The Crow's Foot Rule

The Barker technique imposes an additional constraint upon the drawing, over and above determining what symbols to use to represent different things: Entity types on a drawing are to be arranged so that the crow's feet in the relationships point either to the top of the diagram or to its left. In addition, boxes are stretched so that all relationship lines are straight, without "elbows".

This has the effect of providing some sort of "shape" to the drawing. A drawing with a random assortment of boxes and lines going every which way is very difficult to read. Figure 3.24, for example, shows a data model organized randomly. What is the model about? Hard to say, really. People seem to be visiting someone. A block party?

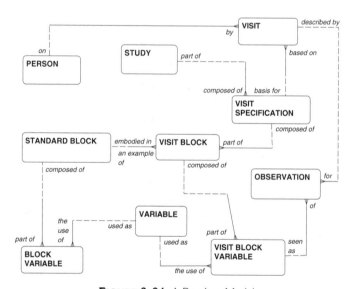

FIGURE 3.24 A Random Model.

Following the positional convention has the effect of placing the reference entity types (those that don't depend on any others) in the lower right, and the intersect or transaction entity types in the upper left. This makes it much easier to see the basic elements in the model, separately from what is done to them. Figure 3.25 is the model from Figure 3.24 rearranged according to this rule. Here it is easier to see that the model is basically about STUDIES of PEOPLE. OBSERVATIONS of VARIABLES are then collected on PEOPLE during these STUDIES.

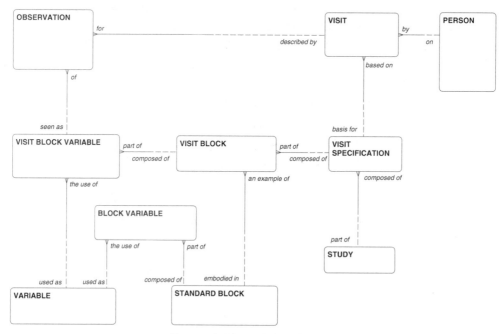

FIGURE 3.25 An Orderly Model.

There are those with the opinion that crow's feet should point down and to the right. While your author stands firmly against this heresy, the fact of the matter is that as long as you are consistent, you will achieve the same result.

Semantic—Data Model Patterns

If you follow the crow's foot rule, you will begin to notice certain things about your models. The aesthetics of the drawing suggest similarities. Figure 3.26, for example, shows a model of PURCHASE ORDERS, each of which is *to* a VENDOR and *composed of* one or more LINE ITEMS, each of which is *for* a PRODUCT TYPE.[8]

---

8. The examples in this section are derived from examples in David C. Hay's Data Model Patterns: Conventions of Thought (New York: Dorset House Publishing, 1996). Used with permission of Dorset House Publishing Co., Inc.

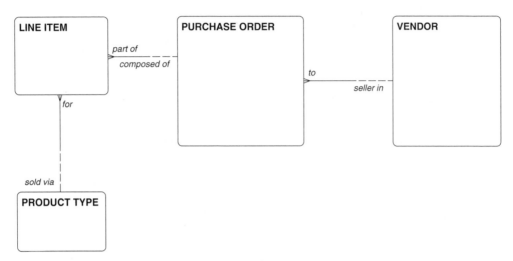

FIGURE 3.26 Purchase Orders.

Figure 3.27, on the other hand, shows a model of sales orders. Sales orders, of course, are handled by a completely different department from purchase orders, so there would seem to be no relationship whatsoever between them. In this figure, a SALES ORDER must be *from* one CUSTOMER and *composed of* one or more LINE ITEMS, each of which is *for* a PRODUCT TYPE.

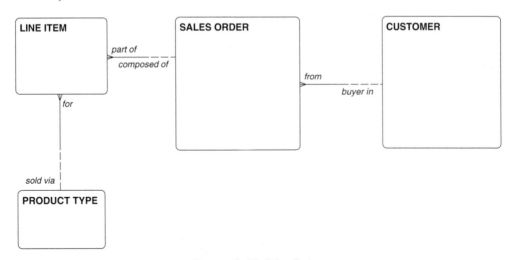

FIGURE 3.27 Sales Orders.

As you look at these two models, what do you see? First, the structures of SALES ORDER and PURCHASE ORDER are identical. Each must be *composed of* one or more LINE ITEMS, each of which is *for* a PRODUCT TYPE. The big difference is that a PURCHASE ORDER must be *to* a VENDOR, and a SALES ORDER must be *from* a CUSTOMER. But what are CUSTOMER and VENDOR? Each of these is fundamentally either a PERSON or an ORGANIZATION. Having said that, we can now recognize that our own enterprise is in fact an ORGANIZATION.

An ORGANIZATION or a PERSON is only a "customer" if it is a *buyer in* a (purchase or sales) ORDER. It is only a "vendor" if it is a *seller in* such an ORDER.[9] Thus, the real model is of an ORDER that has two relationships to PARTY: it must be *from* one PARTY and *to* another PARTY. Each party may be the *buyer in* one or more ORDERS, and each PARTY may be the *seller in* one or more ORDERS. This is shown in Figure 3.28.

The vendor's sales order is exactly the same order as the customer's purchase order. If we are the buyer, we call it a PURCHASE ORDER. If we are the seller, we call it a SALES ORDER. Any order always has both a buyer and a seller. Moreover, some organizations might well be both buyer and seller. The fact of the matter is that our organization is assuming one or the other of those roles.

Note that both PERSON AND ORGANIZATION share roles in an ORDER. In a large model, they will share other roles as well, so it is useful to define a super-type PARTY which is defined as either a person or organization of interest to the enterprise.

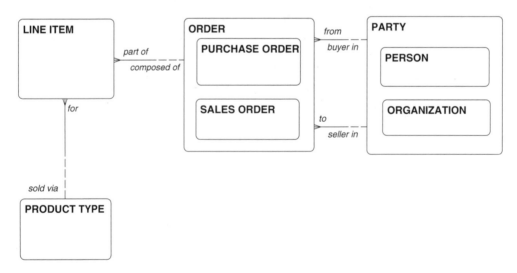

FIGURE 3.28 Orders.

It turns out that this model for ORDER (which could also be called CONTRACT or AGREEMENT, or whatever) is common to any enterprise that does business with others. Once you recognize that this is the generic pattern for orders, you can now use it for

---

9. In this example, that is. In some companies you must be designated as a "vendor" before you can sell something. This would require creation of an entity type linking PARTY to PRODUCT TYPE to portray the role.

almost any company. It may have to be elaborated on, but the underlying structure will be pretty much the same, whether the company is selling advertising for a cable television network, gasoline, pharmaceuticals, aluminum futures, or what have you.

In addition, there are other patterns available that apply to most commercial businesses. Many of these are laid out in *Data Model Patterns*, and a few will be presented below. These can be viewed from a high level, describing common business phenomena, or at a lower level, describing components of those higher-level models.

At the higher level, you have (among others):

- People and organizations
- Geography
- Products, assets, or materials
- Activities
- Contracts

At the lower level, you have (among others):

- Hierarchy/network
- Type

These are described more fully in the following sections.

People and Organizations

As described above, a PARTY is a person or an organization of interest to the enterprise. In Figure 3.29, you can see that not only is a PARTY either a PERSON or an ORGANIZATION, but an ORGANIZATION, in turn, must be either a COMPANY, an INTERNAL ORGANIZATION (such as a department), a GOVERNMENT AGENCY, or an OTHER ORGANIZATION. Depending on your situation, you can define sub-types further, itemizing kinds of COMPANIES, for example.

Note that the sub-type structure is *fundamental*. That is, any PARTY must be either a PERSON or an ORGANIZATION and not both. ORGANIZATION is then further subcategorized. There are in fact other kinds of classification that companies often wish to identify, but these are not so fundamental. These categories could be demographic categories, for example, such as "annual income". These can be accommodated by the entity types PARTY CATEGORY, PARTY CATEGORY SET, and PARTY CLASSIFICATION.

A PARTY CATEGORY is one of those classifications that someone is interested in, such as "Income greater than $50,000 per year". A PARTY CLASSIFICATION is the fact that a particular PARTY falls into that category, such as "Sam has an income of greater than $50,000 per year." Note that the PARTY CATEGORY, "Income greater than $50,000 per year", must be *part* of the PARTY CATEGORY SET, "Annual Income".

Note also that a PARTY CLASSIFICATION must also be *by* someone (a PARTY). This could be the Marketing Department, for example.

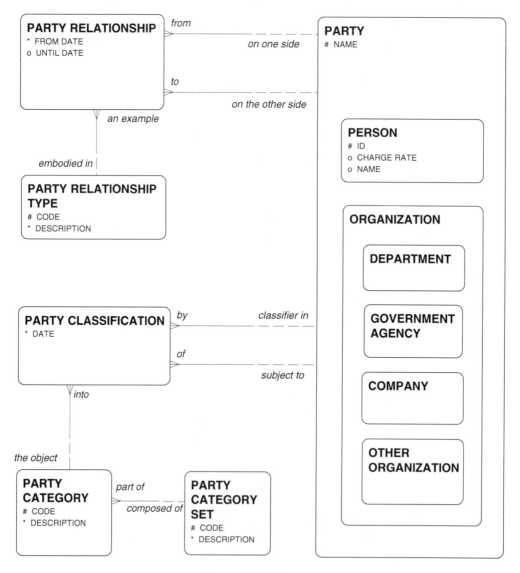

FIGURE 3.29 Parties.

PARTIES are related to each other. An INTERNAL ORGANIZATION may be part of another INTERNAL ORGANIZATION; a PERSON may be married to another PERSON; a PERSON may be a member of an OTHER ORGANIZATION, such as the Teamsters Union or The Data Administration Management Association. Each of these is an example of a PARTY

RELATIONSHIP *from* one PARTY to another. Each PARTY RELATIONSHIP, in turn, is also an example of a PARTY RELATIONSHIP TYPE, such as "organizational structure", "marriage", or "membership". This is also shown in Figure 3.29.

Note that making the entity types more generic makes any systems based on them more robust. For example, new categories of PARTY can be added without changing the data structure. This is at the cost, however, of losing representation of the business rules that lie behind the data. There might be rules that say, for example, that only PEOPLE can participate in the PARTY RELATIONSHIP of PARTY RELATIONSHIP TYPE "marriage", or that a DEPARTMENT in PARTY CATEGORY "sales office" can only report to a DEPARTMENT in PARTY CATEGORY "sales district".

These rules must be documented separately from the model drawing.

Geography

It may seem that an appropriate attribute of party is "Address". But unfortunately, many parties have more than one address. These include "billing address", "delivery address", "home address", and so forth. To have multiple addresses as an attribute of party would thus violate First Normal Form.

What is required is a separate "address" entity type, shown in Figure 3.30 as SITE. A PARTY PLACEMENT is then defined as the fact that a PARTY is *located* at a particular SITE. Thus, not only can one PARTY be located in one or more SITES, but one SITE may be the location of one or more PARTIES.

Note that by recognizing both PHYSICAL SITE and VIRTUAL SITE, the same entity type can be a place to store not only street addresses, but also telephone numbers, web addresses, and e-mail addresses.

A SITE is a particular virtual or real place with a purpose, such as a house, office, or website. A SITE must be an *example* of a SITE TYPE, such as "one-family home", "office building", "archeological dig", "warehouse", and so forth. A PARTY PLACEMENT—the fact that a particular PARTY is located at a particular SITE—must be *an example of* a PARTY PLACEMENT TYPE, such as "home address", "billing address", etc.

Each PHYSICAL SITE, in addition, must be located in at least one but possibly more GEOPOLITICAL AREAS. A GEOPOLITICAL AREA is a kind of GEOGRAPHIC AREA whose boundaries are defined by law or international treaty. A GEOGRAPHIC AREA is simply any bounded area on the earth. If it is not a GEOPOLITICAL AREA, a GEOGRAPHIC AREA may be either an ADMINISTRATIVE AREA (whose boundaries are defined by an enterprise's policies), a SURVEYED AREA (whose boundaries are defined by a survey, in terms of townships, sections, and the like), or a NATURAL AREA (whose boundaries are determined by a natural phenomenon, such as a lake or habitat).

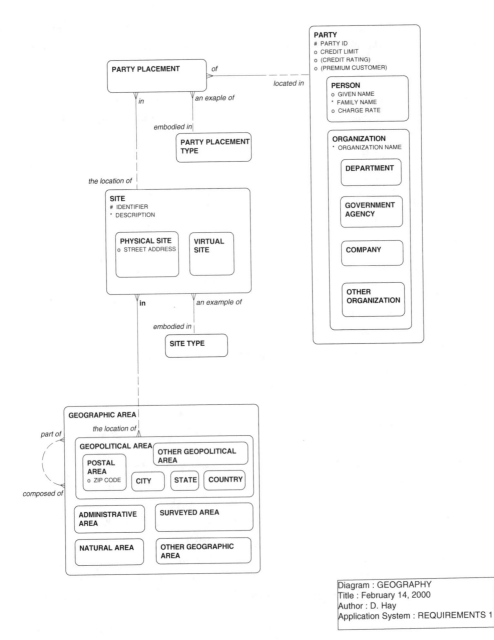

FIGURE 3.30 Geography.

Products

So, what does the company make? What does it use? What does it otherwise manipulate? These fundamentally are products. The word "product" is troublesome, however, because while in principle it refers to anything tangible that can be bought, sold, or handled, in fact many companies' products (like those of banks) are intangible. In many ways, though, even these behave the same as tangible ones, such as computers and steam compressors.

In this model we will constrain PRODUCT to mean something discrete that is bought or sold, distinguishing it from EQUIPMENT which is used in the manufacturing process and MATERIAL such as powder or goo. The super-type we will define that encompasses all of these is ITEM. (In *Data Model Patterns*, this is called ASSET.)

We want to distinguish between ITEM TYPE, which is the definition of a thing, such as might be found in a catalogue or specification sheet, and ITEM, an occurrence or instance of the thing that exists in a physical place. In Figure 3.31 ITEM TYPE is shown with the sub-types PRODUCT TYPE, MATERIAL TYPE, EQUIPMENT TYPE, and OTHER ITEM TYPE, as were described above.

ITEM, on the other hand, distinguishes between INVENTORY, whose primary attribute is "Quantity", and DISCRETE ITEM, whose primary attribute is "Serial number". That is, a DISCRETE ITEM can be identified, piece by piece, while INVENTORY is an undifferentiated quantity of things.

Each ITEM must be (currently) *located at* only one SITE. This implies that an INVENTORY is defined to be that quantity of a particular ITEM that is stored in a particular SITE, just as a DISCRETE ITEM is a single object stored in a particular SITE.

Also an ITEM or ITEM TYPE may refer to anything—finished good, intermediate, or raw material. By itself, an occurrence of ITEM or ITEM TYPE tells you nothing of its composition. For this we need ITEM TYPE STRUCTURE ELEMENT and ITEM STRUCTURE ELEMENT.

At the ITEM TYPE level, an ITEM TYPE STRUCTURE ELEMENT is the fact that a particular ITEM TYPE is a component of another ITEM TYPE. This information is usually found in engineering specifications. That is, each ITEM TYPE may be *part of* one or more ITEM STRUCTURE ELEMENTS, each of which must be *the use* (of that ITEM TYPE) *in* one and only one other ITEM TYPE. Looking at it from the other direction, each ITEM TYPE may be *composed of* one or more ITEM TYPE STRUCTURE ELEMENTS, each of which must be *the use of* one and only one other ITEM TYPE.

An ITEM STRUCTURE ELEMENT is similar. Instead of being concerned with ITEM TYPES, however, it is concerned with actual occurrences of ITEMS. That is, each ITEM STRUCTURE ELEMENT must be *the use in* a physical ITEM and *the use of* a physical ITEM. Actually, an ITEM may contain not only identifiable other ITEMS, but also a quantity of an unidentified ITEM TYPE, such as "water" or "natural gas". Consequently, what the model actually says is that an ITEM STRUCTURE ELEMENT may be <u>either</u> *the use of* an ITEM <u>or</u> *the use of* an ITEM TYPE. (The arc across the two relationships denotes this "exclusive or" concept.)

Ideally, each ITEM STRUCTURE ELEMENT would be based on an ITEM TYPE STRUCTURE ELEMENT. Whether this is possible or not in your company is another question.

Note that attributes of both ITEM TYPE STRUCTURE ELEMENT and ITEM STRUCTURE ELEMENT include "Quantity per" (the amount of the component required to make one unit of the assembly), "Effective date", and "Until date".

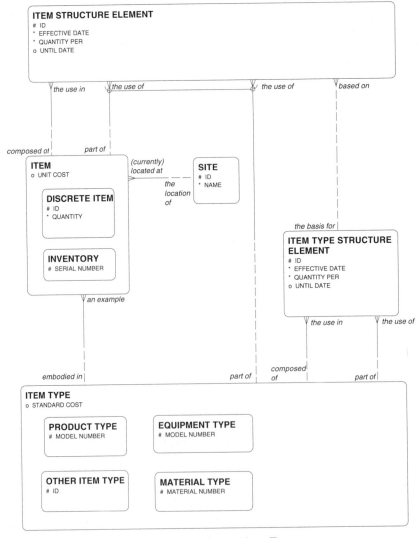

FIGURE 3.31 Items and Item Types.

Activity Type/Activity

The work of an enterprise is defined by its *activity types*. In Column Two (Chapter 4), we will model the nature of activity types. To the extent that activities and activity types are themselves things of significance to the business, however, with data describing them, they will show up here in the Column One model.

An ACTIVITY is an example of either a SERVICE or an ACTIVITY TYPE. If we are talking about something offered for sale, it is probably a SERVICE. If, instead, we are talking about something done inside the company only, it could be called an ACTIVITY TYPE or PROCEDURE. Structurally, these are identical. A SERVICE or ACTIVITY TYPE may be *embodied* in one or more ACTIVITIES. Each ACTIVITY must occur on a particular "Date" (and optionally, "Time"), and must be *performed* at a SITE. All of this is shown in Figure 3.32.

Also shown in Figure 3.32 is the fact that an ACTIVITY may be *part of* a WORK ORDER. A WORK ORDER is a specific authorization for a relatively large effort to be carried out. A WORK ORDER is usually *composed of* one or more ACTIVITIES.

A WORK ORDER must be either a PRODUCTION WORK ORDER (to make an ITEM TYPE) or a MAINTENANCE WORK ORDER (*to fix, install, or replace* a DISCRETE ITEM).

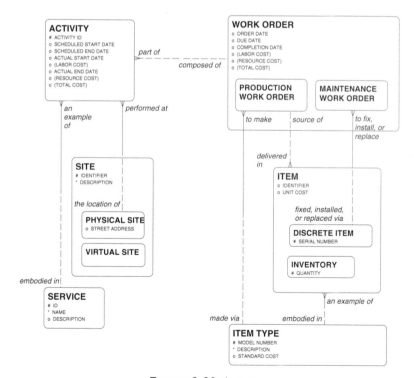

FIGURE 3.32 Activities.

In those companies where the model is concerned primarily with SERVICES that are sold to customers (or bought, for that matter), it may be simpler to make SERVICE a subtype of ITEM TYPE. This has some odd implications, but most relationships actually apply both to SERVICE and the more tangible kinds of ITEM TYPES.

Figure 3.33 expands on the ACTIVITY idea, adding the PARTIES who participate in a WORK ORDER or in a particular ACTIVITY and adding also the consumption of labor and other resources by an ACTIVITY.

Note the attributes shown in this diagram. You can see that ACTIVITY, for example, has a "Scheduled start date", "Scheduled end date", "Actual start date", and "Actual end date". These position the ACTIVITY in time. By specifying scheduled dates only, you can define a planned activity before it is actually carried out. Similarly, WORK ORDER had an "Order date" and a "Due date", as well as a "Completion date".

A WORK ORDER ROLE is the fact that a PARTY (a PERSON or an ORGANIZATION) has something to do with a WORK ORDER. This could be its manager, someone contributing to its execution, or even a beneficiary of it. Each WORK ORDER ROLE must be played by a PARTY, for a WORK ORDER.

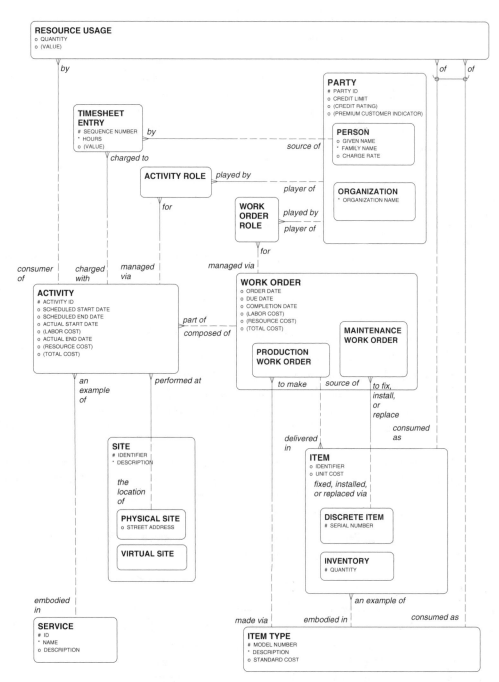

FIGURE 3.33 Activity Management.

Similarly, an ACTIVITY ROLE is the fact that a PARTY has something to do with an ACTIVITY. Each ACTIVITY ROLE must be *played by* a PARTY, for an ACTIVITY.

WORK ORDERS and ACTIVITIES consume both labor and other resources, such as materials. The fact that time is consumed for an ACTIVITY is called a TIMESHEET ENTRY. Each TIMESHEET ENTRY must be by one PERSON and *charged to* a single ACTIVITY. Its most interesting attribute is "Hours": the number of hours (including fractions of hours) spent by this PERSON on this particular ACTIVITY. An attribute of the PERSON is "Charge rate": the dollars per hour charged for this PERSON'S work. This allows us to calculate the derived attribute "(Value)" as the "Hours" from this TIMESHEET ENTRY times the "Charge rate" of the PERSON that is the *source* of this TIMESHEET ENTRY. (Parentheses denote the fact that the attribute is derived.)

The "(Value)" of all the TIMESHEET ENTRIES that are *charged to* an ACTIVITY can then be summed up to yield the derived attribute "(Labor cost)" for the ACTIVITY. The "(Labor cost)" of all ACTIVITIES that are *part of* a WORK ORDER can similarly be summed up to yield the "(Labor cost)" of the WORK ORDER.

A RESOURCE USAGE is the fact that an ITEM or ITEM TYPE is consumed during the course of an ACTIVITY. That is, each RESOURCE USAGE must be *of* either a particular ITEM (a specific DISCRETE ITEM or an INVENTORY), or *of* a generic ITEM TYPE such as "natural gas" or "water".

As with the calculation of labor cost, the cost of resources used combines the "Unit cost" of an ITEM or the "Standard cost" of an ITEM TYPE with the "Quantity" used of the RESOURCE USAGE. The "(Value)" of the RESOURCE USAGE is calculated by multiplying its "Quantity" by either the "Standard cost" of the ITEM TYPE that is *consumed as* the RESOURCE USAGE or the "Unit cost" of the ITEM that is *consumed as* the RESOURCE USAGE. The attribute "(Value)" can then be summed across all the RESOURCE USAGES that are *charged to* an ACTIVITY, to get the "(Resource cost)" of that ACTIVITY. Similarly, the "(Resource cost)" of an ACTIVITY can be summed across all ACTIVITIES that are *part of* a WORK ORDER to compute the total "(Resource cost)" for that WORK ORDER.

The "(Total cost)" of either an ACTIVITY or a WORK ORDER can then be computed by adding together that entity type's "(Labor cost)" and "(Resource cost)".

Contract

The business of any enterprise is contracts—purchase orders, sales orders, leases, and the like. As we have seen, all contracts fundamentally have the same structure. In the introduction to this section we saw that a SALES ORDER and a PURCHASE ORDER are simply examples of different kinds of ORDERS. Here we will generalize the concept even further to the idea of CONTRACT. (ORDER is simply a kind of CONTRACT.) A CONTRACT can be any agreement between two PARTIES, for the supply from one to the other of any product or service. This is shown in Figure 3.34. In addition to a simple SALES ORDER or

PURCHASE ORDER, it could be a lease, a financial instrument, or an employment contract, among others.

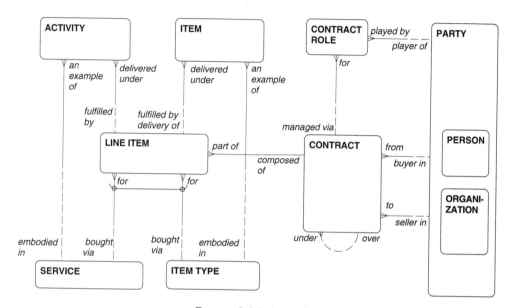

FIGURE 3.34 Contracts.

In most cases, a CONTRACT is simply *from* one PARTY (the *buyer*) and *to* another PARTY (the *seller*). There can be multi-party CONTRACTS, but these are rare enough to leave the model of that to the reader. In addition to the primary PARTIES, however, there can be other PARTIES playing various CONTRACT ROLES. These could be "contract manager", "vendor agent", and so forth.

Each CONTRACT must be *composed of* one or more references to the things being sold—LINE ITEMS. Each LINE ITEM, in turn, must be *for* either a SERVICE or an ITEM TYPE. Again, as mentioned above, if most of the enterprise's ACTIVITIES are bought from contractors or sold to the public, it may be appropriate to make SERVICE or ACTIVITY TYPE simply a sub-type of ITEM TYPE. Then each LINE ITEM must be simply *for* one ITEM TYPE. It seems a little strange, but it works. Virtually all of the relationships defined for ITEM TYPE can also apply to SERVICE.

Note that each CONTRACT may be *over* (the basis for) one or more other CONTRACTS. For example, a blanket purchase order may be the basis for one or more specific purchase orders.

The CONTRACT and its LINE ITEMS describe what has been ordered. The nature of delivery against a CONTRACT depends on what that was. If a SERVICE was ordered, the contract may be *fulfilled* by conduct of one or more actual ACTIVITIES, as described above.

On the other hand, an ITEM TYPE bought via the LINE ITEM may be *fulfilled by delivery* of one or more specific ITEMS.

Note the business rule that requires that ACTIVITY be *an example* of the same ACTIVITY TYPE that the LINE ITEM was *for*. Similarly, each ITEM *delivered under* a LINE ITEM should be *an example of* the same ITEM TYPE that the LINE ITEM is for.

Hierarchy/Network

The above patterns describe aspects of the business in business terms. Close examination of these models, however, reveals that within each pattern there are components that are themselves significant patterns. There are many of these, but two in particular are worth discussing here.

The first is the model of a hierarchy and a network. Note in Figure 3.28 that each CONTRACT may be *over* one or more other CONTRACTS. This is a simple hierarchy of a sort that occurs frequently. Note, however, that each CONTRACT may be *under* only one CONTRACT. This imposes a constraint that may not always be appropriate.

In Figure 3.31, reproduced here as Figure 3.35, each ITEM TYPE was shown as being *composed of* one or more other ITEM TYPES and being *part of* one or more other ITEM TYPES. That is, each ITEM TYPE is *composed of* one or more ITEM TYPE STRUCTURE ELEMENTS, each of which must be *the use of* another ITEM TYPE. Each ITEM TYPE may also be *part of* one or more ITEM TYPE STRUCTURE ELEMENTS, each of which must be *the use in* another ITEM TYPE.

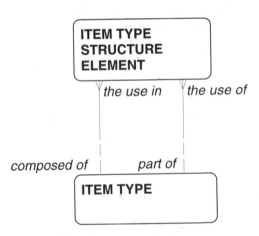

FIGURE 3.35 Product Structure.

An example of such a structure is shown in Figure 3.36. This is sometimes called a *bill of materials*—a list of component assemblies and parts that comprise a manufactured product. Note that the two models of bicycles and all of their components are really ITEM TYPES. Each line connecting two (such as from "Bicycle B" to "Crank Assembly T-23") is represented by an occurrence of ITEM TYPE STRUCTURE ELEMENT. Note that an attribute of ITEM TYPE STRUCTURE ELEMENT is "Quantity per"—the "1" and "24", which is the quantity of the component required to build one of the assembly.

Each "Bicycle B", for example, requires but *1* "Frame X-23", "Crank Assembly T-23", "Front Wheel Assembly K-43", and "Rear Wheel Assembly D-64". On the other hand, "Front Wheel Assembly K-43" and "Rear Wheel Assembly D-64" each require *24* "18" Spokes".

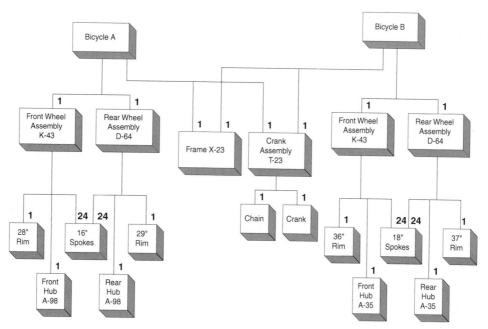

FIGURE 3.36 A Sample Product Structure.

Note that this model pattern can describe more than a product structure. We used it in Figure 3.29 to describe the complete set of possible relationships among parties. A department, for example may be composed of several other departments, and over time it may report to several other departments. A critical-path PERT chart is also a network, relating projected activities to each other. There are many different uses for this configuration.

Type

In Figure 3.29, the fact is that a PARTY RELATIONSHIP, for example, must be *an example of* one and only one PARTY RELATIONSHIP TYPE. That is, the WORK ORDER ROLE TYPE describes the kind of relationship between two PARTIES. The set of PARTY RELATIONSHIP TYPES is defined in advance, before any actual PARTY RELATIONSHIPS exist. The idea of a "...TYPE" entity type that categorizes an entity type occurs throughout any typical complete model. Figure 3.37 shows some of the …TYPE entity types that could appear in our model: a WORK ORDER ROLE TYPE defines the kinds of WORK ORDER ROLES that could be played in a WORK ORDER, such as "authorizer". (See Figure 3.33.) A CONTRACT ROLE TYPE defines the kind of CONTRACT ROLE being played in a CONTRACT, such as "contract manager", "attorney of record", and so on. (See Figure 3.34.) An ACTIVITY ROLE TYPE defines the kind of ACTIVITY ROLE being played in an ACTIVITY—"project manager", "chief engineer", and the like. (See Figure 3.33.) A PARTY RELATIONSHIP TYPE is the kind of PARTY RELATIONSHIP: "spouse", "departmental structure", "union membership", and so forth. (See Figure 3.29.)

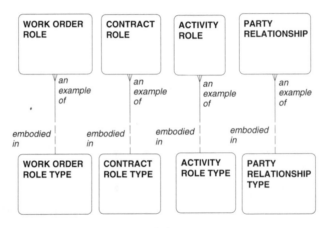

FIGURE 3.37 Types.

Note that each thing must be an example of one and only one thing type. This is exactly the same information conveyed by the sub-type/super-type structure. In Figure 3.38, for example, the occurrences of PARTY TYPE will be "Person", "Organization", "Company", "Department", "Government Agency", and "Other Party".

The advantage of using the …TYPE entity type instead of sub-types and super-types is that it can easily be changed. Rows can be added and deleted as necessary. The advantage of super-types and sub-types, however, is that each can have a different set of attributes. In deciding which approach to take, judgment is required.

Even though this adds redundancy, it can be useful to have both. First, more detailed PARTY TYPES can be specified in an implemented system, without having to restructure the database. Note that each PARTY TYPE may be *a super-type of* one or more other PARTY TYPES.

Second, it is sometimes useful to be able to refer to the …TYPE as an entity type. Another entity type could be related to one or more occurrences of this …TYPE.

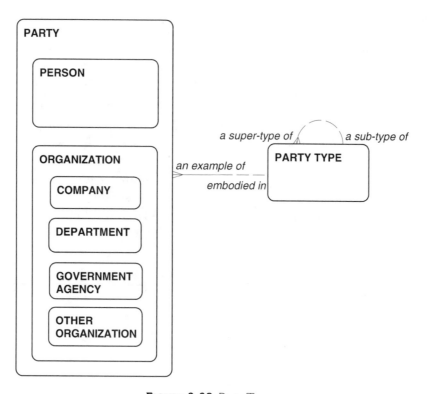

FIGURE 3.38 Party Types.

Entity/Relationship Model Validation

When delivering a data model, it is important to validate it. This happens from two directions. First, someone should proofread it to be sure that it follows the modeling rules and conventions. This means first making sure that the syntax is correct, and then making sure that the positional conventions were followed. Then it means making sure that industry standard conventions for representing standard situations were at least consulted. There should be an explicit reason for each departure from the semantic standard.

Second, it should be reviewed with subject matter experts to ensure that the assertions made in the model are in fact true in the business.

Finally, it should be tested for intellectual rigor. Is it consistent and coherent? This is trickier to do.

John Sharp has in fact devised a way to validate the coherence and correctness of a model systematically, using sample data and focusing on the use of unique identifiers. He has presented it in numerous articles for the *Journal of Conceptual Modeling* (on the World Wide Web at: *http://www.inconcept.com/JCM*). This involves setting up a table of attributes and populating it with sample data, varying one attribute at a time.

In an example from a course that he teaches, Figure 3.39 shows the Barker version of a model presented in the Federal IDEF1X standard [FIPS, 1993]. Some of the entity types have been slightly renamed for clarity. Dr. Sharp uses this to demonstrate his technique.

Note that the unique identifiers for each entity type are shown in the diagram as a combination of attributes (denoted by the octothorpe symbol, #) and relationships (denoted by a line across the relationship). Table 3.17 shows the identifiers of each entity type.

TABLE 3.17 Unique Identifiers

Entity type	Attribute	Relationship
PERSON	"ID"	
SEMESTER	"ID"	
COURSE	"Course Number"	
COURSE OFFERING		*during* SEMESTER
		occurrence of COURSE
CLASS SECTION	"Section Number"	
		of COURSE OFFERING
CLASS ENROLLMENT		*of* PERSON
		in CLASS SECTION

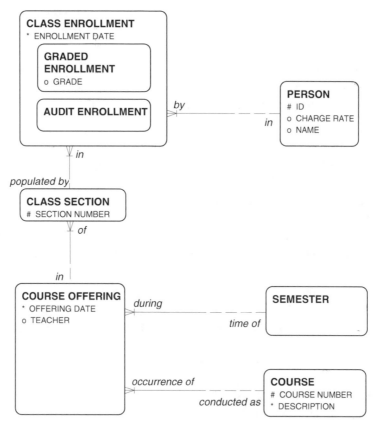

FIGURE 3.39 Validation Exercise—I.

Dr. Sharp's technique begins by expressing a sentence that represents an occurrence of the entity type. In this example, such a sentence might be "Sally (PERSON 234) received an A in Section 2 of Geology 101 (GE101) during the Fall semester of 1999 (F99)." This is represented by the first row of Table 3.18.

TABLE 3.18 Validation Table

Semester ID	Course ID	Section Number	Person ID	Grade	Expert	Model
F99	GE101	2	234	A		
(another)	GE101	2	234	A	Y	Y
F99	(another)	2	234	A	Y	Y
F99	GE101	(another)	234	A	N	Y
F99	GE101	2	(another)	A	Y	Y
F99	GE101	2	234	(another)	N	N

The relation is arranged so that the attributes represent the predicates of a particular entity type. (Predicate, recall, means either an attribute or a relationship to another entity type.)

The rows are arranged to ask, in each case, if a particular predicate can have any other value for the predicate than the one used in the base sentence. For example, in Row Two, is it possible that Sally (PERSON 234) could receive an A in Section 2 of Geology 101 (GE101) during *another semester*?

At the right are two columns, indicating in one case the answer by an expert in the area under discussion, and in the other case the answer dictated by the model. If the answers don't match, the model must be wrong.

In the model, since "Semester ID" is part of the unique identifier of COURSE OFFERING, A COURSE OFFERING, can be for as many SEMESTERS as we want. The expert also says that, at least under current rules, a PERSON can take the same SECTION of the same COURSE more than once. (Note that the rules may change.) Similarly, the model and the expert agree, as they do in all the rows but one—the fourth.

In the fourth row, the question is, can Sally (PERSON 234) receive an A in *another section* of Geology 101 (GE101) during the Fall semester of 1999? It is highly unlikely that she is taking two sections at once, but this is not prevented by the model. In this case, the model says that, since SECTION is part of the identifier of "grade" (in GRADED ENROLLMENT), then it is possible to take as many sections of a course as you want, and there is nothing to prevent the sections from being in the same semester. However, the expert points out that this is *not* possible. You can take only one section of a course at a time. Hence, the model is wrong, or it is at least missing a business rule.

The corrected model is shown in Figure 3.40. Note that CLASS ENROLLMENT is now identified only by COURSE OFFERING, not by CLASS SECTION. It is still a fact that the CLASS ENROLLMENT is *in* a particular CLASS SECTION, but now a given occurrence of CLASS ENROLLMENT *in* a COURSE OFFERING may be in only *one* CLASS SECTION. Note that a business rule must be still be specified: Since each CLASS ENROLLMENT must be *in* a CLASS SECTION that must be *of* a COURSE OFFERING, and each CLASS ENROLLMENT must be *in* a COURSE OFFERING directly, the CLASS OFFERING for a single CLASS ENROLLMENT must be the same for both paths.

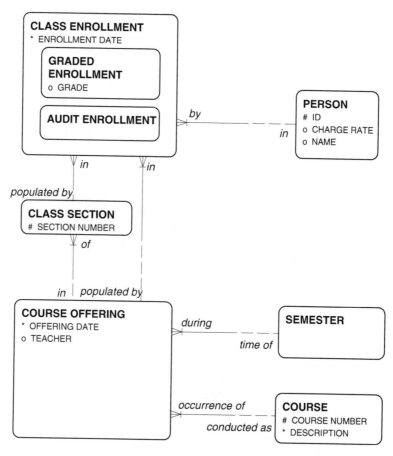

FIGURE 3.40 Validation Exercise—2.

This validation procedure is a very important way to verify that your model says exactly what you think it does. In addition, it identifies business rules that may not be able to be portrayed in the model at all. Note that this validation cannot be done with an object model, since object models do not specify which attributes and relationships are unique identifiers.

The Requirements Analysis Deliverable—Column One

Entity Types and Relationships, with Narrative

A data model is a major product of the requirements analysis process. At the very least, this should be an architect's version, showing the conceptual structures of the company's data. Where appropriate, user views of the data can be included, with the linkages appropriately documented.

The data model can be an object role model, a conceptual entity/relationship diagram, or an object model showing business-oriented classes. If an entity/relationship diagram is used, it should be in either Barker or information engineering notation, to ensure readability. If a UML business class model is produced, it must be with a stripped-down version of UML. It can show only classes, associations, and sub-types. Relationship roles must be labeled in both directions.

Regardless of notations, the relationships should be named as described in this chapter, to ensure that they can be converted into conventional English. Note that each entity type name must be a common natural language term. No abbreviations, acronyms, or references to computer terms are permitted.

In the CASE tool supporting your efforts, each entity type must be described by its name and definition. Optionally, estimates of the number of occurrences, synonyms, and other information may also be included. (See Chapter 2 for a description of how this information can be used to estimate the data capacity required.)

A narrative should accompany the model: Strictly speaking, this is a collection of definitions and relationship sentences, but this structure can be camouflaged, making the narrative look like paragraphs of normal text. The idea is that anyone could read the text and understand it, without necessarily understanding the model graphics.

Also included as documentation of the model should be the business rules (captured for Column Six) that constrain it. At the basic level, this includes rules associated with the data model configuration, such as "no loops in a recursive structure", or the requirement that if there are two paths between two entities, the occurrences at each end of the paths must be the same (or they must be different). In addition, there will be many rules which originate in the business itself.

Attributes

In the course of developing a model, the entity types and relationships are defined first, with perhaps a few attributes defined for each entity type, to clarify its meaning. By the end of the requirements project, however, all known attributes must be specified, with each defined by its name and description, format, optionality, and validation rules.

In assigning attributes, be sure to recognize that some things that appear to be attributes are really relationships to other entity types. Bob Schmidt [Schmidt, 1999] points out that what an entity type really has are *predicates.* A predicate is a piece of information about an entity type. It may be an attribute or a relationship to another entity type. The important thing at the beginning of the effort is to identify the predicates. Once they have all been laid out, which are attributes and which are in fact relationships to other entity types?

This is the approach also taken by object role modeling.

Ask, does this attribute itself have attributes? If so, you have a relationship to a new entity type.

In fact, you should have relatively few attributes for each entity type. You may have a surrogate key, a name or description, and possibly some cost or date data. Nearly every other attribute you may imagine is probably a relationship to another entity type.

As with entity types, each attribute must be a common natural language term. If the UML is used and attributes are shown on the model, show the attribute name only. Be sure to describe attribute characteristics behind the scenes.

Domains

It is a good practice to assign a domain to every attribute. A *domain* is a validation rule for an attribute. It establishes a context. It may consist of a list of values, a range, or an expression of some kind. A domain may also be used to specify a standard format. This is convenient, because once a validation rule has been defined, it can be applied easily to many attributes. It also adds discipline to the attribution process, because it requires the analyst to analyze carefully just what the attribute means.

In addition, many domains are actually specified as ...TYPE entity types. While defining these as entity types/tables adds flexibility and robustness to the final system, the values should be determined up front. WORK ORDER TYPE, REPORTING RELATIONSHIP TYPE, and so forth are effectively domains, and it is the analyst's job to provide at least an initial set of values for these.

Unique Identifiers

As shown above, a data model cannot be validated without knowledge of each entity type's unique identifiers. For this reason, it is important to be sure that the attributes and relationships identifying each entity type be properly identified.

Referential Integrity

Most CASE tools do not permit this annotation, but examine the data model, and for every relationship, note on the "one" end the referential integrity rule for that relationship. Is it *cascade delete*, meaning that if the parent is deleted, all of that parent's children will also be deleted? Is it *restricted,* meaning that the parent cannot be deleted if it has children? Or is it nullify, meaning that the relationship from children to parent is optional, and deleting the parent means that the value of the relationship for each remaining child is reset to "null"?

Data and the Other Columns

Data and Activities

In conjunction with the Column Two part of the project, the Requirements Analysis project should deliver an activity/entity cross reference ("CRUD Matrix"). This allows for finding activities without entity types and entity types without activities. Activities without entities may be spurious, or they may be a sign that something was overlooked in the data model. Entity types without activities may simply mean that maintenance activities were overlooked. (See more on the activity/entity type matrix on page 195.)

Data and Locations

There have always been two issues when one sets out to build a distributed database: Where should the data reside? Where are they to be used? This is one case, however, where technology is rapidly rendering these questions less important. It is now possible to make the data in all entities available everywhere. Still, when the physical database configuration is being laid out, it will be useful to know the locations from which data for each entity type will come, and the locations where they will be used.

Data, People, and Organizations

A very important part of the documentation for a data model is identification of the roles (if not the individual people) who will be responsible for each entity type and attribute. Certain people will "own" an entity type, meaning that those people are ultimately responsible for its data quality. The same or other people are responsible for updating it. Yet others have permission to see it. This matrix is required if data quality is to be established.

Documentation of each entity type should include identification of at least the role responsible for the quality of its information, if not the individual person so responsible.

Data and Timing

In Chapter 7 is defined the "entity life history" technique for describing the states an occurrence of an entity type can go through in the course of its life. Understanding the structure of data, as revealed in an entity/relationship diagram, does not completely reveal the nature of the entities involved. It is in the life history—the succession of states—that this is revealed. State/transition diagrams show that sequence of states. Entity life histories show how timing (events) determines the passage of entities from one state to another.

Data and Business Rules

Fundamentally, business rules are about data. In Row Three, especially, a business rule constrains what data may be or must be created in the course of business operations. The discovery and definition of business rules must be carried out in conjunction with the development of the data model.

Conclusion

The secret to system success is the correct organization of its data. If the data are organized so as to minimize redundancy along the lines of the structure of the business, normal changes to that business will not require significant changes to a system based on those data. Achieving this resiliency in the face of constant business change has been the holy grail of the computer industry for many years. It can be done if requirements are defined in terms of a clear understanding of the inherent structure of the enterprise's data.

The secret to winding up with the right organization of data in a system is to understand how different players view it. The system design must not only accommodate all the different external (business owner's) views that are initially understood, but it must be structured so that it can accommodate future views as well. This is possible only if the underlying, fundamental structure of the data is understood. Hence it is necessary to translate from the external schemata to a conceptual schema, before using this conceptual schema as the basis for database design.

Column Two: Activities

The activities dimension of the Architecture Framework is concerned with what the enterprise *does*. Specifically, what kinds of transformations of material and information take place in the course of doing business? What are the enterprise's activities in carrying out its mission? The modeling of an enterprise's activities is somewhat less coherent than the modeling of its data, because there are many very different ways of viewing activities.

The object-oriented world tends to view the activity and data columns together. Certainly in object-oriented design the activities are designed as adjuncts to the code which defines the data in object classes. In analysis, that is possible to some degree, although it is still useful to address business activities in their own right. These tend to be discovered when you interview someone and ask "What do you do?" Once activities have been modeled separately, a function/entity type matrix (showing what activities create, retrieve, update, or delete occurrences of each entity) can be used to determine which activities go with each entity.

Unfortunately the terms "process", "function", and "activity" are often used interchangeably, and worse still, different authors define the terms slightly differently. The following definitions, however, are close enough to most people's usage to be satisfactory for our purposes. These definitions will be the basis for the rest of this book.

- *Activity* is a general term to describe something that is done. It is used when more specific definition is not available.

- A *process* is an activity performed by the enterprise to produce a specific output or achieve a goal. It may or may not be described in terms of the mechanisms used. Processes are usually represented in terms of their timing relative to each other—either in sequence or in parallel—and they also are usually described in terms of their inputs and outputs. An example of a process is "issue purchase order". Row Two descriptions of activities are typically in terms of processes, although processes may also be terms for Row Three descriptions. These processes may be viewed at a high level or in atomic detail.

- A *function* is a type of activity to carry out an objective of the enterprise. It is described solely in terms of what it is intended to accomplish, and without regard for the technology used to carry it out. This is also described without reference to time. An example of a function is "order material". Functions are used to describe the business in Row Three terms, but they are usually accessible to business owners as well. Functions also begin from a global perspective (what is the mission of the enterprise?) and may be broken down to reveal a considerable amount of detail.

- An *essential activity* is either a *fundamental activity* that performs a task that is part of the enterprise's stated mission or a *custodial activity* that establishes and maintains the system's essential memory by acquiring and storing the information needed by the fundamental activities [McMenamin and Palmer, 1984, pp. 17-20]. In other words, like a function, an essential activity is without reference to technology used, but like a process, it is positioned in relative time. It may also be described in terms of its inputs and outputs. Essential activities are elements of the Row Three perspective. An essential activity might be "Receive shipment", or "Place order".

Data flow diagrams and function hierarchies may break activities into activities more detailed than an essential activity, but by definition the essential activity is at the lowest level of detail that describes an inherent function of the enterprise. Any lower-level activities are described in terms of the particular way the function is carried out in this enterprise.

So, while this chapter might be thought to be about "process modeling", to be more rigorous here it will be called "activity modeling".

This chapter will describe several different approaches to modeling processes and functions. A summary of the different characteristics of each technique is provided at the end of the chapter. It would be nice to be able simply to adopt the best features of each, but unfortunately, use of any of these techniques requires a graphic tool (a "CASE" tool). Tools are available for almost all the techniques described here, but no one tool supports more than one or two, so it is not currently possible to adopt a super-set. Invariably you will be required by circumstances and corporate politics[1] to use only one of the techniques and endure its shortcomings. From this book you will at least be able to tell what those are in advance.

From the Business Owners' View to the Architect's View

Figure 4.1 shows the Framework with Column Two highlighted.

The Row One scope effort for the enterprise should have defined the scope of this project in terms of, among other things, the sets of activities to be addressed: "process control", "facility management", "order processing", and so forth.

Business owners view processes in very concrete terms. Fill out a purchase order. Operate a lathe. Receive a shipment. Most descriptions include at least an implied mechanism for carrying out the activity. The business owner is observing the flow of materials as much as the flow of data. *Physical data flow diagrams* (page 161) and pro-cess models of the sort used in *business process re-engineering* (page 185) are suitable for presenting this view.

The architect's view is of functions or essential activities. An architect is interested only in what actions must be taken to carry out the company's objectives and policies. By definition, if this is done in the context of a system requirements analysis, it is expected that current technology will be replaced with new technology, so we need a description of the underlying functions that is not dependent on the technology involved. This is the realm of the *function hierarchy* and the *essential data flow diagram.*

All of this is not to say that functions are not suitable as a representation of the busi-ness owner's view. They should be described in natural language and validated by sub-ject-matter experts. Their expression of what the business does without regard for technology, however, makes them fundamentally elements of the Row Three perspective.

In summary, then, the analyst must evaluate each physical process to determine what underlying function is being performed. Some processes do not address a corpo-rate function at all but are simply a means for dealing with inadequate current technol-ogy. (An example might be "Re-enter customer data".) Some processes are done simply because "we've always done it that way". Thus one of the tasks is to determine which processes are truly "value added" in that they contribute to the effective operation of the enterprise. (See "A Word About Business Process Re-engineering" on page 185.)

---

1. OK, occasionally by reasoned judgment.

	Data (What)	Activities (How)	Locations (Where)	People (Who)	Time (When)	Motivation (Why)
Objectives / Scope (Planner's view)	List of things important to the enterprise	List of processes the enterprise performs	List of enterprise locations	Organization approaches	Business master schedule	Business vision and mission
Enterprise model (Business Owners' Views)	Language, divergent data model	Business process model	Logistics network	Organi-zation chart	State / transition diagram	Business strategies, tactics, policies, rules
Model of Funda-mental Concepts (Architect's View)	Convergent e/r model	Essential data flow diagram	Locations of roles	The viable system, use cases	Entity Life History	Business rule model
Technology Model (Designer's View)	Data base design	System design, program structure	Hardware, software distribution	User interface, security design	Control structure	Business rule design
Detailed Representation (Builder's View)	Physical storage design	Detailed program design	Network architecture, protocols	Screens, security coding	Timing definitions	Rule specification program logic
Functioning System	*(Working System)*					
	Converted data	Executable programs	Communi-cations facilities	Trained people	Business events	Enforced rules

FIGURE 4.1 Architecture Framework—Activities.

The business owners see the activities being performed by current systems. The architects' view is of the functions being performed by those systems, so they can see how new systems might perform the same functions. The designer will design new processes to carry out those functions.

Table 4.1 compares the terms "process", "function", "activity", and "essential activity".

TABLE 4.1 Activities, Processes, and Functions

	Processes	Functions	Activities	Essential Activities
Include Mechanisms?	May or may not	No	May or may not	No
Show Relative Time?	Yes	No	May or may not	Yes
Atomic?	May or may not be	May or may not be	May or may not be	Yes

The techniques described here have been evolving since the mid-1970s. Because most of them predate it, they vary in the extent to which they address Rows Two and Three of the Architecture Framework. Some are more suitable for one or the other, and others can be used to represent both. Because the interrelationships among the tools and their history is important, they are presented here in historical order, rather than by the rows they address. In each case, the row(s) addressed will be discussed.

Approach

This chapter will describe the examination of activities in terms of the following techniques:

- *Function hierarchy*—A hierarchical representation of the functions of the enterprise. At the top of the hierarchy is the company's mission, broken into the six, seven, or eight primary functions that contribute to that mission. Each of these is broken out in turn. Start with the overall function of an enterprise or section of an enterprise and break this down into component functions and processes. Each of these can then be further broken down, and so forth.
- *Dependency diagram*—A diagram showing activities and how they depend on each other. That is, one activity cannot be carried out until another activity has been completed. How are activities dependent upon each other?
- *Data flow diagram*—A drawing of the flows of data though an enterprise. It includes a box or circle describing each physical process and lines showing the

communications between processes. It also includes representations of data stores, which are the holding of data over time.

- *Essential data flow diagram*—A data flow diagram which is a description of the fundamental processes required to carry out the business of the enterprise. All physical elements have been removed, and the activities have been organized in terms of the events affecting the organization.

- *IDEF0 diagram*—A kind of data flow diagram that places more emphasis on diagraming rigor and activity control and that also shows mechanisms and material movements. It merges the elements represented on both physical and essential data flow diagrams.

- *Business process diagram*—A variation on a physical data flow diagram organized according to participants. Its purpose is specifically to discuss collections of activities with business people, so its notation may be extended to include graphic symbols representing different kinds of activities.

- *UML activity diagram*—A data flow diagram, which, like a business process diagram, is organized in terms of the actors performing the activities.

- *UML interaction diagram*—A diagram showing the interactions between activities and objects (occurrences of entity types).

At the end of the chapter is a matrix comparing the techniques described here. In addition, this chapter will discuss various kinds of detailed activity documentation.

Function Hierarchies

The simplest way to represent a business's operations is with a hierarchy of boxes. The top box of this *function hierarchy* contains the mission of the enterprise. Determine the six, seven or eight principal activities that are required to carry out the mission. Put each of these in a box attached to the top box. Then, for each of these, determine the six, seven or eight activities required to do it that continue this process for as long as seems reasonable.

Typically, this is done to represent functions (Architecture Framework Row Three), not current physical processes (Architecture Framework Row Two). A first pass at the steps in development of the hierarchy may begin with physical activities, but after that first pass it is important to define the activities without regard to current mechanisms: "Place order", not "Fill out purchase order". And, at least at the higher levels, these are functions rather than processes, although as you get further down the hierarchy, you may be inclined to show specific processes (with their implied sequence) rather than functions.

A good way to create a function hierarchy from your interview notes is to use a pad of sticky notes. For each verb in your interview notes, write a function sentence on a sticky note and place it on the wall. When all the sentences have been thus recorded, move the notes around to arrange them into a hierarchy. Insert functions as necessary to collect them together.

Add as the root of the hierarchy the *mission* of the enterprise, discussed in Chapter 8 of this book. Also add at the first few levels of the hierarchy the enterprise's strategies and tactics (also discussed in Chapter 8). Each function identified should be directly contributing to one of these.

Note that, to make the hierarchy comprehensible, you should arrange functions such that between five and nine functions appear on any level. In 1956 G. A. Miller published a paper, "The Magical Number Seven, Plus or Minus Two: Some Limits on Our Capacity for Processing Information" in *The Psychological Review.* In it he observed that the human mind can hold only about seven plus or minus two things in active memory at once. This turns out to be significant, because it is an excellent measure of complexity. More than nine things together constitute something hard to grasp or remember. Fewer than five constitute something so simple as to be uninteresting. To make the function hierarchy interesting, make sure that each level is a set of seven plus or minus two functions. It should be possible to easily comprehend the functions at each level and how they relate to each other.

It is also important for the set of seven plus or minus two functions to be parallel and coherent. Of course they must all be components of their parent function, but they should also be at roughly the same level of detail. If the function is "Take an order", it is appropriate to have subfunctions such as "Receive call", "Record customer information", and so forth, but not "Pick up pencil from the desk".

There are actually four ways you can break down a function [Feldmann, 1998, pp. 150–155]:

- *Decomposition*—The components are themselves functions, in the sense that they do not refer to time or sequence, but rather are simply things that are done to accomplish the parent function.
- *Sequence*—This conveys the sense that processes are carried out as sequential steps to accomplish the parent function or process. Even if they are kept technologically neutral, there is a strong sense of the means by which the parent function is carried out.
- *Organization*—Here the parent function or process is broken into the organizational units that carry out parts of it. This is clearly not a good idea, since the objective of the model is to determine *what* is done, not *how* it is done or *who* does it. This does not reveal the true nature of the function itself.
- *Split by Type*—This is the case where a function or process may be carried out in more than one way. For example, the function "Fabricate product" may be done differently in each of 10 different work centers. Each work center is then broken

out in its own right, revealing its component functions or processes. In a function hierarchy this is acceptable, but it is not quite the same kind of thing as a functional decomposition.

The lowest level should consist of elementary business functions or, in the language of the UML, "actions". These are the most atomic and indivisible functions or processes you can find. In 1992 Richard Barker and Cliff Longman defined an *elementary business function* as one which "when triggered must either be completed successfully, or, if for some reason it cannot be completed successfully, must 'undo' any effects that it had up to the point of failure" [Barker and Longman, 1992, p. 40]. Similarly, in the UML, an *action* is "an atomic computation that results in a change in the state of the model or the return of a value... it cannot be terminated externally" [Rumbaugh, *et. al.*, 1999, p. 122].

Stephen McMenamin and John Palmer, on the other hand, are less concerned with what is absolutely the most atomic activity. As will be described below (p. 162), the lowest level of interest to them is the "essential activity"—the complete response to an external event. This might comprise more than one atomic activity. It could be either an "essential process" in a data flow diagram, or an "essential function" in a function hierarchy. The same criteria apply.

While an essential activity may not be quite as atomic as an elementary business function or a UML action, it is more useful in understanding the nature of the business and it is more amenable to defining a specific process for achieving that understanding. For these reasons, this essential activity approach is described in more detail below.

Figure 4.2 shows a sample function hierarchy.

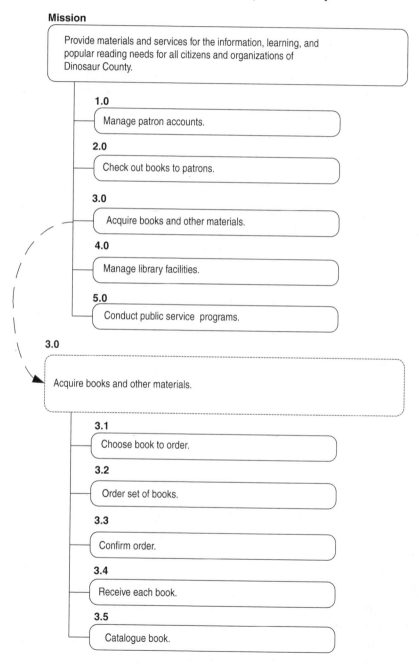

Dinosaur County Public Library

Mission

Provide materials and services for the information, learning, and popular reading needs for all citizens and organizations of Dinosaur County.

1.0

Manage patron accounts.

2.0

Check out books to patrons.

3.0

Acquire books and other materials.

4.0

Manage library facilities.

5.0

Conduct public service programs.

3.0

Acquire books and other materials.

3.1

Choose book to order.

3.2

Order set of books.

3.3

Confirm order.

3.4

Receive each book.

3.5

Catalogue book.

FIGURE 4.2 A Sample Function Hierarchy.

Dependency Diagrams

Once you have established the hierarchical structure of a business's activities (functions and processes), you can determine which activities are dependent on which other activities. That is, to perform an activity, what other activities must be done first? Because sequence is implied, a *dependency diagram* is about activities as processes, rather than as functions, although these processes may or may not be technologically neutral.

There are three ways one process may be dependent upon another:

- *Resource dependency*—a process produces a tangible resource that is required before another process can be executed. For example, "Ship ordered materials" cannot occur until "Pick ordered materials" has been done. This only applies to resource-handling processes.
- *Data dependency*—a process requires data that is produced by another process. For example, "Issue purchase order" cannot be done until after "Receive requisition".
- *Constraint dependency*—a process depends on a constraint that was set in another process. For example, "set up production" determines whether "produce widgets" or "produce gadgets" is performed. This should be avoided, because it implies too great a coupling between the two activities. It would be better for the first process to pass data to the second process for it to act upon.

There are various ways of drawing dependency diagrams. A typical version is presented by Carma McClure and James Martin in their 1985 book, *Diagramming Techniques for Analysts and Programmers*, and is shown in Figure 4.3.

FIGURE 4.3 Dependency Diagram.

Ms. McClure and Mr. Martin have elaborated on the basic concept of a dependency diagram with some annotations [McClure and Martin, 1985, pp. 83–85]. A solid dot next to one end or the other means the process is optional. As shown in Figure 4.4, if it is next to the first process, it means that one may or may not be followed by the other. If it is next to the second, then the first process may or may not be the cause of the second's happening.

It is also possible to identify the cardinality of occurrences of processes. Figure 4.5 shows examples where each occurrence of the second process may be preceded by one or more occurrences of the first process (upper diagram) and each occurrence of the first process may be followed by one or more occurrences of the second process (lower diagram).

You may log into order system without ordering a book.

You may apply a Dewey number to a book without looking it up first.

FIGURE 4.4 Optionality in a Dependency Diagram.

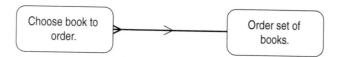

Choose a book to order one or more times before ordering a set of books.

After a set of books are ordered, one or more
books are received, one at a time.

FIGURE 4.5 Cardinality in a Dependency Diagram.

It is common for dependencies to branch. A process may be followed by numerous other processes, or a process may be dependent on one or more processes. These situations are all shown in Figure 4.6. Note that no sequence is implied for the activities that follow "Receive a book shipment".

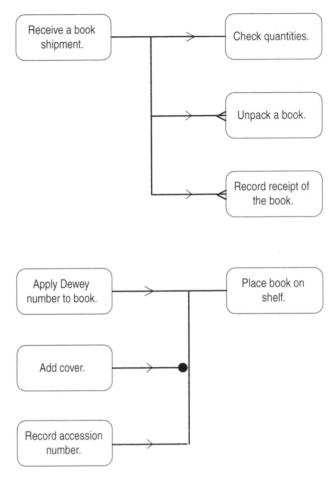

FIGURE 4.6 Branching in a Dependency Diagram.

Data Flow Diagrams

The *data flow diagram* is a specialized kind of dependency diagram. Data flow diagrams are the workhorses of requirements analysis and have been around for longer than almost any other technique. They are specifically concerned with data dependency and show this in terms of the flow of information from one activity to another. Their usefulness is limited by the facts that the nature of the flows in an enterprise changes frequently (so diagrams tend to go out of date quickly) and that many modern enterprises aren't as likely to use data in sequence, instead processing them asynchronously from some central data store. Still, it is worthwhile to understand data flow diagrams and to be able to recognize when they can be useful.

Data flow diagrams were described originally by Tom DeMarco in 1978 and a year later by Trish Sarson and Chris Gane. Their different notations do essentially the same thing. Mr. DeMarco's notation seems particularly suitable when you do not have a CASE tool and must produce the diagrams by hand. Ms. Sarson's and Mr. Gane's are a little more rigorous in identifying each symbol.

Because the activities of a data flow diagram are inherently sequential, they describe *processes* rather than *functions*. Still, it may be appropriate at some level to break down the function hierarchy sequentially, so that the resulting activities can be linked together in a data flow diagram.

The context of a data flow diagram is defined by its *external entities.* An external entity is a party that supplies or consumes information. Note that within the diagram, information is neither created nor destroyed. All the information referred to there originates from one or more external entities and eventually must wind up in one or more external entities. As shown in Figure 4.7, Mr. DeMarco uses a simple box for this, while Ms. Sarson and Mr. Gane use a shadowed box. Ms. Sarson and Mr. Gane also add a one- or two-letter designator to identify the entity.

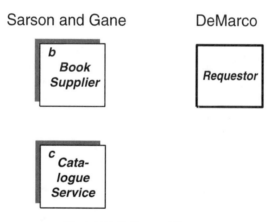

FIGURE 4.7 External Entities.

The central symbol in a data flow diagram is a *process*. In Ms. Sarson's and Mr. Gane's notation, this is represented by a round-cornered rectangle, as shown on the left side of Figure 4.8. It is labeled by a piece of text and a number. Optionally, it may also show the party that performs it. In Mr. DeMarco's notation it is represented by a simple circle with a textual label and a number. Typically a DeMarco diagram does not show who is doing the process. An example of this is shown on the right side of Figure 4.8.

Sarson and Gane   DeMarco

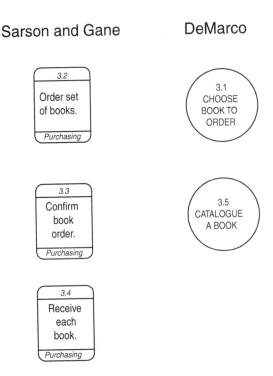

FIGURE 4.8 Processes.

The *data flow* in a data flow diagram is shown by a solid arrow. In Ms. Sarson's and Mr. Gane's version the line tends to be orthogonal (left and right or up and down), with elbow bends. In Mr. DeMarco's notation it is typically curved. Figure 4.9 shows this, with Ms. Sarson's and Mr. Gane's version on the left and Mr. DeMarco's on the right.

There are actually two kinds of data flows. *Information* is simply data passed from one process to another or between a process and a data store; a *message* is information that something has happened, calling for a response from the receiving process. It is an event. Messages are not stored in a data store.

This distinction is not represented in the diagram, but it is important to understand if you want to understand the nature of the flows. Other modeling techniques make this explicit. The IDEF0 technique, described below, does so.

Note that a data flow diagram is concerned only with *data* flows, not *material* flows. Sometimes this can be inconvenient, since the flow of material may be what the department is about. Still, the presence of material may itself be information. A good example is receiving shipped material—but it is the information that the shipment arrived, not the material itself, that is of interest. "Existence of material received" (or simply, "receipt of material") would be the data flow. Ms. Sarson and Mr. Gane do recognize that material flow should sometimes be kept track of, and they introduce a special kind of arrow for this purpose, but it is rarely used.

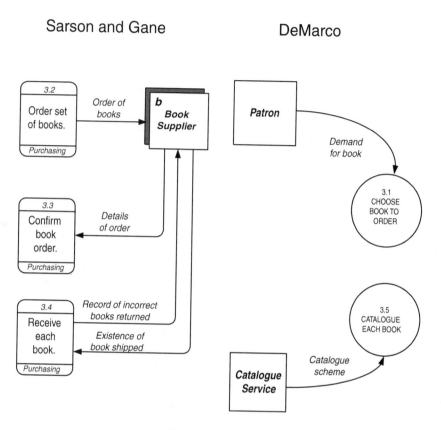

Sarson and Gane   DeMarco

FIGURE 4.9 Flows.

It is often the case that data will reside somewhere temporarily before they are used. An example is a purchase order awaiting receipt of purchased material. This is represented on a Sarson and Gane data flow diagram as an open-sided rectangle (called a *data store*), or, on a DeMarco diagram, as lines above and below (or sometimes just above) text (called a *file*). These are shown in Figure 4.10, again with the Sarson and Gane version on the left and the DeMarco version on the right.

Figure 4.11 shows a complete diagram in the Sarson and Gane notation. From here on, that notation will be used in the example, since it has a slightly more rigorous system of symbol identification.

Sarson and Gane   DeMarco

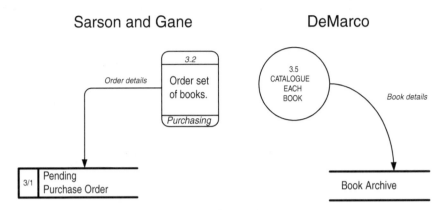

FIGURE 4.10 Data Stores.

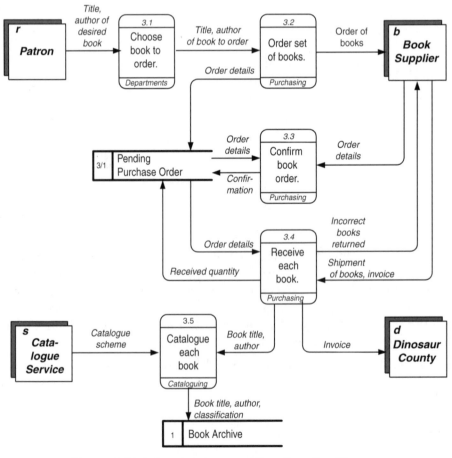

FIGURE 4.11 A Complete Sarson and Gane Data Flow Diagram.

Note, by the way, that the data shown in either flows or data stores represent an observer's *view* of the data. These are, in effect, views of the entities and attributes represented in the entity/relationship diagram. A view can be defined just as an SQL view would be defined, in terms of the entities and attributes it contains. It will be described by a common name, such as "payment", "order details", or some such term. The dataflow and entity models can then be linked together via the strict definition of each of these views.

For example, Figure 4.12 shows a data model and the views of it that could be represented as data stores or flows. In the model, each PURCHASE must be *by* one and only one PARTY and *from* one and only one PARTY. Each PURCHASE, in turn, may be *composed of* one or more LINE ITEMS, each of which must be *for* one and only one BOOK.

The derived attribute "(value)" in LINE ITEM is computed by multiplying "price" in BOOK by "quantity ordered" in LINE ITEM. This in turn is summed across all LINE ITEMS that are *part of* a PURCHASE to calculate "(total value)" as an attribute of PURCHASE. This in turn is summarized across all PURCHASES that are *from* a (vendor) PARTY to calculate "(total purchases)" from that PARTY.

Similarly, "(total value)" for a BOOK is calculated as the total of "value" in LINE ITEM across all LINE ITEMS that are *for* the BOOK.

One data-store view, then, could be "Pending Purchase Orders", from the diagrams described here. This consists of all four entities. Note that for the data flow diagram the only orders of interest were those that had a "Status" of "Pending". In fact, the view could as easily be simply "Purchase Orders". Another might be "Vendor List", showing for each vendor (PARTY that is the *seller in* a PURCHASE) the total purchases for the year. This is created from the PARTY entity, but with the attribute "Total purchases" that is computed as the total of "(Total value)" from all the PURCHASES the PARTY is a *vendor in*. Another view is "Book List", showing for each book its total purchases. This is easily captured from the BOOK and LINE ITEM entities.

"Exploding" Processes

Note that neither the function hierarchy nor the data flow diagram shows the internal logic of a process. This must be done as separate documentation or models, as described below. (See page 187.)

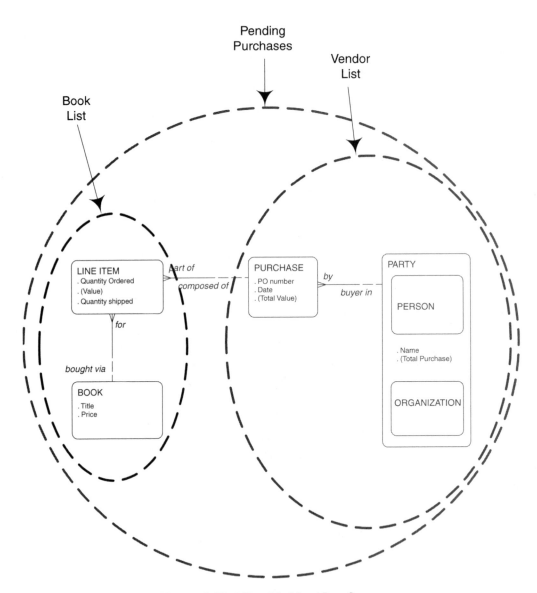

FIGURE 4.12 A Data Model and Data Stores.

As with the function hierarchy, processes in a data flow diagram can be *exploded* into component processes. That is, one diagram may describe the fact that a process shown on a higher-level diagram is composed of six, seven, or eight smaller processes, and then another may in turn take the first of these processes and show its component six, seven or eight processes. Figure 4.13 illustrates this.

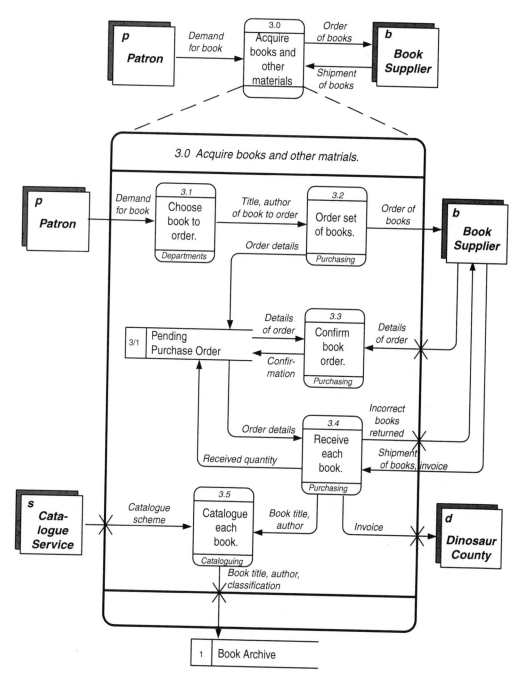

FIGURE 4.13 Explosion of Processes.

Certain rules must be followed when exploding a process:

- All of the flow lines going into or out of a process at the higher level must be represented at the lower level.

- Additional flows into or out of the process may be added at the lower level, but these must be marked with an "X" at the point where each new flow crosses the process boundary.

- Data stores may be added within the lower-level process. In Ms. Sarson's and Mr. Gane's numbering scheme, a sequence number is added to the process number. For example, in Process 3, the first data store is numbered 3/1.

- Similarly, in both techniques, lower-level processes are given a decimal number based on the parent process number (3.1, 3.2, etc.).

    (Sometimes it is more convenient to simply give each process a mnemonic label, like "acbk" for "Acquire books". This is particularly true while the data flow diagram is being developed and many structural changes are being made. Once the diagram has stabilized, the processes may be relabeled with hierarchical numbers.)

- A process on the higher level that communicates with the process being exploded may be shown as a process outside the exploded process boundary on the lower level, or it may be converted to an external entity which is the agent that performs the process.

Note that manipulating diagrams and their exploded children is difficult, especially while adjustments are being made to the models. For this reason, you are well-advised to do a function hierarchy first, to get the levels sorted out, before trying to connect the functions/process to the data flows.

Context Diagram

Creation of a data flow diagram usually starts by creating a ***context diagram***. This is a diagram containing only the highest-level process and the external entities with which it communicates. The process description should not be as flowery as a mission statement. Try to make it succinct. For example, The Dinosaur Public Library's mission statement (p. 149), "Provide materials and services for the information, learning, and popular reading needs for all citizens and organizations of Dinosaur County", has been reduced in Figure 4.14 to "Provide materials and services for all in Dinosaur County". This, then, is surrounded by the external entities "Patron", "Citizen", "Book Supplier", and the "Dinosaur County" government.

The context diagram is useful in determining the environment of the analysis and the players that will be important. It is also the basis for determining the events that will affect the enterprise and the overall body of data that will be needed.

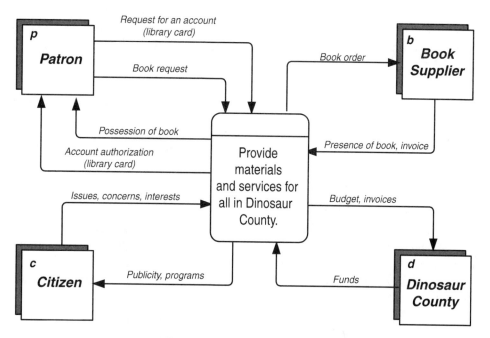

FIGURE 4.14 Context Diagram.

Physical Data Flow Diagrams

There are two kinds of data flow diagrams. A "physical data flow diagram" describes processes in terms of the specific physical mechanisms used to carry them out. This "as is" diagram corresponds to the Row Two perspective ("business owners' view") of Column Two (activities) in the Architecture Framework. This shows the operation of the business in terms known to the people who do it. It is a very good way to capture what goes on and is fairly easy to do.

In an interview, you ask each person, "What reports and forms do you get?", "What do you do with them?", "What reports and forms do you produce?", and "Where do you send these?" A physical process then might be "Fill out purchase order", and data flows from this process might include "yellow copy of purchase order" to "vendor", "blue copy of purchase order" to "accounting", and so forth.

In the physical model, it is appropriate (indeed necessary) to identify who performs each activity. This can be the name either of an individual or of a department (or computer system). Indeed, sometimes the process itself may be no more specifically identified than "Sally's job". Here you have a link between Column Two's activities and Column Four's people and organizations.

This modeling exercise can have amusing results. You complete an interview and realize that you have not heard mention of a report that another worker told you was sent to this person. When you ask about that report, you will get one of the following responses:

- "Oh, that's right. I forgot. When I get that I..."
- "Oh, yes, I get that. But it goes straight to the dustbin. I don't do anything with it."
- "What report?"

The assignment clearly is to make as complete and thorough a record as possible of all the physical data flows in the organization.

Logical ("Essential") Data Flow Diagrams

Tom DeMarco described the distinction between physical and logical data flow diagrams. All he said, however, was that you should "logicalize" the model by replacing physical items with their logical equivalents. "The underlying objectives of the current operation are divorced from the methods of carrying out those objectives" [DeMarco, 1978, p. 27].

Ms. Sarson and Mr. Gane believe that you should start with a logical model in the first place.

Neither of these was as clear as one could be as to exactly what constitutes a logical model and how to tell if you have one, let alone how to get from the physical model to the logical one.[2] Yes, physical mechanisms are easy enough to recognize. But how do you know if you have really captured the correct atomic-level functions at the bottom row?

Enter Stephen M. McMenamin and John Palmer. As mentioned earlier, in their 1984 book *Essential Systems Analysis* they describe a specific procedure for arriving at a set of "essential activities"—the most basic, fully functional description of what an enterprise does.

As with Mr. DeMarco, Messrs. McMenamin and Palmer believe that the place to start is to remove all references to *mechanisms* from processes, data flows, and data stores. An essential data flow diagram must first be *technologically neutral*—true no matter what technology might be employed to carry out the work. This assumes instantaneous response time, no matter what is being done, and infinite storage space. Processing time and storage space are the kinds of constraints that cause current physical systems to have their sometimes peculiar characteristics, so we will assume those constraints away for purpose of identifying the essential processes.

---

2. One is reminded of the cartoon of some years ago, where a blackboard is shown covered by two groups of exceedingly complex equations. In the space between the two groups is the legend "Miracle occurs here".

As defined earlier in the chapter, an *essential activity* is either a *fundamental activity* that performs a task that is part of the system's stated purpose, or a *custodial activity* that establishes and maintains the system's *essential memory* by acquiring and storing the information needed by the fundamental activities.

Where previous authors simply advocated going from a physical data flow diagram to a "logical" one, Messrs. McMenamin and Palmer described very specific steps for identifying fundamental activities:

1. Explode the data flow diagram down to the lowest (atomic) level of detail.

    Richard Barker and Cliff Longman call this level that of an *elementary business function* (one that "when triggered must either be completed successfully, or, if for some reason it cannot be completed successfully, must 'undo' any effects that it had up to the point of failure" [Barker and Longman, 1992, p. 40]).

    This corresponds to an action in UML. Messrs. Rumbaugh, Jacobson, and Booch define an *action* as "an executable atomic computation that results in a change in the state of the model or the return of a value" [Rumbaugh et al. 1999, p. 122].

    When a physical data flow diagram is broken down to its smallest component activities (however this is defined), Messrs. McMenamin and Palmer call these *activity fragments*, some of which are physical mechanisms, some of which are essential.

    Figure 4.15 shows an example where an information flow begins with the arrival of a shipment and ends with flows to data stores ("pending purchase order" and "card catalogue") and flows to an external entity ("Baker and Taylor" and "Dinosaur County" government). Each of the boxes shown represents an elementary business function or essential activity fragment.

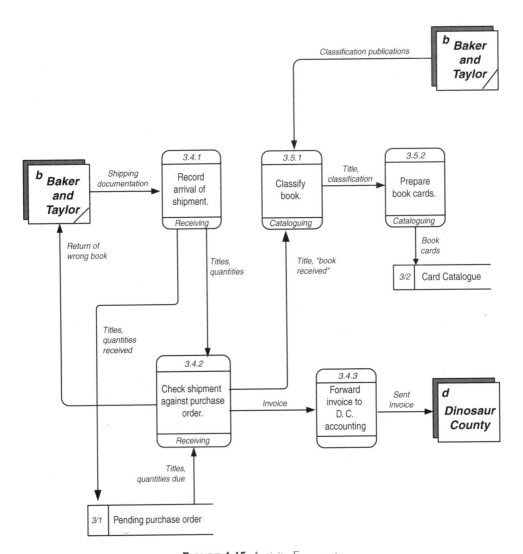

FIGURE 4.15 Activity Fragments.

2. Identify and remove nonessential fragments (mechanisms). These include:

- *References to physical media*—Replace "Gold copy of the purchase order" with "purchase order information". Similarly, replace a "Daily fax" with separate arrows for each flow that is being faxed. Also, remove references to the tools used to perform the activities. For example, replace "Generate CRISP Report" with "Report sales data".

- *Internal validity check*—Remove processes that unnecessarily check internal data. In an essential system, it is assumed that data passed from one component to another are correct. There is no need to add a process to check that. The energy spent coming up with that process could be spent making sure that the first component works correctly. (This does not remove the need for processes that check the validity of data coming from the outside.)

- *Artificial sequence*—Make processes operate in parallel as much as possible. Processes may currently be executed in a sequence that is not required by the function.
- *Redundant activities and data references*—Eliminate multiple processes that update the same data; eliminate multiple data stores that are the same data in different states.
- *Transportation*—Eliminate all processes that say "copy", "send", and so forth.
- *Buffers*—Eliminate data stores with no essential function. There are data stores whose sole function is to wait for the next process to catch up. That is, process A prepares data for process B, and if process B isn't working fast enough and the data must wait, they are placed in a "buffer" data store. This data store has no essential function and should be eliminated.

Figure 4.16 shows the following being renamed or eliminated:

- External entity "Baker and Taylor" becomes both "Book Supplier" and "Classification Service", reflecting the two roles the company now plays. This company has supplied books and cataloguing services in the past, but there is no reason to assume it will continue to do either or both of these things.
- The sequence implied by the connection of 3.4.1 and 3.4.2 is not required. The "Titles, quantity" data flow is removed. A new flow now goes directly from "Book Supplier" to activity 3.4.2. Checking the shipped quantities may be done before or after recording receipt of the shipment. Note that this will require a new communication back to process 3.4.1 ("Return of book") if the book is rejected.
- The activities "Prepare book cards" (activity 3.5.2), and "Forward invoice to Dinosaur County Accounting" (activity 3.4.3) are removed. These activities describe communication only.
- The data flows "shipping documentation" and "classification publications" are renamed. These are the physical manifestations of information. The information involved is "receipt of books" and "classification guidelines".

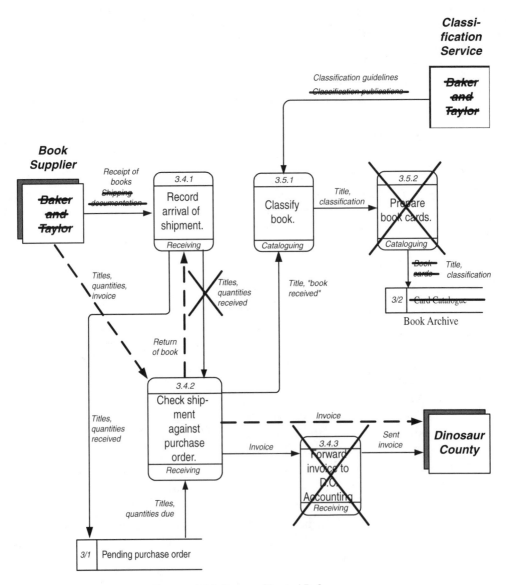

FIGURE 4.16 Remove Physical References.

- The data store, "Card Catalogue" is renamed "Book Archive" (or it could also be "Book Index"). This is a physical repository for storing information about books. Along with that is the renaming of "book cards" to "Title and classification".

  This is a very good example, by the way, of how the technology has traditionally affected our view of processes. Those born before 1980 will remember that the card catalogue has always been a fundamental part of a library. It was a dramatic change to see this replaced by a computer terminal. But in fact the card catalogue and the database are but two different technologies for implementing the same data store.

3. Identify all the real-world events that impinge on the operation. These are things happening in the outside world that cause the enterprise to react. They can be identified from the context data flow diagram. They might include such things as a customer inquiry, a customer order, the receipt of purchased goods, a person applying for a job, and so forth. (We are not concerned here with internal events, such as the completion of a process.)

4. Identify the activity fragments that are carried out in response to each external event.

5. Define a parent activity that encompasses these activity fragments that are the response to that event. This is a "fundamental essential activity".

6. Examine the data stores used by the essential activities. Are there activities that update those stores? If not, define additional "custodial" activities. For example "Manage patron changes" might be a custodial activity.

7. Eliminate any activities that are not fundamental or custodial.

After Step 2, above, the activity fragments left are:

- Record arrival of shipment.
- Check shipment against purchase order.
- Classify book.

The only relevant event is "Receipt of a book", a message from the Book Supplier to "Record arrival of shipment". As it happens, all three of our fragments are performed in response to that event, so we define a parent activity, "Receive each book". This, then, is the "essential activity" shown in Figure 4.17.

Notice, by the way, that "Catalogue book" has wound up as a component of "Receive each book". This was not what we originally expected when we laid out the function hierarchy and the first draft of the data flow diagram in Figure 4.13. The process of determining essential activities has revealed something to us.

Now this would not be true if it were not the case that, as is currently understood, a book is catalogued as soon as it is received. If a book were not catalogued when received, then that activity would be outside the essential activity "Receive each book", just as we originally portrayed it.

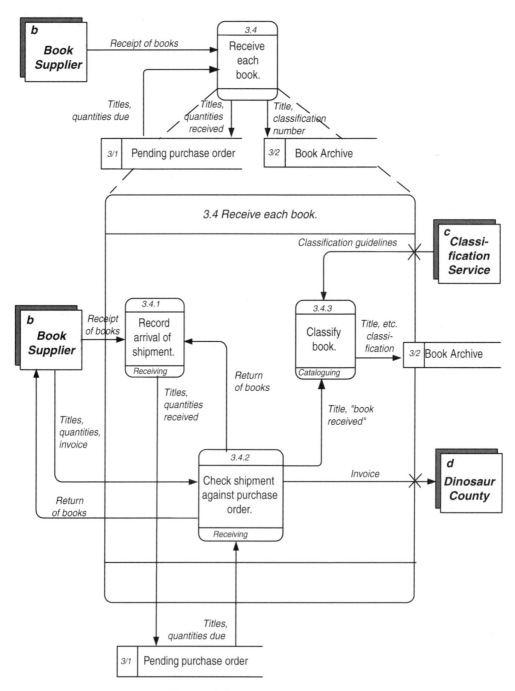

FIGURE 4.17 An Essential Activity.

It may be the case that a particular fragment is used by more than one essential activity. In this case, it is appropriate to break out the fragment as its own essential activity.

Note that an essential activity is the lowest level of detail at which a process (or function) can be described. Indeed it may be that these lower-level activities are the atomic ones, in terms of Barker's definition of an elementary business function or the UML's definition of an action. Those more atomic process fragments, however, that comprise an essential activity are by definition specific to the company and, at least to some extent, are bound to a technology. For example, the company could employ new barcoding technology that would, at the same time the shipment is moved into inventory, perform the necessary checks, recording, and notification. Below the essential level, the activities are chosen by the enterprise as a mechanism for carrying out the essential business function. As a consequence, they could be changed in a new system, so they are not of concern in an analysis diagram.

Above this level, you should have described functions that the company must perform, regardless of the technology used.

Once the essential data flow diagram has been developed, it is possible to examine it to see what parts should be automated and how that automation should work.

IDEF0

In the mid-1970s, Douglas Ross worked with the U.S. Air Force to develop a method for modeling processes on the ICAM (Integrated Computer-Aided Manufacturing) program. Shortly thereafter, he applied the new method to an ITT telephonic system requirements definition effort. The name "Structured Analysis and Design Techniques" (SADT) was coined by Mr. Ross as a result of discussions with ITT. This was based on the principle that graphic models of various kinds should be used to communicate between the different disciplines involved in system development.

In 1981 the Air Force recognized the usefulness of the concepts in SADT and derived from them a series of IDEF (Integrated computer-aided manufacturing **DEF**inition) methods. One of these, IDEF0, addressed the modeling of functions and processes, while a second, IDEF1 (later extended to IDEF1X), addressed the modeling of data structure.

In 1998 Clarence Feldmann wrote a guide to IDEF0, *The Practical Guide to Business Process Reengineering Using IDEF0*. His focus was less on preparing for new computer systems than on simply understanding the nature of an enterprise and how it might be reworked. This section is largely derived from that book.[3]

---

3. Your author would like to express particular appreciation to Mr. Feldmann for his help with this section.

On the surface, IDEF0 models are similar to data flow diagrams, but they are different in several significant ways:

- While a data flow diagram shows only the communication of *data* between activities, an IDEF0 model can also show *material flows* and *control flows* as well. Previously, the distinction between data and messages was described, but it was observed that the data flow diagram does not represent that distinction graphically. Here this distinction is made explicit. A message from one activity to another asserts control over the second activity. It is not merely an input to it.

- An IDEF0 diagram contains neither external entities nor data stores. The input and output lines document external entities and double as data stores, in that, where there is more than one input, data will wait in each flow until other needed flows are present. Arrows into and out of the diagram can, however, be documented separately as to where they are coming from and going to.

- Where a data flow diagram process can only be decomposed to a single lower-level diagram, an IDEF0 activity may be exploded in alternative ways. There are explicit constraints on the ways activities may be decomposed. (See p. 147.) In addition, there is a provision to link an activity to other documentation.

- The activities in an IDEF0 model show constraints, not sequential processes. That is, the execution of an activity is actually controlled by other activities. It is not just an optional branch.

- As normally used, the orientation of the model is toward the operation of the business, not the operation of an information system. Of course the symbols could be used to describe physical activities in all their technical glory, but that is not their intended use. That is, while mechanisms may be explicitly shown on the diagram, these need not affect the organization or the nature of the activities. Fundamentally, the diagram is supposed to be technologically neutral.

Syntax

The basic symbol in an IDEF0 model is a rectangle that represents an *activity*. Figure 4.18 shows this. The four sides of the box represent the four elements of the activity. Arrows coming into the left are *inputs*. An input arrow from the left describes input data that will be transformed by the activity. Arrows going from the box to the right are *outputs*. An output arrow describes the results of the transformation. Arrows going into the box at the top are *controls*. A control arrow describes something that affects the execution of the activity. This could be a message that triggers it, or a set of constraints that affect how the activity works. Arrows going into the box from below describe *mechanisms*, the physical means by which the activity is carried out. A mechanism arrow could describe a physical resource, such as a computer system, or it could describe the people or organizations that perform the activity.

Finally, an arrow from the box at the bottom is a "call" to another activity. This is used to refer either to a common process that is invoked in multiple places or to a process that is at a lower level of abstraction. In the first case, a call might be to a "Report Process" function or to a "Copy and Distribute" function. In the second case, the call arrow refers to a list of types of functions that are performed at this point in the model. For example, the box might be "Perform manufacturing process", and the called models might be "press", "treat", "form", etc.

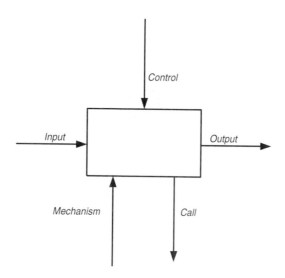

FIGURE 4.18 IDEF0 Activity Box.

As with data flow diagrams, IDEF0 begins with a context diagram, labeled "A-0". This consists of one box for the entire portion of the enterprise being modeled. Figure 4.19 shows an example of this, for the same example that was used previously (Figure 4.14, page 161). Note that the federal standard for IDEF0 specifies the page layout for all IDEF0 diagrams. The "node" shows the position of this diagram in the overall structure. "BAQ", for example is the name of this project, and "A-0" means that this is the overview diagram. The name of the diagram is in the middle, and "DH63" on the right is a diagram number for this sheet of paper. (As you go through various drafts of the same model, each will have a different diagram number.)

Note the following controls that can be shown here that did not appear on the context data flow diagram:

- Market demand
- Patron's account
- Classification guidelines
  (This appeared in a lower-level data flow diagram.)

"Funds" was shown as a data flow on that diagram. Here the flow is "Funds From County".

Also note the addition of the following mechanisms:

- Baker and Taylor (the company from which the library buys books and that helps with classification)
- Circulation system (the current manual set of procedures for checking out and returning books)
- Library staff

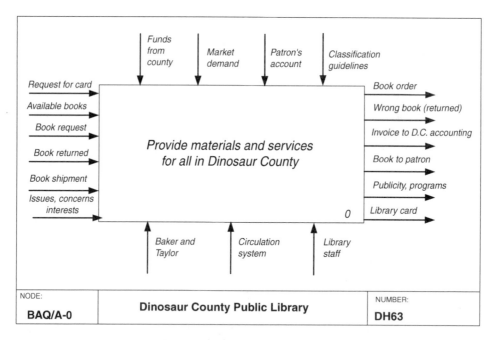

FIGURE 4.19 A-0 IDEF0 Diagram.

For readability purposes, an IDEF0 diagram is limited to no more than six activities. If more detail is required, one or more of these six can be exploded to describe how it works. This is a more rigorous requirement than was ever expressed for data flow diagrams, although the principle has always been around. Mr. DeMarco tended to have fewer processes on a diagram and a deeper explosion structure than Ms. Sarson and Mr. Gane, who liked broader, shallower diagrams. But the rules were never expressed as explicitly as this.

(This is more rigorous than required by Mr. G.A. Miller's 1956 finding that a person can hold about seven plus or minus two elements in his mind at a time. In principle, one could have seven or even up to nine and still achieve the simplicity desired, but six was the number chosen.)

With only six activities per page, it is easy to put the page on a single 8.5 by 11[4] piece of paper. The activities are arranged from upper left to lower right.

Information appears on this diagram that was not on the data flow diagrams. First, the books themselves show up as flows ("book shipment", "received book", "catalogued book", and "wrong book"). We also show the system provided by Baker and Taylor (the book distributor) which is used both for ordering and cataloguing. The bundle which is the "Baker and Taylor" system is split into two parts: the "Order System" and the "Cataloguing System".

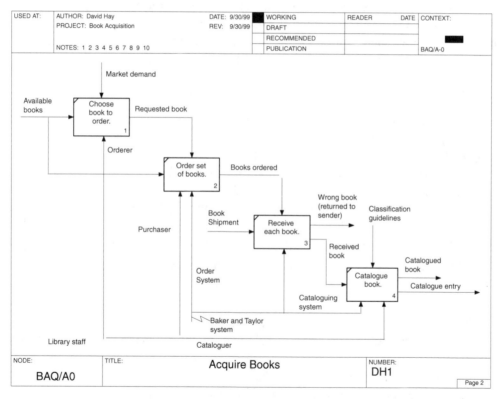

FIGURE 4.20 An IDEF0 Model. (Diagram by Clarence G. Feldmann.)

The players are shown as another resource, "Library Staff", which is split into the "Orderer", "Purchaser", and "Cataloguer". External entities are not shown but are inferred. In the case of the company supplying the books, this is not a problem, although it would be nice to know where the "Classification Guidelines" came from.

4. ... or A4, if you are European...

Being vague on the origin of "Market Demand" is actually desirable in this case, since to characterize that more finely in this model would require more details than are appropriate at this time.

This "Node" is shown as being the top-level diagram (A0) in the application area "BAQ". (Note that "A-0" is the context diagram, while "A0" is the highest-level detailed diagram.)

Note in Figure 4.20 that the physical book shipment is shown, along with information about it. This is different from a data flow diagram's concern with information alone. Note that processing of the shipment is "controlled" by the specification of which books were ordered. If a book received wasn't ordered, it is returned to the sender.

Note also that this example does not show "Catalogue book" combined with "Receive each book", as was done in the essential activity analysis. IDEF0 has no specific provision for determining essential activities, although the process described in the previous section could certainly be applied here.

Rules

One of the strengths of the IDEF0 approach is the discipline it applies to the modeling process. Mr. Feldmann's book, for example, spends an entire chapter describing the "pragmatics" of developing IDEF0 models. He lays out criteria for organizing the project (including defining its purpose and viewpoint), creating the model (including the mechanics of its creation, as well as its validation), conducting peer reviews and critiques, presenting models to an audience, and analyzing the impact of changes that arise out of the modeling effort. In fact much of what he says applies to any modeling effort and is reflected in the material presented in Chapter 2 of this book.

In addition, he presents very specific rules for the formation of the model itself [Feldmann, 1998, pp. 107–122]:

Box Rules

- Identify each activity box with a single-digit number, placing it in the lower right corner.
- Assign each activity at least one *control* arrow and one *output* arrow. (Unlike with data flow diagrams, it is not necessary for an activity to have an *input* arrow.)
- Name each box with a verb phrase consisting of an active verb and a direct object.
- Eventually, represent all covered activities in the lowest level of detail.

Arrow Rules

- Match the arrows going into and out of the activity being decomposed to the arrows going into and out of a decomposed diagram. For example, the explosion of "Receive each book" must have arrows at the boundary describing "Book ship-ment", "Books ordered", etc. This means that alternative decompositions of an activity are possible, as long as the arrows match.

Note that it is not recommended to "split by type", where an activity is split into different versions of the same activity. For example, the activity "Process product" should not be split into one activity for each work center. Those dia-grams are not of the same level of abstraction as the parent. It is better to use the call arrow pointing to different diagrams for each work center.

- Label each arrow with an adjective and a noun.
- Some arrows may constitute groups of flows. If an arrow branching from a main arrow contains less than all the flows in the parent arrow, it must be labeled accordingly.
- Bundle arrows according to the appropriate level of detail of the processes involved.
- Show arrows as orthogonal (north/south or east/west), with rounded corners.
- Do not assign the same name to more than one arrow that goes into or out of one activity.

Diagram Rules

- Each diagram must have between three and six activities represented.

    Identify each diagram by a project abbreviation, plus "A" with a hierarchical code. The context level with one box is called "A-0," and the highest level show-ing the first six activities is "A0". The first-level activities are identified as A1, A2, A3, etc.; the next level, A11, A12,..., A21, A22, and so forth.[5]
- Label the flows connecting between different diagrams. Each flow within a dia-gram may be identified as <source activity number>{I | C | O | M}<flow number on that side>. So, for example, the third input to a process coming from process 2 is labeled "2I3". A flow to the outside of the diagram, then, is labeled with the target diagram identifier, plus the flow definition within that diagram. A flow in dia-gram PRJ/A23, which on that diagram is 4O2, may be labeled to connect with 1I3 on diagram A32. This would be PRJ/A32/1I3.
- Diagrams show constraint. They are not data flow diagrams or flow charts. For example, Figure 4.21 shows a flow chart, with its sequence of steps and its branch, next to an IDEF0 diagram, where the data flows are constrained by the control flow.

---

5. The "A" comes from the fact that the original SADT technique involved activity models and data models. So, activities were designated with an "A" and entities with a "D".

Flow Chart

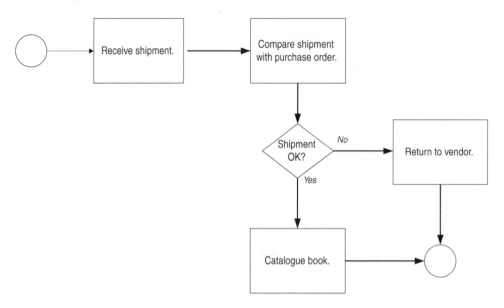

IDEF0 Diagram

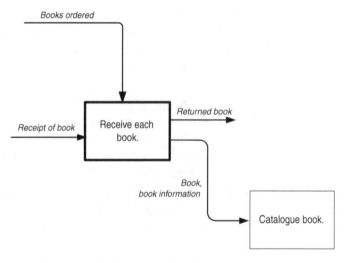

FIGURE 4.21 Constraints, Not Flows.

Model Rules

Restrict a model to a single viewpoint and purpose. The model's purpose must be clearly stated before the effort begins. It will affect how things are represented. The viewpoint is also important in determining how processes will be described: Is it technical? Managerial? Financial?

An important component of viewpoint is the level of abstraction of the model. "Manage the corporation" is at a different level of abstraction than "Run the accounting department", and "manufacture product" is at a different level than "press ingots into sheets", "anneal sheets", and "form boxes".

Note that this is different from "level of detail". A model of "Manage the corporation" may be very detailed in describing the tasks required, but these tasks are very different from the detailed tasks required to "Press ingots into sheets".

There are also specific criteria that can be applied to determine an IDEF0 model's quality (Many of these can also be applied to other process model techniques as well):

- *Model Validation*

  An IDEF0 model must be put through a comprehensive process of review both for technical correctness (did it follow the rules described above?) and factual accuracy (does it reflect the actual nature of the business?) Questions to ask during validation include:

  - What controls each activity?

  - How does the activity respond to erroneous arrow content?

  - Is there any feedback to previously completed activities?

  - Which inputs and controls are used to produce each possible set of outputs?

  - Which events trigger activation of the diagram?

  If the model is of the current operation and is to be used to modify the organization, it must be checked to be sure it is in sufficient detail to provide a basis for developing such modifications. To address this, questions might be:

  - Is there a single organization responsible for performing this activity? If not, further decomposition is needed.

  - Is there sufficient detail to analyze the activity in detail? For example, can you analyze its operating costs? If not, further decomposition is needed.

  - What additional facts does this decomposition diagram provide?

  - Are the facts related to the purpose of the diagram? If they are not, try a different decomposition.

  - Are the facts related to the stated viewpoint? If not, determine where a viewpoint shift occurred.

- *Fog Factor Testing*

  The best test of the readability of a diagram is to evaluate the responses of various readers of the diagram. A more mechanical approach is to simply analyze the components of the diagram. Add together the number of boxes, the number of input, control, and output arrows per box, the number of arrow forks or joins, and the number of arrow crossings. If this number is greater than your corporate threshold (50, for example), then the model is too complex and should be simplified. Put more details in lower-level diagrams.[6]

- *Arrow Label Precision /Arrow Label Description/Precise Control Arrow Content*

  The name chosen for each arrow is critical to understanding the meaning of a model. It must be specific enough to convey accurately what the flow is about. Don't simply say "procedures". Say "accounting procedures" or "assembly procedures" or whatever. Don't simply say "rules" as a control. Specify which rules, or at least what category of rules. And don't just describe the medium, like "computer output" or "daily fax". Describe the contents of the flow.

  Note that a bundle may branch at some point and go to multiple different activities. If, when this happens, an arrow contains less than the full bundle, it must be labeled accordingly. For example, back in Figure 4.20, the bundle "Library Staff" consists of "Orderer", "Purchaser", and "Cataloguer". The cataloguer bundle branches three ways, but all three are the cataloguer, so they don't have to be labeled separately.

  In particular, the names of control arrows must be assigned carefully at each level.

- *Diagram Simplicity*

  The limit of six activities on a diagram helps to keep it from becoming too complex. It is equally important to be sure that the diagram isn't too simple. Are all the activities meaningful? Are all the flows and controls present that are required for a full understanding of the process involved? The way to test this is to imagine different scenarios and make sure that each of them can be handled (described) by the diagram.

- *Arrow Bundle Grouping*

  As the level of detail in successive diagrams increases, naturally the level of detail of the information flows will also increase. At the higher levels, it is reasonable to have data flows that are clusters of elements. These are broken out at lower levels. Even at a particular level, you have choices to make about the extent to which you group flows together. It is certainly possible to make the qualitative assertion that each data flow should be a coherent single thing at an appropriate level of detail,

---

6. This, by the way, is not a bad technique for evaluating *any* model.

although there are few guidelines as to what constitutes an "appropriate level of detail".

Too many flows obviously clutter the diagram. Too few provide too little information about what is happening. In general, any time you have multiple flows between the same two processes, you have the opportunity to bundle them together. The bundling should make logical sense, however. You may still wind up with two or three bundles.

- **Correct Identification of Controls**

While it is better if this is not so, some bundles at a higher level will contain flows that are both inputs to an activity and controllers of it. When they are broken out at lower levels, this will become clear. At the higher level, though, if any part of the bundle is used for control, it should all be considered a control bundle.

It is certainly important, even at a high level, to keep clear the distinction between inputs and controls. An input is something that is modified by the activity to produce an output. A control, on the other hand, determines how the activity works.

- **Viewpoint Focus**

If the diagram seems to show many kinds of data from different viewpoints, the modeler should consult the model's viewpoint definition (described above, p. 177) to see which viewpoint is supposed to be represented on the diagram.

- **Text Selection**

Each diagram should be accompanied by a body of text that explains and clarifies it. This should not, however, be a detailed description of what is on the drawing. That should be self-evident. Rather, the text simply clarifies circumstances, gives examples, and describes business rules that are not apparent on the diagram.

- **Function and Design Separation**

Finally, an IDEF0 diagram should describe the *functions* of the business—what it is or wants to do (including sequential processes)—not the *design* of the business. Yes, mechanisms are added as comments on the bottom of the activity boxes, but the presence of these mechanisms should not in any way affect the shape of the drawing or the descriptions of the activities.

The UML Activity Diagram

Ironically, the object-oriented world, which has moved our orientation so dramatically from processes to objects and classes, has also produced an activity modeling notation. A portion of the UML is devoted to modeling activities. The syntax is an interesting combination of business process re-engineering process diagrams, data flow diagrams, and flow charts.

In a UML activity diagram, an activity is inaugurated by the completion of a prior activity and continues until its completion triggers yet another activity. The effect of this is to provide a model much like the others that have been presented here.

An activity diagram is concerned with activities and actions. The UML defines an "activity" as "a non-atomic execution within a state machine" [Booch, et. al. 1999, p. 457]. In other words, this can be subdivided into smaller activities and ultimately actions. An "action", on the other hand, is "an atomic computation—that is, it cannot be terminated externally" [Rumbaugh, et. al. 1999, p.122]. This is compatible with Richard Barker's definition of an "elementary business function" (one which "when triggered must either be completed successfully, or, if for some reason it cannot be completed successfully, must 'undo' any effects that it had up to the point of failure") [Barker and Longman, 1992 p. 40].

An activity diagram is like a data flow diagram in that it features activities, flows, and data stores. An activity is represented by a round-cornered rectangle. (Messrs. Rumbaugh, Jacobson, and Booch do not specify whether the activities are physical activities or essential activities.) Flows, represented by arrows, always begin at a solid circle in the upper left corner and end with bounded circles at the bottom of the page. If a flow branches, this is shown by a horizontal line, with the detailed flows dropping from it. All the flows must come back together in another horizontal line. Objects are shown in square-cornered boxes, with data flows shown by dashed arrows. Swim lanes are represented by vertical lines dividing the diagram space. Both material flows and data flows are shown.

An activity diagram is different from a data flow diagram in that the flows are organized by *swim lanes* (one for all the activities performed by one *actor*). (They are commonly called swim lanes because the same approach is taken in business process diagrams, described below [page 187], where each actor's activities are arranged horizontally. Here they are vertical, however, so perhaps they should be called "diving lanes".) Also, unlike a data flow diagram, an action diagram starts with a designated start point, ends with a designated end point, and does not represent external entities at all. There is only the actor that is responsible for each swim lane. And unlike for a data flow diagram there are no rigorous rules about maintaining consistency from one level to the next.

A sample activity diagram is shown in Figure 4.22. Note that activities are rounded boxes, and data flows are arrows, as we have seen before. In this case, there are three swim lanes, one each for the activities that are the responsibility of the Department Managers, the Purchasing Department, and the Cataloguing Department. The activities shown are the same as those previously shown for the examples of other modeling techniques.

The treatment of data stores is very different from that in data flow diagrams. Whereas in the essential activity above, data stores are views, each typically composed of multiple entities, in a UML activity diagram, the only data stores are objects (entity occurrences). In fact, however, objects and classes in the object-oriented world are often called *collections* of what a relational model would declare as entity types. So the "objects" of the activity diagram are not that far removed from the views that are data flow diagram data stores.

Note that here a data store is not a class but a representative object (occurrence or instance) of that class. In Figure 4.22, the object labeled "o:Order" represents an instance of the class "Order", not the class itself. This is a subtle distinction not made in other modeling notations. This emphasizes the assertion that the model describes a set of actual objects, not simply an object structure. The expected state of that representative object after the action has taken place may also be indicated. Note that in Figure 4.22 this means the ORDER object appears once for each state (o:Order [pending], o:Order [confirmed], o:Order [received]). Among other things, this means that the object is repeated on the diagram for each state it may be in.

Note an interesting constraint: when flows diverge, this is denoted by a horizontal line; when they come back together again, there must be a matching horizontal line bringing together exactly the same number of flows that were divided above. This means that if there are successive divisions of flows, there must be successive convergence. Some activities may have to wait for the completion of others in the set.

The sample model in Figure 4.22 breaks out the receiving process more than in previous examples, to illustrate both the fork-and-join notation and branching. In the latter case, when the shipment is checked for correctness, it is either accepted and catalogued or returned.

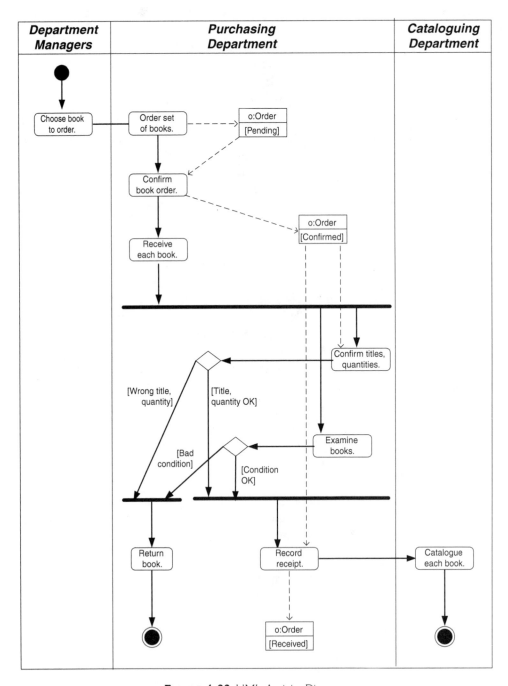

FIGURE 4.22 UML Activity Diagram.

Interaction Diagrams

A more intricate description of the interaction and communication among objects in the UML is the **UML interaction diagram.** There are two versions: the sequence diagram and the collaboration diagram. The **UML sequence diagram** shows a set of objects across the top of a page and the communications among them as a set of parallel lines. A *collaboration diagram* is similar to a data flow diagram, but instead of communications between activities, it shows communication between objects. Both of these diagrams are important for object-oriented design, but it is not clear how effective they are for analysis. Still, they represent an interesting exercise.

A sequence diagram is shown in Figure 4.23. Each is arranged with a set of objects laid out across the top of the diagram. (Again, what are shown are representative objects of a class, not the class.) Down the page are a series of horizontal arrows, representing transactions (activities sending messages), arranged in chronological order, with each showing a communication between two or more objects.

In a sequence diagram, the vertical rectangles represent the life of the object. Where an object is destroyed, an "X" below the rectangle shows this. In Figure 4.23 the object "o:PurchaseOrder" is created in response to the transaction "createOrder" and destroyed by the transaction "closeOrder."

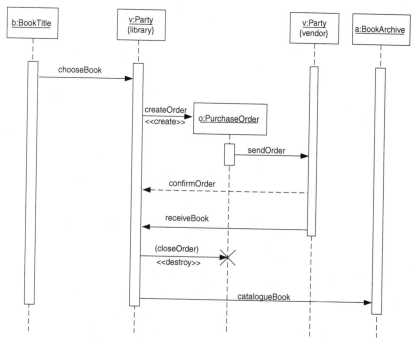

FIGURE 4.23 Interaction (Sequence) Diagram.

Figure 4.24 shows a collaboration diagram. In this, the objects are linked together, and the activities that send messages from one to another are listed along the side of each link. The sequence of the activities is shown in the lists, not graphically, as is the case with the sequence diagram. Figure 4.24 is logically equivalent to Figure 4.23.

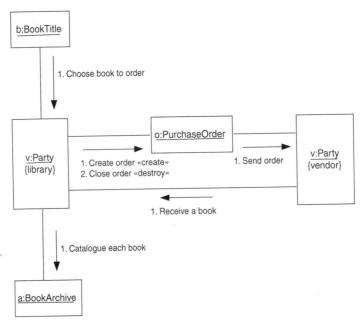

FIGURE 4.24 Interaction (Collaboration) Diagram.

Use Cases

In the late 1990s much was made of the *use case* approach to defining system requirements. According to Paul Harmon and Mike Watson, "A use-case diagram provides a functional description of a system and its major processes. It also provides a graphic description of who will use the system and what kinds of interactions they can expect to have with the system" [Harmon and Watson, 1998, p. 112]. A use case consists of a graphic showing a system as an oval, and one or more actors interacting with it. An *actor* is the person, organization, or computer system that is interacting with a system. In addition, supporting documentation describes the triggers of the use case, the steps taken, and alternative steps that are taken under specific circumstances.

As normally used, then, a use case is not a description of the business. It is a description of a hypothetical system. Therefore it does not belong in Row Two of the "Activities" column (Column Two) of the Architecture Framework, as it does not describe the business user's view of an enterprise's activities. Neither does it belong in Row Three, according to that definition since it does not represent the architecture of an enterprise's activities.

As will be shown in Chapter 5, the definition of "system" can be extended to mean a piece of the business itself, however, and a use case can describe the business owner's view of the interactions with that piece. Ivar Jacobson explores this idea in his 1994 book *The Object Advantage: Business Process Re-engineering with Object Technology*. To the extent that this approach is taken, it is much like a context or a level-one data flow diagram. The actors are "external entities" in a data flow diagram, but the idea of how they interact is the same. The difference is that it does not describe the nature of the communications data, and it is not as rigorously defined. The rules for exploding a process, for example, are not well documented in any of the literature currently available.

A use case, then, presupposes that a boundary has been drawn around a future system and it describes the nature of the interactions with that system. Because it focuses on interactions more than the actual activities performed, it more appropriately belongs in Column Four ("People and Organizations"), either in Row Three (describing the nature of interactions with a part of the enterprise's functions) or Row Four (describing a user interface). For that reason, use cases are described more fully in Chapter 5.

A Word About Business Process Re-engineering

From the outset it was clear that documenting an enterprise's data flows could be more useful to the company than just as the basis for designing new systems. Why is it necessary to produce 15 copies of a production order in the course of producing a lot? Perhaps there are things that we could do to improve the structure of processes, before we even look into automating some of them. Indeed, some of the processes we thought we were going to automate may be completely eliminated.

In the 1990s this recognition took formal shape with the advent of ***business-process engineering***. Suddenly a whole branch of consulting began to specialize in drawing variations on data flow diagrams for the purpose of recommending changes to the structure and processes of an organization. The business process diagram was developed to address this.

Business Process Diagrams

The business-process re-engineering movement has come up with the ***business process diagram***. This has been presented as a new technique, but it really is the data flow diagram in new clothes. Like a data flow diagram, it is a set of boxes representing things the company does, linked by data flows and (optionally) material flows. It is similar to the approach taken in the UML activity diagram, in that the activities are grouped according to who does them.

A business process diagram differs from a data flow diagram in two ways: First, as typically drawn, a business process diagram focuses on the current physical system, with an interest in moving to a new physical system as quickly as possible. The step of looking at the underlying functions, independent of technology, may be overlooked, although processes may be categorized as being "value added" to the extent that they do contribute to the functions of the organization. The current physical nature of the diagrams is emphasized by the replacement, in many cases, of the boxes with icons representing manufacturing, the telephone, forms, and so on.

The second—and more significant—difference is that the processes are organized by the players. That is, as with UML activity diagrams, each participant is designated as being responsible for a *swim lane*, and all processes performed by that participant are shown in that swim lane. (Unlike the UML activity diagram, however, the swim lanes here are horizontal.) An example is shown in Figure 4.25.

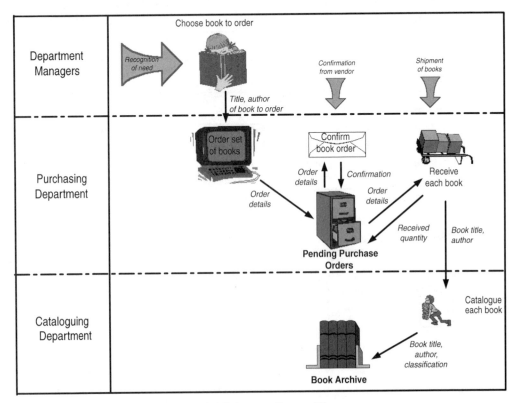

FIGURE 4.25 Business Process Diagram.

One way to enrich any of the diagrams described here is to highlight the processes that really do contribute to the functions of the business. To do this, produce an essential data flow diagram and compare it to the physical business process diagram. Which of the business process diagram processes directly implement fundamental essential processes? Color those green. Which processes are custodial? Color those yellow. Which processes are left over and do not contribute to the value of the firm? Color those red. This is a very useful exercise. With each category shaded a different color, you can then determine how best to eliminate the processes that are not of value to the enterprise.

Detailed Function and Process Documentation

None of the techniques described above does more than identify activities, giving each a name and perhaps a number and description. Aside from exploding a process into smaller processes in a data flow diagram, there is no provision in these techniques for documenting in detail how an activity works. This requires a different approach.

Many processes are trivial on the surface: "record order", "issue work order", and so forth. The data flow diagram shows the information used and the information produced. A paragraph of text in the accompanying model documentation may be sufficient. Some processes, however, require more documentation in order to describe any algorithms used as well as any business rules that apply. Several techniques originally developed for documenting program logic are available for this. Among them are:

- *Structured natural language* and *pseudo-code*—text organized in a formal way
- *Action diagrams*—a kind of hierarchy of the steps required to perform the function
- *Decision trees* and *decision tables*—a way of describing the alternative steps that might be required.
- Other hierarchical techniques, such as HIPO and Warnier-Orr

Structured Natural Language

Structured natural language[7] and pseudo-code are ways of describing specific processes. These typically describe the implementation of business rules, although until recently we didn't realize this. *Pseudo-code* specifically uses key words derived from programming and is similar in many ways to programming languages such as Pascal or C. *Structured natural language* takes a similar approach, but it relaxes some programming constraints to make it more readable for the casual user. Structured natural language is a more appropriate part of a requirements analysis. Carma McClure and James Martin described structured English in their 1985 book, *Diagramming Techniques for Analysts and Programmers*. Figure 4.26 shows an example of structured natural lan-

---

7. We in the United States grew up hearing that this was "structured English", but we live in a global marketplace, now.

guage. Note that there are four basic types of structure in this passage:

- *Sequence*—a series of steps, one following after the other. No key words are involved. A step may be either an information processing or a physical step.
- *Condition*—the application of a test ("if") to determine which step should be taken. This is depicted by using the key words IF, THEN, and ELSE. That is, the structure is IF <condition> THEN <action 1> ELSE <action 2>.
- *Case*—a complex condition, wherein several alternatives are possible. Usually this is in the form IF <condition 1> THEN <action 1> ELSE IF <condition 2> THEN <action 2> ELSE IF...END IF.
- *Repetition or iteration*—a specification that one or more steps are to be repeated one or more times. Repetition is of two types:
  - REPEAT WHILE—operations are continued as long as a condition exists. The condition is tested *before* each iteration. Key words may be DO WHILE, REPEAT WHILE, or LOOP WHILE. For example, a structure might be DO WHILE amount received is less than 1000, THEN receive shipment END DO WHILE. The shipment that would take the total over 1000 would not be accepted.
  - REPEAT UNTIL—operations are continued until a condition exists. The condition is tested *after* each iteration. Key words may be FOR, DO UNTIL, REPEAT UNTIL, or LOOP UNTIL. For example, a structure might be DO UNTIL amount received is greater than or equal to 1000, THEN receive shipment END DO UNTIL. In this case, the shipment of 200 units that takes the total to 1100 would be accepted, since the check is not done until after it is received.

FOR each book to be catalogued:
    Enter query for book title, author;

    Retrieve extended Dewey number;

    IF number of digits to the right of the decimal point of the extended
      Dewey number is GREATER THAN four,

    THEN create DPL Dewey number by truncating all digits more than
      four positions to the right of the decimal point,

    ELSE, accept extended Dewey number as the DPL number

    EndIf;

End for

FIGURE 4.26 Structured Natural Language.

Carma McClure and James Martin cite a set of rules for constructing structured natural language descriptions:

Format

1. The structures are indented to show the logical hierarchy.
2. *Sequence, condition, case,* and *repetition* structures are made clear.
3. The sequence structure is a list of items where each item is placed on a separate line. If the item requires more than one line, continuation lines are indented. The end of an item is punctuated with a semicolon (;).
4. Blocks of instructions are grouped together and given a meaningful name that describes their function.
5. Comment lines are delimited with a beginning asterisk and a terminating semicolon.

Key Words

6. Key words are used to make the structures clear: for example, IF, THEN, ELSE, ENDIF, FOR, REPEAT WHILE, REPEAT UNTIL, END REPEAT, EXIT.
7. Key words are used for logic: AND, OR, GT (greater than), LT (less than), GE (greater than or equal to), LE (less than or equal to).
8. The choice of key words should be an installation standard.
9. The key-word set may be selected to conform to a particular fourth-generation language, but they are still language-independent descriptions.
10. Key words and names that are in the data dictionary are capitalized; names of program blocks are capitalized; other words are not capitalized.
11. End words such as END IF, END REPEAT, and EXIT are used to make clear where the structure ends.
12. Parentheses are used to avoid AND/OR and other ambiguities [Martin and McClure, 1985, p. 170].

Within these constraints, the wording should be chosen to be as easy as possible for end users to understand.

With all due respect to Ms. McClure and Mr. Martin, exception could be taken to Rule 7. In the interest of making the text as comfortable as possible for nontechnical people, the logic key words ("greater than", "less than", etc.) should not be abbreviated. It is arguable whether or not any of the key words should be capitalized. The sentences should certainly be as close as possible to common natural language sentences.

Action Diagrams

Ms. McClure and Mr. Martin also show an *action diagram* (not to be confused with UML's "activity diagram") as a way of continuing the function-hierarchy idea into the workings of an activity itself [Martin and McClure, 1985, pp. 183–209]. The sequences, conditions, cases, and repetitions described above for structured natural language and pseudo-code can be represented as a graphic hierarchy: The statements of actions are listed sequentially with bars to indicate nesting, loops, and branchings of various kinds. Figure 4.27 shows a sample action diagram.

In the diagram, a simple bracket surrounds groups of steps to be considered together. The steps to be performed for each response to an IF statement constitute a special case of bracketing such groups of steps. In that case, the bracket is divided between the steps to be performed if the statement is true and those to be performed if it is false. In this case, the bracket points to the IF, ELSE, and ENDIF statements. Similarly, the bracket points to each element of a CASE structure.

Loops are represented by a thickened bracket with a doubled line at the top, pointing to the DO or FOR statement.

Bracketed groups may be nested inside each other. This provides a hierarchical representation of the steps.

Exits are shown by an arrow pointing to the left with the arrowhead outside the level being exited.

FOR each book to be catalogued:

Enter query for book title, author.

Retrieve extended Dewey number.

IF number of digits to the right of the decimal point of the extended Dewey number is GREATER THAN four,

THEN create DPL Dewey number by truncating all digits more than four positions to the right of the decimal point,

ELSE, accept extended Dewey number as the DPL number.

(ENDIF)

(END FOR)

FIGURE 4.27 Action Diagram.

Decision Trees and Decision Tables

Like the flow charts popular in the 1950s and 1960s, UML activity diagrams may include logical tests and branching. Data flow diagrams and IDEF0 diagrams, on the other hand, do not show branching logic. In these cases, for example, after process 1, either process 2 or process 3 may be performed, arrows are drawn to both of them without describing the constraints that cause one or the other path to be taken. Sometimes this can be mitigated by naming a process: "If it is Tuesday, then...." Sometimes the decision logic is much more important, however, and this deserves a model in its own right. This is particularly true when business rules are involved. Sometimes this logic applies within a process, and sometimes it applies to sets of processes.

A *decision tree* is simply a set of lines drawn to show the possible paths that may be taken, depending on various tests of values. The graphic allows you to represent each alternative value for a variable and map what is to be done next. The technique is actually much more powerful for problem solving than will concern us in this book. Howard Raiffa, in his 1968 book, *Decision Analysis,* describes the technique shown here, as well as kinds of problems in probability theory that the technique can be used to solve.

Figure 4.28 shows a sample decision tree, describing the decisions associated with ordering a book. Was it requested? Has it been reviewed?—and so forth. This example shows only "yes/no" decisions. More complex ones are also possible.

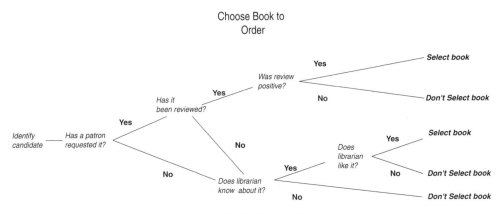

FIGURE 4.28 Decision Tree.

A variation on the decision tree is a *decision table.* This is a table representing a sequence of decisions to be taken in a particular evaluation. A set of conditions is shown on the left, with one row for each permutation of values for the decisions. A column on the right shows each resulting decision, based on the particular permutations in that row. An example is shown in Table 4.2. Each of the decision points is a column in the table. Rows are then established for each combination of yes and no answers to the decision point. In some cases, a question is not applicable because of the answer to the previous one. For example, if the librarian does not know about a book, it is meaningless to ask whether the librarian likes it. In such cases the cell is indicated by "—".

TABLE 4.2 Decision Table

Has patron requested?	Has it been reviewed?	Was review positive?	Does librarian know about it?	Does librarian like it?	Order it?
Yes	Yes	Yes	Yes	Yes	Yes
Yes	Yes	Yes	Yes	No	No
Yes	Yes	Yes	No	—	Yes
Yes	Yes	No	—	—	No
Yes	No	—	Yes	Yes	Yes
Yes	No	—	Yes	No	No
Yes	No	—	No	—	No
No	—	—	Yes	Yes	Yes
No	—	—	Yes	No	No
No	—	—	No	—	No

Other Hierarchical Techniques

Other techniques for documenting program code could be used to document business logic as well. These typically represent a problem as a hierarchical structure. Best known are the "HIPO" (Hierarchical input and output) diagram and the Warnier-Orr diagrams. Each of these can represent either a data structure or a set of activities in hierarchical form. See the 1985 McClure and Martin book for more information.

Implications of Analyzing Activities

Implications for Relational Design

Documentation of the inherent or essential functions of a business sets the stage for creating programs to carry out those functions. If a function simply describes inputs to or retrievals from a database, the only programming required to implement them is specification of simple input or output transactions, probably making use of an appropriate high-level database tool. If an activity is more complex, then more complex logic must be programmed, either for attachment to one of those input/output programs or as a stored procedure to guard the database against invalid operations. In this case, documentation of the detailed workings of the activities will be required, as will detailed specification of the program logic design.

Clearly, the database design, as controlled by the data model (see Chapter 3), will significantly affect the structure of any programs involved. In the old days, a program had to be concerned with the details of inputs and outputs and data definition, as well as with underlying logic. Now these categories of processing are largely carried out by database management systems and fourth-generation languages. All that remains is the central logic and the overall architecture of the programs.

Implications for Object-Oriented Design

To the extent that true entity types behave in the object-oriented sense, the function/entity type matrix can guide the designer to the activities that must be attached to each entity. To the extent that object-oriented analysis simply identified activities that are being called objects, the implementation of these will be, as in the relational approach, pieces of program code. That the code is then attached to dummy objects does not fundamentally change this.

The Requirements Analysis Deliverable—Column Two

There are more modeling techniques for Column Two than for any other, but these techniques are actually related to each other. Clearly a given project will have to choose from among them. Table 4.3 compares them.

The activity models clearly should be derived from the Row One scope document, which, among other things, will determine which functional areas are to be addressed in the first place.

It is important at least to deliver from a requirements analysis project a model of the underlying functions of the business. A function hierarchy is the easiest form of this, but if the communications among the functions are important, an essential data flow diagram may also be used.

If a Row Two diagram is to be made explicit, a process flow diagram, physical data flow diagram, or a UML activity diagram can be used. It is only in Row Two that you identify the actors who are (currently, at least) performing each function. In Row Three you could organize the flow diagram in terms of swim lanes, but these can refer only to general roles in the company. Indeed, identifying what those roles should be is a Column Four activity, so the final form of this should be defined in conjunction with that work.

A Comparison of the Techniques

Table 4.3 shows each of the techniques described in this chapter, along with the particular characteristics that make each unique. A check mark means that the technique completely embraces the characteristics described in the row heading. A blank box means that it has none of the characteristics described in the row heading.

TABLE 4.3 A Comparison of Activity Modeling Techniques

	Function Hierarchy	Physical DFD	Essential DFD	Use Case/ Object Model	IDEF0	Business Process Model	UML Activity Diagram
Physical/ Essential	Essential	Physical	Essential	Unspecified	Essential	Physical	Unspecified
Architecture Row	Two and Three	Two	Three	Two	Three	Two	Two, Three
Data Stores		Views	Entity Types	Typical Objects		Views	Typical Objects
Data Flows		✓	✓	Unlabeled interactions	✓	✓	Unlabeled interactions
External Entities / Actors		External Entities	External Entities	Actors		Events	
Swim Lanes						✓	✓
Material Flows		Sarson and Gane only	Sarson and Gane only		✓		Material flows are not prohibited
Control					✓		
Mech- anisms		✓			✓	✓	
Rules for Decom- position	✓	✓	✓		✓		

As mentioned above, none of the techniques is ideal for all circumstances. One day, perhaps, there will be a CASE tool that will accommodate combining the techniques. In the meantime, we can only do the best we can with what we have.

Regardless of the tool, it is important to understand that the purpose of activity modeling in the requirements analysis process is to first capture the business owners' views of their functions and processes in terms that can be readily understood and confirmed. A further objective is to analyze the current physical state of the business to determine the underlying activities (functions) required to carry out the business of the enterprise. Only then are we in a position to recommend new physical tools and techniques for improving the business's operations.

Activities and the Other Columns

The techniques discussed in this chapter primarily describe activities—Column Two elements. The external entities of data flow diagrams and the performers of processes are borrowed from Column Four (people and organizations). Data flows and stores in data flow diagrams (as well as interest by the object-oriented among us) show that Column One (data) is clearly involved in any activity modeling. The events described in Chapter 7 define essential processes. The locations in Chapter 6 provide a place for activities to take place. And the business rules described in Chapter 8 are constraints on data, but they are often expressed in terms of the activities which implement them.

Activities and Data

The fact that an activity has data being fed to it on one side and produces data on the other is significant to understanding both the nature of the data and the nature of the process. Naturally, an activity diagram focuses on activities and transformations of inputs into outputs. It may not be clear from an activity model, though, whether the same data element is used by more than one activity. Especially for object-oriented design, which is oriented toward the data classes, this input/output documentation is not sufficient. If data stores are resolved to the level of object class, however, this is less of a problem, since, for each entity, you could then see either how it is produced or how it is used. Still, there are better ways to capture this information. Enter the function/entity matrix.

The *function/entity type matrix* is a straightforward approach to linking activities and entities. Entities are lined up along one dimension of a matrix and activities are lined up along the other. It is sometimes called the **CRUD matrix** because, in each cell, you designate whether the entity is (C)reated, (R)etrieved, (U)pdated, or (D)eleted by the activity. Any business rule that is controlling the creation, retrieval, update, or deletion operation can be specified via the cell's annotation. (See Table 4.4 for an example.)

Once this is done, the report sets the stage for an object-oriented implementation of the functions associated with each entity. From the communications among the functions associated with an entity, you can then infer the communications between the entities themselves in the object-oriented sense.

Of course, creation of a function/entity type matrix is also an excellent cross check, because any entity types without activities to at least create and retrieve them are suspect, as are any activities that don't do anything with any data.

TABLE 4.4 A Sample Function/Entity Type Matrix

	PARTY	PURCHASE	LINE ITEM	BOOK TITLE	BOOK COPY
Choose book to order				R	
Order set of books	R	C	C	R	
Confirm order		R	U		
Receive each book		RU	RU		C
Catalogue book				U	

Activities and Locations

Where in the world does each activity take place? Is it always in one location, or is it replicated across the country (or across the world)? There are no formal graphic models for representing this (although creative use could be made of maps and matrices), but certainly the documentation behind each activity should do so.

Examining the function hierarchy or the essential data flow diagrams from Chapter 4, we can look at each function and ask, "Where does it take place?" This is especially significant if our model is a variation on a data flow diagram, where the processes communicate with each other. Two processes that must communicate between different facilities have profound implications on the kinds of systems that can be built to support them.

Each activity diagram (in whatever form), then, can be annotated as to the location or site where the activity takes place. Grouping activities by site is a useful way to understand the geographic architecture of any prospective system. Indeed, rather than representing actors, swim lanes could represent sites or geographical areas.

Activities and People

We have already seen that an important part of documenting activities is documenting who does each of them. Data flow diagrams at least show external entities that are people and organizations who are supplying or consuming information. They may also show the actor in each activity. The use cases that are now so popular go to the heart of the interaction between people and the activities of a business. Chapter 6 discusses use cases further.

All of the activity modeling techniques (except for the function hierarchy) described in this chapter to support Row Two include references to the people or organizations performing the functions. Data flow diagramming and process modeling were described because these techniques emphasize what is being done; use cases were described in this chapter because they are concerned with the nature of the interaction. Indeed, all three of these techniques belong firmly in both columns.

The activities should also be classified as Stafford Beer's System One, Two, Three, Four, or Five activities. (See Chapter 5.)

Activities and Timing (Events)

The secret to understanding the true nature of the functions of an organization (uncluttered by the current mechanisms in place to perform those functions) is the event as a stimulus. Recall that in several modeling techniques it was significant that communications could be either simple data or messages (triggers, events) causing an action to take place.

Functions can also be divided and organized in many different ways, but the set of event types that can affect a company ultimately must be the basis for any rational organization of those functions.

Activities and Motivation

An organization's mission, strategies, and tactics form the structure around which its activities are organized. These, therefore, are the top levels of any hierarchical representation of activities.

As will be shown in Chapter 8, business rules are normally defined in terms of constraints on data not on processes. We have seen, however, that the detailed documentation of activities can reveal business rules. Indeed, they are often implemented by activities and restrictions on activities. The activities and the business rules must be documented together.

Column Four: People and Organizations

5

According to the overall scheme for this book, this chapter should be about Column Three, Locations. It turns out, however, that the models for Column Four, People and Organizations are extremely useful for analyzing the issues raised in Column Three. So, we'll describe Column Four first and then come back to Column Three when we're done.

Figure 5.1 shows the Architecture Framework, with Column Four highlighted. The fourth column of the Architecture Framework is about people and groups of people. It is not possible to view an enterprise without looking at the people who comprise it. Without people there is no enterprise. This column is the one absolute prerequisite—before data, before processes, and before any of the other columns.

This, however, is the one column that, to date, has the fewest available models to describe it. We can draw an organization chart, but this is becoming progressively less satisfactory as a way to represent the true relationships among the people in an enterprise. Technology has completely changed the kinds of communications channels we use, and all companies are now in the throes of trying to understand the full implications of this.

In fact, not only are there few models, but the entire nature of the workplace is changing before our very eyes.

For these reasons, this chapter will be a little less coherent than the others. Instead of a systematic comparison of different approaches, it will present the issues involved in trying to come to grips with how to organize a company. It will draw from two completely different fields: knowledge management and cybernetics.

Like the other chapters, this one will first discuss people and organizations from the Row Two perspective—the business owner's view. In recent years this view has been radically altered by changes, both in society and in technology. The business owners—clerks, engineers, accountants, and managers—are viewing their world quite differently than they might have fifty years ago. These changes are being acknowledged in the new field of knowledge management. The architect's view (Row Three), on the other hand, is supposed to be of fundamental structures that are immune to such changes. To provide such a robust view is surely a challenge. As it happens, there is a modeling approach that can help. It comes from the science of cybernetics. Also in the architect's view is an analysis of the interactions between actors and the business functions. A technique for doing this is use cases.

Knowledge management is the management of an enterprise's capabilities with an emphasis on the knowledge content of the work being done. If *data* are letters and numbers, and *information* is the meaning given to those letters and numbers, *knowledge* is the application of that meaning to achieve objectives. Knowledge management is about effectively employing the information held in an organization.

Cybernetics is the science of communication and control. Developed during World War Two, this is concerned with the mechanisms of control, especially variations on feedback loops.

A *use case* is a technique for representing the interactions between a system and those who affect and are affected by it.

	Data (What)	Activities (How)	Locations (Where)	People (Who)	Time (When)	Motivation (Why)
Objectives / Scope **(Planner's view)**	List of things important to the enterprise - Term 1 - Term 2 - Term 3 ...	List of processes the enterprise performs - Function 1 - Function 2 - Function 3 ...	List of enterprise locations	Organization approaches	Business master schedule	Business vision and mission - Vision ... - Mission
Enterprise model **(Business Owners' Views)**	Language, divergent data model	Business process model	Logistics network	Organi-zation chart	State / transition diagram	Business strategies, tactics, policies, rules
Model of Funda-mental Concepts **(Architect's View)**	Convergent e/r model	Essential data flow diagram	Locations of roles	The viable system, use cases	Entity Life History	Business rule model
Technology Model **(Designer's View)**	Data base design	System design, program structure	Hardware, software distribution	User interface, security design	Control structure	Business rule design
Detailed Represen-tation **(Builder's View)**	Physical storage design	Detailed program design	Network architecture, protocols	Screens, security coding	Timing definitions	Rule specification program logic
Functioning System	*(Working System)*					
	Converted data	Executable programs	Communi-cations facilities	Trained people	Business events	Enforced rules

FIGURE 5.1 The Architecture Framework—People

How to Organize the Enterprise (Row One)

The Row One model must be the enterprise's set of principles and structures that govern the way people in the enterprise interact. The challenge in Row One is to come up with a vision for the enterprise that adequately addresses the needs of its people and accommodates the new approaches to human resource management that are now coming into play. The issues raised in the next two rows must ultimately be addressed by those responsible for setting the direction of the enterprise.

As stated previously, the planner's view is a combination of an enterprise-wide view with the definition of specific projects to be undertaken. The company's overall approach to human resources management is the starting point, followed by specific decisions as to exactly which people or which jobs will be the domain of each project.

Row Two: The Business Owner's View

Times Change...

In the modern enterprise, the business owner is usually concerned with five specific relationships:

- With the boss
- With subordinates
- With colleagues
- With customers
- With vendors

The relative weight of these relationships changed dramatically in the second half of the twentieth century. In the past, only certain departments dealt with customers and vendors. The dominant relationship for most people was with the boss, with the relationship to subordinates coming in a close second. Immediate colleagues were part of the employee's world, but these were relatively few. Most communication was up and down the chain of command. Education about one's specialty and one's industry was via books and university courses outside the company.

This picture has now changed. Thanks to the wonders of modern communication, each employee is in direct contact not only with many more fellow employees, but also with colleagues outside the company who are specialists in the same fields or participants in the same industry. Moreover, decisions do not always have to be made by going up and down the organization chart. Decisions instead are now often based on collaborations among people from what used to be disparate organizational units.

Now many specialties are pursued by organic groups of people from many enterprises all over the world, who, on a daily basis, exchange ideas electronically about the best ways to do things.

Most significantly, nearly everyone has some direct involvement with clients, customers, and vendors—or at least has the facility to do so. Probably the most important relationship of all has become that of every employee to the company's customers.

A Very Short History of the World

To put this cell of the Architecture Framework (the business view of people and organizations) into perspective, it is important to understand the remarkable place at which we stand in human history. That history is, of course, far more complex than can be described in a few pages here, but a few points are worth noting.

Before the nineteenth century, people worked primarily on farms or as single artisans producing products one at a time. Wealth was measured in acreage of land. This period, which lasted for millennia, is often called *the agricultural age*. Early in the nineteenth century, things changed dramatically. Now people began to work in factories, producing hundreds or thousands of copies of the same product at once. Instructions were passed down an organizational hierarchy, and performance monitoring was passed up the hierarchy. The nineteenth and the first half of the twentieth century have been called *the industrial age*.

The driver of this new economy changed from land to capital. Where before, wealth was determined by an aristocrat's land holdings, now anyone could produce wealth with a factory, if one could accumulate enough capital to build it.[1] The people who worked in these factories simply carried out the owner's instructions for making wealth. Where before, serfs did the labor that created the wealth from the land, now factory workers played the same role, creating wealth from capital.

In response to all this, Karl Marx, Charles Dickens, and others wrote of people's alienation when they worked simply as appendages to machinery. People didn't own the equipment they used. They were interchangeable. The jobs were narrow and offered no intrinsic satisfaction. Divisions grew up between owners and management on the one hand, who wanted the most output for the least money, and labor on the other, who wanted at least a living wage and respect for their efforts.

In spite of these conflicts, because of the nature of the work to be done, this remained the most economically attractive alternative well into the twentieth century, at least in the west. The Soviet Union tried to change the premises in 1917, and while the factories were then owned by the State instead of by private capitalists, and some attempts were made to provide for the general welfare, the underlying dynamic was no different. The

---

1. Aristocrats were decidedly troubled by this.

economies were different, but the economics didn't change, and the work was still alienating. Eighty-four years later, the experiment was abandoned.

In the second half of the twentieth century things changed again. Suddenly information and knowledge became more important than physical capital. A company that is smarter in getting the most use out of a physical device will be more successful than one that is not. Marx's observations are no longer relevant, at least in the developed world, because the relationships between labor and capital have fundamentally changed. We each own our own knowledge, and this knowledge turns out to be the company's most important asset.[2]

For this reason, the age we are now in is called *the information age*. There are those who would call it *the knowledge age.*

Actually, as Jonas Ridderstråle and Kjell Nordström asserted, Marx, Ho Chi Minh, Lenin, and Chairman Mao Zedong were all *right*. "They were right because they subscribed to the Marxist view that the workers should own the major assets of society, the critical means of production. We now do. And, perhaps, we did all along but we just didn't have the insight to realize it" [Ridderstråle and Nordström, 2000, p. 17].

While factories certainly have not gone away, fewer people work there, and even working there has changed. Much less of the work is done with unskilled labor. More of the work in manufacturing, for example, requires technical (knowledge-related) skills.

Now the worker chooses what to work on and how to go about it. Because the company is dependent upon the worker's knowledge, it must permit this to happen. It is in the nature of knowledge that it is communal, so people are no longer working on isolated tasks. The working environment is becoming clusters of people who share an area of interest or an objective.

Most significantly, their motivation is now in the work itself, not just the benefits bestowed by the corporation.

We own the means of production because those means are in our own heads. The physical capital on the balance sheet is no longer as important as the collective knowledge of the enterprise. The management of knowledge itself has become the primary focus of progressive companies today.

Thomas Stewart, in his 1997 book by that name, lists three kinds of "intellectual capital":

- *Human capital:* the value of the knowledge held by a company's employees

---

2. Of course there is still a large part of the world living under the assumptions of the old economy — with the result that the gap between the rich and poor appears to be getting wider. The biggest challenge of the twenty-first century will be how to somehow bring the majority of the Earth's humans into this new world.

- *Structural capital:* the physical means by which knowledge and experience can be shared
- *Customer capital:* the value of the company's franchise and its ongoing relationships with its customers (and vendors)

Each of these is critical to a modern company's operation, but none of them show up in its chart of accounts.

Human Capital

A company often has much more knowledge and expertise than it realizes. Many companies are very poor at exploiting the knowledge they have. Traditional corporate organization has often prevented companies from gaining full benefit of employees' expertise. Many companies hold thousands of patents that they don't even know they own.

Microsoft is one of the most successful companies of all time, yet it produces virtually no physical product and has relatively little physical capital. True, it does deliver physical media, such as compact disks, but customers are not buying the media. They are buying the knowledge that is encoded on the media. Consider the microchip in your computer: The value of all the chips produced in a year exceeds the value of all steel produced in the same period [Stewart, 1997, p. 13].[3] The value is not in the material, of course: it is in the design of the chip and in the design of the complex machines that make it. The value is in the *knowledge* required to build them.

Even companies that sell physical products, such as automobiles, have had to radically increase the intellectual content of their products. To compete, a car must now be more sophisticated, economizing on weight, cleverly getting the engine not to emit harmful gases, and providing just the right "feel". All these things come from the auto maker's investment in knowledge and expertise, not from its investment in steel and rubber.

In 1998, The Berkshire Hathaway Company's net worth was $57.4 billion, the largest of any American corporation. The company sells insurance and other financial instruments, plus shoes, jewelry, other manufactured products, and ice cream. The company's market value, however, was only one-third that of knowledge companies Microsoft and General Electric [Berkshire Hathaway, 1998, p. 4].

Structural Capital

The second component of intellectual capital for an enterprise is the technical infrastructure that makes a company's knowledge accessible. This includes everything from the Internet—for sharing ideas and thoughts on various subjects—to data warehouses that publish the operational data for a company. Success in accumulating structural

---

3. Not bad for what is essentially sand, eh?

capital directly affects an enterprise's success in the marketplace. Wal-Mart, for example, has revolutionized the retailing business by building what may be the world's most sophisticated information systems to support it. The company became the nation's largest corporation (in sales) in 2002, while during the same year its nearest competitor, K-Mart, declared bankruptcy.

Customer Capital

In the days of smokestack capitalism, the economy consisted of factories producing thousands of copies of the same thing. Marketing consisted of persuading lots of people that the thing was exactly what they wanted. The customer was at the mercy of the producer.

Now, the balance of power is devolving onto the customer. Customer relations is turning out to be the "hot button" of modern business. Customers expect custom-made products. (Land's End just published an ad for swimsuits that are cut precisely for your shape.) This means that the company's relationship to the customer—its ability to understand clearly what the customer wants—is critical. Companies that have established such relationships are worth a great deal more than companies that have not.

Requirements for Knowledge Management

So, what does all this mean to those of us who build systems? Knowledge management can be divided into two areas. *Natural knowledge management* is concerned with the way people learn and communicate with each other directly. In the past it has not been concerned with technology, but this is slowly changing. *Artificial knowledge management* is all about information processing using technological tools. This is the current concern of our operational systems and our data warehouses.

While we in the information industry have traditionally focused on artificial knowledge management, natural knowledge management is important too, and our success from now on will be measured in terms of our ability to manage both.

As we provide tools to support knowledge management, we must keep in mind these things:

- **We must understand the role of systems**

  Systems don't create knowledge; knowledge is the *interpretation* of information. Systems manipulate data and turn it into the information to be interpreted. The quality of system design will make it easier or harder for users to take the next step and turn information into knowledge. For us to build "good" systems it will be necessary to understand each user's process of turning information into knowledge. We must understand in detail how a system supports each task.

- **We must design systems to support knowledge management**

The job is not to push out more data. The job is to allow a user naturally to retrieve the *right* data. This requires skill in designing the presentation of data and in designing the user's interactions with technology. This is the fundamental criterion we must apply in designing our data marts: are they presenting the right amount of the right data for the user to make decisions? We must get inside each user's job to understand just what that user must know to make the required decisions.

Edward Tufte has a series of three wonderful books on the graphic presentation of information. While his insights are oriented toward graphic presentation, they are very appropriate in the design of any management reports. As he puts it:

> Confusion and clutter are failures of [drawing] design, not attributes of information. And so the point is to find design strategies that reveal detail and complexity—rather than to fault the data for an excess of complication. Or, worse, to fault viewers for a lack of understanding. [Tufte, 1990]

This means that our systems designers must be skilled in presenting data, but it also means that as analysts, we must provide designers with a clear understanding of what it is that people want to see.

We must also expand the domain of our systems to include "fuzzier" data. We must go beyond artificial knowledge management and begin to tackle natural knowledge management.

This means not just compiling data in databases about such things as sales and patents and employee characteristics, but also making available better communications tools, so that people can work together on projects, even if they are not physically in the same place. This is particularly true of research kinds of projects where the process is one of pure intellectual exploration. Also important is the need to capture the results of knowledge creation in meaningful, accessible ways. Electronic mail and products such as Lotus Notes have taken us a long way in this direction, but there is more to do.

The New Workplace and Knowledge Management

The study of knowledge is both very old and very new. Philosophers have been writing about it for millennia. But attention to the relationship of knowledge to the structure of the workplace is relatively new. Most of what has been written about this topic has been published since 1990.

The changes described in this chapter have had a profound effect on the nature of the workplace. The traditional model of an enterprise has always been its organization chart. This has sometimes been a reflection of the structure of the work that the enterprise does, but not always. The boss wanted something and transmitted instructions to the employees. Their messages were then returned to the boss, describing how successful they had been in carrying out the instructions. The definition of work ultimately came from the boss. The worker contributed very little to the definition of the task.

For factory workers carrying out well-defined tasks this worked reasonably well. The boss described the tasks and the employees carried them out.[4]

Where the tasks are intellectual, however, the hierarchical approach doesn't work at all. As "knowledge workers", many of us no longer work for a "boss" who simply tells us what to do and makes sure that we do it to a specification. The boss may describe an objective, but the employee is now responsible for understanding the objective, plus the business environment, available technology, constraints, and the impact of various options on achieving that objective. The boss cannot possibly know all that is involved and is dependent on the worker's knowledge and skill.

Many of us have become "consultants" (even within our own companies), hired to assist "clients", using our expertise and knowledge. The worker is now in the position not only of assisting the client in achieving objectives, but also of telling the client whether the objective is reasonable in the first place and, if it is not, recommending alternative objectives.

Instead of focusing on the politics of keeping various bosses happy, our entire transaction with the client now comes down to whether or not we are providing a useful service. Not only is the client free to let us go if we are not being useful, but we probably want to go if the environment is not one where we can be productive. This is a much happier arrangement than we have known in the corporate world, where we always had to be alert to making the right people happy, in ways that often had nothing to do with our skills or abilities—or the job at hand, for that matter.

Our motivation is no longer security and money.[5] We work on projects because they stimulate our imagination and intellect. We will work for a company as long as it provides interesting and meaningful projects. When it stops doing so, we will go somewhere else.

This has a profound effect on how companies are managed. Suddenly managers must be alert to the dynamics of their departments in ways they never were before. This has not been easy. For years, employees at a Canadian software company lobbied management to revamp their products to make them more integrated, more reliable, more robust, and more effective. Their pleas fell on deaf ears, but at one point the company published a brochure, falsely claiming that the products had exactly the qualities the employees were trying to promote. Management's intransigence, along with its lack of understanding of what the employees were trying to do, caused 20 of the company's 25 employees to quit. Twelve of them created a competing company.

4. Yes, there were those pesky problems with Karl Marx and the labor unions, but they were all dealt with, right?
5. Well, not so much...

On a happier note, one company has launched a four-year plan and has organized its personnel entirely around it. It is a matrix, where the rows are groups of projects and the columns are areas of expertise. There are three columns that are the basis for maintaining quality work: Applications, Data, and Technology. The rows address such project areas as "People and Organizations", "Physical Assets", "Finance", and so forth. The people, then, all work at the intersection of a row and a column. The idea is that each person is supposed to be working toward implementation of one or more projects as expeditiously as possible. But each also has the obligation to do quality work, as defined by the column involved. Data people are obligated, for example, to follow the best practices in industry in organizing and acquiring quality data—even if it may affect the project plan.

This is one example. Other companies have different kinds of matrix organizations (or hierarchical ones) as well.

Thomas Stewart describes the opinion of Frank Walker, president of GTW Corp., that in the years to come there will ultimately be only four types of career:

- The *top executive* sets strategy: It is the land of presidents and CEOs and executive vice presidents.
- *Resource providers* develop and supply talent, money, and other resources; they are the chief financial officers, chief information officers, human resources managers, temporary services firms, and heads of traditionally functioning departments like engineering and marketing.
- *Project managers* buy or lease resources from resource providers, negotiating a budget and getting people assigned to the project and putting them to work to achieve a particular objective.
- *Talent*: chemists, finance personnel, salespeople, bakers, candlestick makers (and presumably the odd systems analyst or two) actually carry out the work. [Stewart, 1997, p. 204]

The fact of the matter is that the business owner's view is of a world that is changing under our feet at an astounding rate. This affects our personal lives, how we relate to our work, and how our employers relate to us. We have incredible new opportunities for creativity and self-discovery, but it comes at the cost of an overwhelming amount of uncertainty and chaos. Companies must deal with this, and we must deal with it as individuals. Is there anything out there that can help us come to terms with all this change?

As it happens, there may be....

Row Three: The Nature of a (Human) System

If the perspective of the business owner is now one of incredible change, what Row Three view can accommodate all this change?

While the organization chart is no longer adequate to describe the nature of an organization, cybernetics expert Stafford Beer in his 1979 book, *The Heart of Enterprise*, offers a model that can help us understand the fundamental structure of an organization and how its pieces work together—even in times of great change. This model, which will be presented in the following pages, yields exactly the insights necessary to address the issues of a modern corporation. It provides a handle on the nature of an enterprise's struggles with change, and on what it must do to deal with those struggles. This model, which addresses Row Three architecture, can be used to evaluate Row Two realities and thereby help us define an appropriate response.

Mr. Beer's model is based on the cybernetic concept of variety. *Variety*, in the information theory sense, is the number of states that a situation can have. The theoretical definition of *information* is that it is the quantity of variety in a communication. This turns out to be a very good way to measure the degree of *complexity* of the situation. This is significant in discussing management, since fundamentally, *complexity is what management manages.* Finally, we have a way of evaluating this, just as money is used to evaluate the ebb and flow of wealth in a company.

The concept of variety also helps us realize what we are dealing with as individuals when we confront the complexities and uncertainties of modern life. The variety of the world around us is proliferating at a prodigious rate. Especially in the information technology industry, we are constantly confronted with new things to be learned and changes to what we think we already know. Our ability to deal with that variety is an important skill, which can significantly affect our careers. Variety provides a way to measure the uncertainty and complexity in the world.

The problem, however, is that variety itself isn't all that easy to measure.

A light has a variety of two: on and off. Well, of course you may try to turn it on and the light bulb is burned out. So the variety is actually three: one on and two off. But then, the main switch for the house may be off, so variety turns out to be four. Or there is a general power failure, so there is a variety of five— and so forth.

As another example, what is the variety of this?

$$X \quad X \quad X$$

If you assume that each "X" represents presence of something, then the variety is 2^3, or 8. On the other hand, if each is a letter of the alphabet, then the variety is 26^3 or 17,576. Or each position could be represented by a letter or a digit, which makes the variety 36^3 or 46,656. Other assumptions can increase the variety of these three X's even more.[6]

---

6. For example, one X may be missing, so the variety is really 2^4, or 16. If more were missing, of course the variety could be much greater.

One point evident in both of these examples is that variety is not an absolute number. It is a function of both the *purpose* of the system and the *perceptions* of the viewer. Another point is that variety, even of simple situations, can proliferate way out of control.

The viewer by definition, then, must filter out the extensive variety that is possible, because the magnitude of possibilities is too much to cope with. What managers do, fundamentally, is to *destroy variety* via filters of various kinds. Managers break their companies into divisions. They set objectives. They "manage by exception". All of these are techniques for reducing the variety they must deal with.

In the old days, for many people, things were simpler. The variety in their world was constrained because they lived in the small town they had always lived in, and their values and views of the world were already formed by that community. They were unlikely to encounter views that differed significantly from their own. Or they worked for a large corporation that provided structure and instructions and protected them from the variety of the outside world. In other words, the number of choices (variety) in their lives was much more limited than it is today.

As we become more global and more mobile in our movements from town to city and from organization to organization, however, these filters are no longer available to us. Now what?

A System

To properly address the problem of variety, it is necessary to discuss **systems**. We are not speaking now of a system as a collection of computer components, but rather as any arrangement of components *that is self-perpetuating*. This includes everything from corporations and governments to the human body. (Mr. Beer's original work was in physiology, and many of the insights he presents came from that field.) The enterprise, as described by John Zachman, for example, is a very good example of such a system. Mr. Beer's work is concerned with the quest to understand the fundamental structures and phenomena that govern any such system.

One filter used to reduce variety in order to manage a system is to divide it into smaller parts that have less variety. The question is, how to do that? It turns out that the only meaningful approach is to recognize that all systems are fundamentally *recursive*. That is, each system is a complete system *within* another system. In turn, each system *contains* one or more other systems. As you look at the world around you, you will discover that this is the way it is organized. Your family is in a community; the community is in a state; and so on. Every system you can name is part of and managed by a larger system.

Since variety depends at least partly on the purpose of the system exhibiting it, what is the purpose of any particular system? Because systems are so various, from British Rail to an English Sheepdog, it is reasonable to ask, what is the purpose of each? Upon close analysis it turns out that they all have *the same* purpose: *to continue to exist.* Virtually all of the actions taken by any system are directed to that end.

As defined above, **cybernetics** is the science of communication and control. Mr. Beer makes extensive use of the works of H. Ross Ashby, a cyberneticist who wrote in the 1950s. Ashby postulated a series of *natural laws* that apply to any control mechanism. He proposed that control mechanisms must follow these laws if they are to work, just as airplanes must account for the laws of aerodynamics if they are to fly. An excellent example of his work is *An Introduction to Cybernetics*, written in 1956, which explains these laws in very clear language.

Mr. Beer takes Dr. Ashby's work a step further when he then asks the question:

> Since we now know that the purpose of a system is to continue to exist, and that the system must follow natural laws, what are the characteristics of a system that will allow it to continue to exist?

We can use the laws of aerodynamics to determine characteristics required of an airplane to allow it to fly. How can we use the laws of cybernetics to determine the characteristics required of a system to allow it to continue to exist? Expressed in another way, what are the characteristics of what he calls a **viable system**? Specifically, how can variety be managed so that the system can get on with its work?

What does this have to do with people, by the way? As it happens, in any organization, it is the people that are the organization's fundamental components. As Mr. Beer puts it, people are *The Heart of Enterprise* (hence, the title of his work). At any level, a person's job in an organization is *to manage variety.*

The assignment to understand what makes an enterprise viable is an assignment to understand the required nature of interactions among human beings, and how they collectively manage variety. How can a system be divided so that the variety of each component is manageable?

Management

How do you manage a system? The basic cybernetic model, shown in Figure 5.2, has a *process* of some sort,[7] with a *controller*—an agent controlling it. It also has information *channels* for communicating between the controller and the process. The controller makes use of a *set point*, a reference value that serves as a target value for the process. The process generates information (*values* of specified *variables*) about its performance which is communicated through a channel to the controller. This information is continuously compared to the set point, and, depending on the result of the comparison, the

---

7. This is the Chapter 4 definition of "process", meaning an activity that is one of a set of activities carried out in sequence. In this case we are leaving ambiguous the extent to which mechanisms are part of the definition of the process.

controller may then send *commands* to the process through a different channel. If the values are too low, one set of commands is sent. If they are too high, a different set is sent.

The signals from the process to the controller constitute *feedback*. This configuration of process and controller is called a *feedback loop*.

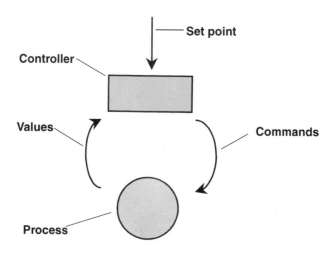

FIGURE 5.2 The Feedback Loop.

Loops like this are most visible in physical control mechanisms like thermostats and manufacturing process control. In a thermostat the set point is a desired temperature. If the actual temperature goes below that, a signal goes to the furnace to turn it on. When it goes above the setpoint, a signal goes to the furnace to turn it off. In process control, a set point might be a value of a measured variable, such as oil pressure. If the oil pressure in the process goes too low (or too high, depending on the situation), a signal is sent to a motor to open (or close) a valve.

Feedback loops are also present in any organization. The manager has some vision of what is desired, and he issues instructions to the operational groups. Information about the organization's performance is then returned and evaluated. A sales target could serve as a set point, for example, such that if sales went below that target, steps would be taken to increase sales.

In manufacturing, this was formalized during the 1970s and 1980s with the integration of Master Production Scheduling, Materials Requirements and Capacity Planning, and Shop Floor Control systems. The master schedule laid out the products to be produced over time, Material Requirements Planning and Capacity Planning determined what materials and other resources would be required to satisfy the schedule, and Shop Floor Control provided feedback about what was actually happening so that the schedule could be adjusted as necessary.

In his search for the viable system, Mr. Beer expands on this simple model. He starts by pointing out that the system does not operate in a vacuum. Each process exists within its *environment*. The model then, actually has three components: the environment, the process (which he calls "operations"), and the managing controller. Because of some things he's going to do with the model later, Mr. Beer chooses to rotate it 90 degrees, as shown in Figure 5.3.

Note that in this diagram management does not interact directly with the environment. Only the operational element does that. There is in fact an interaction between management and the environment, but it is of a different kind than is shown here and will be discussed further below.

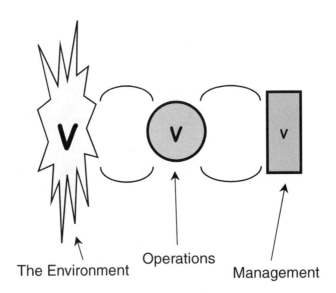

The Environment   Operations   Management

FIGURE 5.3 The Feedback Loop, Expanded.

At this point we introduce one of Mr. Ashby's natural laws of cybernetics: *the Law of Requisite Variety* [Ashby, 1956, p. 206]. That is:

Only variety absorbs variety.

A particular management has at its disposal only a finite amount of variety—a specified number of available actions to take. The Law of Requisite Variety means that management can only deal with an amount of variety equal to the amount at its disposal.

For example, if a process can assume 15 different states, the Law of Requisite Variety says that the controller must have a variety of exactly 15. This is reasonable, since, if the process assumes the 15th state and the controller's variety is only 14, the controller won't know what to do. By the same token, if the controller is capable of a 16th response, this is irrelevant.[8]

If the variety in the world is increasing at the rate we perceive it to be, this puts a tremendous pressure on management to increase the variety at its disposal as much as possible. This can be done via education, management techniques, and other methods. Ultimately, however, management cannot keep up. This is also part of the natural law.

In Figure 5.3, the "V" in each component refers to the relative variety handled by that component. The world at large has a great deal more variety than your typical process operation, which in turn has more variety than management. Consequently, Environment's V is larger than Operations' V, which is larger than Management's V. Think of all the potential customers out there, with myriad tastes, which may well change from day to day. In your company, you have a finite number of products and options to offer for sale. No matter how sophisticated you become, you will never be able to match the variety of the world.

The operation, in turn, has more variety than management. Your typical manager is responsible for a department of perhaps 15 people, each of whom has a collection of ambitions, talents, and personality quirks. This is in addition to whatever technology is being used, the particulars of the department's operations, and much more. On top of that, there is the obligation to learn all the new things that are happening in the company's industry. There is no way that the manager has the variety needed to match the variety of the operation. The manager cannot respond to every event that takes place in the organization. The implications of *sets* of events must be understood.

The Law of Requisite Variety, then, requires the introduction of **amplifiers** and **attenuators (filters)** to make the variety perceived at each point the same as the variety at the disposal of each point. (See Figure 5.4.) In other words, an attenuator filters the variety to the exact amount that can be processed by the receiver. The business filters what it sees in the world. It perceives the market only in terms that it is capable of understanding. In Figure 5.3, this is the filter on the left side. Similarly, management filters what it sees of a company's operations. Ultimately the manager can perceive only as much as can be acted upon. In Figure 5.4, this is the filter on the right side.

---

8. Mr. Ashby wrote in mathematical terms, and the power of his work is in its engineering applications. In human organizations, his principles can be observed only in the most general terms. We can say that one job involves much more variety than another, but we cannot quantify that. For our purposes here, however, this is not a problem. We are concerned here only with *relative variety*.

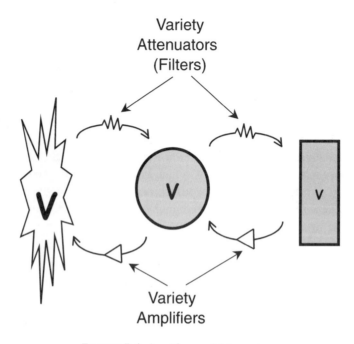

Variety
Attenuators
(Filters)

Variety
Amplifiers

FIGURE 5.4 Amplifiers and Attenuators.

Going in the other direction, an amplifier multiplies the effects of management's decisions to make them responsive to the variety of the operation (shown on the right side of Figure 5.4), just as another amplifier can multiply the effects of an operation to make it responsive to the environment (shown on the left side of Figure 5.4).

This recognition led Mr. Beer to formulate his *First Principle of Organization:*

> Managerial, operational and environmental varieties, diffusing through an institutional system, tend to equate; they should be <u>designed</u> to do so with minimal damage to people and to cost [Beer, 1979, p. 97].

To say that varieties equate is to say that the variety left after some is consumed by filters must be equal to the amount of variety that can be perceived by and dealt with by management. Similarly, the variety generated by management (which is equal to the amount perceived) must be augmented by amplifiers so that it is equal to the variety that can be dealt with by operations. As stated above, we are saying here that the incoming variety of a controller is exactly equal to the variety disposed by it.

The *design* point is at work when the filters are designed so that the controller sees the *right* set of things. A successful company analyzes the world and determines the two or three or four things it is capable of reacting to. It then designs the appropriate filters to provide information on just those things.

Similarly, the manager has to filter the information received from operations. If reports and display screens are well designed, the manager will be in a position to make intelligent decisions about the operation. If, instead, the more common filters "blind ignorance", "prejudice", "politics", and being "intellectually challenged" are used, then the decisions may prove to be a bit less successful.

The inability to see things is itself a filter.

An *amplifier* takes the manager's simple decisions, such as "increase staff by 50%", and expands their information content to incorporate all the specific implications of those decisions. Similarly, the enterprise's marketing efforts constitute amplifiers to disseminate the enterprise's message from operations to the world at large. The enterprise may advertise on TV, for example, to encourage many people to look at its website. The website, in turn, can communicate more than the advertising campaign could, further increasing the variety of the message.

To the extent that the company designs these filters and amplifiers well, it will be successful in the marketplace. To the extent that it doesn't, it won't.

If we are to design these amplifiers and filters, we must give thought to their characteristics. These are addressed in Mr. Beer's *Second Principle of Operation*:

> The four directional channels,[9] carrying information between the management unit, the operation and the environment, must each have a higher capacity to transmit a given amount of information relevant to variety selection in a given time than the originating sub-system has to generate it in that time [Beer, 1979, p. 99].

The important element that this principle introduces is *time*. Is the channel sufficient to convey what must be conveyed in the time allowed? For example, there is a crisis in the plant, and among other things, the computer network is down. An indicator light in the main office communicates that "The Framis isn't working". That's a filter all right, but it in fact filters out critical information required for the manager to respond. This is an example of a communications channel without sufficient capacity to transmit required information. More useful would be a telephone call saying "The Framis is down because of flooding!" That's a channel that can convey the information required.

As another example, consider a worker having trouble with an online system. She tries several things and nothing works. She is already considerably frustrated when she calls the help line. She tells them "This system is [*expletive deleted*]! I can't get it to work! I just can't!" This is a highly filtered message to the help desk, without enough information getting through to allow the help desk to determine the exact cause of the problem.

---

9. ... environment to operations, operations to controller, controller to operations, and operations to the environment.

As another example, many top management reports are made up of *averages* of critical data, such as sales or expenses. But the averaging process may lose key points that are required to make an intelligent decision. In many cases, too, there are people lobbying and promoting particular policies, very carefully protecting the boss from meaningful knowledge about what is really going on.

These are examples of communication channels whose variety is not adequate to the task of managing the enterprise.

We can examine these amplifiers and attenuators in more detail through Mr. Beer's *Third Principle of Operation:*

> Wherever the information carried on a channel (capable of distinguishing when a given variety crosses a boundary), it undergoes **transduction**; and the variety of the transducer must be at least equivalent to the variety of the channel [Beer, 1979, p. 101].

That is, a translation ("transduction") takes place when the operation communicates with the controller. The channel must not only have the requisite information capacity, but it must be able to deal with the specific states that are being transmitted, so that it can correctly translate the variety into terms management can understand. A Board of Directors listening to a senior manager's presentation might well have the information capacity to understand a very sophisticated presentation. But if the manager presents a gray, ambiguous situation in black-and-white terms, the translation process is being subverted.[10]

We often make mistakes in our evaluation of people, thanks to the "halo" effect. Because people are well mannered and well dressed, we translate these signals into the assumption that they are therefore intelligent and knowledgeable. In fact we have perceived much less variety than is there for us to see, or than we could understand if our filters weren't subverting the translation process. Indeed, prejudice itself may be characterized as a problem of variety: we can see only two states—"us" and "them".

---

10. Edward Tufte's 1997 book, *Visual Explanations,* is an excellent exposition on how to present information (especially numerical information) effectively. Among others it tells the story of the case made by Space Shuttle engineers against launching the Challenger in 1986. A typewritten listing of O-ring damage at various temperatures was presented, with notes written in the margins. Many different aspects of the damage incurred were described, along with the conclusion that the Shuttle should not be launched if the temperature was less than 53° (F). Management ignored the report. A much more effective report would have been a simple graph showing failure rates by launch temperature. Clearly the failure rate was off the scale where the temperature was below 50° (F). (The temperature predicted for the launch was between 26° (F) and 29° (F)). This was clearly a case of poor transduction.

A Model of the Viable System—System One

OK, let's take this view of feedback loops and see if we can come up with a more sophisticated model of the viable system—one that will give us some guidance as to how to design those attenuators and amplifiers.

First, looking at the original configuration in Figure 5.2, what if something happens in the circular operation presented that is *outside* what the controller knows how to deal with? There is a fire in a plant, for example. This isn't in the procedure book. Once the mess is cleaned up, what is needed is a mechanism for reviewing the basic feedback loop and evaluating its set points and other structures to be sure that the loop can handle this situation next time. In this case, next time there should be a procedure in place for mitigating the effects of a fire.

An *adjuster organizer* is a mechanism for modifying a basic feedback loop's set points and other structures. (See Figure 5.5.) This enables the inner loop to handle a new situation. This adjuster organizer in the outer loop can adjust the feedback process itself, responding to things that the inner loop could not. In the fire example, the adjuster organizer implements the new procedure for mitigating the effects of fire. In principle, the adjuster organizer also is controlled by a set point, although this could be something as crude as "the company falls apart". That would be a trigger for the adjuster organizer to act.

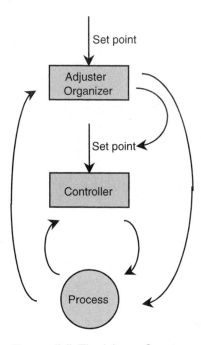

FIGURE 5.5 The Adjuster Organizer.

This brings us to the idea of recursion. Assume for a moment that we have a set of systems of the sort shown in Figure 5.4, and that they are inside some sort of meta-management that provides them with adjuster organizers to perform the necessary feedback adjustments, as shown in Figure 5.5. The adjuster organizer constitutes a meta-management. A *meta-management* is a controller at one level of recursion that is responsible for managing a set of systems at the next level of recursion down.

A set of systems, each with its environment, process, and controller, are represented in Figure 5.6 as what Mr. Beer calls *System One*. These systems exist in the context of some meta-management, whose exact nature we have yet to discover, but whose function will be to oversee the feedback loops of all the Systems One.

Figure 5.6 is a considerably simplified representation. The fact that there are only three Systems One is arbitrary, for purposes of this demonstration. Naturally, in a real system there could be more or fewer. In addition, the lines of communication from the first to the second and from the second to the third are not meant to imply that there are no lines from the first to the third. To draw them, however, would unnecessarily clutter the diagram. Similarly, the lines from the meta-management to each of the three Systems One are not meant to imply that the meta-management communicates only to the third System One via the first two. Again, in the interest of clarity, the detailed lines were left out.

In fact there are *18* channels connecting the various parts of this three-part set of Systems One.[11] If there were four Systems One instead of three, the total number would increase to 34. "Thus does variety proliferate," says Mr. Beer.

---

11. Two each between each operation and its environment, two each between each operation and its management, and two each between each System One management and the meta-management. Adding links from each System One management to each other System One management brings the total to 24.

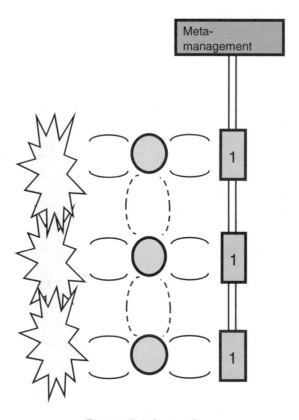

FIGURE 5.6 System One.

(In the diagram, for neatness' sake, the "1" appears only on the management box. In fact, each entire assembly of environment, operations, and management constitutes a System One.)

Note that the dashed lines showing connections between operational circles may be strong or weak. They are almost certainly there. Labor unions, for example, have always been very good at communicating across operational units. Twenty years after Mr. Beer wrote his book, the technology of electronic mail has greatly increased the extent of these communications channels. The meta-management should know this and take it into account.

Freedom

This brings up an important issue that has been part of the discussion of human systems over the centuries: the emotive concept of *freedom.* Much has been written about it and much passion has been expended. It turns out that cybernetics has a few things to say on the subject.

If you look at the model for System One, you see that each of the Systems One appears to be and ought to be autonomous. It would seem desirable for each to be able to react to the environment exactly as it sees fit. If we are talking about Systems One that are our households, in the metasystem that is our local government, this certainly seems to be the case.

And yet in both the operational and the managerial columns, it is reasonable to expect that a meta-manager is going to exert some interventions, if only to ensure that the Systems One don't work at cross purposes. The meaning of "cross purposes", of course, is defined by the meta-management. The Meta-management seeks a cohesiveness that is not necessarily perceived as possible or even desirable by the Systems One, but which is directly connected to the meta-management's mission.

Thus the meta-management will intervene in the operation and management of Systems One. This intervention comes in the form of communication on the vertical plane between it and the Systems One, at right angles to the horizontal management of each System One. In intervening, the metasystem will reduce the variety available to each System One. A corporate salary policy, for example, constrains each manager as to what can be offered to employees as compensation.

The nature and extent of the intervention will vary, depending on the organization and the circumstances of the intervention. The extent to which freedom is *perceived* to be constrained will also depend on the organization as well as its perceived purposes. A military organization, for example, places extensive constraints on the range of actions available to soldiers, which constrain their freedom considerably. These constraints are perceived to be essential to the survival of the unit, however, so (for the most part) the soldiers go along with it. A commune, on the other hand, whose purpose is to spread peace and love, provides many fewer constraints on its citizens—consistent with its purpose.

It is interesting that the nature of the intervention's effect on variety is usually misunderstood. This can be to the detriment of the organization. For example, a project that is intentionally *not* autocratically managed may require endless committee meetings to ensure that all interests are accounted for, and even these may be in the unwritten context that what is done must follow corporate policy, even if that policy isn't explicitly expressed. Participants wind up with less freedom than they would have if objectives were more clearly expressed and they could focus on those that pertained to each of them. A management intervention to clarify objectives in this case would *increase* freedom.

Mr. Beer lays out the following chain of argument as to how to deal with the issue of vertical interventions and their effects on the autonomy of Systems One [Beer, 1979, pp. 157–158]:

(i) For the management unit (an element of a System One), handling horizontal variety in the elemental operation is difficult, since it has less variety than its own operation—which in turn has less variety than its own environment. It must design amplifiers and attenuators in order to regulate the double loop, if it is to meet the Three Principles of organization.

(ii) Since the elemental operation is part of a whole, which is a cohesive system, its related elemental Systems One *intervene* (in the vertical plane) with each other in these horizontal variety equations. This intervention is a mark of the total cohesion, but it tends to vitiate elemental autonomy.

(iii) If the meta-management, in its turn, intervenes in the activities of a System One, it is likely (on the whole) further to diminish the variety disposed by the management unit of each operation.

Therefore

The meta-management should make minimal use of variety amplifiers in its dealings with management units in a downward direction. But this is difficult, since even "policies" and "guidelines" tend to be perceived from the other direction as massive constraints.

This is the cybernetic *argument for autonomy (or freedom), as distinct from the ethical, political, or psychological arguments. Unlike these others, it has no emotive content. It is basically mathematical.*

(iv) If minimal variety amplification is desirable, the question arises whether there need be any meta-management intervention in elemental operations. The minimum is zero, in principle.

(v) However, if there were *zero* meta-management intervention, elemental operations (in pursuit of their individual targets) would inevitably exhibit activities that were not consonant with each other—and which might be downright contradictory.

Therefore

The meta-management must make some intervention, and should make only that degree of intervention that is required to maintain cohesiveness in a viable system. For a viable system cannot disintegrate without losing its viability.

(vi) Cohesiveness is, however, a function of the *purpose* of the system. Viable systems of concentrated purpose will be closely knit, highly cohesive. Viable systems of general purpose will be more loosely coherent.

(vii) But systemic purpose (as we saw) is a subjective phenomenon, rather than a property of the system independent of its instigators, participants, and observers. Thus the mathematical extent to which meta-management will minimally vitiate the elemental variety disposable, above zero subtraction, is determined within the total systems framework as earlier described. In other words, the extent to which the meta-management can help depends on the overall situation.

Therefore

> Freedom is in principle a computable function of systematic purpose as perceived [Beer, 1979, p. 158].

So, as with the horizontal management lines, the amplifiers and attenuators along the vertical axis must also be designed. If they are not, they will simply "grow"—not necessarily to the advantage of the organization. More significantly, they will grow in ways that are not perceived (and certainly not understood) by the managers involved.

In Chapter 8 is a model of an organization's ends and means. It specifically deals with what it calls "elements of guidance" (business policies and business rules) that amplify management decisions, and "assessments" that provide a filtered view of the effect of the environment (there described as "influences") on the organization's ends and means.

In modern times there is a particularly pernicious "nutrient medium" in which this growth takes place—the computer. The computer allows us unlimited options in the way communications are established. When Mr. Beer wrote his book, the situation was bad enough, but in the 20 years since then, these options have increased exponentially. Our intelligence in employing these options, alas, has not increased nearly as much.

Thus, buried in the middle of Chapter 5 of this book is its most important point:

> **Requirements analysis** is the examination of an organization to determine the most effective amplifiers and attenuators to build. What are needed? How are those now in place ineffective or counterproductive? What should they look like, given the purpose and organization of the enterprise?

So, what does that vertical axis look like in the viable system?

System Two: Dampen Waves

We have established that it is desirable for each System One to have a certain amount of autonomy to conduct its own affairs, but it is also desirable to moderate autonomy and to promote their cooperation.

The first problem with a set of Systems One is their tendency to step on each other's toes or to oscillate. Oscillation occurs when the action of one System One causes an adverse effect on another System One. The reaction of the second exacerbates the situation in the first, which reacts in a way even worse for the second. This continues until the entire situation degenerates completely.

As an example of how subsystems can work at cross purposes, a production order is placed on production line 1 for widget A-6, which requires parts P-4, P-6, and P-8. It is due January 15. The parts needed are then allocated in inventory and therefore are not available to any other orders. An order for widget B-10 is placed on production line 2 for delivery January 17, requiring parts P-32, P-17, and also P-8. The production line 2 foreman discovers that (after the allocation to A-6) there are not enough P-8s to complete the order, although more are coming in on January 24. Therefore, the order for B-10 must be held for one week.

Meanwhile, however, it turns out the P-4 parts are defective. This means that A-6 cannot actually be made until more parts are received on January 30.

Since production line 1 and production line 2 don't communicate with each other, there is no way for production line 2 to learn that, in fact, the P-8 material *is* available and the order for B-10 *can* be completed.

This kind of problem is common in business, especially in manufacturing, and the informal communications between operations are often not sufficient to address it. What is needed is some oversight that can take into account the set of operations in the various Systems One and coordinate them. This argues for the creation of **System Two**. System Two's purpose is to control oscillation between pairs of Systems One.

In Figure 5.7 we have added triangles to represent this new (sub)system. Note that System Two does not instruct any System One as to what it should do, beyond what is required to coordinate between the different Systems One. For this reason, it is not part of the meta-management. This function is represented in the manufacturing world, for example, by materials management, whose job is to prevent precisely the disruptions described above. In this case, System Two would be aware of the requirements and limitations of both production lines and be able to release parts that could not otherwise be used. Without instructing the plants in any way as to how to manufacture, or even what to manufacture, it simply coordinates supply and demand to ensure that the right *quantity* is manufactured each week.

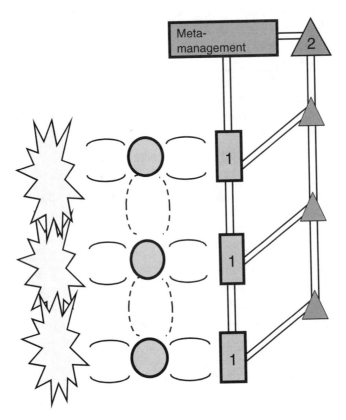

FIGURE 5.7 System Two.

System Three: Achieve Synergy

Ah, you say, but, in addition to System Two, there still has to be some management over the set of Systems One to direct them to one or more corporate (metalevel) goals. Meta-management is still required to direct the set of Systems One.

In Figure 5.8 *System Three* appears as the first recognizable component of the meta-management. It is shown as a *component* of the meta-management rather than its entirety, because we don't know yet what other components might be present.

Note that System Two is not part of the meta-management box, because it isn't really supervising System One. It is not at the meta-level of recursion. It is simply providing a service, and it lives at the same level of recursion as System One.

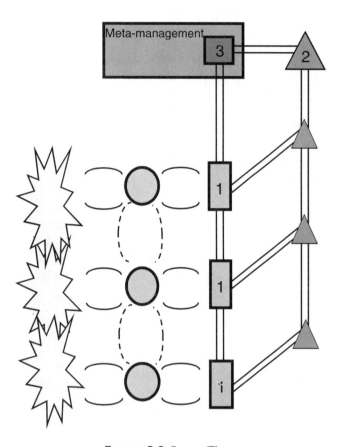

FIGURE 5.8 System Three.

System Three's job is to *integrate* the operations of the collected Systems One. It deals with issues that each System One cannot see. Since it is desirable for Systems One to have as much autonomy as possible, this doesn't simply mean "you do what I tell you". Rather, as described above, integration is the "minimal meta-systematic intervention that is consistent with cohesiveness within the purposes of the viable system. These purposes are not, of course, objective properties of the system; they are formulated by those who have charge of it, which include its initiators, its owners, its employees, its customers, and its observers" [Beer, 1979, p. 202].

As part of the meta-management, System Three is in communication with *all* the Systems One simultaneously. It knows what is going on *inside* the firm, *now*.

The actual interventions taken by System Three will depend on its purposes, but we can assume that one purpose will include getting the most out of *the set* of Systems One. That is, the objective is *synergy*, an increased output for the whole, even if it means directing that one or more of the components be less than fully productive.

System Four: Opportunities

It is important to pause here and remember what is being described. This model is not advising how an organization *ought* to be run. It is describing what *must be present* in any viable system. Normally systems (enterprises) aren't described this way. Mr. Beer has created a new language for describing how an enterprise must work. So far we have acknowledged that any system must be viable and that it must exist in the context of a higher-level system. Moreover, a set of viable systems must be regulated, first by a system that dampens oscillations and then by a system which generates synergy across the set of systems to achieve a meta-level goal.

Any viable enterprise must have these elements. One which does not will not long survive.

Note, however, that while these are *necessary* conditions for survival, they are not *sufficient*. What we have so far is an automobile that is idling. The component systems are operating and System Three is working to maximize their total output, but this in no way accounts for changes that will be necessary (at this level of recursion) to adjust to changes in the environment. What we have so far is not sufficient for the system to make "progress".

What is required is *innovation*. It is necessary for a viable system to be constantly examining the environment to find new opportunities and to ward off risks.

In 2000, Jonas Ridderstråle and Kjell Nordström, two leather-clad Swedish college professors with shaved heads, wrote a very witty and entertaining book on the modern world called *Funky Business*. In it, they describe "Funky, Inc.", their view of what the modern company should be. Among other things, "Funky, Inc. is extremely innovative. In a real-time, globally linked surplus society it is just a matter of a few weeks, days, or even hours before our friends from Bangalore, New York, Kuala Lumpur, Paris, Gdansk, Tokyo, Seoul, London, or Santiago come here to copy our recipes. To remain unique, we must constantly sharpen our competitive edge. Alan F. Shugart, Chairman of disk drive giant Seagate Technology Inc., goes as far to say that 'Sometimes I think we'll see the day when you introduce a product in the morning and announce its end of life at the end of the day' [Shugart, 1997]. And IT guru Kevin Kelly says 'Wealth flows directly from innovation... not optimization... wealth is not gained by perfecting the known' [Kelly, 1998]" [Ridderstråle and Nordström, 2000, p. 152].

To deal with this change, we must add a *System Four*. Figure 5.9 shows this. Here, System Four's primary communications are not with other parts of the system but with the *environment*. Note that there are really two domains in the environment that System Four must deal with. The first is the *accepted environment*, which is the part of the environment that Systems One already address. The second, more important part of the environment that System Four must be about is the ***problematic environment.*** It is in the second environment—the one not seen by Systems One—that System Four has the ability to identify the true opportunities (and risks) to the business. (Note the discussion of the "adjuster organizer" in Figure 5.5, above.) What things are going on in the world that the operating divisions are not in a position to see?

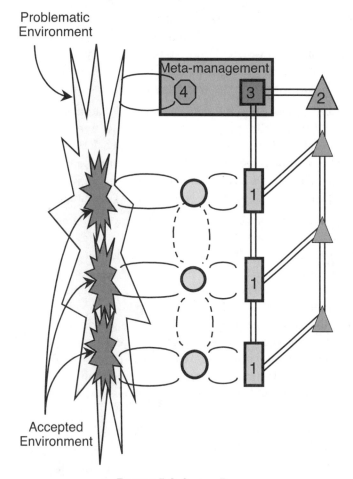

FIGURE 5.9 System Four.

In one real example, a book store conglomerate was initially unable to understand the implications of the World Wide Web. And yet that bit of environment has suddenly raised its ugly head and completely changed the business of selling books. It required a company with an active System Four to spot that. (More significantly, it took a brand-new company willing to look at the world clearly to see that. Existing companies, dominated by their Systems Three, could not for some time.)

If System Three is about "inside and now", System Four is clearly about "outside and then". System Three's domain is the system and its operations; System Four's domain is the world at large.

Note, by the way, that "innovation is not only a matter of technology—nuts and bolts. In fact, technology is often only a small part of it. Innovation concerns every little aspect of how an organization operates—administrative innovations, marketing innovations, financial innovations, HRM [human resources management] innovations, and service-concept innovations. Going for total innovation, therefore, requires rethinking every little aspect of how we operate" [Ridderstråle and Nordström, 2000, p. 153].

More significantly, innovation is not just a matter of listening to the environment and determining "what the public wants". The truly innovative company provides goods and services the public didn't know it wanted. Did 3M ask the public if it should invent Post-it Notes? Did Starbucks ask the public if they wanted a cup of coffee available on every street corner? The trick to *real* innovation is to create new things and then make them widely available. Real innovation often involves educating the consumer.

All this talk about innovation raises one of the more interesting aspects of System Four. Even though we have emphasized here that the model does not correspond to an organization chart, it is not hard to find corporate analogies for Systems One and Three, as well as, with a bit more difficulty, System Two. Most companies, however, do not have a formal "System Four Department". Some have "Research and Development". Some have "Market Research". Some have "Corporate Development". For most companies, though, the real System Four consists of a random collection of insightful, clever, *and forceful* employees who could literally be working *anywhere* in the company. Somebody with enough nerve and aggressiveness may be willing to stir up trouble until someone in authority finally responds to a good idea. Unfortunately, the way most companies are organized, excellent ideas from people with less nerve and aggressiveness are often lost.

What we more often have is a market research department that has little contact with research and development. The information services department is disconnected from corporate planning. Each of these reports as a staff function to different parts of the enterprise. The existence of System Four as an essential condition for the enterprise's viability has often gone unrecognized.

An interesting side effect of the move toward knowledge management is that the System Four function is finally being dealt with in some companies. It has been hard to institutionalize it, but people are beginning to be appreciated and rewarded for their creativity and insight. Even so, in most real companies, this System Four functionality has not been adequately integrated. As Messrs. Ridderstråle and Nordström point out, this has profound implications on twenty-first century business—for two reasons.

The first reason is the incredible increase in the rate of change in the environment. When the world was relatively stable, a CEO could charge a small group of people to study a change in the world about them, and occasionally they would come up with a useful idea. This is no longer adequate. The survival of the firm depends on its ability repeatedly to respond and adapt quickly to its environment.

Not only is technology changing more rapidly than even the most agile enterprise can accommodate, but the very institutions and values of our newly global society are changing. This means that, among other things, markets are now international, consumers demand specific products for their needs, and the old structures of corporation and government are becoming obsolete. The company that cannot cope with these changes will soon no longer be in business.

For example, one company realized a few years ago that its status as a premier glass manufacturer in Mexico was insignificant if it was simply a minor player in North America.

The second reason for profound implications is that the allocation of responsibility for responsive behavior in the past is inappropriate for supporting true innovation. Before, innovation was mostly carried out by what were called "staff" functions—supporting management as a kind of extension of it. The idea of "staff" suggests the taking on of routine activities that managers are not interested in doing themselves. That does not describe what is required of System Four in the modern era. System Four is now concerned with technologies that are probably outside the sphere of competence of the boss. It must be carried out by people with more experience in specific areas than the boss, and with more autonomy than they have ever known before.

There is, of course, another basic problem with System Four: All these good ideas about the environment and the future often disrupt the nice, pretty equilibrium of System Three. This means that there will always be a fundamental conflict between Systems Three and Four. Implementation of integrated manufacturing planning techniques, for example, can make a company much more responsive to the marketplace and can significantly reduce inventory costs. Such techniques, however, can conflict directly with the corporate culture of manufacturing via more informal systems [Wight, 1975].

As a further example, it is ironic that in the 20 or so years since Mr. Beer wrote his book, a lot of the acceleration of technology has been in the information processing arena. The World Wide Web, for example, has completely changed the marketplace in which most companies operate. In principle, this means that much of a company's potential for innovation should reside in the information technology department. The problem, however, is that, while it may promote change in the information processing *tools*, the information technology department has often been the one where it is *most difficult* to absorb change. Systems in place are hard to modify, and the people working in information technology departments are often wedded to older structures. "We can't do that, because the systems we have won't permit it". This will be the epitaph of many companies in the twenty-first century. How do we resolve this conflict?

System Five: System Identity

Resolution of this conflict requires the introduction of the last component of meta-management: *System Five*. This system resolves differences in point of view between System Four and System Five, based on its understanding of the identity of the viable system.

System Five is the only one that rates its own Row in the Architecture Framework. It represents the *identity* of the firm. It defines the enterprise's *scope*. We are a bank and not an oil refinery. What does that mean? What does it mean about our data, functions, planning cycles, locations, business rules, and yes, our people? System Five is the part of the meta-management that knows *why* we are in business, and therefore System Five is the ultimate arbiter of disagreements between Systems Three and Four. (See Figure 5.10.)

This doesn't mean that being System Five is easy, especially these days. The pressures of the global marketplace challenge everything about the way companies have been run. Responding adequately could mean wrenching changes that may be difficult or impossible to carry out. But it is System Five that must ultimately make the decision whether or not to proceed.

The inclusion of System Five completes the definition of meta-management. Now we can see how the recursion works. This meta-management is really the controller of a System One at recursion's next level. (See Figure 5.11.) Note that, contrary to what was said at the beginning of the chapter, in fact there is communication between the controller of System One and the environment, but as we saw above, it is of a different quality than the communications from the process and the environment.

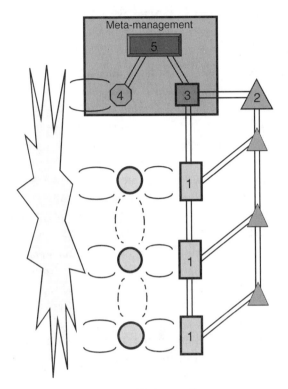

FIGURE 5.10 System Five.

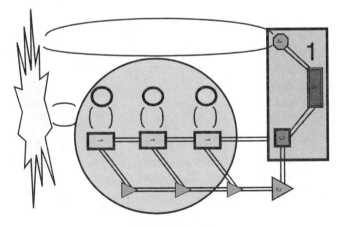

FIGURE 5.11 The Next Recursion.

Extra Communication Channels

Notice that what are represented here are system *functions*, not necessarily an actual physical organization. For example, each operating division might have its own Finance Director, Marketing Vice President, and Manufacturing Management. The same positions might exist in the corporate management. It is not unreasonable for the corresponding functions to meet across divisions, perhaps with the corporate manager sitting in as well. In this case, it is the *group* that is serving as System Three.

In a small organization, a single person might serve as Systems One, Two, and Three, although it is important for all to realize that any particular message from that person to the operating groups is *either* a System One message, a System Two message, or a System Three message. In a one-man consulting organization, for example, the entrepreneur may decide what kind of business to pursue (System Four), schedule projects so that they don't overlap (System Two), and perform the work (System One).

One way that the organization chart is misleading is that each box on it does not necessarily represent a viable system in its own right. It may simply be a component of the parent, without having any of the characteristics of a viable system that are being promulgated here. The Systems One depicted in the model here do *not* correspond to such things as "finance", "sales", and "manufacturing". Each System One must itself be a viable, self-contained system. This means that manufacturing and its connection to the outside world, sales, must be part of the same System One. Dissecting a System One into subsystems, based on the tasks each performs, is *not* the same as identifying its component Systems One.

As much as the independent consultant, for example, would love to have the "company" concerned only with using skills, it can't be done. The entrepreneur must also do all the tasks (accounting, marketing, etc.) required to make the company into a viable system.

Note that, by virtue of Ashby's Law, the total variety on the vertical plane (including System Two) must equal the sum of the variety on the horizontal plane. The set of Systems One, after all, constitute the operating unit for a System One at the next level of recursion. All the variety in this operational unit has to be accommodated (albeit with attenuators and amplifiers) in its communication with the manager.

Viewing the viable system in its present configuration, this presents a problem for our earlier assertion that there should be minimal intervention by System Three into the activities of Systems One. Rather, the variety equation requires considerable intervention, almost to the extent that meta-management is taking on the responsibility of the System One managers. Figure 5.12 shows this with its emphasis on the vertical communications.

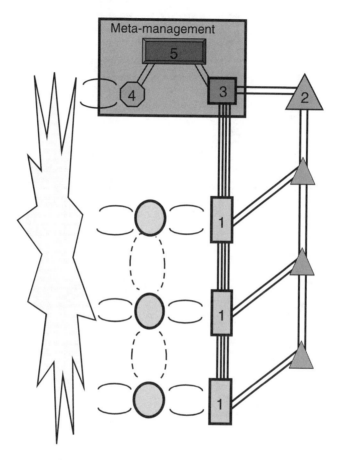

FIGURE 5.12 Horizontal and Vertical Variety.

There is an alternative, however, which is shown in Figure 5.13. The idea here is that the meta-management can directly interrogate the operations. Some authors and managers call this "management by walking around". It provides important information to meta-management, which allows it to convey much less information down the management channel. For example, drivers are given a set of rules to follow in driving, so that it is not necessary for the state to control each trip. This direct communication allows monitoring of the operation to ensure that it is running well. If it is, communication with Systems One is limited. This in turn allows the variety equation to be satisfied, even as it reduces the amount of direct intervention by System Three into the System One Managements.

Note that care must be taken to design these direct communications between System Three and operations, so that they do not interfere with the smooth operations of System One.

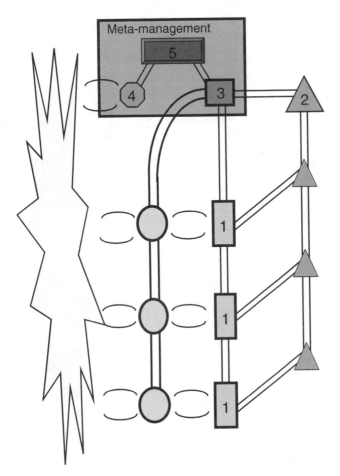

FIGURE 5.13 Direct Information.

Implications of This Model

Mr. Beer's model provides considerable food for thought about how companies really work. In particular, there are two implications: First, it correctly characterizes the number-one problem for a business as information overload; second, it provides insights as to how we should look at our own jobs.

Information Overload

How do I manage a multibillion-dollar company in a world where the business environment changes almost daily? And the problem isn't even that there is insufficient information about what is going on. It is that there is *too much* information. Not only is there too much information about what is going on within our organizations, there is way, *way* too much information about what is going on in the environment.

Variety has always been what management has been about, and it has grown much worse in modern times. To say that we are suffering from "future shock" is to say that the variety of our environment has exploded.

What this means for systems designers is that our number-one job is to create the amplifiers and filters necessary to enable a manager to survive. For filters, we must design reports that provide enough information, richly enough, to be useful in managing the enterprise, without providing so much that the important items cannot easily be identified.

Vice presidents, for example, are not going to go through a two-inch-thick report to find the four pieces of information they need. On the other hand, in 2001, a two-page summary of Enron's financial status clearly wasn't adequate to understand what was wrong at that company.

For amplifiers, we must set up structures such that a single command from above can easily be translated into a complex set of instructions to all involved.

Moreover, as we design these systems, we must understand which system we are serving: Systems One, System Two, System Three, System Four, or System Five.

And what does this model tell us about the movement toward knowledge management?

Knowledge is the application of *information* to useful ends. That is, knowledge is the variety that has been filtered to equal the variety of the manager perceiving it.

The meaning of knowledge management, then, is twofold:

First, the ability to absorb variety is now the most important trait anyone brings to the job of being manager. This capacity for dealing with variety is a direct function of intelligence and education. To deal with all that is going on around the enterprise, managers simply have to work smarter than they ever did in the past.

Second, to the extent that the world still will always have more variety than the manager can absorb, information systems are required that digest the information and produce the specific sets of information that allow for ready interpretation. To the extent that our information systems simply add to the noise, they provide no value to the enterprise.

To the extent that they provide exactly what is needed, they are indispensable.

Jobs

Traditionally, enterprise organization has emphasized the relationships between Systems Three and One. Systems Two and Four, if they existed at all, were diffused throughout the enterprise.

The cybernetic systems tended to look like this.

- The CEO usually played System Five.
- Middle Management mostly performed System Three functions.
- Research and development, market research, and random, clever, *pushy* people were System Four.
- Interdisciplinary Committees formed System Two.
- And of course the workers were System One.

Now, however, technology permits much more interaction among all the players. The management role at System Three doesn't disappear, but many more people can participate in it, as well as Systems Two and Four.

Now you get something like the following configuration, in terms of the four twenty-first century jobs described previously (see page 209):

- The CEO is still System Five.
- Resource managers (inventory control, human resources, finance, etc.) are System Two.
- Each effort is often independent of others, so project leaders play the role of System Three.
- And it's the talent—scientists, technicians, programmers and analysts, and others—that are both Systems One and Four.

Our Personal Lives

In addition to the issues of variety that are present in managing organizations, similar issues are present as we manage our personal lives. Each one of us (forget about the enterprise for a moment) must suddenly deal with innovation, changes in technology, and a vast amount of new things that must be learned—this week.

But we all have a limited "channel capacity", and we each deal with this fact in our own way. We select which magazines we don't read and, of those we do, which articles (or paragraphs) in them we don't pay attention to. We carefully don't hear discussions about subjects that are troubling or that might challenge our preconceptions. Similarly, we amplify our knowledge in the way we use those tidbits in conversation to give the impression that we know more than we do.[12]

---

12. Yes, we all do that, admit it.

As individuals, we destroy the variety we experience as well, and we amplify the variety at our disposal.

The assignment is to somehow organize our lives so that the gleaning of tidbits is systematic and at least leaves us aware of the things we are supposed to know, even if we don't quite know them yet. We also try to broaden our education as a way to increase channel capacity.

Of course we go to conferences and seminars and the occasional class to try to improve at least our intellectual tools for dealing with variety, if not our knowledge directly.

And we don't always succeed. There are religious wars about the best data modeling techniques to use, because none of us command enough variety to comprehend the full array of techniques that are out there and the implications of each.

Perhaps understanding this model will allow us all to accept our limitations and get on with our lives.

System Use

So, how do we go about designing systems that mitigate variety correctly? More significant to this book, how do we describe the particular requirements for mitigated variety?

This opens the door for a new technique called use cases.

The *use case* is a kind of diagram showing "actors" interacting with a hypothetical system.

According to Paul Harmon and Mike Watson in their 1988 book, *Understanding UML: The Developer's Guide*, "A use case diagram provides a functional description of a system and its major processes. It also provides a graphic description of who will use the system and what kinds of interactions they can expect to have with the system" [Harmon and Watson, 1998, p. 112].

The decision as to what systems should be built doesn't come until the end of the requirements project, but once the general idea has been established that a particular part of the business should be automated, it is possible to imagine a system that would do it. Given such an imagined system, it is possible to imagine also the kinds of interactions that a person might have with such a system.

But previously we recognized that an enterprise is itself a system, however, so this definition can be extended to describe a piece of the business and the interactions with that piece. To the extent that this approach is taken, it is much like a context or a level one data flow diagram. The "actors" are "external entities" in a data flow diagram, but the idea of how they interact is the same. Ivar Jacobson explores this idea in his 1994 book, *The Object Advantage: Business Process Reengineering with Object Technology.* This approach can make use cases effective in capturing a business owner's view of interactions with the enterprise.

The technique differs from data flow diagramming, however, in that less attention is paid to the data content of each flow, and the process of "exploding" higher level processes to component processes is less well articulated.

But the use case can be helpful, however, for its focus on the nature of the interaction itself. To the extent that this is in terms of the mechanical details of the user interface, it is firmly in Row Four, the "Designer's View", but if it simply discusses the content of the interaction without describing the technology involved, it is a legitimate Row Three technique for the people and organization column.

The technique originated as a graphic one, with ellipses for "systems", and stick figures for the "actors". (See Figure 5.14.)

The problem with this approach is that, as we've said, it doesn't describe the data, nor does it really describe the nature of the interaction at all. In recent years, it has become evident that the use case is not as significant for its graphics, as it is a vehicle for organizing text descriptions. An excellent description of this more verbal approach is Alistair Cockburn's 2000 book, *Writing Effective Use Cases.* His view of the use case puts it squarely in Column Four: it is inherently a *contract* between an actor and a system. It is all about the nature of the interaction.

FIGURE 5.14 A Use Case

To Cockburn, a use case description must have the following parts:

- *Name*—A description of the goal of the use case.
- *Scope*—The boundaries of the use case. The nature of this depends on whether the use case is for analysis or design.
  - *Analysis: Functional Scope*—This is described in terms of the actors involved and their goals. A *use case brief* summarizes the scope.

- *Design: Design Scope*—The set of hardware and software systems to be addressed.

Each use case must be clearly identified as to whether it is for analysis or design. In this book, we are only concerned with those used for analysis.

- *Level*—What is the level of detail for the use case? This may be very high summary, summary, user-goal, sub-function, or too low.

  Level, here, is described more subjectively than for data flow diagrams. The reference point is the "user-goal"—the level where a person would be expected to complete a single task. This is similar to the "essential activity" level described for essential data flow diagrams in Chapter 4, but the criteria for determining it are different. A user-goal could be at a lower level than an essential activity that is the complete response to an external event, but it may not be. For example, a user goal could be the cataloging of a book received by the library, when the essential activity is the entire receiving process.

- *Stakeholders and Interests*—A list of the actors and each actor's goal. An actor is typically a role, such as "inventory manager" or "data entry clerk", not a named individual. A *stakeholder* is someone who has a vested interest in the behavior of a system, but who may or may not interact with it directly. A *primary actor* is an actor that calls on the system to deliver one of its services. The primary actor is often, but not always, the one who triggers the use case.

- *Preconditions*—What the use case must determine to be true before it can start. For example, before calculating charges associated with a sale, the customer must be known.

- *Success Guarantee*—What interests of the stakeholders will be satisfied when the use case is complete, whether through a normal path or one of the alternate paths. For example, if the use case describes a depositor's withdrawal from a bank, success consists of the depositor's actually receiving funds.

- *Minimal Guarantee*—What the use case must deliver, even if the "Success Guarantee" is not met. In the bank withdrawal example, even if the transaction cannot be completed (if there are insufficient funds, for example) the depositor must at least be notified as to the reason.

- *Trigger*—The external event that causes the use case to happen. This is the same external event described for essential data flow diagrams. To the extent that the trigger only causes the steps described here, the use case is for an essential activity.

- *Main Success Scenario*—The sequences of steps that take place if all goes well. While one or more of these steps may be described in lower level use cases, they don't have to be. Describing them simply as components of this use case may be sufficient.

- *Extensions*—Attached to steps in the main success scenario, an extension is a list of steps to be followed if the condition for the main step is not fulfilled. For example, if a step in use case "Get paid for car accident" is "1. Claimant submits claim with substantiating data", an extension could be "1a. Submitted data is incomplete", followed by the steps to be taken under these circumstances.

So, to summarize, in describing the roles people and organizations play in interacting with components of the enterprise, a use case can be an effective tool. Care must be taken, however, to ensure that what are being represented are truly interactions with a business function, and not interactions with a system that hasn't been defined yet.

Requirements Analysis Deliverable—Column Four

The Row One scope should have identified the part of the organization to be addressed by each particular project.

For a particular project, then, as described above,

> **Requirements analysis** is the examination of an organization to determine the most effective amplifiers and attenuators to build. What are needed? How are those now in place ineffective or counterproductive? What should they look like, given the purpose and organization of the enterprise?

The assignment of the system developer is to provide the tools to reduce the variety experienced by a manager. It is *not* to provide *more* information, it is to provide *less* information, but the *right* less. To do this, the systems analyst must understand not only what the business player says, but also what the true role of that business player is in the organization—in cybernetic terms.

To be sure, it will be necessary to deliver organization charts, matrix management charts, or charts describing how the enterprise is to be organized. In particular, it is necessary to articulate the structure of the part of the enterprise to be addressed by this project. Having said that, the Column Four deliverable must also include:

- Identification of the parts of the organization that correspond to the five systems of a particular enterprise
- Identification of the amplifiers and filters required
- Definition of the entities, functions, locations, events, and business rules that must be brought together to construct each filter and amplifier
- Description of the interactions of various players in carrying out the functions of the five systems (use cases)

Are we supporting System Two, the simple coordination of different Systems One? Are we serving System Three, which is trying to find the synergy among Systems One? Are we perhaps reporting on the world at large for System Four, required as we are to provide enough information about the world to be useful, even as we filter that information so that it can be absorbed? Or, are we supporting System Five, helping that system understand the specifics of a System Four proposal, along with its implications on the operation of System Three and the lower levels?

The answer to these questions will dramatically influence the kinds of systems we build.

Note that the very act of drawing the models described elsewhere in this book acts to reduce variety. This is a very confusing enterprise. By selecting things to look at (entity types, processes, events, etc.), we are able to look at a piece of it and thus are able to grasp significant truths about the enterprise as a whole. By discussing these models with a manager, we give that manager tools for understanding the variety of the enterprise.

Ultimately *all* of the systems we build will feature ***exception reporting.*** The trick is to design the logic for determining which exceptions to show. Something like a use case can be helpful in identifying the nature of these exceptions.

To do all this effectively, we must truly understand the particular information that is required to perform the job. This ultimately is why data modeling is more important than process modeling. If you can understand the variety equation for a particular managerial task, you know what is needed from a system that supports that task. To know just the nature of the task itself is actually less important.

People, Organizations, and the Other Columns

People and Data

A very important part of the documentation for a data model is identification of the roles (if not the individual people) who will be responsible for each entity and attribute. Certain people will "own" an entity, meaning that those people are ultimately responsible for its data quality. The same or other people are responsible for updating it. Yet others have permission to see it. This matrix is required if data quality is to be established.

Documentation of each entity should at least include identification of the role responsible for the quality of its information, if not the individual person so responsible.

People and Activities

All of the activity modeling techniques (except for the function hierarchy) described in Chapter 4 include references to the people or organizations performing the functions. Data-flow diagraming and process modeling were described in Chapter 4, because these techniques emphasize what is being done; use cases were described in this chapter because they are more concerned with the nature of the interaction. Indeed, all three of these techniques belong firmly in both columns.

In addition to their basic definitions in the models, all activities should also be classified as System One, Two, Three, Four, or Five activities.

People and Locations

Where people are significantly influences the way Systems One through Five described here work. Each person is in a particular location, and the roles each plays may be for different locations. It is incumbent on management of an organization to place the people who must communicate most extensively in the same location. The extent to which they are in disparate places will affect the quality and nature of the communications channels that can be built among them.

People and Timing

In the cybernetic model of the organization presented here, the main topic is communications, with no distinction being made between simple data and events. One event that was significant, however, was an operation's going outside its operating values (set points). Ultimately, this is the event that requires the management entity to act. With all the events that management must respond to from the outside world, this internal event is also critical.

The analysis project must clarify which events affect which parts of the organization.

People and Motivation

As stated previously, Chapter 8 contains a model of an organization's ends. It specifically deals with what it calls "elements of guidance" (business policies and business rules) that amplify management decisions, and "assessments" that provide a filtered view of the effect of the environment (there described as "influences") and operations on the organization's ends and means.

An element of guidance represents a message sent by management to its operating divisions. Business policies and business rules must be carefully designed to account for the issues described here.

Similarly, an assessment is the retrieval of information from the operating organizations, interpreting what happened, which influences caused it to happen, and the effects of these events on the enterprise's ends and means.

Business rules may be specific to the organization involved. There may be good and valid reasons for a rule to be applied to one division and not another. This must be documented.

Column Three: Locations

6

In John Zachman's original framework there were only three columns: data, function, and location. In 1989, the elements that concerned developers were primarily data and processes, although the implications of distributed systems were significant as well, and it was clear that any requirements analysis project would have to address them. Location was easily as important as data and processes. Only later did Mr. Zachman realize that there were three other columns as well.

The problem is that location is not really another column: It is a third dimension. That is, each of the other columns has a location dimension to it. It's as though the real Architecture Framework were as shown in Figure 6.1, with "Location" as a distinct dimension. We want to know the location of the data, the location of the activities, and so on.

Thus, more than any other column, location is intimately associated with the other columns, and it cannot be examined in isolation. Indeed, its relationships with the other columns can be very complex.

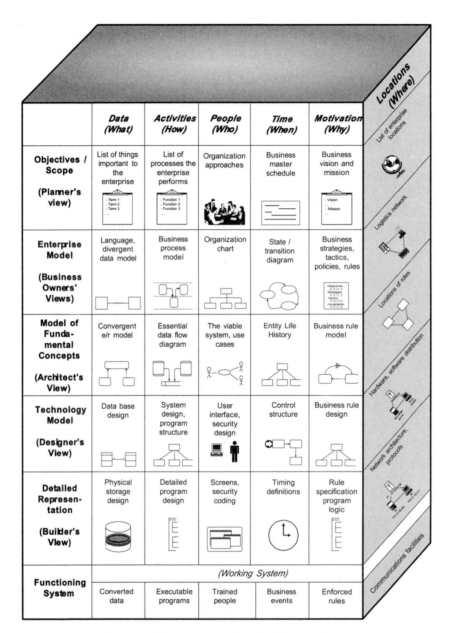

	Data (What)	Activities (How)	People (Who)	Time (When)	Motivation (Why)
Objectives / Scope (Planner's view)	List of things important to the enterprise - Term 1 - Term 2 - Term 3	List of processes the enterprise performs - Function 1 - Function 2 - Function 3	Organization approaches	Business master schedule	Business vision and mission - Vision - Mission
Enterprise Model (Business Owners' Views)	Language, divergent data model	Business process model	Organization chart	State / transition diagram	Business strategies, tactics, policies, rules
Model of Fundamental Concepts (Architect's View)	Convergent e/r model	Essential data flow diagram	The viable system, use cases	Entity Life History	Business rule model
Technology Model (Designer's View)	Data base design	System design, program structure	User interface, security design	Control structure	Business rule design
Detailed Representation (Builder's View)	Physical storage design	Detailed program design	Screens, security coding	Timing definitions	Rule specification program logic
Functioning System	*(Working System)*				
	Converted data	Executable programs	Trained people	Business events	Enforced rules

Locations (Where)
- List of enterprise locations
- Logistics network
- Locations of roles
- Hardware, software distribution
- Network architecture, protocols
- Communications facilities

FIGURE 6.1 Locations and the Architecture Framework.

The only graphic modeling technique for this column (both Rows Two and Three) is the trusty map. In the business owner's view (Row Two), one can lay out the geography of the city, state, country, or Earth, and place offices, warehouses, and plants on it.

In the architect's view (Row Three), these sites may be shown on a map as well, but the important thing is to document all the other columns for each site. This is a kind of network map, with the aesthetics left up to the mapmaker. In whatever way it is represented, though, in Row Three this network must be linked to the information in the other five columns.

Row Two—Geography

Ultimately, the business owner's view of location is geographic. Where do we do business? How do we communicate among these locations? What is the business content of those communications?

Obviously, this is less of a concern if a company's entire operation is in one location, although the locations of customers and communications with them keep the issue of geography relevant.

The issue of location has become more complex since the early 1980s. Before 1980, all data processing was done in centralized locations. This was because the economics of computing were such that it was cheaper to do it all on large, central computers. In about 1980, those economics changed radically. Mini-computers and personal computers made it reasonable for divisions to have their own computing facilities. Corporate information systems management resisted this, of course, because it threatened control that it had always exercised. As it happened, corporate management lost the battle, because the new economics were too persuasive. The issue remained, however, that some information still had to be *communicated* to management for business purposes. Now that economics didn't place that information there in the first place, it was necessary to define the *business* requirement for these communications. This was a new kind of problem.

Now, with better understanding of the whole idea of system requirements and of the options for decentralization, it should be possible to conduct a more rational dialogue. Indeed, we are now in a position to ask the question previously ignored: What communications are required among offices to address the true functions of the business?

The viable system considerations from Chapter 5 are important here. In examining a company's locations, it is important to ask the question: How much System One work is being done here? System Two?—and so forth. The answers will have a profound influence on the kinds of systems and communications that should be built.

Note, by the way, the difference between the concept of "location" and that of "site". A *location* (or "geographic area") is simply a place on the earth, like Cleveland, or Death Valley. It has a boundary, defined in terms of specific points. A *site* (also called a *facility*) is a place with a purpose, such as a house, office building, factory, or warehouse. One characteristic of a site, of course, is its location (although sometimes that can change), but site and location are not the same thing. (See page 119 for the data model of SITE and GEOGRAPHIC AREA.)

In requirements analysis, we are primarily concerned with sites, but in describing them, we will make generous use of our knowledge of geography.

There are many possible configurations of companies, reflecting the fact that there are many kinds of companies. Some of the general configurations of sites are:

- Headquarters and field offices
- Production networks
- Distribution networks
- Research networks
- Customer locations

Specific sites where the enterprise does business might include:

- Offices
- Kiosks
- Toll booths
- Archeological digs
- Oil wells

Headquarters and Field Offices

There are variations on this theme, as described below, but ultimately the question of communications among sites is about the relationship of headquarters to its outlying sites. The nature of these communications can be understood in terms of Stafford Beer's viable system (described in Chapter 5). Systems Three, Four, and Five are typically in an enterprise's headquarters. They control the operational elements in the field—Systems One and Two. The operational elements deal with the outside world and respond accordingly, feeding data about their performance back to the controlling units. If the data show an aberration, then the controlling system issues instructions to correct their efforts. Communication is essential for the feedback loop to work.

If the headquarters and field offices are in the same place, this problem is nothing other than the set of management issues described in Chapter 5. If not, the communications links must be explicitly addressed in more detail.

It is important to make sure that communication between the field and headquarters contains the information (variety) necessary for headquarters to evaluate the field facilities' performance. More often than not, these are in the form of financial reports, but they may also include other kinds of performance statistics. Similarly, communications from the headquarters to the field may contain some direct instructions, but more often they consist of policies, constraints, and operating conditions. These establish what in process control are called "set points" against which the operating elements' performance will be judged.

The pre-1980 practice of also sending information to headquarters to be processed was for economic reasons (only headquarters could afford a computer) and not relevant to the viable system model.

Production Network

In the specific case where manufacturing takes place in several facilities, communication among those facilities is essential. In terms of Mr. Beer's viable system, this is largely the province of System Two—coordinating the flow of resources to various places—but System Three comes into play as well, in that communications are required for the overall management of the operation.

System Two's role in production is to make sure that each production step is aware of the production demands from the next operation upstream, and that its requirements in turn are properly communicated downstream. At the sales point, there are forecasts of expected sales, which are translated into production requirements for the finished products. These in turn must be translated into demand for the first level of subassemblies. These then are translated into requirements that generate demand for the next level of subassemblies, and so forth. Where it is done well, this entire calculation typically is performed in a central materials management site, and the resulting production schedules are then communicated to the sites involved. This permits balanced use of inventory. The calculation is the same whether the production is all in one building or worldwide. Components that are in multiple sites, however, raise implications for the communication networks that will be required.

For example, one pharmaceutical company had five major plants producing bulk pharmaceuticals and 26 plants packaging finished products—scattered all over the world. The logistics of bulk supply had to be managed centrally, with the instructions transmitted to all sites.

The System Three requirement is about management's making a set of plants more productive by examining the way each plant is working and then recommending changes in appropriate policies, constraints, or operating principles.

For example, a special case of a production network is an oil field. Numerous wells are scattered over the landscape, with both primitive and sophisticated means for monitoring them. Specifically, instruments may be attached to wells that are connected electronically to a central controlling computer, or alternatively, a worker may simply visit each well in his pickup truck and make observations. Either way, the data must be brought to the field office and analyzed, with proper steps then being taken to respond to circumstances.

Distribution Network

Requirements for communication among nodes of a product distribution network are similar to those for a production network. Again, System Two makes sure that supply and demand are coordinated, while System Three ensures that the inventory of the set is optimal, even if this means that the inventory in one site may not be.

Research Network

In one pharmaceutical company, new compounds are identified and research is planned at corporate headquarters in the American Midwest. The actual research, however, is conducted via clinical trials held at subsidiaries all over the world. This, of course, means extensive communication of research protocols (instructions as to how to carry out the research) to the field. Data are collected at each site, and initial reviews of the data are conducted there. Some research is conducted centrally, as well, with data that are collected and reviewed there. From the outset headquarters wants to be able to see the data for preliminary analysis, but the volume required is such that the data don't have to reside there. At a specific point in the process, however, use of the data in the field diminishes, and serious analysis begins at headquarters. Remote sites still have access to the data, so that they can respond when questions arise.

When a project was defined to address these requirements in the late 1980s, the economics of database management systems at the time suggested that the data be captured in the field with remote access to them being available from headquarters. Then, for the second part of a study, the data were physically moved to headquarters, with remote access then being provided to field sites. The economics could change in the future, requiring changes to the physical architecture of the system. The requirements for access would not change, however.

Customer Locations

It is common for an enterprise to have to keep track of its customer locations. Maps are a useful mechanism for this. A company may be concerned with locations outside its operational offices. For example, an automobile insurer must keep track of the locations where accidents happen. This might mean recording accidents on a map. The Los Angeles Film Board, as another example, issues permits to production companies, allowing them to make movies, commercials, and the like on the streets of Los Angeles. This requires extensive mapping facilities to define the exact territory for each permit.

The Set of Sites

All of these examples show that the set of sites where the enterprise operates is significant in defining the nature of that operation. The last pair of examples, by the way, shows that site may be an issue not only for placement of future systems, but also for the content of these systems.

Row Three—Network (and the Other Columns)

The business owner's view of facilities is concerned simply with what operations are where. The architect's view, however, is concerned with the relationship between sites and each of the other columns. It is not very meaningful, in an architectural sense, to say simply, "Where are we located?" The questions are, "Where do we perform various functions?" "Where do people work?" "Where are the data?"—and so forth.

Column One: Where Are Data Created? Where Are They Used?

There have always been two issues when one sets out to build a distributed database: Where should the data reside? Where are they to be used? This is one case, however, where technology is rapidly rendering these questions less important.

In recent years, database management systems have made it possible to define distributed databases such that the person making an inquiry need not know anything about where the data are stored. The system simply goes to get the results of the inquiry, wherever they might be. There are, of course, performance considerations when the bulk of data most people require is from distant sites, but as communications speeds increase, these are also becoming less important. During requirements analysis, however, it behooves the analyst to estimate the volume of communications that may be required between each pair of sites.

Also, previously it was important to know where users were, so facilities could be provided to allow them to access data. If a new system is to be implemented using client/server technology, this is still important. If the World Wide Web is to be used, however, all potential users already have the required tools on their desktops, so nothing need be done but to design and implement web sites that are, upon completion, accessible worldwide.

Column Two: Which Functions Are Where?

Examining the function hierarchy or the essential data flow diagrams from Chapter 4, we can look at each function and ask, "Where does it take place?" This is especially significant if our model is a variation on a data flow diagram, where the processes communicate with each other. Two processes that must communicate between different facilities have profound implications on the kinds of systems that can be built to support them.

Each activity diagram (in whatever form), should be annotated as to the location or site where the activity takes place. Grouping activities by site is a useful way to understand the geographic architecture of any prospective system. The swim lanes in a process model or a UML activity diagram, for example, could be used to represent either sites or geographic locations.

Column Four: Which Roles Are Where?

Where people are significantly influences the way Systems One through Five described in Chapter 5 work. Each person is in a particular location, and the roles each plays may be for different locations. It is incumbent on management of an organization to place the people who must communicate most extensively in the same location. The extent to which they are in disparate places will affect the quality and nature of the communications channels that can and must be built among them.

Column Five: What Events Are Where?

An important aspect of defining essential activities, as described in Chapters 4 and 7, is the definition of "external event". If an entire enterprise is in one facility, this is clearly an event from the world outside the enterprise. The whole process of developing an essential data flow diagram presupposes that internal events—where one activity triggers another activity—are not included. On the other hand, if one activity is in Cleveland and it triggers an activity in Los Angeles, it is hard for the folks in Los Angeles not to consider this an "external" event. None of the data flow diagramming techniques (including IDEF0 and use cases) provides a very good way of dealing with this.

Ultimately, this means that business decisions about what should happen where are significant to the overall efficiency of an organization. It would have been nice, when such decisions were made, if the company looked at events and the activities required to respond to them and then placed all the activities responding to one business event in the same place.

This may not have happened. If it did not, the event of communications between plants must be taken into account during the requirements analysis project, and the activity models must reflect this, even if the results are not tidy. What otherwise would have been a single essential activity may have to be broken into two—one for the part that takes place at each facility.

Column Six: Which Business Rules Are Where?

Ideally, a single set of business rules applies to the entire enterprise. In reality, however, it may be necessary to vary the rules by facility. Different locations may be run differently, may have different customs, or may be subject to different laws. For example, different offices of a car rental agency may have different rules for late return of a car, depending on when they are open. Office hours might be different in different sites, and different legal systems may apply.

The Requirements Analysis Deliverable— Column Three

The Row Two deliverable could be as simple as a map showing the enterprise's various locations, with different icons showing the kinds of facilities in each.

Ultimately, however, the analysis project should deliver a location dimension for all its other deliverables:

- For each entity, where are the data collected, and where are they used?
- For each activity, where is it performed?
- What is the volume of data to be communicated from one location to another?
- For each organization, where is it located, and with what other organizations in what other sites does it interact?
- For each event, where does it take place, and what is the location of each response to that event?
- For each business rule or business policy, which sites are affected?

Column Five: Timing

## 7

Introduction

The Timing column is intimately associated with other columns. To be meaningful, timing must be "of" something, usually either activities or data events. Moreover, often the business rules from the Motivation column also figure into any discussion of timing.

Timing is ultimately about events. These can be either business events—things happening in the world that the business must respond to—or temporal events—triggered by the passing of time. The latter often appear in the form of formal schedules. This chapter will first discuss schedules and then deal with other events.

Figure 7.1 shows the Architecture Framework with Column Five highlighted.

	Data (What)	Activities (How)	Locations (Where)	People (Who)	Time (When)	Motivation (Why)
Objectives / Scope (Planner's view)	List of things important to the enterprise - Term 1 - Term 2 - Term 3 ...	List of processes the enterprise performs - Function 1 - Function 2 - Function 3 ...	List of enterprise locations	Organization approaches	Business master schedule	Business vision and mission - Vision - Mission ...
Enterprise model (Business Owners' Views)	Language, divergent data model	Business process model	Logistics network	Organi-zation chart	State / transition diagram	Business strategies, tactics, policies, rules Objectives Strategies Tactics Constraints
Model of Funda-mental Concepts (Architect's View)	Convergent e/r model	Essential data flow diagram	Locations of roles	The viable system, use cases	Entity Life History	Business rule model
Technology Model (Designer's View)	Data base design	System design, program structure	Hardware, software distribution	User interface, security design	Control structure	Business rule design
Detailed Represen-tation (Builder's View)	Physical storage design	Detailed program design	Network architecture, protocols IP 137.39.65.788 IP 324.33.56.765 234.21.43.111	Screens, security coding	Timing definitions	Rule specification program logic
Functioning System	*(Working System)*					
	Converted data	Executable programs	Communi-cations facilities	Trained people	Business events	Enforced rules

FIGURE 7.1 The Architecture Framework—Timing.

Row One: Scope

The enterprise's orientation toward time is determined at the scope level. Does the organization do long-term planning, and if so, for how far into the future? In making decisions about investments, is it concerned with the next quarter or the next five years? To what extent is the company driven simply by the events that have an impact on it?

These choices, among other things, affect systems-development projects. The strategy taken in developing and implementing systems is very different for companies that are concerned only with this quarter's profits than for those that are committed to the longer-term future.

The timing component of the project's scope project will have a significant effect on how systems-development projects will be addressed. See Chapter 2 for a discussion of the impact of having too little time for a project.

Row Two: The Business Owner's View

As stated before, Row Two of the Architecture Framework is about what business owners see. These include business events and the business activities that are performed in response to them.

Schedules

Temporal events are caused by the passage of time. *Ongoing events* are the cyclical passage of the beginning of a day, the first day of a month, the first day of a year, and so on. Often activities are defined to be performed in response to these. *Scheduled events* occur at specified dates and times.

Ongoing events may be defined as part of the normal activities of the business. Accounting is an area where these are important. The "monthly close", for example is a series of activities to be done at the end of each month, in order to account for the expenses and revenues of that month.

The development of schedules, in turn, requires a structured approach to the work flow and activities of the organization. "First you . . . ", "Then you . . . ", and so on. In addition, the development of a schedule may itself be in response to temporal or other events.

For example, an annual temporal event (such as "October 1") may trigger creation of the annual budget, and this can include a schedule of events for next year's sales, purchases, and production. Over the course of the budget process, budgetary requirements are analyzed and then translated into specific timed goals, targets, and constraints on departments. Once the budget and annual plan are approved, the company must then live with in the budgetary and timing constraints—unless exceptional circumstances permit otherwise.

An annual plan does not necessarily specify when things are to happen during the upcoming year, but it could. Typically, it simply determines how much money is available each month.

A master production schedule, on the other hand, is a very different kind of schedule. It defines specifically what to do and when. Here, the schedule puts specific constraints on what can be done in the manufacturing process. This schedule is a set of instructions as to what to buy and when, as well as what to manufacture and when. Since it has a smaller scope, it is developed much more quickly and more frequently than an annual budget. With the help of computers, its development can be an interactive process, with changes in response to circumstances being made almost continuously, with their implications being determined immediately. As an alternative, its creation may be triggered by an ongoing temporal event, say, Monday.

Keep in mind that the events we discuss here are business changes. These are things that happen in the world. We are not concerned here with system events, like clicking on a mouse button.

Events and States

A non-temporal *business event* is something that happens in the world, requiring the enterprise to react. Business events might include, for example:

- Receipt of an order,
- Receipt of a shipment,
- Receipt of an application for employment, or
- Recognition that an inventory balance is incorrect.

Note that in each of these cases, there are business functions that the enterprise must perform in response to the event. When an order is received, for example, the enterprise sets out to fulfil it. When a shipment is received, it is either applied to an open order or added to inventory. When someone applies for a job, steps are taken to determine both the qualifications and appropriate opportunities for that person. When an inventory balance is recognized as incorrect, it must be checked and corrected. Moreover, steps may also be taken to prevent the error from happening again.

Note that the events described in this chapter are intimately connected to the activities (described in Chapter 4) which are performed in response to them.

Besides triggering activities, a business event may affect the *state* of one or more entity types. When a request for products is received, a Sales Order is created and put into the state "pending". When the last products are shipped, this order is changed to the state "complete". When a machine is turned on, its state goes from "off" to "standby", and then when it is put into gear, it goes from "standby" to "operational".

State/Transition Diagram

One way to represent the link between events and entity types (or object classes) is a *state/transition diagram*, a representation of the states an entity type passes through in response to events. It is described in many works, including Richard Barker's and Cliff Longman's 1992 *CASE Method: Function and Process Models*. The UML version of this is described in most UML texts, including the 1999 *The Unified Modeling Language User Guide* and Martin Fowler's 2000 version of his *UML Distilled*. A state/transition diagram shows the sequence of states an entity type goes through as it responds to events.

Figure 7.2 shows a sample state/transition diagram. This describes the state of a PURCHASE ORDER. Here it is in terms of a Row Two (business) perspective, but more than most of the diagramming techniques presented in this book, it is also a good basis for a Row Three view as well. State/transition diagrams can represent both Row Two and Row Three events and states.

The solid dots represent the initial and final states of the entity type. Once a purchase order is issued, it begins its life in the "Pending" state. Receipt of the last delivery moves it to "Complete". (Receipt of a delivery before the last one does not change the state of the purchase order.) If the order is in the state "Complete", finding something unsatisfactory causes the ordered product to be returned to the vendor. This event (and its resulting activity) then changes the status of the order back to "Pending". When the last physical asset to be returned has been returned, if it is determined that the physical asset will not be replaced, the purchase-order state is changed back to "Complete".

In this particular example (and this varies from company to company), we will assume that there is a specific process for closing a purchase order, once all materials have been received (or returned). The explicit decision to close the order is required to change the state from "Complete" to "Closed".

Note that while the order is still "Pending" it is possible that the material ordered is no longer needed, resulting in cancellation of the order. This determination changes the status from "Pending" to "Cancelled".

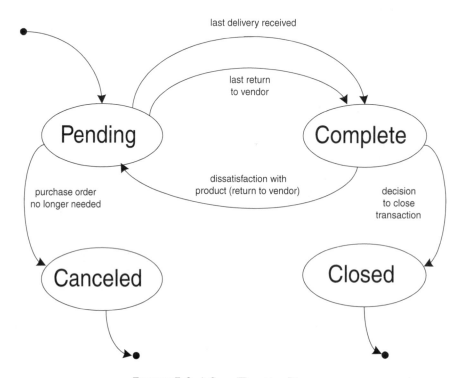

FIGURE 7.2 A State/Transition Diagram.

Row Three: The Architect's View

In Row Two of the Architecture Framework, the concern is with the business activities that take place in response to events such as those just described. Row Three is more concerned with the data-transformation activities responding to each event.

Events and States

One way in which the architect's view differs from the business owners' is that the entity types subject to a Row Three state/transition diagram (for example) are those that have been generalized into an architect's data model. The state/transition diagram for Row Two presented in Figure 7.2, for example, might be very similar to one for Row Three, but in Row Three, instead of being described for a PURCHASE ORDER, the states are described for the more general concept, CONTRACT or ORDER.

Generalizing the entities in Row Three will, of course, also require us to generalize the states as well. Whereas a purchase order may go through many more specific states than are shown in the example in Figure 7.2, "pending", "complete", "closed", and "canceled" may be as specific as we can get in a Row Three model.

In addition, note that while the triggers of a Row Three state/transition diagram are still events in the world, the actions that cause the state change are *data* actions. That is, they are the creation, deletion, or modification of data—specifically, in our example, of the data describing the CONTRACT. Moreover, the "state" of the entity type is the state of the data, not of the thing in the world that the data represent.

Two techniques are added to our repertoire as we move to the architect's view:

- *Essential data flow diagram*—Organization and presentation of an enterprise's activities in terms of the events that trigger them.

- *Entity life history*—Descriptions of the structure of the events and activities that affect each entity type.

Essential Data Flow Diagrams

As discussed in Chapter 4, Stephen McMenamin and John Palmer, in their 1984 *Essential Systems Analysis*, describe the ***essential data flow diagram.*** What is important about an essential data flow diagram (or the "essential" level in a function hierarchy) is that its structure is determined by the *events* in the world that affect the company. That is, an ***essential activity*** is defined as the complete response to an external event. To summarize what was written in Chapter 4, the process of developing an essential data flow diagram from a physical data flow diagram is as follows:

1. Explode the data flow diagram down to the lowest level that seems reasonable, producing a set of "activity fragments".

2. Identify and remove nonessential activity fragments (mechanisms). These include references to physical media, internal validity checks, buffers, and so forth.

3. *Identify all the real-world events that impinge on the activity fragment.* These are either temporal events or things happening in the outside world that cause the enterprise to react. These may be identified from the context data flow diagram. As described above, these might include such things as a customer inquiry, a customer order, receipt of purchased goods, a person applying for a job, and so forth. (We are not concerned here with internal events, such as the completion of a process.)

4. For each external event, identify the activity fragments that are carried out *in response to* that event.

5. Define a parent activity that encompasses these activity fragments that are the response to that event. This is a ***fundamental essential activity.***

6. Examine the data stores used by the essential activities. Are there activities that update those stores? If so, define additional ***custodial*** activities. For example "Manage customer reference data" might be a custodial activity.

7. Eliminate any activity fragments that are not part of a fundamental or custodial essential activity.

It may be the case that a particular fragment is used by more than one essential activity. In this case it is appropriate to break out the fragment as its own essential activity.

Note from this description that an essential activity is not necessarily the lowest level at which a business can be described. The more atomic process fragments that comprise an essential activity are, however, specific to the company and, at least to some extent, are technologically bound. For example, instead of separately verifying an order, recording its receipt, and updating appropriate inventories, the company could employ new bar-coding technology that would do all the necessary checks, recording, and notification at the same time the shipment is moved into inventory.

Below the essential level, the activities are chosen by the enterprise as a mechanism for carrying out the essential business function. As a consequence, they could be changed in a new system. Consequently, while they may be the proper object of a business process re-engineering effort, they are not of concern in an analysis diagram. The analyst is interested only in the essential level and above—the description of the things an enterprise *must* do, regardless of the technology it uses.

Thus, it is the *events* described in the Timing column that profoundly affect the definitions of activities described in the Activities column. In addition, it is events that ultimately determine the boundaries of business process engineering.

Entity Life Histories

The characteristic of object classes in object models that distinguishes them from entity types in entity type relationship diagrams is the specification of their behavior. Since system objects (Row Four artifacts) are themselves pieces of code, using a kind of pseudocode to describe this behavior in design object models makes sense. The behavior description can easily be included in an extension of the object-class box, as specified for the UML. See Figure 7.3 for an example from Martin Fowler's 2000 book, *UML Distilled*.

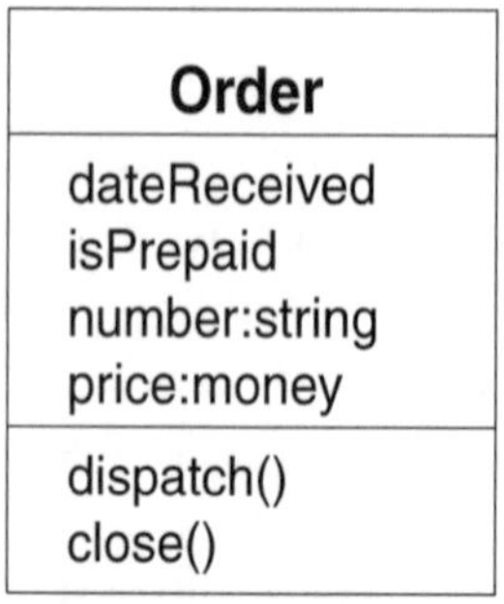

Order
dateReceived
isPrepaid
number:string
price:money
dispatch()
close()

FIGURE 7.3 An Object Class (with Behavior).

Here, "dateReceived", "isPrepaid", "number", and "price" are all attributes. (UML requires specifying the format of each attribute—"date", "boolean", etc.) The lines "dispatch()" and "close()" are the names of program modules that carry out the behaviors of an Order. Behavior for an instance of a class (an object) is invoked in response to triggers (events) sent from other objects.

It seems a reasonable extension to suggest, then, that when entity types representing things in the world are specified in Rows Two and Three, entity/relationship models could also be extended to represent the behavior of these entity types, along with their triggers. What steps, for example, are required to create an occurrence of an ORDER, and what causes them to be followed?

The problem is that the behavior of a real-world entity type is often much more complex than a simple list of steps. While it is appropriate to want to know what functions are performed around the entity type, this is much more than a simple narrative added to an entity type box.

One way of addressing the question of an entity type's behavior is to create a matrix associating each entity type with the activities that affect it. We saw the function/entity type matrix in Chapters 3 and 4, and it is described further on page 267 below.

A more sophisticated approach is the *entity life history diagram*. The technique was originally described by Michael Jackson (no, not the popular singer) in his 1983 book, *System Development*, and it is incorporated into the "Structured Systems Analysis and Design Method" (SSADM) widely used in Europe. The materials presented here are based largely on the work of Keith Robinson and John Hall of Model Systems Consultants, Inc. Specifically, the material is from their 1991 white paper, *Logical Data Modeling and Process Specification*.[1]

While the essential data flow diagram shows the relationships of events to activities, the entity life history diagram shows the relationship of events to data.

The entity life history diagram is a comprehensive representation of the things that can happen to an entity type—the events that cause it to change state and the functions that are performed when it does. It combines the data model with the state/transition diagram for a more robust description of each entity type's behavior than could be given in entity type boxes.

A Data Model

Figure 7.4 shows an example of a data model for a purchasing environment. The model describes contracts used to acquire materials. For purposes of this exercise, the referential integrity constraints, usually documented behind the scenes, are shown explicitly. The letters in parentheses next to the relationship names describe the referential integ-

---

1. Your author wishes to express his particular appreciation to John Hall for his assistance with this chapter.

rity rules: The symbol "(c)" designates the "cascade" rule that if an occurrence of a parent entity type is deleted, all children are to be deleted. The symbol "(r)" is for the "restricted" rule that a parent may not be deleted if children exist.

The central entity type in this model is CONTRACT, which is an agreement by a PARTY to pay for specified ASSET TYPES which are to be supplied by another PARTY. A CONTRACT must be *composed of* one or more LINE ITEMS, each of which is *to buy* a particular ASSET TYPE. Note the "(c)" by the relationship from CONTRACT to LINE ITEM. This means that if a CONTRACT is deleted, all its associated LINE ITEMS will be deleted as well. The "(r)" by the *from* and *to* relationships between PARTY and CONTRACT means that a PARTY cannot be deleted if any CONTRACTS are associated with it.

An ASSET TYPE is the definition of a product, material, or other physical thing of interest to the organization. A PHYSICAL ASSET is a physical example of an ASSET TYPE. An ASSET TYPE, for example, could be an IBM ThinkPad Model 600, as described in IBM's advertising. A PHYSICAL ASSET, then, is the ThinkPad 600 (serial number 47-DCH54) owned by your author.

A PHYSICAL ASSET must be either a DISCRETE ITEM—uniquely identifiable with a serial number or something similar—or an INVENTORY—a quantity of undifferentiated things. The aforementioned author's computer is an example of a DISCRETE ITEM, while a collection of 50 light switches in a hardware store is an example of an INVENTORY.

Because a PHYSICAL ASSET is a physical example of an ASSET TYPE, it must be *(currently) located at* one and only one SITE. A SITE, in turn, is a location which serves a particular function, such as a warehouse location or a work center.

The entity type representing transactions that move material in, out, and through the plant is MOVEMENT. When a PHYSICAL ASSET is received against a purchasing CONTRACT, for example, a MOVEMENT (a RECEIPT) is recorded *from* the PARTY (PERSON or ORGANIZATION) that sold it *to* a particular SITE. Should the PHYSICAL ASSET be found to be faulty, it may be returned via another MOVEMENT (a RETURN) *from* the SITE *to* the PARTY that sold it.

Sometimes it is necessary simply to transfer material *from* one SITE *to* another, so TRANSFER records this. Sometimes the meaning of MOVEMENT can also be extended to include INVENTORY ADJUSTMENTS based on physical counts of the INVENTORY, and these INVENTORY ADJUSTMENTS increase or reduce the balance. An increase can be recorded as a MOVEMENT *to* an INVENTORY with no "from" indicated, and a decrease can be recorded as a MOVEMENT *from* an inventory with no "to" identified.

To summarize, each MOVEMENT may be *from* a SITE or *from* a PARTY and may be *to* a SITE or *to* a PARTY.

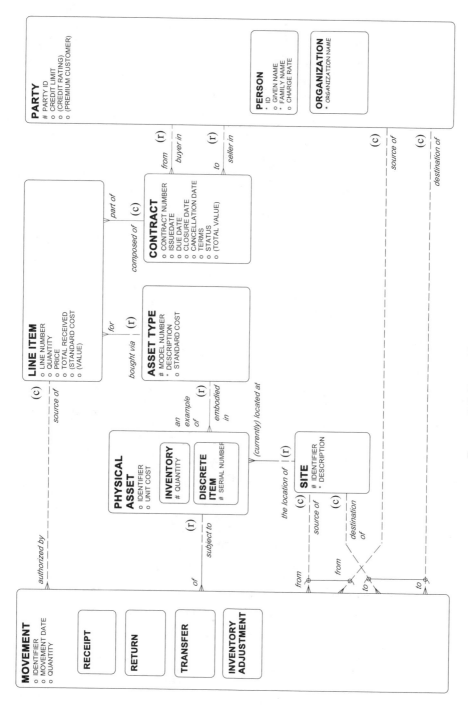

FIGURE 7.4 Entity / Relationship Model.

Note the **business rules** that say when a MOVEMENT is *of* INVENTORY *from* one SITE, the "Quantity" of the INVENTORY at that SITE must be reduced by the "Quantity" of the MOVEMENT. At the same time, if the MOVEMENT is *to* another SITE, the "Quantity" of the INVENTORY at the destination SITE must be increased by the MOVEMENT "Quantity". If a single DISCRETE ITEM is moved, the link to its SITE must be disconnected and a new link to the destination SITE must be created.

Events

Each entity type is primarily controlled by the following events:

Party:	What events cause a PARTY...	
	...to be born?	PARTY recognized
	...to be changed?	PARTY data found incorrect
	...to die?[a]	PARTY no longer needed
Site:	What events cause a SITE...	
	...to be born?	New SITE recognized
	...to be changed?	SITE description is incorrect
	...to die?	SITE not needed
Asset type:	What events cause an ASSET TYPE...	
	...to be born?	New ASSET TYPE recognized
	...to be changed?	ASSET TYPE data found incorrect
	...to die?	ASSET TYPE discontinued
Physical asset:	What events cause a PHYSICAL ASSET...	
	...to be born?	DISCRETE ITEM received (not last)
		DISCRETE ITEM received (last)
	...to be born?	INVENTORY defined
	...to be changed?	INVENTORY quantity found to be incorrect
		INVENTORY found unsatisfactory (not last)
		INVENTORY found unsatisfactory (last)
	...to move?	Transfer of PHYSICAL ASSET required
	...to die?	INVENTORY no longer needed (and
	...to die?	DISCRETE ITEM no longer needed (and destroyed)
	...to die?	DISCRETE ITEM found unsatisfactory (not last)

DISCRETE ITEM found unsatisfactory (last)

Contract: What events cause a CONTRACT...

...to be born?	CONTRACT issued
...to be changed?	CONTRACT found incorrect
	CONTRACT closed
...to die?	CONTRACT no longer needed (and canceled)
...to die?	CONTRACT found obsolete (and canceled)

Line item: What events cause a LINE ITEM...

...to be born?	New LINE ITEM needed
...to be changed?	"Price" incorrect
	"Quantity" incorrect
	PHYSICAL ASSET received (not last)
	PHYSICAL ASSET received (last)
	PHYSICAL ASSET found unsatisfactory (not last)
	PHYSICAL ASSET found unsatisfactory (last)
...to die?	LINE ITEM no longer needed

a.   *Note that to "die" in this case may simply mean to be rendered inoperative, not necessarily to be physically deleted from a database.*

Event/Entity Type Matrix

A first cut at describing the functions affecting each entity type is the *function/entity type matrix* (also known as the CRUD matrix). As stated above, an essential activity is the complete response to an event. Each event listed above, therefore, will trigger an essential activity or, in these terms, a function. The function/entity type matrix, then, can be modified to be an "event/entity type" matrix. Table 7.1, then, shows all of the events affecting each entity type.

A few things should be noted about this matrix. First, where a relationship is "restricted" [represented by "(r)" on the data model], an attempt to delete one entity type "reads" the controlling entity type to see if the deletion is permitted. For example, the event "ASSET TYPE discontinued" reads the entity type LINE ITEM to see if it can be done. Similarly, where a relationship "cascades", the deletion of the parent entity type also deletes all the children. For example, discontinuance of an ASSET TYPE also deletes all related occurrences of MOVEMENT. This means it "deletes" MOVEMENT.

Also, whenever a child is created (for example, INVENTORY), the parent entity types are "read" (in this case, SITE and ASSET TYPE).

Note: In the above list, these are *events*—something that happens in the world—not our reaction to what happens. Consequently, for example, you have "DISCRETE ITEM no longer needed", not "DISCRETE ITEM destroyed". For clarity, though, in some cases, the typical response is included in parentheses.

TABLE 7.1 Event / Entity Type Matrix

#	Event	Party	Site	Asset type	Physical asset	Contract	Line item	Work order	Move-ment
	Party								
1	PARTY recognized	C							
2	PARTY data found incorrect	U							
3	PARTY no longer needed	D				R			D
	Site								
4	New SITE recognized		C						
5	SITE description is incorrect		U						
6	SITE not needed		D		R				D
	Asset Type								
7	ASSET TYPE recognized			C					
8	ASSET TYPE data found incorrect			U					
9	ASSET TYPE discontinued			D	R		R		
	Asset								
10	PHYSICAL ASSET received (not last)		R(DI)[a]	R(DI)	U(Inv) C(DI)			U	C (Receipt)
11	PHYSICAL ASSET received (last)		R(DI)	R(DI)	U(Inv) C(DI)	U		U	C (Receipt)
12	PHYSICAL ASSET found unsatisfactory (not last)				U(Inv) D(DI)			U	C (Inv Return) D (DI)
13	PHYSICAL ASSET found unsatisfactory (last)				U(Inv) C(DI)	U		U	C (Inv Return) D (DI)
14	New INVENTORY defined		R	R	C				

TABLE 7.1 Event / Entity Type Matrix (Continued)

#	Event	Party	Site	Asset type	Physical asset	Contract	Line item	Work order	Move-ment
15	INVENTORY "quantity" found to be incorrect				U				C (Inv. Adj.
16	Transfer of PHYSICAL ASSET required		R(DI)		U[b]				C (Transfer)
17	INVENTORY no longer needed (and discontinued)				D(Inv)				D
18	DISCRETE ITEM no longer needed (and destroyed)				D(DI)				D
	Contracts								
19	CONTRACT issued	R		R		C	C		
20	CONTRACT found incorrect					U			
21	CONTRACT deemed incomplete (and closed)					U			
22	CONTRACT no longer needed (and canceled)					U			
23	CONTRACT found obsolete (and deleted)					D	D		D
	Line Item								
24	New LINE ITEM needed			R		R	C		
25	Price incorrect						U		
26	Quantity incorrect						U		
27	LINE ITEM no longer needed			R			D		D

a. "Inv" means INVENTORY; "DI" means DISCRETE ITEM.

b. Note that if the movement is of INVENTORY, then two occurrences of INVENTORY are affected—the "from" INVENTORY and the "to" INVENTORY.

Asset Type

An entity life history always has an entity type in the center of the top of the diagram. This is the entity type whose history is being characterized. The events that affect it are shown as boxes below it. There are three constructs for these boxes:

- *Sequence*—the events on a row will be encountered in the sequence shown. This is the case if there are no special markings.
- *Iteration*—an event may occur one or more times, or not at all. This is shown by an asterisk (*) in the upper right corner of the event box.
- *Selection*—only one of the events shown in a row may occur for each occurrence of the event above. This is shown by a small circle (o) in the upper right corner of the event box.

Figure 7.5 shows the entity type ASSET TYPE, with its attributes "Model number", "Description", and "Standard Cost". The first row below the entity type is an example of "sequence", in that each occurrence of ASSET TYPE must first be "recognized", have a "life", and ultimately become "discontinued". Note that there are no special marks on these boxes.

"Asset type life" consists of "Asset type event", an example of an "iteration". This is shown by an asterisk in the upper right corner of the box. During an "Asset type life" an ASSET TYPE may have one or more "Asset type events" or none.

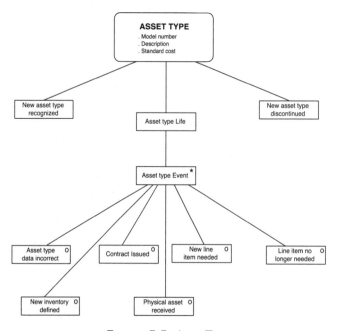

FIGURE 7.5 Asset Type.

Below "ASSET TYPE event" is example of "selection". For each "Asset type event", one and only one of the following events may occur:

- "ASSET TYPE data incorrect", resulting in correction of the data,
- "CONTRACT issued", including the creation of associated LINE ITEMS referring to existing ASSET TYPES. (See the discussion of LINE ITEM below on page 276.)
- "New LINE ITEM needed", calling for creaticn of a LINE ITEM that refers to an existing ASSET TYPE.
- "LINE ITEM no longer needed", calling for deletion of the association between a line item and this ASSET TYPE.
- "New INVENTORY defined", resulting in creation of an INVENTORY of an ASSET TYPE.
- "PHYSICAL ASSET received", creating an occurrence of a PHYSICAL ASSET that is an example of the ASSET TYPE.

Note that the set of events that constitute the "leaves" of the hierarchy tree correspond exactly to events in the function/entity type matrix (Table 7.1, above).

Physical Asset

Figure 7.6 shows the entity life history for PHYSICAL ASSET. The PHYSICAL ASSET entity type is shown, along with its sub-types INVENTORY and DISCRETE ITEM. That is, as described above, a PHYSICAL ASSET must be either a specific DISCRETE ITEM, identified uniquely with a "Serial number", or simply an INVENTORY, whose "Quantity" may vary over time. Note that the attribute of PHYSICAL ASSET, "Identifier", is "inherited", so it applies both to DISCRETE ITEM and INVENTORY. (An "Identifier" is simply a sequence number uniquely identifying each PHYSICAL ASSET.)

A particular PHYSICAL ASSET begins its life when it is recognized, either by receipt of a DISCRETE ITEM or by definition of an INVENTORY.

The center of the diagram shows that a PHYSICAL ASSET'S "Physical asset life" consists of one or more "Physical asset events", or it may have none at all. Each "Physical asset event", in turn, must be either a "Movement life", or a "Reference life".

Note that, since there can be one or more "Physical asset events", one of them can be a "Movement life" and another can be a "Reference life". It is just that a single "Physical asset event" can be only one of those.

An occurrence of "Movement life" may consist of one or more "Movements". Each "Movement", then, must be affected by one of the events shown in the next row:

- "INVENTORY received", which updates the "quantity" of an INVENTORY
- "INVENTORY found unsatisfactory", which results in a MOVEMENT of the INVENTORY being returned to a vendor (the "quantity" is returned to its original value)

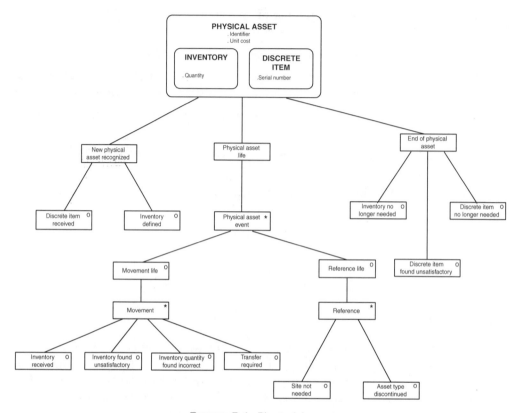

FIGURE 7.6 Physical Asset.

- "INVENTORY "quantity" found incorrect", which results in its being updated
- "Transfer of PHYSICAL INVENTORY required", which results in either a DISCRETE ITEM being unlinked from one SITE and linked to another, or one INVENTORY "Quantity" being reduced and another incremented

An occurrence of "Reference life", similarly, consists of one or more occurrences of "Reference", where each "Reference" must be the occurrence of either "SITE not needed" or "ASSET TYPE discontinued". In either case, the event results in an attempt to delete the specified entity type. This in fact may be thwarted by the existence of a PHYSICAL ASSET.

The effect of this structure is that a PHYSICAL ASSET event may be a combination of movements—say, receipt of INVENTORY plus finding INVENTORY unsatisfactory. Similarly, a PHYSICAL ASSET event may consist of more than one reference.

The "End of a PHYSICAL ASSET" must be from either "INVENTORY no longer needed (and discontinued)", a "DISCRETE ITEM found unsatisfactory" (and returned to a vendor), or a "DISCRETE ITEM no longer needed (and destroyed)".

Site

Figure 7.7 shows the entity life history for SITE. SITE is shown as an entity type with the attributes "Identifier" and "Description". A site's life begins with a "New SITE recognized" and ends with a "SITE not needed". In between, its "SITE life" consists of one or more "SITE events". Each "SITE event" either recognizes that a "new INVENTORY [is] defined", identifies that the "site description is incorrect", recognizes that a DISCRETE ITEM is received, or recognizes that a "transfer (in) is required". Note that other events that affect INVENTORY do not directly affect SITE, so they are not shown here. (In fact, SITE may be read for its "description", for example, but for simplicity this is not shown.)

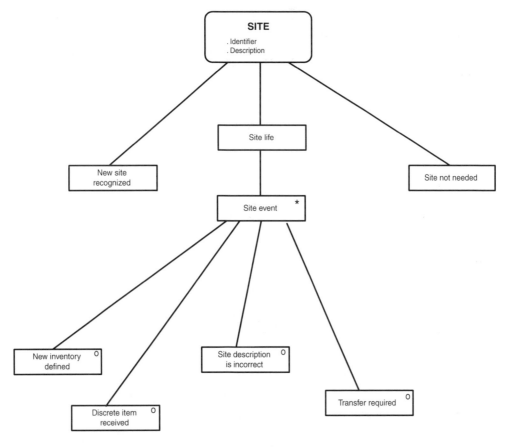

FIGURE 7.7 Site.

Note that the same Site event may appear in more than one entity life history. "Transfer (of a physical asset) required" affects both SITE and PHYSICAL ASSET.

Contract

Figure 7.8 shows the entity life history for CONTRACT. CONTRACT is shown with attributes for "Contract number", various dates, "Terms", and "Status". A particular contract begins with "CONTRACT issued" and ends with a three-step process involving first being complete, then ending, and then finally being deleted when it is found to be obsolete. In between, as with the other entity life histories we have seen, is "CONTRACT life".

Specifically, the contract's life consists of one or more "Contract events", where each "Contract event" must be either:

- "CONTRACT found incorrect", resulting in corrections being made to it,
- "PARTY no longer needed", resulting in an attempt to delete the PARTY, which is thwarted because of the existence of the CONTRACT, OR
- "New LINE ITEM needed", resulting in the addition of a LINE ITEM to the CONTRACT.

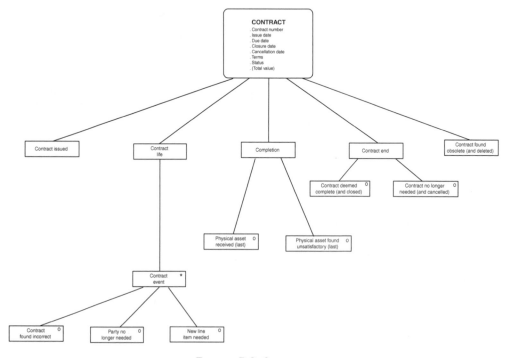

FIGURE 7.8 Contract.

As was seen in the state/transition diagram for PURCHASE ORDER in Figure 7.2, ending a CONTRACT takes place in one of two ways. Either it can be completed and closed, or it may be cancelled. That model is not concerned if it is physically deleted.

First, the "PHYSICAL ASSET received (*last*)" (on the last LINE ITEM) changes the "status" attribute of CONTRACT" from "pending" to "complete". If one or more of the purchased PHYSICAL ASSETS are found unsatisfactory, they are returned to the vendor that sold them. Until the last occurrence of this, the state of the CONTRACT is unaffected by receipt of items against it. (It might be appropriate to record receipt of a "not last" PHYSICAL ASSET on a LINE ITEM (see next section), but it is not appropriate to record that fact on a CONTRACT). If the last occurrence of "PHYSICAL ASSET found unsatisfactory" happens after the last occurrence of "PHYSICAL ASSET received", this will be the transaction which completes the CONTRACT.

The policy of the company may be to consider the CONTRACT closed simply by virtue of having been complete. In this example, however, it is necessary for someone specifically to deem it complete and close it. This is one of the options for "CONTRACT end". An alternative way for a CONTRACT to end is to discover that it is "no longer needed" and cancel it. In the state/transition diagram for PURCHASE ORDER in Figure 7.2, this event changed its state to "Cancelled".

At some later date, regardless of how the contract was completed and ended, and depending on policies and schedules for archiving, the CONTRACT occurrence is "found obsolete" and physically deleted ("CONTRACT deletion").

Line Item

Figure 7.9 shows the entity life history for a component of a CONTRACT, the LINE ITEM. Normally, the LINE ITEM is born at the same time as the CONTRACT ("Contract issued"). Once the CONTRACT has been created, however, LINE ITEMS may be added or dropped. The former ("New line item needed") is an event that is part of "Line item birth", while the latter ("Line item no longer needed") is part of "Line item end".

"Line item life", like other lives, may consist of one or more "Line item events". Two events trigger changes to LINE ITEM data ("Price incorrect" or "Quantity incorrect"). Other events include "Receipt of PHYSICAL ASSET (not last)" and "PHYSICAL ASSET not satisfactory (not last)". The "not last" means that all receipts and returns other than the last ones simply update or query the LINE ITEM without affecting its life span. The last receipt or the last return is the signal that the LINE ITEM'S life is over.

The options for ending a LINE ITEM'S life are more complicated. A LINE ITEM can end its life as a "Normal line item end", or it can be canceled when a "LINE ITEM [is] no longer needed". The normal end for a line item consists of "Receipt of physical asset (last)" or "physical asset not satisfactory (last)".

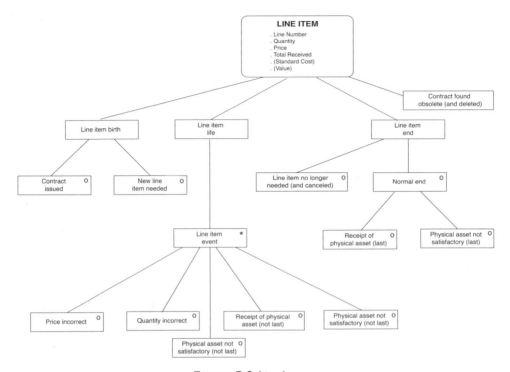

FIGURE 7.9 Line Item.

Movement

Figure 7.10 shows the entity life history for MOVEMENT. Note that since MOVEMENT is a transaction entity type, occurrences are normally only created, although the first row shows the possibility of a MOVEMENT's being both created and deleted.

Creation may be triggered by one of the four events shown in the third row under "Creation":

- "PHYSICAL ASSET received", which creates a MOVEMENT, as well as either creating an occurrence of DISCRETE ITEM or updating the "Quantity" of an INVENTORY
- Transfer [of a PHYSICAL ASSET] required, which results in a MOVEMENT that represents either a DISCRETE ITEM's being unlinked from one SITE and linked to another, or one INVENTORY's "Quantity" being reduced and another's incremented
- PHYSICAL ASSET not satisfactory, which results in a MOVEMENT that represents the PHYSICAL ASSET's being returned to a vendor.
- INVENTORY quantity incorrect, which results in creation of a MOVEMENT to adjust it.

There are six circumstances under which a MOVEMENT transaction might be deleted:

- The PARTY to which or from which things were moved is no longer needed (and deleted).
- The SITE to which or from which things were moved is no longer needed (and deleted).
- The DISCRETE ITEM that was moved is no longer needed (and deleted).
- INVENTORY no longer needed (and discontinued).
- The LINE ITEM under which the MOVEMENT took place is no longer needed (and deleted).
- CONTRACT found obsolete (and deleted).

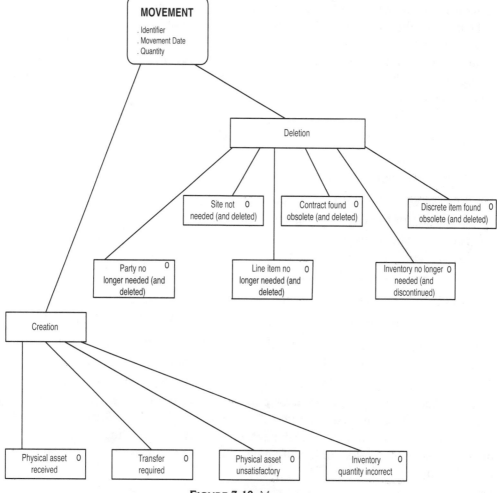

FIGURE 7.10 Movement.

Activity Fragments

So far, we have diagrammed the relationships between events and entity types (or object classes). The next assignment is to fold in the functions (or activities). In this context we will call them activity fragments, since they are described at a very low level of detail. Specifically, activity fragments are described in terms of the specific actions taken on various entity types in response to each event. In object-oriented terms these are the behaviors or "methods" of each entity type in response to each event or "message".

The principles of essential systems analysis say that the atomic process in the functional analysis of a business is that which is a complete response to an event. In other words, each of the events portrayed here triggers a single essential business activity. Moreover, each business event is atomic. And, while there may be component activities that constitute the way the work is carried out, the essential activity must complete in order to pass an entity from one business state to another. That is, complete external events and essential business activities have a one-to-one correspondence. To write programs, however, it is necessary to break these activities down into the manipulations appropriate to managing a body of data.

So, for example, the event "CONTRACT issued" would be implemented by an essential activity, but this can be described by eight activity fragments:

1. Create CONTRACT.
2. Tie CONTRACT to *from* PARTY.
3. Tie CONTRACT to *to* PARTY.
4. Create one or more LINE ITEMS, and tie them to a CONTRACT.
5. Set CONTRACT (Issue date).
6. Set CONTRACT (Due date).
7. Set CONTRACT (Status) to "open".
8. Set CONTRACT (Terms).

(The activity fragments for each of the other events are described in Table 7.3, below.)

To understand how each of these activities works, however, it is necessary to understand the predicates of each of the entity types they will act upon.

Predicates (attributes and relationships) of some of the entity types are shown in Table 7.2. Each attribute is shown to be a fixed or replaceable attribute, a fixed relationship,[2] or part of the unique identifier. This determines, among other things, whether the predicate can be changed, once it is set. An activity fragment may change the value of a replaceable predicate, but it could never change the value of a unique identifier or a fixed predicate.

---

2. For the sake of this exercise, all relationships are assumed to be fixed. In a real situation it is possible that events could have the affect of reassigning a relationship to a different occurrence of an entity type.

TABLE 7.2 Predicates

	Entity Type	Predicate	Predicate Type
1.	ASSET TYPE	Model number	Unique identifier
		Description	Replaceable attribute
		Standard cost	Replaceable attribute
2-a.	INVENTORY	(PHYSICAL ASSET) identifier	Inherited unique identifier
		(PHYSICAL ASSET) unit cost	Inherited replaceable attribute
		Quantity	Replaceable attribute
		an example of ASSET TYPE	Inherited relationship
		(currently) located at SITE	Inherited relationship
2-b.	DISCRETE ITEM	(PHYSICAL ASSET) identifier	Inherited unique identifier
		(PHYSICAL ASSET) unit cost	Inherited replaceable attribute
		Serial number	Fixed attribute
		an example of ASSET TYPE	Inherited relationship
		(currently) located at SITE	Inherited relationship
3.	SITE	Site identifier	Unique identifier
		Description	Replaceable attribute
4.	CONTRACT	Contract number	Unique identifier
		Issue date	Fixed attribute
		Due date	Replaceable attribute
		Closure date	Fixed attribute
		Cancelation date	Fixed attribute
		Terms	Replaceable attribute
		Status	Replaceable attribute
		from PARTY	Fixed relationship
		to PARTY	Fixed relationship
5.	LINE ITEM	Line number	Part of compound unique identifier
		Quantity	Replaceable attribute
		Price	Replaceable attribute
		Total received	Calculated attribute
		part of CONTRACT	Relationship, part of compound unique identifier

TABLE 7.2 Predicates (Continued)

	Entity Type	Predicate	Predicate Type
		for ASSET TYPE	Fixed relationship
6.	MOVEMENT	Movement identifier	Unique identifier
		Movement date	Fixed attribute
		Quantity	Fixed attribute
		from SITE	Fixed relationship
		from PARTY	Fixed relationship
		to SITE	Fixed relationship
		to PARTY	Fixed relationship
		authorized by CONTRACT	Fixed relationship

These predicates are an important aspect of the activity fragments that take place in response to events.

There are five combinations of parent and child deaths.

- Parent's death kills current children.
- Parent's death occurs after child's death.
- Parent's death does not affect current children but prevents new children.
- The death of the last child causes parent's death. (A soft example of this is the situation where closure of the last LINE ITEM closes the CONTRACT.)
- Parent's death cuts a changeable relationship from parent to child.

Table 7.3 lists the activity fragments which respond to the events in CONTRACT's entity life history.

TABLE 7.3 Activity Fragments

CONTRACT issued

1. Create CONTRACT.
2. Tie CONTRACT to *from* PARTY.
3. Tie CONTRACT to *to* PARTY.
4. Create one or more LINE ITEMS, and tie them to a CONTRACT.
5. Set CONTRACT (Issue date).
6. Set CONTRACT (Due date).
7. Set CONTRACT (Status) to "open".
8. Set CONTRACT (Terms).

CONTRACT found incorrect

9. Update CONTRACT (Terms).

10. Update CONTRACT (Due date).

PARTY no longer needed

11. Prevent deletion of PARTY

New LINE ITEM needed

12. (4, above)

PHYSICAL ASSET received (last)

13. Update CONTRACT (status) = "complete".

PHYSICAL ASSET found unsatisfactory (last)

14. Update CONTRACT (status) = "open".

CONTRACT deemed complete (and closed)

15. Update CONTRACT (status) = "closed".

16. Update CONTRACT (closure date).

CONTRACT no longer needed (and cancelled)

17. Update CONTRACT (status) = "canceled".

18. Update contract (cancellation date).

CONTRACT found obsolete (and deleted)

19. Cut CONTRACT occurrence from *from* PARTY.

20. Cut CONTRACT occurrence from *to* PARTY.

21. Delete each LINE ITEM for this occurrence of CONTRACT.

22. Delete contract occurrence.

The activity fragments shown in Table 7.3 fall into the following categories:

- Occurrences are created, initializing key attributes and sometimes other (fixed and replaceable) attributes.
- Relationships between a parent and its children may be tied, cut, or swapped.
- "Non-key" attributes may be set. Replaceable attributes may be replaced, initialized, incremented, or decremented as frequently as necessary.
- Unique identifier attributes may not be changed. Fixed attributes and non-changeable relationships may not be changed once they are set, but they do not necessarily have to be set when the occurrence is created.
- Occurrences and their children (if permitted) may be destroyed, after being cut from their parents.

For each entity life history, then, for each event, we can identify the definition, tying, cutting, and updating required. Figure 7.11 shows the activity identifiers attached to each triggering event in the entity life history.

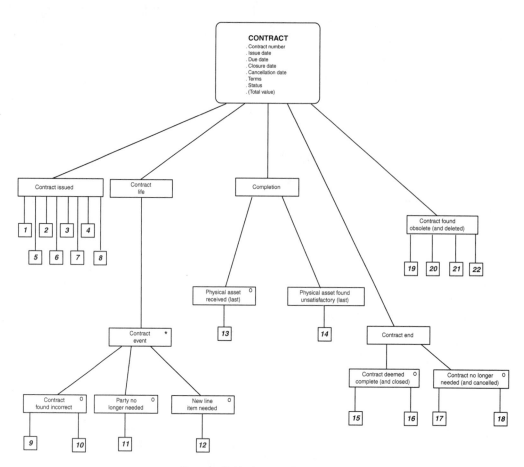

FIGURE 7.11 Activity Fragments.

The activity fragments shown here can be made more sophisticated by adding the use of state variables, but that is beyond the scope of this book. Also subject to further discussion is the process of rotating the model 90 degrees so as to capture the full effects of an event on all entity types. This model, called the *event process outline*, takes an event (such as "Contract cancellation") and shows the complete set of effects it has on various entity types. A variation on this latter technique is used in object-oriented design and called a *sequence diagram* in the UML.

The Requirements Analysis Deliverable— Column Five

Essentially, there are three kinds of deliverables from Column Five:

- State/transition diagrams from the business owners' perspectives
- State/transition diagrams from the architect's perspective
- Essential data flow diagrams (architect's perspective)
- Entity life histories (architect's perspective)

The business owner's state/transition diagram is a very good way of understanding the interactions of events, entity types, and processes. In addition to its use for planning systems, it is also very useful for business process re-engineering.

The architect's state/transition diagram forms a good basis for developing the entity life history, which has more detail about the nature of entity types' reactions to events.

The events that are identified in the state/transition diagram and the entity life history then can be the basis for developing essential data flow diagrams.

Timing and the Other Columns

Timing and Data

Understanding the structure of data, as revealed in an entity/relationship diagram, does not reveal the true nature of the entities involved. It is in the life history—the succession of states—that this is revealed. State/transition diagrams show that sequence of states. Entity life histories show how timing (events) determine the passage of entities from one state to another.

Timing and Activities

In the search for understanding of the true nature of the functions of an organization, the event as a stimulus causing functions to occur is the answer. Recall that in several modeling techniques it was significant that communications could be either simple data or messages (triggers, events) causing an action to take place.

Functions can also be divided and organized in many different ways, but the set of event types that can affect a company ultimately must be the basis for any rational organization of those functions.

Timing and Locations

As described in Chapter 6, everything in a company takes place somewhere. Events and state changes are no different, although they are usually located in the same place as the entity types whose states are being changed. More than that, however, location can affect the way we define what constitutes an external event. We have repeatedly said that internal events—one activity's triggering another—are not our concern. The problem is when a closely related department is, in fact, in a remote location. If they were in the same place, the activity in one department would trigger the activity in another, but both would be part of a single essential activity, because both were components of a reaction to something happening in the world. If, on the other hand, the organization performing the first action were in New York City and the organization performing the second were in Los Angeles, the trigger would certainly look like an external event to the people in Los Angeles. This has to be accounted for during analysis.

Timing, People, and Organizations

In the cybernetic model of the organization presented in Chapter 5, the main topic is communications, with no distinction being made between simple data and events. One event that was significant, however, was an operation's going outside its operating values (set points). Ultimately, this is the event that requires the management entity to act. Of all the events that management must respond to from the outside world, this is the one internal event that is critical.

The analysis project should clarify which events affect which parts of the organization.

Timing and Motivation

Goals and strategies typically are not expressed in terms of time or the events to which they are responding. Objectives and tactics must be so expressed, however. Business policies and business rules often deal with external events and recommended ways of dealing with them.

One way to discover rules is to study events and determine the decisions made in response to each.

Conclusion

Entity life histories bring together in one model the entity types (object classes), events, activities, and activity fragments that constitute an organization's essential activities. They present the effects of events and activity fragments on entity types in more business-oriented terms than does a simple function/entity type matrix, and they prepare the way for the object-oriented thinking about the *behavior* of entity types.

Entity life histories are particularly useful when significant entity types have sequential behavior. This is especially true when analyzing how sequences may be broken and how they can be repaired.

Column Six: Motivation

Introduction

Interest in business rules is not a recent phenomenon, but its role in systems development has escalated significantly in recent years. Figure 8.1 shows the Architecture Framework with Column Six highlighted.

When the computer industry began, there were programs. All attention was paid to writing programs that performed functions. Beginning in the 1970s and more fully during the 1980s, people began to focus on data. Then, John Zachman published his architecture in 1987, adding location, reflecting the fact that distributed systems were all the rage. In 1992, he and John Sowa expanded these notions of "what", "how", and "where" to include "who", "when", and "why": people and organizations, timing, and motivation. The first five elements were fairly well understood. It was less clear what to do with "why".

It seemed that from the scope point of view motivation consists of things like mission and vision, and the business owners' views are concerned with things like objectives and goals, but none of this was formalized, and it was uncertain what should be done with the other rows.

	Data (What)	Activities (How)	Locations (Where)	People (Who)	Time (When)	Motivation (Why)
Objectives / Scope (Planner's view)	List of things important to the enterprise - Term 1 - Term 2 - Term 3 ...	List of processes the enterprise performs - Function 1 - Function 2 - Function 3 ...	List of enterprise locations	Organization approaches	Business master schedule	Business vision and mission - Vision ... - Mission ...
Enterprise model (Business Owners' Views)	Language, divergent data model	Business process model	Logistics network	Organi-zation chart	State / transition diagram	Business strategies, tactics, policies, rules
Model of Funda-mental Concepts (Architect's View)	Convergent e/r model	Essential data flow diagram	Locations of roles	The viable system, use cases	Entity Life History	Business rule model
Technology Model (Designer's View)	Data base design	System design, program structure	Hardware, software distribution	User interface, security design	Control structure	Business rule design
Detailed Represen-tation (Builder's View)	Physical storage design	Detailed program design	Network architecture, protocols	Screens, security coding	Timing definitions	Rule specification program logic
Functioning System	*(Working System)*					
	Converted data	Executable programs	Communi-cations facilities	Trained people	Business events	Enforced rules

FIGURE 8.1 The Architect Framework—Motivation.

At about the same time, Ronald G. Ross recognized that the rules determining the integrity of a business's data were not adequately dealt with in the systems development process:

> Specific integrity rules [of an enterprise], even though "shared" and universal,... traditionally have not been captured in the context of its [data] models. Instead, they usually have been stated vaguely (if at all) in largely uncoordinated analytical and design documents, and then buried deep in the logic of application programs. Since application programs are notoriously unreliable in the consistent and correct application of such rules, this has been the source of considerable frustration and error. It sometimes also has led, unjustly, to distrust of the data model itself [Ross, 1987, p. 102].

In the early 1990s business rules and the "why" column began to come together with the formation of The Business Rules Group as a project within GUIDE, IBM's user group. In 1994, Mr. Ross then published the first edition of his *Business Rules Book*, and Barbara von Halle began writing articles on business rules for the data industry magazine, *Data Base Programming and Design*.

Suddenly business rules began to attract attention as a way of improving systems by better describing the world they addressed.

It was discovered that just describing what processing should be done and what data should be manipulated was not sufficient. There are rules and constraints that control processing and that constrain data values—and failure to address these is failure to address a major part of the effort.

In 1988, for example, one analyst dutifully prepared data models and function models for a large communications company and turned these over to a programmer, so that the latter could produce a system to process invoices. It quickly became evident, however, that very complex rules were associated with the invoices and the accounts to which they should be credited. These were not described in the analyst's models. The programmer was now forced to spend many hours with the accountants to learn these rules—something that should have been done by the analyst. [1]

Since business rules are derived from business policies, and these in turn are the direct implementation of business goals and objectives, they seemed at home in Column Six, the "why" column.

One of Mr. Ross' insights was that, contrary to what might be supposed, in the context of system development a business rule is ultimately about data, not about processing. It is a constraint on what data may or must be updated. If a particular row in a table can be updated only when certain constraints are met, it does not matter which process is trying to do the updating: The rule lives with the data.

---

1. Yes, that analyst would be your author.

To be sure, the rules themselves are not part of the data, even though they act upon them. Indeed, business rules are often implemented through program processing. In recent years there has been a movement to build "rules engines" specifically to separate the definition and execution of business rules both from the database and from other processing. But again, if a rule constrains what can be updated in a database, that rule applies no matter what processes try to do the updating.

In 1995 The Business Rules Group (the GUIDE organization mentioned above) published a white paper, *Business Rules: What Are They Really?*, describing the nature of business rules from a Row Three perspective. This addressed the question of how rules interact with data, and it described categories of rules from the architect's Row Three perspective. In 2000 The Business Rules Group published a second paper, *Organizing Business Plans: The Standard Model for Business Rule Motivation,* describing the business owners' Row Two approach to business rules. The paper presents a data model of such concepts as "mission", "vision", "strategy", "tactics", and so forth. It discusses a business's ends and means and the role that rules and business policies play in establishing and managing these. It defines more precisely than ever before these motivation terms, which tend to be used cavalierly in modern business.

The second paper describes why a business does what it does, while the first paper describes why a system should behave the way it does.

The Business Rules Group Motivation Model is shown in Appendix C. This was created without cardinality or optionality designations. An extended model with these included is in Appendix D.

Most recently, in 2002, Ms. von Halle has published an extensive discussion of business rules, *Business Rules Applied*. In it she describes in detail just how business rules should be captured and organized as part of a system development project.

The first part of this chapter is based on the Business Rules Group Motivation model and on Ms. von Halle's book. The remainder is a description of various techniques for representing business rules.

Row One: Scope

Business Rules Applied begins its discussion of scope with a description of the "business context [that] includes the organization's mission, strategies, objectives, policies, and business performance metrics. These represent the reasons for the system and the measurements by which it will be deemed a success, even as it changes over time" [von Halle, 2002, p. 8]. In the book, Ms. von Halle goes on to say that as scope is being defined, it is important to establish that business rules will in fact be captured as a distinct part of the systems development effort.

The Business Rules Group, in its Motivation Model, asserts that the scope of an organization's motivation is its vision and mission. *Vision* is a statement about the future state of the enterprise, without regard to how it is to be achieved. That is, an automobile company's vision might be that it will be the foremost marketer of high-quality, prestige automobiles.

A *mission*, on the other hand, is the means to achieve a vision. It defines the ongoing operational activity of an enterprise. While expression of the mission is part of the "why" of an organization, it clearly drives the scope of the first five columns of the Architecture Framework. The car company's missions, then, might be to increase sales by 10% per year and to always be ranked in the top three by the J. D. Powers Company.

As we have done in this book, Ms. von Halle includes an organization's mission in the scope effort, in terms of its data, processes, locations, people and organizations, and events. To this she adds that scope should include definition of business performance metrics, business and technical constraints, and business and technical risks.

Thus, the vision and mission of an enterprise should be established before a system development project is launched. It is reasonable to believe that when a requirements analysis effort begins, the vision and its associated missions will be available to the requirements team. This provides priorities for a project, and with that an important part of its context. If these items are not initially available to the requirements team (which is often the case), it is to the team's advantage to seek them out.

Row Two: Business Owners' Views

When the time comes to analyze the enterprise from the business owners' viewpoint, the focus turns to the objectives, goals, strategies, and tactics that constitute business motivation at this level.

These are terms that are commonly used but rarely defined precisely. The Business Rules Group Motivation paper is an attempt to define them in a rigorous, precise way. That group's definitions follow here.[2] In addition, it is important to address the question of how to discover rules. In *Business Rules Applied*, Ms. von Halle has some useful tips as to how to do this, and these follow the definition sections below.

According to the Business Rules Group's Motivation Model, the business owners' views of motivation are in terms of

- Ends
  - Goal
  - Objective

---

2. The definitions are reproduced by permission of the Business Rules Group.

- Means
  - Cause of action
  - Element of guidance
- Assessment
- Influence

End

An *end* is a statement about what the business seeks to accomplish. The important thing to remember about an end is that it does not include any indication of *how* it will be achieved.

Analysis of an organization (a department or a whole enterprise) begins with examination of the ends of that organization. Previously, we saw that the enterprise's first end is its *vision.* That is a statement about the future state of the enterprise, without regard to how it is to be achieved. Another kind of end is *desired result*—a state or target that the enterprise intends to attain and maintain. While a vision is an end that is a statement about the future state of the enterprise, a desired result is an end that amplifies a vision. A desired result is either a goal or an objective.

Goal

A *goal* is a desired result that has the following characteristics:

- It is ongoing, usually described for an extended period of time.
- It is qualitative, rather than quantitative.
- It is expressed in general rather than specific terms.

More specifically, a goal is a statement about a general state or condition of the enterprise, which is to be brought about or sustained over time through appropriate means. A goal amplifies a vision and should be relatively narrowly defined. It can then be *quantified by* an objective. For example, a pizza parlor may have the goal of delivering pizza on time most of the time.

Objective

Another kind of desired result is an *objective.* This is a statement of a specific time-targeted, measurable, attainable target that an enterprise seeks to meet in order to achieve its goals. It quantifies a goal.

Compared to a goal, an objective is short-term and does not continue beyond its timeframe (which may be cyclical).

Specifically, an objective is:

- *Measurable*. It must include some explicit criteria for determining whether the objective is being met in practice. These criteria may be fairly exacting (for example, "to be on time 95% of the time"). At the very minimum, the criteria must provide a basis for making a yes-or-no determination (e.g., "the compressor must be up and running"). It should be noted that such criteria may be the basis for certain business rules, created specifically to compute or derive the relevant evaluation.
- *Attainable*. It is self-evident that objectives should be attainable. If they are not, the business plans are unrealistic and will likely fail.
- *Time oriented*. This is either an absolute time reference (e.g., "by January 1, 2001") or relative time reference (e.g., "within two years") that should be included in each objective. This timeframe indicates when the objective is to be met.

Our pizza company's objective is, for the next three months, to deliver each pizza within 30 minutes of the call.

Means

Revealing an organization's ends sheds new light on the means at its disposal to meet them. The Business Rules Group's Motivation Model presents means in a particularly interesting way.

The particular components of means are properly the subject of the other five columns of the Architecture framework—especially the activity models. Mission, strategies and tactics define the *direction* of the company, however, so they are discussed here. They should be captured as part of any requirements analysis project, regardless of how they are categorized.

A *means* is a device, capability, regime, technique, restriction, agency, instrument, or method that may be called upon, activated, or enforced to achieve one or more ends.

According to the Business Rules Group's Motivation Model, a means is either a course of action or an element of guidance.

Course of Action

A *course of action* is a means that is an approach or plan for configuring some aspect of the enterprise, involving things, processes, locations, people, timing, or motivation undertaken to achieve ends. It must be either a strategy or a tactic.

A *strategy* is a resource, skill, or competency that the enterprise can call upon—accepted by the enterprise as the *right* approach to achieve its goals, given the environmental constraints and risks. More than that, a strategy represents the right approach to achieve its goals, given the environmental constraints and risks the enterprise faces. A strategy for the pizza company could be to provide enough people and vehicles to meet demand. This is to address the goal of delivering pizza on time most of the time.

A *tactic* represents part of the detailing of a strategy. A strategy tends to be longer term and broader in scope, while a tactic tends to be shorter term and narrower in scope. In the pizza company, tactics include hiring three new people and buying one more van. This is to address the objective of delivering each pizza within 30 minutes of the call.

A strategy, then, implements one or more goals, while a tactic implements one or more objectives.

A strategy is a course of action that is *a component of* a plan for a mission. A tactic, in turn, is a course of action *to implement* a strategy. That is, a tactic is a particular set of steps taken to achieve a strategy, which in turn is a set of steps taken to achieve a mission.

Note that mission, strategies, and tactics are legitimate first levels in a function hierarchy, as it is developed as a Column Two activity model. This is described further in Chapter 4.

Courses of action may enable other courses of action. For example, one tactic, which is *to implement* a marketing strategy (such as an advertising campaign), might enable or increase the effectiveness of another tactic (such as a direct mail program).

Note, by the way, that a system development project itself is a course of action. Typically, it is in the nature of a tactic *to implement* a system development strategy. This means that in addition to the company's vision and mission referred to above, the context for any project must include articulation of the strategy it is to implement, along with the goals and objectives driving both the strategy and the tactics. Here is where the system development project is wedded to the enterprise's overall mission and strategies.

Element of Guidance

A second kind of means in the Business Rules Group Motivation Model is element of guidance. An *element of guidance* is either a business policy or a business rule. This is a declarative statement (or set of such statements) defining or constraining some aspect of an enterprise. It is intended to assert business structure or to control or influence the behavior of the enterprise.

A course of action may be constrained by one or more elements of guidance, and an element of guidance may be a constraint on one or more courses of action. Indeed, each element of guidance may either be the source of a course of action or a guide to it.

A *business policy* is an element of guidance that is a statement (or set of statements) whose purpose is to guide the enterprise. A *business rule,* on the other hand, is a specific directive, intended to influence or guide business behavior, *derived from* (in support of) a business policy. Business rules are the constraints that determine the everyday workings of business.

Each business policy may be composed of one or more other business policies and may be the basis for one or more business rules.

For example, a business policy may be that expenses are not reimbursed unless they are for business purposes. A business rule that supports this business policy may be that "entertainment expenses" that are not directly associated with marketing the company's products are not reimbursable.

An element of guidance must be subject to an *enforcement level*—a value that specifies the severity of action imposed in order to put or keep a business rule or business policy in force. A set of enforcement levels might include the following:

- "Strictly enforced"—if you violate the rule, you cannot escape the penalty.
- "Deferred enforcement"—strictly enforced, but enforcement may be delayed (e.g., waiting for a resource with required skills).
- "Pre-authorized override"—enforced, but exceptions are allowed with prior approval. (For example, if you call in, you may be late for work.)
- "Post-justified override"—if not approved, you may be punished. (If you explain why you were late, you may be able to get away with it.)
- "Override with explanation"—comment must be provided with violation.
- "Guideline"—not enforced.

An element of guidance may support one or more goals or objectives.

Assessment

An *assessment* is a measure of the effect an *influence* has on either a means or an end, where an *influence* in turn, is the act, process, or power of producing an effect without apparent exertion of tangible force or direct exercise of command. An influence is often without deliberate effort or intent. This could be an *external influence* such as technology, a supplier or vendor, or a regulation. Or it could be an *internal influence* such as the company's infrastructure, resource quality, or corporate culture.

An assessment asserts that the influence constitutes a *strength, weakness, opportunity,* or *threat* for an organization. (Some business analysts refer to these elements by the acronym "SWOT".) The influence is also expressed as either a risk or a potential reward (an impact value). This determination is a judgment about the influences in which these things operate.

A *strength* is an assessment that asserts that an influence can positively affect an enterprise's employment of either a means or the achievement of an end (an advantage or area of excellence, for example).

A *weakness* is an assessment that asserts that an influence exists within the enterprise that can have a negative impact on its employment of a means or achievement of an end (such as an area of inadequacy).

An *opportunity* is an assessment asserting that an influence (in this case, something in the environment) can have a favorable impact on the organization's employment of a means or the achievement of an end.

A *threat* is an assessment asserting that an influence (also something in the environment) can have an unfavorable impact on the organization's employment of a means or the achievement of an end.

An *impact value* is an evaluation that quantifies or qualifies an assessment in specific terms, types, or dimensions. An impact value is either a risk or a potential reward. An assessment in terms of *risk* indicates the possibility of a loss. This loss could be expressed either as a probability (e.g., "5% probability of a project's failing") or as an absolute number (e.g., "There is a risk that we will lose $500,000 on this venture.") An assessment in terms of *potential reward* indicates the possibility of a gain. As with risk, a potential reward may be expressed as a probability or an absolute number.

An assessment, then, is a judgment that an influence affects the employment of a means or the achievement of an end, in terms of that influence's risk or potential reward. Specifically, it asserts that an influence constitutes a weakness, a strength, an opportunity, or a threat *for* either an end or a means, *in terms of* an impact value (a risk or a potential reward).

The Business Rules Group paper presents as a case study a fictional car rental agency, EU-Rent. The assessments in that example include the following:

- It has an *opportunity* to reach its objective of increasing its market share (thereby achieving a potential reward) faster via the internal influence of changing its infrastructure—by opening a new office.

- It has a *threat* of failure to reach its objective (which represents a risk) from the same influence of changing its infrastructure—by opening a new office.

- It has a *strength* that offers a potential reward of meeting its objective of increased staff recruitment. This assertion of strength is a judgment about the internal influence of changing its infrastructure—by opening a new office.

- It appears to have a *weakness*, which is a risk it incurs that it will miss its objective of increased market share if the strategy doesn't work.

Discovering Rules

The business owner's view of motivation, then, comes down to his understanding of corporate mission, goals, and objectives, plus the business policies and rules he must work under to carry out these mission, goals, and objectives. The question now is, how do we find out what those rules are?

Ms. von Halle describes the discovery process in detail in *Business Rules Applied*. She distinguishes between discovering the initial requirements for addressing rules and discovering the details of the rules themselves.

To discover the initial requirements, she begins by analyzing the processes and events, such as those described in Chapters 4 and 7 here for essential data flow diagrams. Even if processes and events are not that rigorously modeled yet, they can be listed and mapped to each other early in the analysis process. One way to do this is via use cases, which can be structured to describe each event and the processes that are in response to it.

Once these interactions between events and processes have been identified, it is possible to identify the *decisions* implicit in each process. Whichever way a decision goes, by implication, one or more rules are in effect to determine the way that decision is made. It is possible to identify the mental processes associated with the decision, and from these to infer the existence of rules. Then, in the descriptions of these rules are things referenced and knowledge created. These elements can be correlated with the data model (or object class model) to be sure they are accounted for. Finally, this evaluation identifies the action taken as a result of this set of rules interacting with the event.

In short, orientation toward business rules during requirements analysis constitutes a move from simply discovering organizational behavior to unearthing decisions and rules behind it. "You quickly shift your focus from events and processes (the doing aspect) to the discovery and formal analysis of the decision making (the intellectual aspect) behind a business event" [von Halle, 2002, p. 73].

Once the decisions involving rules have been discovered, it is then a matter of following up to describe the rules themselves. This involves:

- Identifying sources—i.e., who can reveal and authenticate each rule?
- Defining a road map—from business events, optionally through use case steps, to business decisions, and then to rules
- Selecting or confirming standard ways of describing rules (some options are described below)
- Planning rule discovery time and commitment
- Authenticating the rules—verifying their correctness
- Giving the rules business value

From this point, the process merges with the Column One process of modeling data. That is, each rule is identified as to the entities, attributes, and relationships involved in its expression.

Row Three: Architect's View

The move during requirements analysis from the business owners' views of motivation to an architect's view is best described in terms of

- Classes of rules
- Quality criteria for defining a formal business rule
- Ways of expressing rules, including,
  - Natural language
  - Ron Ross notation
  - Object role modeling
  - Rule patterns

Classes of Rules

Ms. von Halle cites at least seven different schemes for classifying rules today [von Halle, 2002, pp. 29–30]. She then consolidates these, eliminating those specific to where they are from, or how they might be manipulated in a computer system to come up with the following scheme:

- Terms and definitions
- Facts
- Rules
  - Derivations
    - Mathematical derivations
    - Inferences
  - Constraints
    - Mandatory constraints
    - Suggested guidelines
  - Action-enabler rules

This is very similar to the scheme described in the first Business Rules Group Paper.

In addition to the classifications described here, mandatory constraints may be viewed in two additional categories:

- Data integrity constraints—constraints based on maintenance of the integrity of the data model
- Business-oriented constraints—constraints imposed by the business for its own reasons

Data integrity constraints can be inferred by studying the data model and looking to common sense. An example would be a rule that the "ship date" in a CONTRACT cannot be before the "order date".

A business-oriented constraint is based purely on business policies. For example, a business-oriented constraint might prohibit entry of an ORDER from a customer PARTY if the current CREDIT RATING "value" of the PARTY is below a specified threshold.

In some cases the model can help identify rules, but they must still be confirmed by the business community. For example, it may be the case that the dates of occurrences of an entity such as STATUS should not overlap. That is, the "Effective date" of one occurrence must be equal to (or not be before) the "Until date" of the previous occurrence. This seems reasonable, but it should be confirmed.

Terms and Definitions

A *term* is exactly what it sounds like. It is a word used in the business. More important is the *definition* of a term, the specification of a meaning for that term as it is used. By defining it, we recognize that it is a term of importance, and we specify exactly what it means. In an analysis project, this may not necessarily be easy, since terms are often not used consistently or coherently in common usage. One of the major assignments of the requirements analysis team is always to recognize what terms are important and to capture coherent and consistent definitions. This is often difficult.

Terms and definitions originate as the primary components of the business owners' views of a Column One data model. They are then refined to become the entity types of an architect's Column One data model.

Terms are often shown on the data model as entity type names and attribute names. In Figure 8.2, the entity types PARTY, CONTRACT, LINE ITEM, and so forth are all terms. So are the attributes "Contract Number", "Standard Cost", and so on. The definitions are not shown on the drawing, but these must be documented behind the scenes. CASE tools used to produce diagrams typically have a mechanism for capturing the definition of each entity type/term in a repository of some sort. Note, by the way, that there are many terms in an organization that will not show up in an entity/relationship model. These also should be captured and documented. As a product of the requirements analysis project, it is worthwhile to publish a glossary describing the entire vocabulary of the enterprise.

Facts

Facts also reside in the Column One data model. A *fact* is the linking of terms to produce useful concepts. Facts are what are presented in data models, when entities are related to each other, when attributes apply to entities, and when sub-types are defined.

In Figure 8.2, that a PARTY may be *a buyer in* a CONTRACT is a fact. That "Quantity" is an attribute of LINE ITEM is a fact. That PERSON is a sub-type of (that is, a kind of) PARTY is a fact. In the Business Rules Group's first paper, terms and facts are collectively referred to as "structural assertions".

Facts are represented on a data model by explicit relationships, the presence of attributes, and by the super-type/sub-type structures.

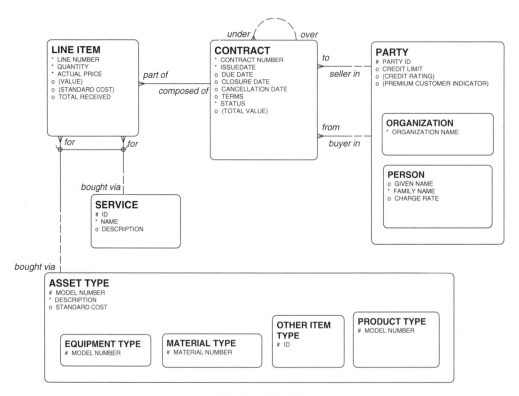

FIGURE 8.2 A Model of Contracts.

Rules

Rules can be either derivations, constraints, or action enabler rules. These are fully the domain of Column Six.

Derivations

A *derivation* is a rule that creates new information from existing information. This may be a *mathematical derivation*, which is a mathematical calculation. (For example, "Age" is equal to the "System Date" minus the "Birth Date".) Or it may be an *inference*, which is the drawing of logical conclusions from facts. (For example, if the scheduled "delivery date" has passed and the material hasn't been delivered, this implies that the shipment is "late".)

Derivations can be shown on the data model as attributes. The algorithm used to derive the attributes, however, *cannot* be shown in the model and must be documented in the repository supporting the drawings (along with the definition of the attribute). Some derivations are shown in Figure 8.2, indicated by attribute names in parentheses.

Note that in an entity/relationship model, nothing is said about whether the values will be calculated when data are entered or when they are retrieved. It is possible in some database tools to define a "computed attribute", which is stored simply as a formula. Then when the attribute is queried, it is calculated. This can be very expensive, however, if the attribute is queried frequently and it is derived from attributes that are relatively stable. In that case, it would be better to store the computed value. The point is that this is a *design* decision, which depends on the expected use of each attribute. During analysis, all we are concerned with is recognizing that the derivation takes place. We don't care if it is calculated "going in" or "coming out".

A *mathematical derivation* is a mathematical calculation of an attribute. It may be obtained through several kinds of manipulations of attributes on the models.

The first derivation is a simple arithmetic operation on multiple attributes within an entity. An example of this in Figure 8.2 is "(Value)" in LINE ITEM, which is derived for a LINE ITEM by multiplying the "Quantity" ordered in the LINE ITEM by its "Actual Price".

The second way to derive an attribute value is to *infer* a value from a parent to a child entity. An example of this on the model above is "(Standard Cost)" in a LINE ITEM which is the same as the "Standard Cost" in the ASSET TYPE that is *bought via* that LINE ITEM.

A third way to do a calculation is to *aggregate* a collection of values for occurrences of a child entity to a parent entity. This could be a *sum* or an *average*, for example. An example of this is "(Total Value)" in a CONTRACT, which is the sum of occurrences of the "(Value)" attribute in the LINE ITEM occurrences that are *part of* that CONTRACT.

An *inference* is the drawing of logical conclusions from facts. It is typically evaluated to a value of "true" or "false", although it may have more than two values. In Figure 8.2, an example of an inference is shown by "(Premium Customer Indicator)" in PARTY. This attribute takes a value "True" or "False", based on a predefined threshold for "Credit Limit".

Constraints

A *constraint* is any restriction applied to data. This is referred to in the first Business Rules Group paper as an *action assertion*. A constraint affects values that can be assigned to attributes, or indeed even occurrences of entities that can be created in the first place. Examples of constraints that might apply to the model in Figure 8.2 are as follows:

- "Total Value" of a CONTRACT may not be greater than the "Credit Limit" of the PARTY that is *buyer in* that CONTRACT.
- "Due Date" in a CONTRACT may not be earlier than "Issued Date" in the same CONTRACT.
- "Price" in a LINE ITEM may not be less than "Standard Cost" of the ASSET TYPE ordered plus 10%.

In each case, the assertions must be documented in the repository supporting the drawings, typically in the documentation of the attributes constrained by the rules (in this case, "Total Value", "Due Date", and "Price").

Note that the expression of constraints above is very precise, in terms of the navigation required of the data model. These are Row Three business rules. In Row Two, there are corresponding rules, expressed in more conventional English:

- One may not buy more from us than one's credit limit permits.
- The contract may not be delivered before it is placed.
- Sales price must be at least 10% more than the standard wholesale cost.

A good example of constraints on the data model are *referential integrity* constraints. These concern "parent-child" one to many relationships. Specifically, a referential integrity rule defines which circumstance applies if a parent is deleted that participates in a one-to-many relationship:

- The rule is *cascade delete* if deletion of the parent automatically means deletion of all the children. Deletion of a PURCHASE ORDER resulting in the deletion of all LINE ITEMS is an example of this.
- The rule is *restricted* if deletion of a parent is not permitted if children exist. For example, it may not be possible to delete a PRODUCT TYPE if there exist LINE ITEMS ordering that PRODUCT TYPE.
- The rule is *nullify* if the children can exist without any occurrence of the parent. Deletion of the parent then means deleting occurrences of the relationship between all children and that parent. For example, if it is optional for a PRODUCT to be *in* a PRODUCT CATEGORY, deleting a PRODUCT CATEGORY simply means that now any PRODUCTS that were in that PRODUCT CATEGORY now are in none.

For the most part, constraints cannot be portrayed on an entity/relationship diagram. Only a few specific kinds of constraints can be expressed in most kinds of entity/relationship models:

- At least one occurrence of an entity must be related in a specified way to an occurrence of another entity. (In Figure 8.2, each CONTRACT must be *composed of* at least one LINE ITEM.) This is an ***optionality constraint.***

- No more than one—or some other specified number of—occurrences of an entity may be related in a particular way to another entity. (Each CONTRACT must be *to* only one PARTY.) This is a ***cardinality constraint,*** the assertion that an occurrence of an entity type may be related to no more than a specified number of occurrences of another entity type.

- An attribute is required to have a value when an occurrence of an entity is created. ("Description" is a required attribute of ASSET TYPE.)

- An occurrence of a super-type must be an occurrence of one and only one sub-type. (A PARTY must be either a PERSON or an ORGANIZATION, but one PARTY cannot be both.) This is a constraint that is implicit in some modeling notations. It is not always present.

The Barker entity/relationship notation provides for one additional constraint: each occurrence of an entity must be related in a specified way to one or another different entity, but not both. In Figure 8.2, this is shown by the arc across two relationships from LINE ITEM. This is saying that each LINE ITEM must be either *for* one PRODUCT or *for* one SERVICE, but not both. Other notations, such as information engineering and IDEF1X, cannot show this.

Some notations can show additional constraints. The UML, for example, can show some labeled interrelationship constraints. A dashed line between entities ("object classes" in a UML model) may represent not only the "exclusive or" of the Barker notation but also "inclusive or", or any other inter-relationship constraint. Where a constraint cannot be shown in this way, a note can be added to the model, describing it.

Object role modeling (ORM) can show many other kinds of constraints, as described below. In addition to simple inter-relationship rules, ORM is more closely based on formal logic and set theory, and constraints involving sets of roles or comparisons between sets of role sequences may also be shown.

A constraint may be a ***mandatory constraint*** that must be followed or just a ***guideline*** that is a recommendation without penalty for not following it.

Action Enabler Rules

An ***action enabler rule*** is a statement that tests a condition, and upon finding it true, initiates another business event, message, or activity.

For example an action enabler rule in Figure 8.2 might be "If a CONTRACT'S "Due date" is greater than two weeks from today, send a backorder notice to the customer PARTY."

Quality Criteria

Business Rules Applied includes nine specific criteria to be applied to business rule definitions to ensure that they are sound and coherent [von Halle, 2002, pp. 309–310]:

- *Relevant/justified*—Is the rule truly required within the scope of the analysis?
- *Atomic*—Does it represent a single condition that cannot be further decomposed?
- *Declarative*—Does it describe states of an entity, decisions, or computations, rather than the processes by which these are achieved?
- *Intelligible/precise*—Can the rule's intended audience clearly understand it unambiguously?
- *Complete*—Does the rule possess all the intellectual properties required for its use?
- *Reliable*—Does the rule originate from a source authorized to decide that the rule is as the business desires?
- *Authentic*—If it is copied from one form to another, is each representation faithful to the original rule? That is, is the precise description of a business rule's effects on entities and attributes true to the original natural language expression by subject-matter experts?
- *Predictable*—Does the rule return the same conclusion, regardless of who invokes it or how it is invoked?
- *Unique/non-redundant/minimal*—Are there no uncontrolled redundant rules?
- *Consistent*—Are there no rules which arrive at different conclusions, given the same set of conditions?

Rule Descriptions

There are many ways that business rules can be described, and as of this writing, the industry has not established any standards. Some traits are becoming clear, however.

Natural Language

Simple natural language (such as English) is a good choice. This, however, is tricky. For Row Two audiences, this must be clear and uncomplicated. For Row Three audiences, it must be rigorous and tied to the data or object-class model. These may be two very different descriptions.

As an example, in the oil industry an oil field consists of "facilities", which are collections of equipment organized for a business purpose. An oil well is a facility, as are a steam generating plant and an oil processing plant. Each facility is an example of a facility type, such as "oil well", "steam-generating plant", or "oil-processing plant".

Each of these has one or more names. Each *facility name* is an example of a *facility name type*. For example, for regulatory reasons, each well has a "permit name" that is its official name for the regulatory agency, although an oil-processing plant does not. Most facilities also have nicknames, and some kinds of facilities have formal names. The model of this is shown in Figure 8.3.

One rule can be expressed with the following two expressions:

- The FACILITY NAME chosen must be of a FACILITY NAME TYPE that is appropriate for the FACILITY TYPE involved (Row Two description).

- The FACILITY NAME TYPE that the FACILITY NAME is *an example of* must be designated as appropriate for the FACILITY TYPE that this FACILITY is *an example of*. This is done via the existence of a FACILITY NAME APPROPRIATENESS that is *of* the NAME TYPE and *to* the FACILITY TYPE (Row Three description).

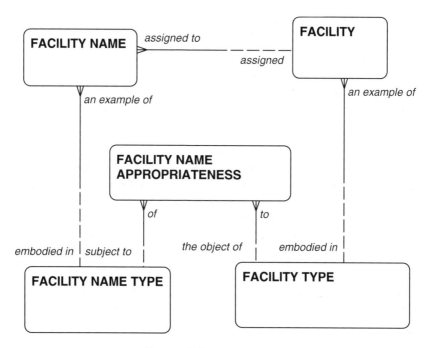

FIGURE 8.3 Facility Names.

Object Constraint Language

The second version of the rule above is an example of a formal way of describing a business rule. This makes the rule more difficult to understand, but it guarantees that it makes logical sense, and this is the form a programmer will require in order to convert the rule into code.

Another formal language for describing rules is part of the UML. The *object constraint language* is a syntax for describing constraints in an unambiguous language. It is described in a 1999 book by the developers of the language, J. Warmer and Anneke Kleppe. The syntax is intimately associated with UML, however, including its design structures such as interfaces. As such, it is too intricate for inclusion here, but it does show promise as a way of describing rules rigorously, if not clearly.

Ronald Ross Notation

For many companies the limitations of data modeling to show constraints has meant that this kind of business rule must be documented in natural language in the repository supporting the model. Not satisfied with documenting rules behind the scenes, Ronald G. Ross has developed a graphical notation for representing constraints. He explains it in his book (originally published in 1994, but updated in 1997), *The Business Rule Book.*

Mr. Ross sees two basic kinds of constraints:

- An *integrity constraint.* This is something that *must be true* about an entity, relationship, or attribute, by definition.
- A *condition.* This is something that determines whether a subsequent rule or action is invoked. It may evaluate to either true or false. Depending on the condition, other constraints may apply. Alternatively, this is an assertion that may be made true by another constraint.

In addition, he has developed a set of 31 standard rule types that he has organized into categories to form what he calls a kind of "periodic table". Each rule type describes the effect of one or more constraining objects (*correspondent* in Mr. Ross's language) on a constrained object (*anchor*). A *constrained object* is an entity, attribute, or relationship in a business rule whose value will be affected by implementation of the rule. A *constraining object* is an entity, attribute, or relationship in a business rule whose value affects the outcome of the rule.

On the left side of Figure 8.4 is an integrity constraint, represented by the arrowhead with the "X" in it.[3] An integrity constraint must be true. The "X", a label for the rule type, means that any occurrence of party must have a value for the attribute "address". Party is the constrained object (anchor), and "address" is the constraining object (correspondent). The "X" is the symbol for one of Mr. Ross' rule types. This rule type is called "must exist". That is, this rule type asserts that each occurrence of PARTY must have a value for the attribute "Address".

---

3. This is a modification made to Mr. Ross's notation to adapt it to the Barker notation. In his original notation, attributes are shown in circles, outside the entity box.

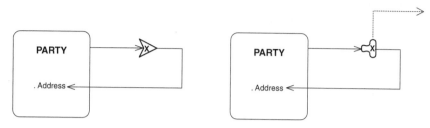

FIGURE 8.4 A Business Rule.

On the right side of Figure 8.4 is a condition. In this case, the "X" rule means "test for existence". This says that *if* an occurrence of PARTY has a value for the attribute "Address", *then* carry out the next part of the rule. Note that rule elements can indeed be strung together to make complex rules.

As in the above case, most rule types may be used as either an integrity constraint or a condition to describe a particular situation. Some rule types, by their nature, can be only one or the other.

Note that even if an atomic rule is a condition, it invariably fires off another rule, so both integrity constraints and conditions in this notation qualify as "constraints" as described above by Ms. von Halle.

Mr. Ross contends that this list of rule types is atomic and fundamental. While extensive, Mr. Ross does not claim that the list is exhaustive. There are undoubtedly more to be discovered. The list is divided into the following seven categories:

- *Instance verifiers* require—or test for—an occurrence of an object (entity type, attribute, or relationship) to be present at the creation of, during the life of, etc. an occurrence of another object.
- *Type verifiers* require—or test for—occurrences of objects to be mutually exclusive, mutually dependent, and so on.
- *Position verifiers* require—or test for—occurrences of objects to be created in a particular order.
- *Functional verifiers* require—or test for—occurrences of an object to be unique, ascending, fluctuating, and so on.
- *Comparative evaluators* define comparisons (less than, equal to, etc.) between the attributes of two occurrences of the same or different objects.
- *Mathematical evaluators* are used in a rule to derive values.
- *Projection controllers* cause things to happen.

The first five represent "mandatory constraints" in Ms. von Halle's classification scheme described above. "Mathematical evaluators are "derivations" and "projection controllers" are "action enablers" in that scheme.

Instance Verifiers

In Figure 8.4 the X is an example of the *instance verifier* "Mandatory". A Mandatory rule either asserts that something must exist, or it is a test of whether or not something exists.

Another kind of instance verifier is "Limit", which prescribes a number of occurrences of an entity. For example, a CONTRACT may be limited to six LINE ITEMS.

Type Verifiers

Figure 8.5 shows a kind of *type verifier,* an example of the second category of constraints. This one is "Mutually Exclusive" (ME). (This constraint can, in fact, be represented in some entity/relationship notations.) Here, each LINE ITEM must be <u>either</u> *for* one PRODUCT, <u>or</u> *for* one SERVICE. Other type verifiers include "Mutually Inclusive", "Mutually Prohibited", and "Mutual".

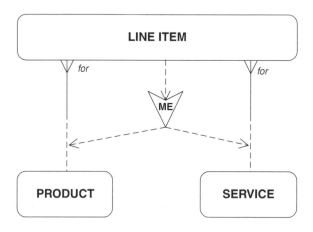

FIGURE 8.5 Type Verifiers.

Position Verifiers

Figure 8.6 shows an example of a *position verifier.* This one is called "Position" (POS). It is an example of a rule that takes an argument, which is the particular position in sequence being sought. In this case, the rule means that if the SECTION in question is the fifth in a REPORT, then....

Because by definition this rule type refers only to one of the occurrences of SECTION, it must always be a condition, not an integrity constraint. You cannot assert that every SECTION must be fifth in a REPORT.

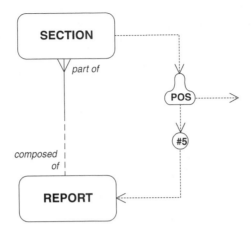

FIGURE 8.6 Position Verifiers.

Other position verifiers include "Low" and "High" (the SECTION that is the lowest or highest in sequence invokes the next rule), and "Old" and "New" (the SECTION that is oldest or newest invokes the next rule). The position verifier "Chron" takes an argument that is the object's position in chronological order. For example, the rule may fire if the object is the third to take place.

Functional Verifiers

Figure 8.7 shows two examples of a kind of *functional verifier*. A functional verifier is a rule about an occurrence of an entity, relative to other occurrences in the entity. In this example, the "Unique" rule addresses whether occurrences of RENTAL AGREEMENT have unique "Effective Dates". In the integrity constraint on the left, the "Effective Date" of each occurrence of RENTAL AGREEMENT must be unique. In the condition on the right, the argument "not" makes the rule mean, "If the 'Effective Date' of an occurrence of RENTAL AGREEMENT is *not* unique, then...."

Other functional verifiers include "Fluctuating", "Ascending", "Descending", "Non-renewable", and the nonspecific "Functional".

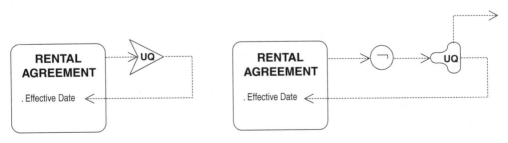

FIGURE 8.7 Functional Verifiers.

Comparative Evaluators

A *comparative evaluator*, as its name implies, compares two elements in the data model. In the "Less-Than" integrity constraint shown in Figure 8.8, the "Order Date" must be less than the "Due Date". Other comparative evaluators include "Equal-To", "Not-Equal-To", "Greater-Than", "Greater-Than-or-Equal-To", and "Less-Than-Or-Equal-To".

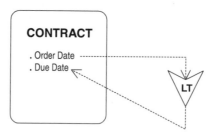

FIGURE 8.8 Comparative Evaluators.

Mathematical Evaluators

A *mathematical evaluator* derives an attribute from other attribute values. In Figure 8.9, "Value" is calculated from "Quantity" and "Price" according to the formula "Value = Quantity x Price". The solid line points to the result, and the dashed lines point to components of that result. There are numerous other kinds of mathematical evaluators, such as "Sum", "Add", "Subtract", and the like.

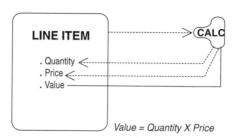

FIGURE 8.9 Mathematical Evaluators.

Projection Controllers

Where other kinds of rules restrain values, *projection controllers* cause things to happen. A value may "Enable" another value or another rule, "Copy" the value of the anchor to a correspondent, or cause an action to be "Executed". In the latter case, the notation reaches beyond the data model to represent the function executed. Here a Column Six business rule is invoking a Column Two activity.

Figure 8.10 shows an example of an "Enabler". In this case, being *in charge of* a PROJECT makes an EMPLOYEE a MANAGER.

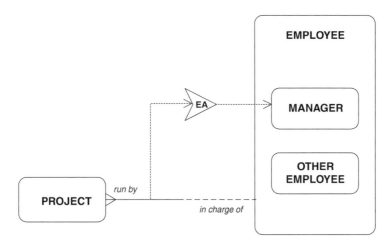

FIGURE 8.10 Projection Controllers.

The examples here are simple atomic rules. Real rules are combinations of these. Complex configurations are possible, and it is also possible to create templates reflecting patterns that can be reused.

Object-Role Modeling (ORM)

Object-role modeling is a modeling technique that views the world simply in terms of objects playing roles (parts in relationships). Originally developed in Europe in the early 1970s, and once going under the name of "NIAM", it has been significantly extended over the years by researchers in Europe, Australia, and the United States. It is described in detail in Appendix B. It is significant in the business rules world because it provides a means of describing many inter-attribute and inter-entity rules.

Entity Types, Attributes, and Relationships

Entity types are represented in ORM as simple ellipses or circles. As in entity/relationship (e/r) diagrams, entity types are related to each other via named relationships. Each relationship consists of one *role* for each participant in it. (There can be more than two entities participating in a relationship.)

The objects in an ORM diagram are entity types and value types. An *entity type* is the same as we have seen before—a thing of significance to the organization. A *value type* is a classification of value, similar to a *domain* in e/r modeling. Examples include "monetary amount", "date", and so forth

Entity types and value types are the "objects" in object role modeling.

Essentially, a *fact* is simply an object's playing a role. A *role* is the half of a relationship reading in one direction. Two or more entity types playing roles with respect to each other constitute a ***relationship*** In Figure 8.11, Sales Order and Person are real-world entity types, while Date is a value type. (Solid ellipses denote entity types, while dashed ellipses denote value types.) When a value type serves as an identifier (as in the Person "ID" and the Sales Order "nr"), it is shown inside the ellipse as a ***label*** of the entity type, indicating that it is a unique identifier. In a value type, its data type (such as "mdy", meaning "month/day/year") is shown below the value name.

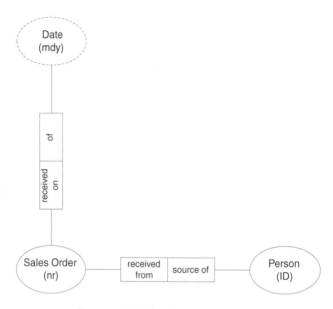

FIGURE 8.11 An Object Role Model.

There are no rules about role names, beyond the fact that they should be readable as sentences. Given that, your author has taken the liberty of constraining names to a modification of the form used in the Barker e/r notation. In the example, each Sales Order is *received from* a Person, and each Person is the *source of* a Sales Order. A Sales Order also plays a role with respect to the value type Date. Specifically, each Sales Order is *received on* a Date, and each Date is *of* a Sales Order. These relationships are further described in the following sections.

Note that the relational concept of "attribute" doesn't really apply here. The "Receipt date" that would be an attribute of Sales Order here is represented by the *received on* role.

About Constraints

ORM is much more versatile than other modeling languages in its ability to represent business rules and constraints. The following sections show how this is so. ORM certainly does not represent all possible constraints on data, but it is able to represent a large proportion of them.

Mandatory Roles

First, like e/r modeling, ORM has the ability to show that a role is mandatory. In ORM, this is shown with a dark dot between the object and the role involved. In Figure 8.12, the role from Sales Order to Person is mandatory. Each Sales Order <u>must be</u> *received from* one Person. The same symbol is also used to show that an attribute is mandatory. In the figure, each Sales Order <u>must be</u> *received on* a Date.

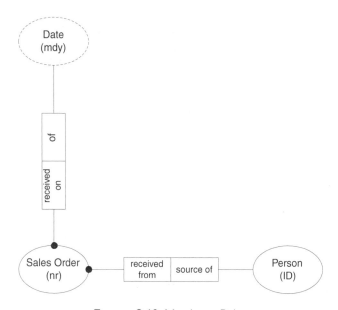

FIGURE 8.12 Mandatory Roles.

Uniqueness

The notion of whether an occurrence of an entity type is associated with one entity type or multiple occurrences of an entity type is known in the e/r modeling world as "cardinality". Usually this is shown by the absence or presence of a crow's foot or asterisk next to the entity type which is singular or multiple.

In ORM, the question is asked differently. It is not, "How many occurrences of another entity type are objects of this role?" Rather it is, "How many times may the same entity instance play this role (at any given state of the database)?" That is, "May an object instance playing that *role* do so multiple times?" In Figure 8.13 each Sales Order has a single occurrence of the role "received from" a Person. That is, each Sales Order must be *received from* one and only one Person. This is shown by the horizontal arrow over the "received from" role box. "Source of", the Person role, on the other hand is not unique. There is no horizontal arrow. This means that a Person may be *source of* a Sales Order multiple times.

Figure 8.13 also shows that relationships in ORM do not have to be binary. *Arity* is the number of entity types permitted to participate in a relationship. In entity/relationship modeling, relationships can only have an arity of 2. (This means that each relationship can only be between two entity types.) In ORM, relationships can have an arity of more than 2. In Figure 8.13, Sales Order, Product, Quantity, and Money amount come together in a single relationship. In this case, there are two entities and two value types, but there could easily also be additional entities or value types in the relationship.

Among other things, this example shows that this concept of uniqueness turns out to be much more versatile than the simple concept of cardinality. For example, a horizontal arrow is across both the "sold via" and "to sell" roles in the relationship between Sales Order and Product. What this means is that it is only the *combination of* a Sales Order's selling and a Product's being sold that is unique. A Sales Order may be to sell one or more Products, and a Product may be sold via one or more Sales Orders. This is the ORM version of the many-to-many relationship.

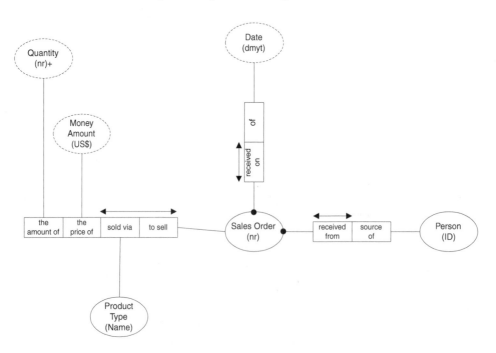

FIGURE 8.13 Uniqueness.

It is not necessary to create an intersect entity. Because the arity of the relationship is not limited to two, attributes of the intersection (such as Price and Quantity, in this case) can simply be added with more roles.

The model in Figure 8.13 has an interesting problem in ORM terms: The facts shown are not **elementary**. The relationship between Sales Order and Product appears to be analogous to the way one would set up a line item table. There are references to the Sales Order and to the Product, plus references to two attributes of the relationship, "Price" and "Quantity". In fact, the model in Figure 8.13 can be made more elementary by converting it to the two models in Figure 8.14.

The rule is that there can be no more than one role more than the roles which determine uniqueness. Neither "the amount of" nor "the price of" participates in the uniqueness constraint on the relationships. Only one such nonunique role is permitted. In relational terms, this means that no table can have more than one non-key attribute. It seems like a strict rule, but it does guarantee that you are looking at the most atomic information possible. Figure 8.14 shows the elementary facts that result from implementing this rule.

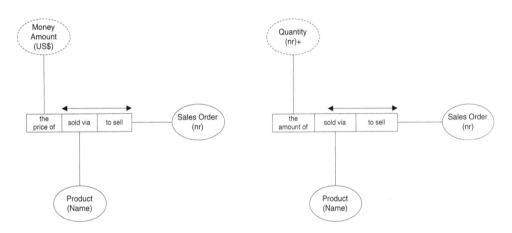

FIGURE 8.14 Elementary Facts.

The concept of uniqueness applies equally to entities and attributes. In Figure 8.15, people take courses, and each person receives a ranking. Only one person can be first, second, and so forth in a course. In the model, then, each combination of Person and Course is unique. That is, there must be only one Ranking for each Person/Course combination. This is shown by the upper arrow across "enrolled" and "presented". But it is also true that in a Course, given a Ranking, there is only one Person occupying that rank. Thus, a second uniqueness bar represents the fact that each Course/Ranking combination is also unique.

Note that, with more than two roles in a relationship, the Barker naming convention breaks down, since the resulting sentence has more than one object. You cannot say "each COURSE may be *presented to* one PERSON and one RANKING". So, the roll names are now simply "enrolled" and "presented".

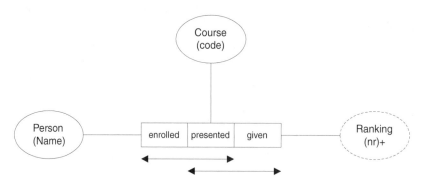

FIGURE 8.15 More on Uniqueness.

Objectified Relationships

While it is not necessary to resolve many-to-many relationships in ORM, it is sometimes useful to do so. Figure 8.16 shows the creation of "Line Item" from the intersection between the "sold via" and "to sell" roles. Line Item in this case is an *objectified relationship* and behaves in all respects like an entity type. This then makes it possible to apply the additional roles for Quantity and Price as attributes of this new entity type. We also add a new attribute Line Number.

Notice the circled "U" symbol connecting the Line Number "for" role with the Sales Order "to sell" role. This means that that combination of roles is unique. This is called an *external uniqueness* identifier. This means that a given Sales Order plus a given line number is a unique combination. Note that adding the Line Number role as part of the identifier of the "Line Item" relationship allows the combination of Sales Order and Product to be not unique, if we choose to make it so. This allows the same product to appear twice on one Sales Order. If we don't want that to happen, we must add back the double-headed arrow that was in the previous drawing.

Notice also that now the "attributes" of Line Item are shown as separate relationships to value types. Therefore we need not limit ourselves to one non-key attribute. Each relationship is already an atomic fact.

Occurrence Frequency

The notation for "one or more" in ORM is simply the absence of a uniqueness constraint. For example, in Figure 8.16, each Person may be *source of* one or more Sales Orders. Back in Figure 8.15, each Ranking may be given to any number of Course/Person combinations. Similarly, each Person may be enrolled in one or more Courses, each with its own Ranking, and each Course may be given to one or more People.

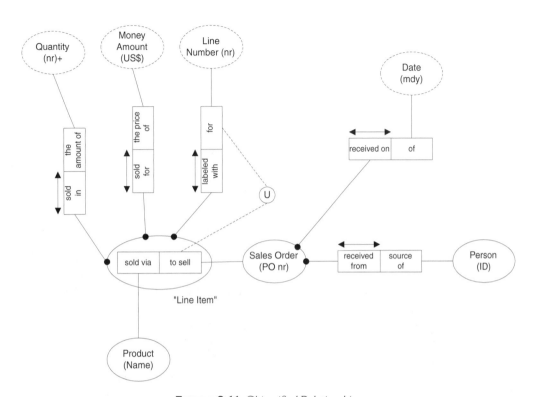

FIGURE 8.16 Objectified Relationships.

A *cardinality constraint* may be specified by adding a number to the role. For example, "<=8" could be placed next to the "enrolled in" role to designate that each Person may be enrolled in no more than 8 Courses. This is shown in Figure 8.17. Similarly, each course is restricted to no more than 30 People, so "<=30" appears next to the "presented" role. More complex rules could also be specified for the "enrolled in" role, such as "2... 8" or "3, 5, 8" for requiring at least 2 but allowing no more than 8, or for insisting on exactly either 3, 5, or 8 courses.

Unlike with e/r modeling, you can also specify the cardinality of an object itself. An *object cardinality constraint* is a number that defines the maximum or minimum number of occurrences that are possible for a given object at a given time. In the example in the figure, no more than 50 courses may be offered at one time. The octothorp (#) means that the count of objects can be no greater than 50.

Using the number "1" with a role or roles is equivalent to adding the double-headed arrow uniqueness constraint across that role. This is also shown in Figure 8.17, showing that "enrolled in" and "presented to" constitute one uniqueness constraint, and "presented to" and "give" are another.

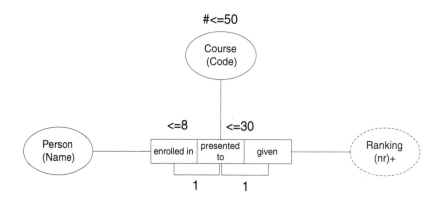

FIGURE 8.17 Occurrence Frequency.

Derivations

One important kind of business rule is the derivation. With the ORM notation you may or may not choose to show derived values graphically on the diagram, but in either case, ORM accommodates defining them in the technique. Derived attributes are not shown as value types, but they are shown on diagrams as being formally defined in terms of other attributes. In Figure 8.18, for example, each Line Item has explicit roles of [Quantity], which is *the amount of* the Line Item, and [Unit Price], which is *the price of* the Line Item. Note the addition of ***rolenames*** for the roles shown in square brackets. "Unit Price" is the name of the "the price of" role. [Value] is the name of the "the value of" role, and describes the complete value of the line—Unit Price times Quantity.

The formula for Value is displayed separately, as text. Specifically, Line Item.Value = Line Item.Unit price * Line Item.Quantity. This is an informal specification. The formal definition is shown on the diagram below the informal one. In the formal definition, "iff" is from logic and means "if and only if", which is to say that the left side of the expression is identical in meaning to the right side.

Note that this example shows how value types really do represent domains and not attributes. Both "the value of" and "the price of" roles are played by the value type (domain) Money Amount, which is expressed in United States dollars.

Value Constraints

One constraint that is very common has to do with the values that an attribute can take. In e/r modeling, if the list is discrete, this is often addressed with a "Type" entity, or with a domain. If the attribute is continuous (accepting any real number), minimum and maximum values may be set in a domain definition. In either case, the model doesn't actually show the legal values. Since these domains constitute a significant element in the configuration of the final system, it would be good if they were more visible. In ORM they are. A ***value constraint*** is a list of possible values for an attribute.

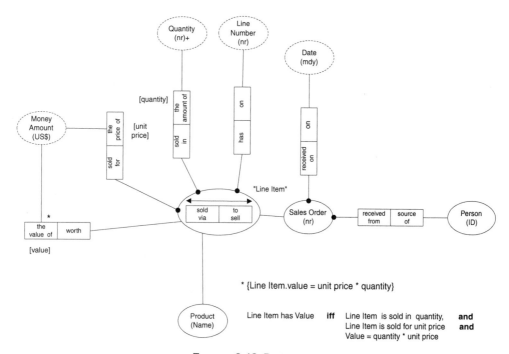

FIGURE 8.18 Derivations.

In Figure 8.19 we have added some new entities. First we determined that each Person has a Sex. The values available for "Sex" are "M" and "F", as shown in the brackets. For purposes of this exercise, we have asserted that only 10 line items per order are possible. This is done indirectly by saying that Line Number can have only the values 1 through 10. Since the uniqueness constraint says that a Line Item can have only one Line Number, then that effectively limits us to 10 Line Items. In addition, because of the nature of the products we are selling (undisclosed here), the Quantity that appears on a single line item can be no larger than 300 units.

Another addition to the model is Sales Order Type. ORM is not clear as to whether it is an attribute of Sales Order or another entity type. As it happens, it doesn't matter. If the only thing you need is the name of the Sales Order Type, it can simply be an attribute—constrained by the list of available values. (It is usually implemented in a relational database as a separate table, with one row for each of the legal values, but that doesn't concern us here.) In this case, a Sales Order can be an example of a "Blanket" order, an "Emergency" order, or a "Call" against a blanket order.

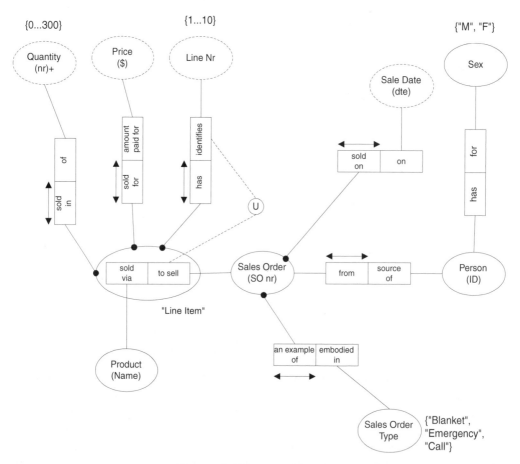

FIGURE 8.19 Value Constraints.

Set Constraints—Subsets

Figure 8.20 shows part of the model of an airline's flight schedule. This part describes the actual departure and arrival of a Flight Segment, where a Flight Segment is defined as a single trip, without stops, between two airports. Continental Airlines flight 635, for example, departed Los Angeles for Houston at 2:10 p.m. on August 17, 2001, and it arrived at 7:30 p.m. Both the departure and arrival roles are examples of the value type Time, expressed in "day, hour, minute".

There is a rule here that says that a plane may not arrive if it has not departed. That is, the set of Flight Segments that show Arrival Times have to be a ***subset*** of the Flight Segments that show Departure Times.

This is shown on the diagram by the dashed arrow. It shows that a Flight Segment may have departed without arriving yet, but it cannot have arrived if it has not departed.

Note that both these roles are optional. A Flight Segment may not have taken off at all.

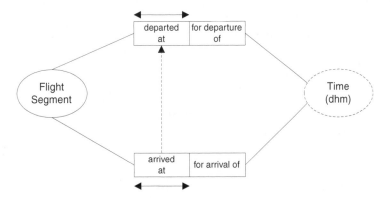

FIGURE 8.20 Subset Constraint.

Set Constraints—Join Subset Constraint

In an example described previously, an oil field consists of "facilities", which are collections of equipment organized for a business purpose. An oil well is a Facility, as is a steam generating plant, or an oil processing plant. Each Facility is an example of a Facility Type, such as "oil well", "steam generating plant", or "oil processing plant".

Each of these has one or more names. Each Facility Name is an example of a Facility Name Type. For example, for regulatory reasons, each well has a "permit name" that is its official name for the regulatory agency, although an oil processing plant does not. Most facilities also have nicknames, and some kinds of facilities have formal names.

On page 305, we saw the rule

> "The FACILITY NAME TYPE that the FACILITY NAME is *an example of* must be designated as appropriate for the FACILITY TYPE that this FACILITY is *an example of*. This is done via the existence of a FACILITY NAME APPROPRIATENESS that is *the of* the NAME TYPE and *to* the FACILITY TYPE (Row Three description)."

Note that, while the e/r model in Figure 8.3 has the entity type FACILITY NAME APPROPRIATENESS to support the rule, the rule itself cannot be represented on that diagram.

The ORM version of this rule is that

> "The Facility/Facility Name relationship is a subset of the possible associations between Facility Type and Facility Name Type."

This is represented in Figure 8.21. The notation that describes this rule has two parts. First, the line between the two "an example of" roles is called a conceptual join path. A *conceptual join path* is a connection between two relationships suggesting that they are in fact related to each other. This asserts a complete fact that each Facility Name is *an example of* one Facility Name Type *that* is *appropriate for* a Facility Type *that* is *embodied in* a Facility. Going in the other direction, each Facility is an example of one Facility Type *that* is the basis for a Facility Name Type *that* is embodied in a Facility Name.

The second part of the rule, then, is the assertion that the set of facts expressed by the "for"/"labeled by" relationship must be a *subset* of the set of facts expressed by the FacilityName/Facility projection to the conceptual join path.

Note that in Figure 8.21 the subset constraint was applied to two roles. Here it is to the entire relationship between two role sequences.

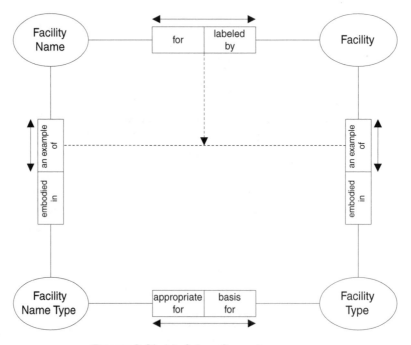

FIGURE 8.21 Join Subset Constraint.

Set Constraints—Equality

Figure 8.22 shows a variation on the subset constraint shown above. In this example we see scheduled flights, rather than actual ones, so for each occurrence of a scheduled departure time there must be a scheduled arrival time as well, and vice versa. This *equality constraint* is shown by the double-headed dashed arrow.

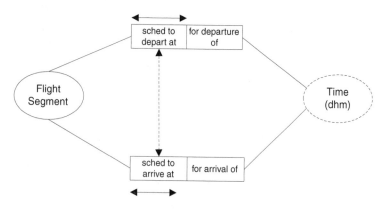

FIGURE 8.22 Equality Constraint.

Set Constraints—Exclusion

Getting back to our Sales Order model, we can extend it to permit purchasing services as well as products. In Figure 8.23, a Sales Order must be <u>either</u> *to sell* a Service, <u>or</u> *to sell* a Product, or both. The relationships involved are circled, and a line is drawn between them. The solid dot in the circle on that line is the same "mandatory" indicator we saw for relationships and entity types, but here it is saying that the pair is mandatory, although either or both elements could be selected. Because both may apply, this is called an *inclusive or* constraint.

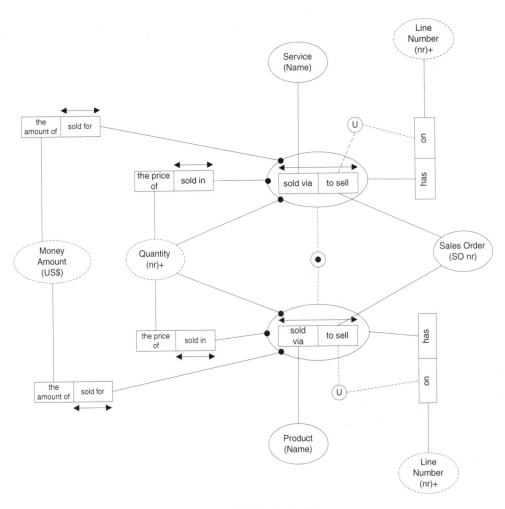

FIGURE 8.23 Inclusive Or.

To use our sales example to demonstrate the next constraint, we must promote the objectified relationship Line Item to a real entity. This allows us to discuss the alternative things a Line Item might be about. Figure 8.24 makes the assertion that a Line Item may be for either a Product or a Service, but not both. The "X" in the circle means "exclusive or". Because there is no solid dot, it also means that the Line Item could be for neither a Product nor a Service.

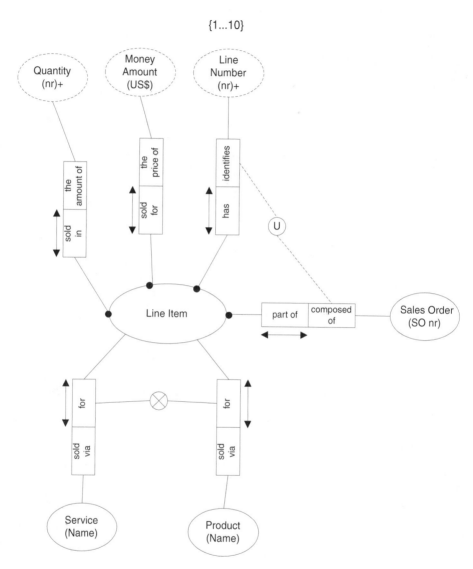

FIGURE 8.24 Exclusive Or—Version 1.

This introduces one flaw in this model. If we want to require that a line item <u>must be</u> *for* either a Product or a Service, we need the symbol shown in Figure 8.25. This is the "X" with the mandatory dot over it.

To summarize, there are two forms of *inclusive or*:

• Absence of a constraint means that the central entity type may be in either role (or neither) (or both).

- Dot without X means that it must be one or the other (or both).

And there are two forms of *exclusive or*:

- X without dot means that it may be one or the other (or neither) (but not both).
- X with dot means that it must be one or the other (but not both).

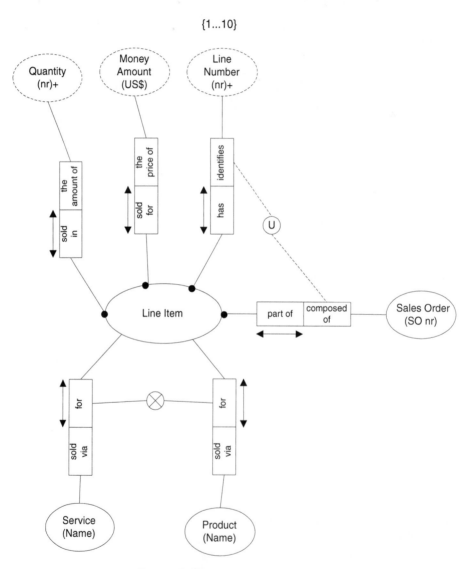

FIGURE 8.25 Exclusive Or—Version 2.

Ring Constraints

When occurrences of an entity are related to other occurrences of the same entity, this is a *ring* in ORM. It is common in the description of manufacturing product structures, but it also appears when describing such things as logistics networks and other inter-entity type relationships. Figure 8.26 shows a product structure, where a Product may be composed of one or more other Products, and a Product may be a component of one or more other Products. The Quantity value tells how many of the component are required to create one of the parent.

This structure can be represented easily enough in an e/r diagram, but it is not possible to describe a series of constraints that might apply.

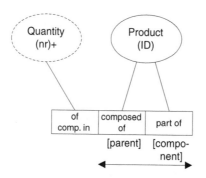

Parent	Component
Bicycle	Bicycle
Bicycle	Wheel
Wheel	Spoke
Wheel	Bicycle
Bicycle	Spoke
Spoke	Bicycle

FIGURE 8.26 A Ring.

The table below the diagram shows some possible values for the structure. Given the drawing as it is, these are all legal values. Upon examination, however, it is apparent that some of these combinations should not be legal.

The first problem is that it should not be possible for a "Bicycle" to be a component of a "Bicycle". This violates our understanding of the nature of things in the world. The ring should not be what is called *reflexive*. It should be *irreflexive*.

Figure 8.27 shows this constraint added. It is in the form of the notation °*ir*. Note that the designation applies to the set of both roles.

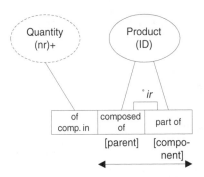

Parent	Component
Bicycle	Bicycle
Bicycle	Wheel
Wheel	Spoke
Wheel	Bicycle
Bicycle	Spoke
Spoke	Bicycle

FIGURE 8.27 Irreflexive.

There are still some problems with the sample data. Note that a Bicycle can contain a Wheel, and a Wheel can contain a Bicycle. In the world, it is unlikely that this **symmetry** is the case, so we need a constraint that will prevent it. The constraint ($^o as$) in Figure 8.28 makes it **asymmetric**.

Note that if it is not permitted to have a pair that is another pair in reverse, that includes the situation where the pair is itself in reverse. That is, if the relationship is asymmetric, it is also irreflexive. The $^o ir$ is unnecessary.

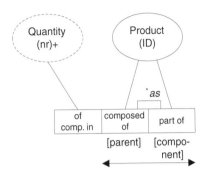

Parent	Component
Bicycle	Wheel
Wheel	Spoke
Wheel------------	-Bicycle---------
Bicycle	Spoke
Spoke	Bicycle

FIGURE 8.28 Asymmetric.

Another problem with our sample data is that a "Bicycle" consists of a "Wheel", a "Wheel" consists of a "Spoke", and a "Bicycle" also consists of a "Spoke". While the construction of some products may allow such ***transitiveness***, we are going to say for purposes of this exercise that it isn't allowed. The constraint "^{o}it" shows the relationship to be ***intransitive*** in Figure 8.29.

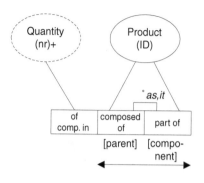

FIGURE 8.29 Intransitive.

The remaining problem with the sample data in our example is that a "Bicycle" is composed of "Wheels", and a "Wheel" is composed of "Spokes", but a "Spoke" is composed of "Bicycles". This kind of loop is not permitted in the real world, so our model must reflect this. This is a more general case of the asymmetry constraint shown in Figure 8.28. This is called *acyclic*. It is added as a constraint in Figure 8.30.

Other Constraints

This section has described some of the constraints that can be expressed directly with the ORM notation. Like all notations, ORM cannot describe all of the constraints that might apply. Supplementing the notation with formal predicate logic statements, however, allows all to be expressed overall.

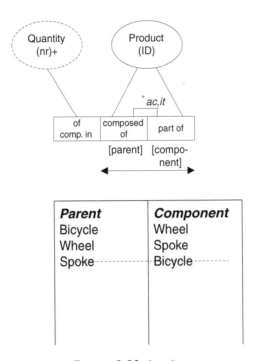

Parent	Component
Bicycle	Wheel
Wheel	Spoke
Spoke------------	-Bicycle--------

FIGURE 8.30 Acyclic.

For example, in Figure 8.31 we are interested in a little more information about the Person at the other end of the Sales Order transaction. Specifically, each Person must be evaluated with a Credit Limit. By adding another derived value, "sales order value", computed as the sum of the "line item values" of all associated Line Items, we can express the rule that the total value of the Sales Order may not be greater than the credit limit of the Person doing the buying.

Notice in this model that the value type "Money Amount" is used both to mean line item value and sales order value. This is the difference between an ORM value type and an e/r model's attribute. Here a value type plays the role of an attribute, in this case more than once. In e/r modeling, a domain may be shared by different attributes, but that does not show on the model.

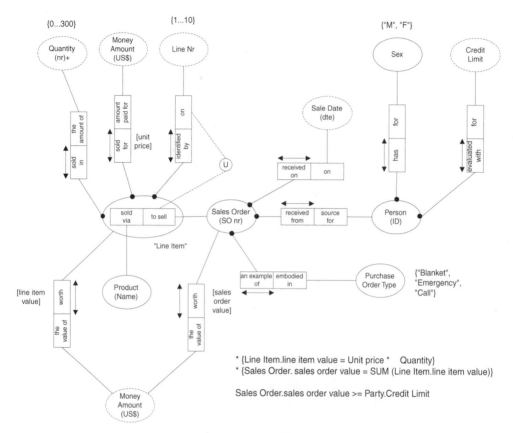

FIGURE 8.31 Credit Limit.

Rule Patterns

Ms. von Halle proposes the use of what she calls *rule patterns*. Predicated on the realization that rules (as opposed to terms and facts) are nearly always conditional, she argues for setting up rule-pattern tables, where the columns are:

- Rule identifier
- One or more conditions
- The effect of the rule

Such tables can then be used to identify rule-integrity problems.

The rule just described above (The FACILITY NAME chosen must be of a FACILITY NAME TYPE that is appropriate for the FACILITY TYPE involved), then, can be represented by the rule pattern in Table 8.1.

TABLE 8.1 Rule Patterns

Rule ID	If FACILITY NAME **Appropriateness** (FACILITY TYPE, FACILITY NAME TYPE)	FACILITY NAME (of FACILITY NAME TYPE) *for* FACILITY (of FACILITY TYPE)
R1	Exists	Permitted

This means that if an occurrence of FACILITY NAME APPROPRIATENESS exists that links a particular FACILITY NAME TYPE with a particular FACILITY TYPE, then it is permitted for a FACILITY NAME (of the specified FACILITY NAME TYPE) to be assigned to a FACILITY (of the specified FACILITY TYPE).

Another set of rules apply to the model in Figure 8.32. Here, PRODUCTION is the fact that a WELL is producing a particular PRODUCT TYPE at a given point in time. The rules are that (a) a WELL may be *producer of* one or more PRODUCTIONS *of* different PRODUCT TYPES, but (b) a WELL may be *producer of* only one PRODUCTION at a time. That is, the "Start date and time" of a PRODUCTION must be *after* the "End date and time" of prior PRODUCTIONS, and the "End date and time", if any, must be *before* any subsequent PRODUCTIONS. Only one PRODUCTION may have a null "End date and time". That is, a well may produce both crude oil and natural gas, but not at the same time.

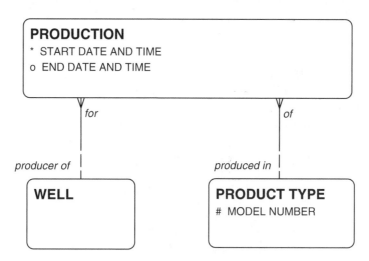

FIGURE 8.32 Production.

The rule pattern for this situation is shown in Table 8.2.

TABLE 8.2 Production Rules

For PRODUCTION:

ID	IF START DATE of occurrence 1 after START DATE of occurrence 2	AND START DATE of occurrence 1 after END DATE of occurrence 2	AND END DATE of occurrence 1 after START DATE of occurrence 2	THEN allowed?
R2	Yes	Yes	Must happen	Yes
R3	Yes	No	Must happen	No
R4	No	Can't happen	Yes	No
R5	No	Can't happen	No	Yes

The table shows all permutations of placements of start and end dates of two occurrences of the PRODUCTION entity type. For each permutation, the rightmost column says whether it is allowed.

In some cases, the value in one column dictates the value of another column. In R2 and R3, for example, if the START DATE of occurrence 1 is *after* the START DATE of occurrence 2, then the END DATE of occurrence 1 *must be after* the START DATE of occurrence 2. Similarly, in R4 and R5, if the START DATE of occurrence 1 is *not after* the START DATE of occurrence 2, then the END DATE of occurrence 1 *cannot be after* the END DATE of occurrence 2.

In R2, the START DATE of the first occurrence is *after* both the START and END DATES of the second occurrence, so it is allowed. In R3, the START DATE of the first occurrence is *after* the START DATE of the second OCCURRENCE, but *before* its END DATE, so it is not allowed. In R4, the start date of the first is *before* the START DATE of the second occurrence, but its END DATE is AFTER the START DATE of the second occurrence, so it is not permitted, In R5, both the START DATE and the END DATE of occurrence 1 are *before* the start date of occurrence 2, so it is allowed.

Business Rule Patterns—CASEtech, Inc.

Peter Brenner, Ed Campbell, and David Wendelken of CASEtech, Inc. have developed an extensive catalogue of business rule patterns. Unlike Ms. von Halle's patterns or the other notation and classification schemes described above, these are described in simple English, and they are accompanied by PL/SQL subroutines. They are intended to be captured in a tool, so that a particular rule can be implemented inheriting characteristics of the pattern. The patterns they have collected correspond to many of Ron Ross's and ORM's examples described above.

The approach here differs from the others, however, in that one purpose of the patterns is to provide a vocabulary with which to describe business rules to the public at large. As described earlier, it is often difficult to describe a rule in a style that is both rigorous enough to be implementable and simple enough to be clearly understood. Patterns can be taught, however, and then it is simply a matter of referring to them.

For example, two sets of relationships are "cousins" if they connect the same two entity types. The "cousin" rule states that "If two different relationship paths from an entity type back to the same 'ancestor' entity type exist, the two paths from *any occurrence* in this entity type must be traced back to *the same occurrence* in the ancestor entity type" [based on Brenner, et. al. 2002, p. 7]. The "no cousin" rule states that the two paths from any occurrence must be traced to *different occurrences* in the ancestor entity type.

For example, Figure 8.33 shows that there are two paths from PITCH to PLAYER. Each PITCH must be *by* one PLAYER, and it must be *during* one AT BAT which in turn must be *by* one PLAYER. In this case, the "no cousin" rule pattern is invoked: it is not permitted for a player to pitch to himself.

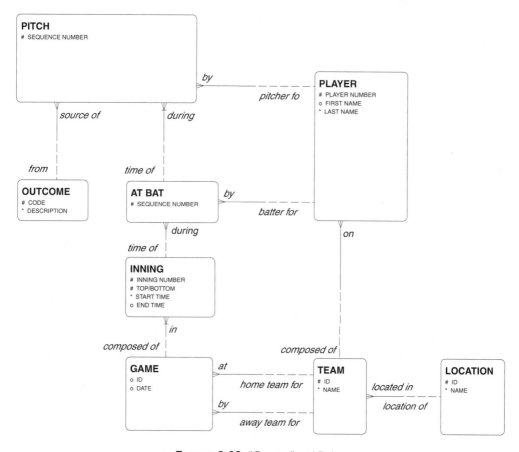

FIGURE 8.33 "Cousins" and Rules.

Figure 8.33 also shows another cousin situation in the multiple paths from AT BAT to TEAM. In this case the "cousin" rule is invoked. The PLAYER who is *the batter for* an AT BAT must be in fact *on* a TEAM that is either *the home team for* or *the away team for* the GAME with the INNING that is *the time of* that AT BAT.

Other patterns include:

- *A or B*—Only one or the other of two specified items may have a value. This is similar to an "arc" on two or more relationships, but it applies to two attributes or an attribute and a relationship.
- *Mandatory wait*—A data item, although optional at first, becomes mandatory when other data items have a certain value. For example, we must have an employee's social security number within three days after they start work.
- *Min max*—The first value must be less than the second value, if both are present.
- *No circle*—A many-to-one or many-to-many relationship from an entity type to itself exists. We do not allow circular relationship patterns. For example, an entity type occurrence cannot be a "parent" of itself, no matter how many other "children" rows intervene. The alternative rule permitting such an arrangement is called the "circle" pattern.
- *No overlap*—An occurrence has starting and ending range values, which must not overlap those of another occurrence.
- *Positive number*—The constrained item must be a positive, numeric value.

Requirements Analysis Deliverable—Column Six

At the conclusion of a requirements analysis project, the following should be produced.

- Restatement of vision, goals, and objectives of the enterprise, especially with respect to this project. As appropriate, include a discussion of the mission, strategies and tactics that will address the vision, goals, and objectives.
- Business policies that pertain to the subject area under consideration.
- All applicable business rules, specifically constraints and action-enabler rules. Terms and facts should have been defined under Column One (Data). Derivations, cardinality, and optionality may be shown in the Column One data model, but their definition is a Column Six responsibility. Several means of describing the rules are available.
  - English (or your natural language) is required (Row Two).
  - Rule patterns provide a structured way to represent them (Rows Two or Three).
  - Ross notation or ORM provide graphic approaches (Row Three).
  - Other techniques may be developed in years to come.

Motivation and the Other Columns

Motivation and Data

Fundamentally, business rules are about data. In Row Three, especially, a business rule constrains what data may be or must be created in the course of business operations. The discovery and definition of business rules must be carried out in conjunction with the development of the data model.

Motivation and Activities

An organization's mission, strategies, and tactics form the structure around which its activities are organized. These, therefore, are the top levels of any hierarchical representation of activities.

Business rules are normally defined in terms of constraints on data, not on processes. We have seen here and in Chapter 4, however, that the detailed documentation of activities can reveal business rules. Indeed, they are often implemented by activities and restrictions on activities. The activities and the business rules must be documented together.

Motivation and Locations

Ideally, a single set of business rules applies to the entire enterprise. In reality, however, it may be necessary to vary the rules by facility. Different locations may be run differently, may have different customs, or may be subject to different laws. For example, different offices of a car rental agency may have different rules for late return of a car, depending on when they are open. Office hours might be different in different sites, and different legal systems may apply.

Motivation, People, and Organizations

This chapter discusses an organization's mission, goals, and objectives. It specifically deals with "elements of guidance" (business policies and business rules) that amplify management decisions, and "assessments" that provide a filtered view of the effect of the environment (there described as "influences") and operations on the organization's ends and means.

An element of guidance represents a message sent by management to its operating divisions. Business policies and business rules must be carefully designed to account for the issues described here.

Similarly, an assessment is the retrieval of information from the operating organizations, interpreting what happened, the influences which caused it to happen, and the effects of these events on the enterprise's ends and means.

Business rules may be specific to the organization involved. There may be good and valid reasons for a rule to be applied to one division and not another. This must be documented.

Motivation and Timing

Goals and strategies typically are not, but objectives and tactics must be expressed in terms of the events to which they are responding. For example, we want to increase market share by 10% *in the next six months.* Business policies and business rules often deal with external events and recommended ways of dealing with them.

One way to discover rules is to study events and determine the decisions made in response to each.

Conclusion

If someone invents a new microchip or a new kind of display-screen technology, it can be a simple matter to build a manufacturing plant, create a marketing organization, and distribute the new technology worldwide in a matter of months. OK, not simple, maybe, but in fact our era is marked by the number of times just this has been done.

If someone comes up with a good idea for the process by which technology is created, however, this can be distributed only one way: The innovator must teach someone the new method. That person must then teach someone else. Maybe that person can teach a class of 20. The innovator can write a book, although that means less control over what is learned from that book. Altogether, this is a much slower process. Moreover, it is prone to all the errors we experienced in playing "Telephone" when we were children. The method that is taught a year after it has been invented may be very different from what the originator had in mind.

Creating system development methods has not been easy. For us to have come as far as we have in developing approaches to requirements analysis is truly remarkable. We all live in hope that the next method or the next technique will suddenly make it easy to build large complex systems. It is a foolish hope. Developing systems will never not be hard.

But techniques are being developed all the time, and progress is being made. It hasn't necessarily gotten easier to build systems, but the systems we are building are vastly more sophisticated than those built just 20 or 30 years ago. And this is not just because the technology is better. It is because we are continually getting smarter in our ability to build systems that are actually useful to someone.

This book is the first chapter of a story that is just beginning. This is an incredible time to be alive. We get to participate in an incredibly dynamic industry, and we get to be in on building its future.

A
The Zachman Framework

ENTERPRISE ARCHITECTURE - A FRAMEWORK ™

	DATA — What	FUNCTION — How	NETWORK — Where	PEOPLE — Who	TIME — When	MOTIVATION — Why	
SCOPE (CONTEXTUAL) / *Planner*	List of Things Important to the Business; ENTITY = Class of Business Thing	List of Processes the Business Performs; Process = Class of Business Process	List of Locations in which the Business Operates; Node = Major Business Location	List of Organizations Important to the Business; People = Major Organization Unit	List of Events/Cycles Significant to the Business; Time = Major Business Event/Cycle	List of Business Goals/Strategies; Ends/Means = Major Business Goal/Strategy	SCOPE (CONTEXTUAL) / *Planner*
BUSINESS MODEL (CONCEPTUAL) / *Owner*	e.g. Semantic Model; Ent = Business Entity, Reln = Business Relationship	e.g. Business Process Model; Proc. = Business Process, I/O = Business Resources	e.g. Business Logistics System; Node = Business Location, Link = Business Linkage	e.g. Work Flow Model; People = Organization Unit, Work = Work Product	e.g. Master Schedule; Time = Business Event, Cycle = Business Cycle	e.g. Business Plan; End = Business Objective, Means = Business Strategy	BUSINESS MODEL (CONCEPTUAL) / *Owner*
SYSTEM MODEL (LOGICAL) / *Designer*	e.g. Logical Data Model; Ent = Data Entity, Reln = Data Relationship	e.g. Application Architecture; Proc. = Application Function, I/O = User Views	e.g. Distributed System Architecture; Node = I/S Function (Processor, Storage, etc), Link = Line Characteristics	e.g. Human Interface Architecture; People = Role, Work = Deliverable	e.g. Processing Structure; Time = System Event, Cycle = Processing Cycle	e.g. Business Rule Model; End = Structural Assertion, Means = Action Assertion	SYSTEM MODEL (LOGICAL) / *Designer*
TECHNOLOGY MODEL (PHYSICAL) / *Builder*	e.g. Physical Data Model; Ent = Segment/Table/etc., Reln = Pointer/Key/etc.	e.g. System Design; Proc. = Computer Function, I/O = Data Elements/Sets	e.g. Technology Architecture; Node = Hardware/Systems Software, Link = Line Specifications	e.g. Presentation Architecture; People = User, Work = Screen Format	e.g. Control Structure; Time = Execute, Cycle = Component Cycle	e.g. Rule Design; End = Condition, Means = Action	TECHNOLOGY MODEL (PHYSICAL) / *Builder*
DETAILED REPRESENTATIONS (OUT-OF-CONTEXT) / *Sub-Contractor*	e.g. Data Definition; Ent = Field, Reln = Address	e.g. Program; Proc. = Language Statement, I/O = Control Block	e.g. Network Architecture; Node = Address, Link = Protocol	e.g. Security Architecture; People = Identity, Work = Job	e.g. Timing Definition; Time = Interrupt, Cycle = Machine Cycle	e.g. Rule Specification; End = Sub-condition, Means = Step	DETAILED REPRESENTATIONS (OUT-OF-CONTEXT) / *Sub-Contractor*
FUNCTIONING ENTERPRISE	e.g. DATA	e.g. FUNCTION	e.g. NETWORK	e.g. ORGANIZATION	e.g. SCHEDULE	e.g. STRATEGY	FUNCTIONING ENTERPRISE

© John A. Zachman, Zachman International

B

A Comparison
of Data Modeling Techniques
(Syntactic Conventions)

Peter Chen first introduced entity/relationship modeling in 1976 [Chen 1976, 1977]. It was a brilliant idea that has revolutionized the way we represent data. It was a first version only, however, and many people since then have made improvements on it. A veritable plethora of data-modeling techniques have been developed.

Things became more complicated in the late 1980s with the advent of a variation on this theme called "object modeling". Now there were even more ways to model the structure of data. This was mitigated somewhat in the mid-1990s with the introduction of the UML, a modeling technique intended to replace at least all the "object-modeling" ones. As will be seen in this appendix, it is not quite up to replacing other entity/relationship approaches, but it has had a dramatic effect on the object-modeling world.

This appendix presents the most important of these techniques and provides a basis for comparing them with each other.

Regardless of the symbols used, data or object modeling is intended to do one thing: describe the things about which an organization wishes to collect data, along with the relationships among them. For this reason, all of the commonly used systems of notation are fundamentally convertible one to another. The major differences among them are aesthetic, although some make distinctions that others do not, and some do not have symbols to represent all situations.

This is true for object-modeling notations as well as entity/relationship notations.

There are actually three levels of conventions to be defined in the data-modeling arena: The first is *syntactic,* about the symbols to be used. These conventions are the primary focus of this appendix. The second defines the organization of model diagrams. *Positional* conventions dictate how entity types are laid out. Richard Barker has defined a very effective set of positional conventions [Barker 1990]. These are described in Chapter 3 (page 113). Finally, there are conventions about how the *meaning* of a model may be conveyed. *Semantic* conventions describe standard ways for representing common business situations. These are described briefly in Chapter 4 (pages 114–132). You can find more information about these in books by David Hay [Hay, 1996] and Martin Fowler [Fowler, 1997].

These three sets of conventions are, in principle, completely independent of each other. Given any of the syntactic conventions described here, you can follow any of the available positional or semantic conventions. In practice, however, promoters of each syntactic convention typically also promote at least particular positional conventions, if not the semantic ones as well.

In evaluating syntactic conventions, it is important to remember that data modeling has two audiences. The first is the business community that uses the models and their descriptions to verify that the analysts in fact understand their environment and their requirements. The second audience is the set of systems designers, who use the structures in the models and the business rules implied by them as the basis for computer system designs.

Different techniques are better for one audience or the other. Models used by analysts must be clear and easy to read. This often means that these models may describe less than the full extent of detail available. First and foremost, they must be accessible by a non-technical viewer. Models for designers, on the other hand, must be as complete and rigorous as possible, expressing as much as possible.

The evaluation, then, will be based both on the technical completeness of each technique and on its readability.

Technical completeness is in terms of the representation of:

- Entity types and attributes
- Relationships
- Unique identifiers
- Sub-types and super-types
- Constraints between relationships

A technique's *readability* is characterized by its graphic treatment of relationship lines and entity-type boxes, as well as its adherence to the general principles of good graphic design. Among the most important of these principles is that each symbol should have only one meaning, which applies wherever that symbol is used, and that each concept should be represented by only one symbol. Moreover, a diagram should not be cluttered with more symbols than are absolutely necessary, and the graphics in a diagram should be intuitively expressive of the concepts involved. Your author has written several articles on this subject [e.g., Hay, 1998.]

Each technique has strengths and weaknesses in the way it addresses each audience. As it happens, most are oriented more toward designers than they are toward the user community. These produce models that are very intricate and they focus on making sure that all possible constraints are described. Alas, this is often at the expense of readability.

This document presents seven notation schemes:

- *Peter Chen*—He's the man who started it all.
- *Information Engineering*—Clive Finkelstein and James Martin combined data modeling with an approach to systems development.
- *Richard Barker*—His is the notation used in Europe's SSADM methodology and by the Oracle Corporation.
- *IDEF1X*—This technique is supported and extensively used by the United States Department of Defense.
- *Object Role Modeling (ORM)*—This is a different approach to modeling facts and data.
- *The Unified Modeling Language (UML)*—This is the latest technique supported in the object-oriented world.
- *The Extended Markup Language (XML)*—This is not strictly a data-modeling language, but it demonstrates some interesting data-structure ideas.

For comparison purposes, the same example model is presented in the following sections using each technique. Note that the UML is billed as an "object modeling" technique, rather than as a data (entity/relationship) modeling technique, but as you will see, its structure is fundamentally the same. This comparison is in terms of each technique's symbols for describing entity types (or "object classes", for the UML), attributes, relationships (or object-oriented "associations"), unique identifiers, subtypes, and constraints between relationships.

At the end of the individual discussions is your author's argument in favor of Mr. Barker's approach for use in requirements analysis, along with his argument in favor of UML to support object-oriented design and IDEF1X to support relational database design.

Peter Chen

Peter Chen invented entity/relationship modeling in the mid-1970s [Chen, 1977], and his approach remains widely used today. It is unique in its representation of relationships and attributes. Relationships are shown with a separate diamond-shaped symbol on the relationship line, and attributes are shown in separate circles, instead of as annotations on each entity type.

A sample model, representing Chen's method, is shown in Figure B.1. This same example will be used to demonstrate all the techniques that follow. The model shows entity types, attributes, and relationships. It also has examples of both a super-type/sub-type combination and a constraint between relationships.

In the diagram, each PURCHASE ORDER is related to a single PARTY and to one or more examples of either one PRODUCT or one SERVICE.

The diagram also includes two entity types (EVENT and EVENT CATEGORY) in an unusual relationship. In most "one-to-many" relationships, the "one" side is mandatory ("... must be exactly one"), while the "many" side is optional ("... may be one or more"). In this example, the reverse is true: Each EVENT *may be* in *one and only one* EVENT CATEGORY (zero or one), and each EVENT CATEGORY *must be* a classification for *one or more* EVENTS (one or more). That is, an EVENT may exist without being classified, or it may be in one and only one EVENT CATEGORY. An EVENT CATEGORY can come into existence, however, only if there is at least one event to put into it.

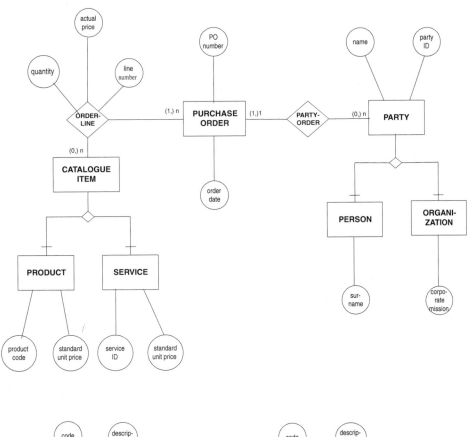

FIGURE B.1 A Chen Model.

Entity Types and Attributes

Entity types are represented by square-cornered boxes, with their *attributes* hanging off them in circles. An entity type's name appears inside the rectangle, and an attribute's name appears inside the circle. There are no special marks to indicate whether attributes are mandatory or optional, or whether they participate in the entity type's unique identifier.

Names of entity types and attributes are common terms, and in multiword names, the words are separated by hyphens.

Relationships

Mr. Chen's notation is unique among the techniques shown here in that a relationship is shown as a two-dimensional symbol—a rhombus on the line between two or more entity types.

Note that this relationship symbol makes it possible to maintain a "many-to-many" relationship without necessarily converting it into an associative or intersect entity type. In effect, the relationship itself is playing the role of an associative entity type. The relationship itself is permitted to have attributes. Note how "quantity", "actual price", and "line number" are attributes of the relationship *Order-line* in Figure B.1.

Note also that relationships do not have to be binary. As many entity types as necessary may be linked to a relationship rhombus.

Cardinality/Optionality

In Mr. Chen's original work, only one number appeared at each end, showing the maximum cardinality. That is, a relationship might be "one-to-many", with a "1" at one end and an "n" at the other. This would not indicate whether or not an occurrence of an entity type had to have at least one occurrence of the other entity type.

In most cases, an occurrence of an entity type that is related to one occurrence of another *must* be related to one, and an occurrence of an entity type that is related to more than one *may* be related to none, so most of the time the lower bounds can be assumed. The event/event category model, however, is unusual. Having just a "1" next to event, showing that an event is related to one event category, would not show that it might be related to none. The "n" which shows that each event category is related to more than one event would not show that it *must be* related to at least one.

For this reason, the technique can be extended to use two numbers at each end to show the minimum and maximum cardinalities. For example, the relationship *party-order* between PURCHASE ORDER and PARTY shows 1,1 at the PURCHASE ORDER end, showing that each PURCHASE ORDER must be with no less than one PARTY and no more than one PARTY. At the other end, "0,n" shows that a PARTY may or may not be involved with any PURCHASE ORDER and could be involved with several. The EVENT/EVENT CATEGORY model has "0,1" at the EVENT end and "1,n" at the EVENT CATEGORY end.

In an alternative notation, relationship names may be replaced with "E" if the existence of occurrences of the second entity type requires the existence of a related occurrence of the first entity type. See "Unique identifiers" below for more about this.

Names

Because *relationships* are clearly considered objects in their own right, their names tend to be nouns.

The relationship between purchase-order and person or organization, for example, is called *order-line*. Sometimes a relationship name is simply a concatenation of the two entity type names. For example *party-order* relates party and purchase order.

Entity type and relationship names may be abbreviated.

Unique Identifiers

A *unique identifier* is any combination of attributes and relationships that uniquely identify an occurrence of an entity type.

While Mr. Chen recognizes the importance of attributes as entity-type unique identifiers [Chen, 1977, p. 23], his notation makes no provision for showing this. If the unique identifier of an entity type includes a relationship to a second entity type, he replaces the relationship name with "E", makes the line into the dependent entity type an arrow, and draws a second box around this dependent entity type. (Figure B.2 shows how this would look if the relationship to party were part of the unique identifier of PURCHASE ORDER). This still does not identify any attributes that are part of the identifier.

FIGURE B.2 Existence-Dependent Relationship.

Sub-types

A *sub-type* is a subset of the occurrences of another entity type, its *super-type*. That is, an occurrence of a sub-type entity type is also an occurrence of its super-type. An occurrence of the super-type is also an occurrence of exactly one or another of the sub-types.

Though not in Mr. Chen's original work, the technique was extended to include this by Mat Flavin [Flavin, 1981] and Robert Brown [Brown, 1993].

In this extension, sub-types are represented by separate entity-type boxes, each removed from its super-type and connected to it by an "isa" relationship. (Each occurrence of a sub-type "is a[n]" occurrence of the super-type.) The relationship lines are linked by a rhombus, and each relationship to a sub-type has a bar drawn across it. In Figure B.1, for example, PARTY is a super-type, with PERSON and ORGANIZATION as its sub-types. Similarly, a CATALOGUE ITEM must be either a PRODUCT or a SERVICE.

Constraints between Relationships

The most common case of constraints between relationships is the "exclusive or", meaning that each occurrence of the base entity type must (or may) be related to occurrences of one other entity type, but not more than one. These will be seen in most of the techniques which follow below.

Mr. Chen does not deal with constraints directly at all. This must be done by defining an artificial entity type and making the constrained entity types into sub-types of that entity type. This is shown in Figure B.1 with the entity type CATALOGUE ITEM, which has mutually exclusive sub-types product and service. Each purchase order has an *order-line* relationship with one CATALOGUE ITEM, where each CATALOGUE ITEM must be either a PRODUCT or a SERVICE.

Comments

Mr. Chen was first, so it is not surprising that his technique does not express all the nuances that have been included in subsequent techniques. It does not annotate characteristics of attributes, and it does not show the identification of entity types without sacrificing the names of the relationships.

While it does permit showing multiple inheritance and multiple type hierarchies, the multibox approach to sub-types takes up a lot of room on the drawing, limiting the number of other entity types that can be placed on it. It also requires a great deal of space to give a separate symbol to each attribute and each relationship. Moreover, it does not clearly convey the fact that an occurrence of a sub-type *is* an occurrence of a super-type.

Information Engineering

"Information engineering" was originally developed by Clive Finkelstein in Australia the late 1970's. He collaborated with James Martin to publicize it in the United States and Europe [Martin & Finkelstein, 1981], and then Martin went on from there to become predominantly associated with it [Martin & McClure, 1985]. Mr. Finkelstein later published his own version [Finkelstein, 1989; Finkelstein, 1992]. Because of the dual origin of the techniques, there are minor variations between Mr. Finkelstein's and Mr. Martin's notations The information-engineering version of our test case (with some of the notations from each version) is shown in Figure B.3.

In the example, each PARTY *is vendor in* zero, one, or more PURCHASE ORDERS, each of which initially *has* zero, one or more LINE ITEMS, but eventually it must have at least one LINE ITEM. Each LINE ITEM, in turn, *is for* either exactly one PRODUCT or exactly one SER-

VICE. Also, each EVENT *classifies* zero or one EVENT TYPE, while each EVENT TYPE must be (related to) one or more EVENTS

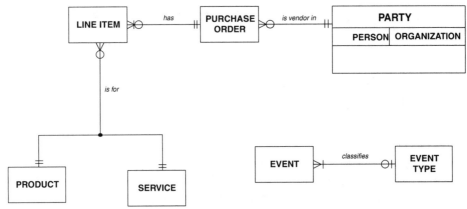

FIGURE B.3 An Information-Engineering Model.

Entity Types and Attributes

Mr. Finkelstein defines entity type in the designer's sense of representing "data to be stored for later reference" [Finkelstein, 1992, 23]. Mr. Martin, however, adopts the analyst's definition that "an entity type is something (real or abstract) about which we store data" [Martin & McClure, 1985, 249].

Entity types are shown in square-cornered rectangles. An entity type's name is inside its rectangle. Attributes are not shown at all. Mr. Finkelstein shows them in a separate document, the "entity type list". Mr. Martin has another modeling technique, called "bubble charts", specifically for modeling attributes, keys, and other attribute characteristics.

Names of entity types are common terms, and the words in multiword names are separated by spaces.

Relationships

Relationships are shown as solid lines between pairs of entity types, with symbols on each end to show cardinality and optionality.

Names

Mr. Martin names relationships with verbs, often only in one direction. Mr. Finkelstein doesn't name relationships at all.

Cardinality/Optionality

Each relationship in information engineering has two halves, with each half described by one or more symbols. If an occurrence of the first entity type *may* or *may not* be related to occurrences of the second, a small open circle appears near the second entity type. If it *must* have at least one occurrence of the second, a short line crosses the relationship line instead. If an occurrence of the first entity type can be related to no more than one of the second entity type ("one and only one"), another short line crosses the relationship. If it can be related to more than one of the second entity type ("one or more"), a crow's foot is put at the intersection of the relationship and the second entity-type box.

For example, in Figure B.3, a PARTY *is vendor in* zero, one, or more PURCHASE ORDERS. A PURCHASE ORDER, on the other hand, (*is to*) one and only one PARTY.

Mr. Finkelstein has a unique notation, also shown in the figure. Note that each purchase order *initially* may have one or more line items, but *eventually* it *must* have at least one. That is, it is possible to create a purchase order without having to fill in the line items immediately, but at least one must be added later. The bar across the line between the circle and the crow's foot shows this.

Unique Identifiers

Unique identifiers are not represented in an information-engineering data model. Mr. Martin shows them separately in "bubble diagrams".

Sub-types

Mr. Martin represents sub-types as nested boxes inside the super-type box. This is shown in the figure. Mr. Finkelstein portrays them as separate boxes, with a linked with "isa" relationship lines, as used in the Chen notation described above.

Constraints between Relationships

In information-engineering notation, a constraint between relationships is shown by the relationship halves of the three (or more) entity types involved meeting at a small circle. If the circle is solid, the relationship between the relationships is "exclusive or", meaning that each occurrence of the base entity type must (or may) be related to occurrences of one other entity type, but not more than one. This is shown in the figure, where each LINE ITEM *is for* either one PRODUCT or *is for* one SERVICE, but not both. If the circle is open, it is an "inclusive or" relationship, meaning that an occurrence of the base entity type must (or may) be related to occurrences of one, some, or all of the other entity types.

Comments

Information engineering is widely practiced. It is reasonably concise and attractive, consistent, and has a minimum of clutter. It is, however, missing important notations for attributes and unique identifiers, although some CASE tools have added these. Mr. Martin's approach to sub-types is compact and therefore desirable if models are to be presented to the nontechnical community, while Mr. Finkelstein's is not. Mr. Finkelstein's notation for "initially may be but eventually must be" is a very ingenious solution to a common modeling situation, not found in any other notation.

Richard Barker's Notation (as Used by Oracle Corporation)

The next notation was originally developed by the British consulting company CACI and is part of the European methodology, SSADM. It was subsequently promoted by Richard Barker [Barker, 1990] and adopted by the Oracle Corporation for its "CASE*Method" (subsequently renamed the "Custom Development Method" [Oracle, 1996]).

Figure B.4 shows our example as represented in this notation. In the diagram, each PURCHASE ORDER must be *issued to* one and only one PARTY and may be *composed of* one or more LINE ITEMS, each of which in turn must be *for* either one PRODUCT or one SERVICE. Also, each EVENT may be *in* one and only one EVENT TYPE, while each EVENT TYPE must be *a classification for* one or more EVENTS.

Entity Types and Attributes

Entity types in Barker's notation are shown as round-cornered rectangles. Attributes may be displayed inside the entity-type boxes.

Officially, attributes are shown with small open circles for optional attributes, solid circles for required attributes, and octothorps (#) for attributes which participate in unique identifiers. Often in practice, however (and throughout this Appendix), dots are used for all required and optional attributes not in a unique identifier.

Relationships

Relationships are shown as lines, with each half solid or dashed, depending on whether that part of the relationship is mandatory or not. The presence or absence of a crow's foot on each end shows that end as referring to, respectively, up to many or no more than one occurrence of that entity type. Naming conventions allow the relationship at each end to be read as a concise, disciplined, but easy-to-understand sentence.

Cardinality/Optionality

Relationships are in two parts, one representing the relationship going in each direction. In a relationship half, different symbols address the upper and lower boundaries of the relationship: A dashed line near the first, subject, entity type shows that the relationship is optional and means "zero or more" (read as "may be"), and a solid line represents a mandatory relationship that means "at least one" (read as "must be"). A "crow's foot" next to the second entity type represents "up to many" (read as "one or more"), while no crow's foot represents "up to one" (read as "one and only one").

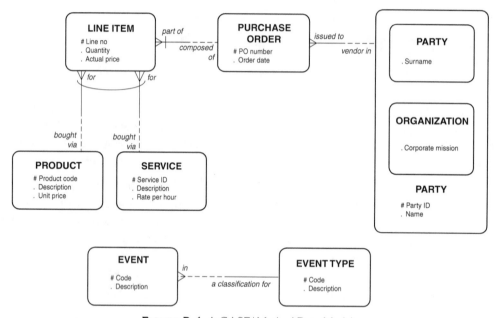

FIGURE B.4 A CASE*Method Data Model.

Names

The Barker notation is unique in the way it names relationships. Relationship names are prepositions or prepositional phrases, not verbs, so that normal and meaningful English sentences can be constructed from them. The sentences are of the structure:

> Each
> <entity type 1>
> {must be | may be}*(If the line is solid or dashed)*
> <relationship>
> {one or more | one and only one}*(If there is or is not a crow's foot)*
> <entity type 2>

For example, in Figure B.4, "Each party <u>may be</u> a *vendor in* one or more purchase orders," and "Each purchase order <u>must be</u> *issued to* one and only one party."

Unique Identifiers

A unique identifier is any combination of attributes and relationships which uniquely identifies an occurrence of an entity type. ***Attributes*** which are parts of the definition of a unique identifier are shown preceded by octothorps (#). ***Relationships*** which are part of the definition of a unique identifier are marked by a short line across the relationship near the entity type being identified.

For example, in Figure B.4, each occurrence of PARTY is identified by its "Party ID", and the unique identifier of LINE ITEM is a combination of the attribute "Line number" and the relationship *"part of* one and only one PURCHASE ORDER." Since the marked relationship represents the fact that each LINE ITEM is partly identified by a particular PURCHASE ORDER, it implies that the PURCHASE ORDER's unique identifier "PO number" participates in identification of the LINE ITEM as well. When implemented, a column derived from "PO number" will be generated in the table derived from LINE ITEM. It will serve as a foreign key to the table derived from PURCHASE ORDER and will be part of the primary key of the table that is derived from LINE ITEM.

Note that Mr. Barker's notation distinguishes the unique identifier in the conceptual model from the "primary key" which identifies rows in a physical table. The unique identifier is shown, while the primary key is not. Similarly, since a foreign key is simply the implementation of a relationship, this is not shown explicitly here either.

Sub-types

Barker's notation shows sub-types as boxes inside super-type boxes, according to the approach to set theory laid out by Leonhard Euler in the 18th Century. This has the advantage of taking up much less room on the diagram, and it emphasizes the fact that an occurrence of a sub-type *is* an occurrence of the super-type. The super- and sub-types are not simply related to each other. This does mean, however, that multiple inheritance (multiple super-types for one sub-types) and multiple type hierarchies (multiple ways of dividing a super-type into sub-types) cannot be represented by a Barker model.

In Barker's notation, sub-types are ***exclusive***, meaning that overlapping sub-types are not allowed. Sub-types are also ***complete***, meaning that sub-types are supposed to account for all occurrences of a super-type, although in practice this latter rule is often bent by adding the sub-type OTHER. In Figure B.4, PERSON and ORGANIZATION are sub-types of PARTY.

Constraints between Relationships

The only constraint between relationships available in Mr. Barker's notation is the *exclusive or*. An arc across two relationships represents the fact that each occurrence of an entity type must be (or may be) related to occurrences of one or more other entity types, but not more than one. For example, Figure B.4 shows that each LINE ITEM must be *either for* one PRODUCT *or for* one SERVICE.

Comments

Several things distinguish this notation from those described elsewhere. These are factors that make the Barker technique the most desirable to use in a requirements analysis project. The technique results in models that are much better for presenting to the public at large than those produced by any other.

First, this notation uses relatively few distinct symbols. There is only one kind of entity type. Whether it is a role, an intersection, or another kind of association between two entity types, it is represented by the same round-cornered rectangle. The full range of relationship types is shown by line halves, which may be solid or dashed, and by the presence or absence of a crow's foot on each end. Unique identifiers, where it is important to show them, are shown by either the hash marks next to an attribute, or a small mark across a relationship line, and dependency is implied by the use of a relationship in a unique identifier. Attributes may be shown with indicators of their optionality.

Other notations are, to varying degrees, more complicated than that.

Second, sub-types are shown as entity types *inside* other entity types. Most other notations place sub-types outside the super-type, connected to it with "isa" relationship lines. This takes up much more space on a diagram and does not convey as emphatically the fact that an occurrence of a sub-type *is* an occurrence of the super-type. Moreover, it is not easy to see that an attribute of or a relationship to a super-type is also an attribute of or a relationship to every sub-type of that super-type.

Third, Barker's notation permits "exclusive or" constraints between relationships, which show that an occurrence of one entity type may be related to occurrences of either of two or more other entity types. This is more than is available in some notations, and less than in others.

The last, and perhaps the most important thing to distinguish this technique from the others is a rigorous naming standard for relationships. Relationship names are prepositions, not verbs. A little reflection should reveal why this is appropriate, since it is the preposition in English grammar, not the verb, that denotes a relationship. (Verbs suggest functions, which are featured in other kinds of models.) The implied verb in every relationship sentence is "to be", expressed as either "must be" or "may be".

Note that in the examples of notations without this discipline, the verbs often include "is" anyway.

This use of prepositions makes it possible to use common English sentences to represent relationships completely. It is not always easy to come up with just the right word, but the exercise of trying to do so improves significantly your understanding of the true nature of the relationship.

This discipline could certainly be followed with the other techniques, but none of the books your author has found to describe these techniques endorses it.

IDEF1X

IDEF1X is a data-modeling technique that is used by many branches of the United States Federal Government [FIPS 1993] [also see Bruce 1992]. The IDEF1X version of the sample model is shown in Figure B.5.

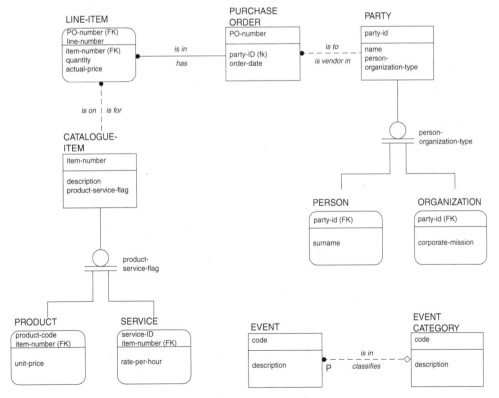

FIGURE B.5 An IDEF1X Model.

Entity Types and Attributes

Entity types in IDEF1X are shown by round-cornered or square-cornered rectangles. Round-cornered rectangles represent "dependent" entity types—those whose unique identifier includes at least one relationship to another entity type. "Independent" entity types, whose identifiers are not derived from other entity types, are shown with square corners.

The name of the entity type appears outside the box. The box is divided, with identifying attributes (here referred to as the "primary key") above the division and nonidentifying attributes below.

In multiword entity type names, the words may be separated by hyphens, underscores, or blanks.

Relationships

In IDEF1X, relationships are asymmetrical: Different symbols for optionality are used, depending on the relationship's cardinality. Unlike the other notations, symbols cannot be parsed in terms of optionality and cardinality independently. Each set of symbols describes a *combination* of the optionality and cardinality of the entity type next to it.

In addition to a relationship line from an entity type, the foreign key that would implement the line in a relational database design is shown as an attribute of that entity type.

If a relationship is part of an entity type's unique identifier, it is shown as a solid line; if not, it is shown as a dashed line.

Table B.1 shows, for IDEF1X and the Barker notation, all the possible combinations of cardinality and optionality on both ends of the relationship.

Cardinality/Optionality

As seen in the table, optionality is shown differently for the "many" and the "one" sides of a relationship. Most of the time, a solid circle next to an entity type means zero, one, or more occurrences of that entity type. If there is no other symbol next to the entity type on this "many" side of a relationship, the relationship is optional. See lines 1-3, and 7 in Table B.1. That is, the solid circle stands for zero, one, or more ("may be... one or more") if it is by itself. Adding the letter P makes the relationship mandatory (meaning "must be one or more")[1]. Adding a "1" also makes the relationship mandatory, but this changes the cardinality of the relationship to exactly one. It changes the meaning of the solid circle from "may be one or more" to "must be one and only one". (See lines 4, 6, 8, and 10 in the table.) Adding the letter Z keeps the relationship optional, but that changes the cardinality of the solid circle to "may be one and only one".

---

1. Meaning that the relationship is <u>P</u>ositively required.

So a solid circle may mean "must be" or "may be", and it may mean "one or more" or "one and only one", depending on the other symbols around it. That is to say, the solid circle does not convey any inherent meaning in itself.

Absence of a solid circle next to an entity type means that only one occurrence of that entity type is involved ("one and only one"). If there is no symbol next to the entity type on the "one" side of the relationship, the entity type is mandatory ("must be one and only one"), as shown in lines 1, 2, 4, 5, 11–18.

Placing a small diamond symbol next to the entity type means that the other entity type in the relationship may be related to one and only one occurrence ("zero or one") of that entity type. (See lines 3, 6, 16, and 19.) This, then, is an alternative way to specify an optional one-and-only-one occurrence as an entity type. We saw above that you could also use a solid circle with a letter Z under it (see lines 21–24.)

Since the solid circle—which usually represents "may be one or more"—always appears on the "many" side of a relationship, the use of the solid circle in a many-to-many relationship makes each end optional. Adding the letter "P" on one or both ends makes the end so modified mandatory (see lines 7 through 10).

TABLE B.1   Comparison of Barker and IDEF1X Notations

	CASE*Method Notation	IDEF1X Notation	CASE*Method Description	IDEF1X Description
1	B ⊳⊢----- A	B •—— A	Each A may be... one or more B's. Each B must be ... one and only one A. (A partially identifies B.)	One to zero or more (dependent)
2	B ⊳----- A	B •------- A	Each A may be... one or more B's. Each B must be ... one and only one A.	One to zero or more
3	B ⊳------- A	B •-----◇ A	Each A may be... one or more B's. Each B may be ... one and only one A.	Zero or one to zero or more
4	B ⊳—— A	B •-----P A	Each A must be... one or more B's. Each B must be ... one and only one A.	One to one or many

TABLE B.1   Comparison of Barker and IDEF1X Notations (Continued)

	CASE*Method Notation	IDEF1X Notation	CASE*Method Description	IDEF1X Description
5	B ⊳—∈ A	B •ₚ— A	Each A must be... one or more B's. Each B must be ... one and only one A. (A partially identifies B.)	One to one or many (dependent)
6	B ⊳- - — A	B •ₚ- - ◇ A	Each A must be... one or more B's. Each B may be ... one and only one A	One to zero or many
7	B ⊳- - -∈ A	B •—• A	Each A may be... one or more B's. Each B may be ... one or more A's	Zero or many to zero or many
8	B ⊳—∈ A	B •ₚ— •ₚ A	Each A must be... one or more B's. Each B must be ... one or more A's.	One or many to one or many
9	B ⊳- -∈ A	B •— •ₚ A	Each A may be... one or more B's. Each B must be ... one or more A's.	Zero or many to one or many
10	B ⊳- - -∈ A	B •ₚ— • A	Each A must be... one or more B's. Each B may be ... one or more A's.	One or many to zero or many
11	B —— A	B •₁- - - - A	Each A must be... one and only one B. Each B must be... one and only one A.	One to one
12	(Same as 11)	B - - - -•₁ A	(Same as 11)	
13	(Same as 11)	B •₁- - -•₁ A	(Same as 11)	
14	(Same as 11)	B - - - - A	(Same as 11)	

TABLE B.1   Comparison of Barker and IDEF1X Notations (Continued)

	CASE*Method Notation	IDEF1X Notation	CASE*Method Description	IDEF1X Description
15	B ⊢——— A	B •——— A ₁	Each A must be... one and only one B. Each B must be... one and only one A. (B partially dependent on A.)	One to one (dependent)
16	B ------- A	B •---◇ A ₁	Each A must be... one and only one B. Each B may be... one and only one A.	Zero or one to one
17	B ⊢——— A	B •----- A z	Each A may be... one and only one B. Each B must be... one and only one A.	One to zero or one
18	B ⊢----- A	B •——— A z	Each A may be... one and only one B. Each B must be... one and only one A. (A partially identifies B.)	One to zero or one (dependent)
19	B ------- A	B •-----◇ A z	Each A may be... one and only one B. Each B may be... one and only one A.	Zero or one to zero or one
20	(Same as 19)	B ◇-----• A z	(Same as 19)	
21	(Same as 19)	B •-----• A z z	(Same as 19)	
22	(Same as 19)	B ◇-----◇ A	(Same as 19)	

The two ways of showing that an occurrence of one entity type "must be" related to a single occurrence of another mean that there are four different ways to represent a mandatory one to one relationship. These are shown in lines 11–14. Similarly, optional one-to-one relationships can be shown in four different ways, as shown in lines 19–22. One-to-one relationships that are partly optional and partly mandatory can be shown in two ways, depending on which way the model is oriented, as shown in lines 16–17.

Note: The variations in notation above, which have no meaning in the conceptual model, turn out to be significant in the physical design. The difference between representations for "may be one and only one" has to do with the fact that the diamond implies an optional foreign key in the opposite entity type, while the circle with the Z simply says that there may or may not be a child occurrence. In the other cases of multiple representation of the same concept (11–14, and 19–22), the culprit is again physical implementation. Each of the different symbol sets is implemented in a different way. Indeed, some of the symbol combinations cannot be implemented as expressed.

In other words, the symbols are deeply linked to the *implementation* of the tables, not the *logic* of the situation. Thus, IDEF1X is fundamentally a physical database design modeling technique, not one appropriate for doing conceptual design.

Names

A relationship name is a verb or verb phrase, where multiple words are separated by spaces. Relationships are identified in both directions.

Unique Identifiers

As stated above, a unique identifier is represented in IDEF1X by the primary key which will implement it in a relational database. Since all relationships are shown by foreign-key attributes, the primary key may consist of any combination of foreign-key and non-foreign-key attributes. If a foreign key is present in the unique identifier primary key, then the otherwise dashed relationship line becomes solid, and the entity-type box acquires round corners.

Sub-type

IDEF1X shows sub-types as separate entity-type boxes, each removed from its super-type and connected to it by an "isa" relationship. (Each occurrence of a sub-type "is a[n]" occurrence of the super-type.)

There are two kinds of sub-types. In Figure B.5, the circle with two horizontal lines under it is a *complete* subtyping arrangement: All occurrences of the parent must be occurrences of one or the other sub-type. A circle with only one horizontal line below it is an *incomplete* subtyping arrangement: The sub-types do not represent all possible occurrences of the super-type.

All sub-types extending from a single sub-type symbol are mutually *exclusive*. Sub-types may be shown to be *overlapping* by being descended from different sub-type symbols attached to the same super-type entity type.

In IDEF1X, the unique identifier of the sub-type must always be identical to the identifier of the super-type. This point is reinforced by including the foreign key

("(FK)") designator next to the unique identifier of the sub-type, referring to the unique identifier of the super-type. Optionally, a "role name" may be appended to the front of the foreign-key name in the sub-type. In Figure B.5, the role names "product-code" and "service-id" are roles, appended to "item number" for the primary keys of product and service. Note that, since the keys themselves remain identical to the key of the super-type, appending role names does not change their format in any way.

An attribute used to discriminate between the sub-types is placed next to the sub-type symbol. For example, "person-organization-type" is shown in Figure B.5 to distinguish between occurrences of person and organization. If the sub-types were implemented in a single table for the super-type, this would become a separate column for discriminating between occurrences of the different sub-types.

Constraints between Relationships

IDEF1X does not have an explicit way to represent constraints between relationships. Instead of saying "A" is related to "B" or to "C", it is necessary to define an entity type, "D", and then use the sub-type notation. Thus you would say "A" is related to "D", which must be either a "B" or a "C".

The ability to express exhaustiveness and exclusivity in sub-types does carry over to this situation.

This is shown in Figure B.5 with the creation of CATALOGUE ITEM as a super-type of PRODUCT and SERVICE.

Comments

IDEF1X symbols do not map cleanly to the concepts they are supposed to model. A concept that should be represented by a single symbol requires several together, and it requires different symbols under different circumstances. That is, particular situations can be represented by more than one set of symbols, while the same symbol can mean different things, depending on context. Which symbol is used to describe a particular situation is heavily dependent on the context of that situation and on how the relationship will be implemented, not just on the situation itself.

For example, the symbol to be used for optionality depends on the cardinality of the relationship. The solid circle symbol can mean anything, depending on its setting. Similarly, a cardinality/optionality combination may be represented in different ways. This is because what is being represented is not a *conceptual* structure, but an *implementation* method.

The effect of all this is that it is prohibitively difficult to teach a nontechnical viewer to read an IDEF1X diagram.

A dominant graphic feature of any relationship line is its being solid or dashed. Barker's notation uses this feature to distinguish between relationships that are required and those that are not. Among those relationships that are, those participating in a unique identifier may be simply marked with an extra line across them, but this level of detail is often not required.

In IDEF1X, however, the solidity of a line describes the participation of one entity type in the unique identifier (primary key) of the other. This requires the analyst to begin the efforts by analyzing dependency—before addressing the optionality or cardinality of the model's relationships.

In a real modeling situation, however, an analyst in fact normally starts by examining which entity types are required for which other entity types, and how many occurrences are involved. The details of keys or identifiers are typically not addressed until much later.

And corrections to the model are unnecessarily difficult: If you make a single error in cardinality or optionality (say, the one-to-one mandatory relationship should really be optional), then several symbols must be changed.

While it does permit showing multiple inheritance and multiple type hierarchies, the multibox approach to sub-types takes up a lot of room on the drawing, limiting the number of other entity types that can be placed on it. It also requires a great deal of space to give a separate symbol to each attribute and each relationship. Moreover, it does not clearly convey the fact that an occurrence of a sub-type *is* an occurrence of a super-type.

IDEF1X may be a good modeling tool to use as the basis for database design, but it does not follow the rules of good graphic design (as described at the beginning of this appendix), making it unnecessarily difficult to learn and difficult to use as a tool for analyzing business requirements jointly with users.

Object-Role Modeling (ORM)

NIAM was once an acronym for "Nijssen's Information Analysis Methodology", but more recently, since G. M. Nijssen was only one of many people involved in the development of the method, it was generalized to "Natural language Information Analysis Method". Indeed, practitioners now also use a still more general name, "Object-Role Modeling", or ORM [Halpin, 2001].[2]

---

2. Your author is grateful to Dr. Halpin for providing information to supplement his book, and for his comments and suggestions about this appendix. Any remaining errors, however, are your author's and not his.

ORM takes a different approach from the other methods described here. Rather than representing entity types as analogues of relational tables, it shows *relationships* (that contain one or more "roles" in ORM parlance) to be such analogs. Like Mr. Barker's notation, it makes extensive use of language in making the models accessible to the public, but unlike any of the other modeling techniques, it has much greater capacity to describe business rules and constraints.

With ORM, it is difficult to describe entity types independently from relationships. The philosophy behind the language is that it describes "facts," where a fact is a combination of entity types, domains, and relationships.

A sample ORM model is shown in Figure B.6

Entity Types and Attributes

As shown in Figure B.6, an entity type is portrayed by an ellipse containing its name. An ellipse may also represent a *value type*, which is similar to a domain. A value type's playing a role in a relationship with an entity type is equivalent to an "attribute" in an entity/relationship diagram.

Entity-type *labels* play roles as identifiers, and these may be shown as dashed ellipses, although as a shorthand, identifying value types may also be shown within the entity-type ellipse in parentheses, below the entity-type name. Nonidentifying attributes always are portrayed as roles played by value types—ellipses outside the entity-type ellipse.

Thus, relationships not only connect entity types to each other but also value types to entity types as attributes. ORM is unique in being able to raise the question: What is the exact relationship of an attribute to its entity type? In particular, it can describe the optionality and cardinality of attributes.

Attributes can be combined if they have the same domain or **unit-based reference mode**. For example, in Figure B.6, the *list price of* Product, the *rate for* a service, and the *cost of* a Line Item are all taken from the domain "Monetary amount". Similarly, this figure asserts that product names and service names are taken from the same set of names.

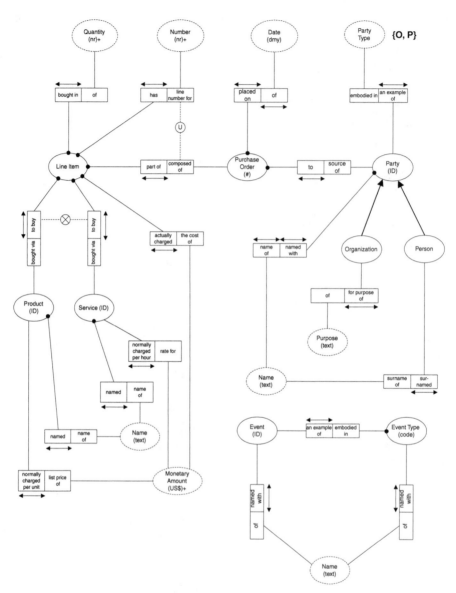

FIGURE B.6 An ORM Model.

Relationships

ORM presents relationships between two entity types as "roles" that entity types and domains play in the organization's structure. Relationships are assembled from one or more adjacent boxes containing role names and connected to the entity types by solid lines. Relationships are not limited to being binary. Tertiary and higher-order relation-ships are permitted.

Where most methods portray *entity types* in terms that allow them to be translated into relational tables, ORM portrays the *relationships* to be converted to tables. That is, the two parts (or more) of the relationship become columns in a "relation" (table). In effect, these are the foreign keys to the two entity types. Attributes of one or more of the related entity types also then become part of a generated table.

A relationship may be "objectified", when it takes on characteristics of an entity type. This is most common in the case of many to many relationships. Note in Figure B.7 that the many-to-many relationship between purchase order and product has been circled. Instead of creating a formal entity type, as is done in many other systems of notation (and as was done above), the relationship simply becomes a "nested fact type" or "objectified relationship". This nested fact type may then be treated as an entity type having other entity types or attributes related to it. In Figure B.7, for example, the nested fact type Line Item *is bought in* a quantity.

This is an alternative to simply defining line item as an entity type, as was done in Figure B.6. That was done in that figure because of the exclusive relationship between it and product and service. (See the discussion of constraints between relationships, below.)

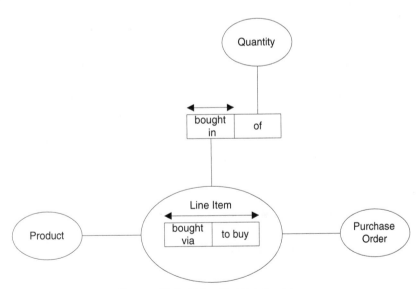

FIGURE B.7 Objectified Relationships.

Cardinality/Optionality

Cardinality is addressed differently in ORM than in the other methods. Here it is tied up with the uniqueness of occurrences of a fact (relationship). By definition, each occurrence of a fact applies to a single occurrence of each entity type participating in the relationship. That is, if each Party may be *the source of* <u>one or more</u> Purchase Orders, then a Party's participation in the *source of* role is not unique. On the other hand, if each Purchase Order must be to <u>one and only one</u> Party, then Purchase Order's participation in the *to* role *is* unique. That is, there is only one occurrence of a Purchase Order's being *to* a Party.

An entity type's uniqueness with respect to a relationship is represented in ORM by a double-headed arrow. If the relationship is one-to-many, the arrow is on the side of the relationship closest to the "many" side—that is, closest to the side of the entity type that is related to only one other thing. So in our Purchase Order / Party example, the arrow is under the Purchase Order *to* role, since it is unique.

As another example, in Figure B.6, the line item itself can appear only once in a *part of* role (that is, it can appear only once in a PURCHASE ORDER) because of the double-headed arrow under *part of*. Each PURCHASE ORDER is to one and only one party, since the arrow is over "*to*". The PURCHASE ORDER, on the other hand, can be *composed of* more than one LINE ITEM, because LINE ITEM can appear in the set of relationship occurrences more than once. This is shown by the absence of the double-headed arrow on the PURCHASE ORDER's side of the relationship.

If the relationship is one-to-one, the bar appears over each half. For example, there is a double-headed arrow over both sides of the relationship between the entity type PARTY and the domain "Name". This means that each party can have at most one "Name", and each "Name" can be used for at most one PARTY. This is a one-to-one relationship.

If the relationship is many-to-many, the arrow crosses both halves of the relationship, showing that both halves are required to identify uniquely each occurrence of the relationship. In the objectified relationship model (Figure B.7) note the arrowheads over both *bought via* and *to buy*.

Optionality: A relationship may be designated as *mandatory* by placing a solid circle next to the entity type which is the subject of the fact. For example, in Figure B.6, each PURCHASE ORDER must participate in the *to* relationship with party.

Names

Entity type and attribute names are the real-world names of the things they represent. Relationship names are verb phrases, and it is permitted to use "is" or "has". There is nothing to prevent use of the Barker convention, however, and that was done in this example. (This becomes problematic, however, in relationships that are not binary.) In some usages, past tense is used to designate temporal relationships that occurred at a point in time, while present tense is used to designate permanent relationships. Some standard abbreviations are used, such as "nr" (number, as a data type), and "US$" (money, as a data type). Spaces may be removed from multiword entity-type names, but all words in a name have an initial capital letter.

Unique Identifiers

As described above, labels may be shown as dashed ellipses, although as a shorthand, they also may be shown within the entity-type ellipse in parentheses, below the entity-type name. If nothing else is shown, these are the unique identifiers of the entity type. Where both a label and some other identifier are involved (such as a system-generated unique identifier), the unique identifier is shown under the name, and the label is shown as another attribute, (albeit with the dashed circle). For example, in Figure B.6, party is shown as *identified by* "ID," but it also is *named with* the label party name.

If two or more attributes or relationships are required to establish uniqueness for an entity type, a special symbol is used. In Figure B.6, the combination of "number" being *line number for* a Line Item and Purchase Order being *composed of* a Line Item are required to identify uniquely an occurrence of the Line Item entity type. This is shown by the **uniqueness constraint**, represented with a circled "u" between the *line number of* and the *composed of* roles. This implies that a given number (such as "2"), while it is *a line number* for only one line item, could apply to more than one purchase order, and a given purchase order could be related to more than one line number. The combination of "Line Number of" and purchase order must be unique, however.

Sub-types

A sub-type is represented as a separate entity type, with a thick arrow pointing from it to its super-type. In Figure B.6, organization and person are each sub-types of party, as shown by the arrows. In addition, a "type" attribute is defined as the flag which distinguishes between occurrences of the sub-types ("party type" in Figure B.6). If the sub-types are **exhaustive** (covering all occurrences of the super-type), a constraint is shown next to the "type" attribute. If they are **exclusive** (non-overlapping), a double-headed line is shown over half of the relationship between the entity type and its "Type".

In Figure B.6, the sub-types of party are exclusive, because the double-headed arrow over is *an example of* party type, meaning that a party is *an example of* one and only one party type. It is exhaustive because only the options "P" (person) and "O" (organization) are available for Party Type.

Constraints between Relationships

In the ORM system of notation, constraints between relationships are shown as circles linked to the relationships involved. An "exclusion constraint" (shown in the figure between the Product and Service relationships from line item) says that one or the other relationship may apply, but not both. The "X" in the symbol means that a Line Item may not be for both a Product and a Service. The dot over the middle of the "X" (⊗) means that a Line Item *must* be for a Product or a Service, but not both. If there were a dot by itself, it would mean that one or the other must apply, but both could apply as well. With no constraint, one or the other, both, or neither could apply.

(See the discussion of ORM constraints in Chapter 8 on pages 311–332.)

Comments

In many ways, ORM is the most versatile and most descriptive of the modeling techniques presented here. It has an extensive capability for describing constraints that apply to sets of entity types and attributes. It is not oriented just toward entity types and relationships, but toward objects and the roles they play—where an "object" may be an entity type or a value type (domain). It is constructed to make it easy to describe diagrams in English, although it lacks a discipline for constructing the English sentences.

Cardinality is shown via uniqueness constraints, and optionality is shown by making a relationship mandatory or not. Interestingly enough, this approach means the optionality and cardinality of attributes can be treated in exactly the same way. Must there be a value for an attribute? Can there be more than one?

Unlike all the flavors of entity/relationship modeling described here, ORM makes domains explicit.

All this expressiveness, however, is achieved at some aesthetic cost. A ORM model is necessarily much more detailed than an equivalent data model, and as a consequence, it is often difficult to grasp the shape or purpose of a particular drawing. Also, because all entity types, attributes, and relationships carry equal visual weight, it is hard to see which elements are the most important.

While it does permit showing multiple inheritance and multiple type hierarchies, the multibox approach to sub-types takes up a lot of room on the drawing, limiting the number of other entity types that can be placed on it. Moreover, it does not clearly convey the fact that an occurrence of a sub-type *is* an occurrence of a super-type. ORM also requires a great deal of space to give a separate symbol to each value type and relationship to it.

All of this could be mitigated by a CASE tool that permitted a model to be drawn in one form and then converted automatically to the other. The entity/relationship version could be used to convey the overall shape of the model and the important relationships, while the ORM version could portray the relationships in more detail.

The Unified Modeling Language (UML)

The Unified Modeling Language (UML) is not billed as a "data-modeling" but as an "object-modeling" technique. Instead of entity types, it models "object classes". Close examination of its models, however, shows these to look suspiciously like entity/relationship models. Indeed, Ivar Jacobson even calls these classes in a business-oriented model *entity type objects* [Jacobson, 1992, p. 132].

Because of a confluence of ideas, techniques, personalities, and politics, UML promises to become a standard notation for representing the structure of data in the object-oriented community. It was developed when the "three amigos" of the object-oriented world, James Rumbaugh, Grady Booch, and Ivar Jacobson, among others, agreed to adopt as standard a variation on a notation originally developed by David Embley and his colleagues [Embley et al., 1992]. The UML was published by the Object Management Group in 1997 [OMG, 1998]. Messrs. Rumbaugh, Jacobson, and Booch have written significant texts on UML: a reference manual [Rumbaugh, Jacobson, & Booch, 1999], a user guide [Booch, Rumbaugh, & Jacobson, 1999], and a guide to their methodology [Jacobson, Booch, & Rumbaugh, 1999], although many other books on the subject are also available.

As a system of notation for representing the structure of data, when used for analysis, the UML *static diagram* is functionally the exact equivalent of any other data-modeling, entity-type/relationship modeling, or object-modeling technique. Its *classes* of *entity-type objects* are really entity types, and its *associations* are relationships. It has specialized symbols for some things that are already represented by the main symbols in other notations, and it lacks some symbols used in e/r diagrams. It does, however, have a more extensive ability to describe interrelationship constraints.

Yes, the UML does add the ability to describe the behavior of each object class/entity type, but the data-structure part of the technique is fundamentally no different from any other data-modeling technique in what it can represent. It also adds notation details most useful when it is applied to object-oriented design.

In addition, the UML includes other kinds of diagrams besides static object diagrams. These include use cases, activity diagrams, and others. They do not concern us here, however.

Figure B.8 shows the UML version of our example.

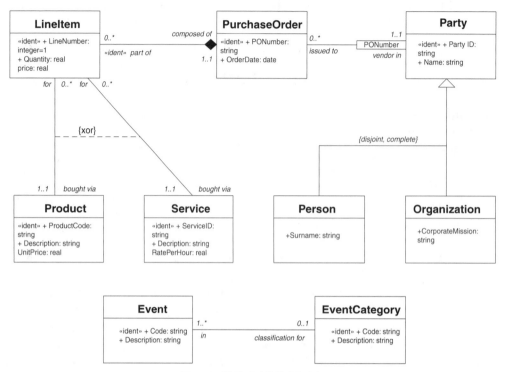

FIGURE B.8 A UML Model.

Entity Types (Object Classes) and Attributes

As stated above, in object models, entity types are called classes. A class in the UML static model is a square-cornered rectangle with three divisions. The top part contains the class name. The middle section contains a list of attributes. The bottom, if included, contains descriptions of behavior. Since the UML is used mostly for design, these behavior descriptions are usually in the form of pseudo-code, C++, or simply program names, or simply references to programs.

An attribute can be referred to by one or more of the following elements:

- *Stereotype*—This extends the attribute concept defined by the person preparing the diagram. (See below.)
- *Visibility*—In terms of the object-oriented code which may implement the class, is this attribute visible to all (+), to only those classes which are sub-types of this class (#), or to this class only(-)? This is only meaningful if a model is used for design. It is not meaningful in design models.
- *Name*—This is the only required element.

- *Multiplicity*—Object orientation is not constrained by the relational notion that an object may have only one value for an attribute. This parameter lets you define that it may have more than one, up to five, or whatever. If the lower limit is zero, then occurrences of the related entity type are optional.
- *Type*—This is the data type of the attribute (number, character, etc.). The values for this depend on the model's environment.
- *initial value*—Here can be specified a default value.
- *{other}*—Additional named properties may be added, such as "tag=<value>".

There are no spaces between the words in names. The class is called PurchaseOrder instead of Purchase Order.

The UML introduces the concept of *stereotype*, which is an additional annotation that can be used to enhance the standard UML notation. If you don't like something about UML, you can change it! A stereotype is identified by being surrounded by guillimets (« »), and can be used to extend entity type, attribute, and association definitions. In Figure B.8, the stereotype «ident» extends the model to denote unique identifiers. (See "Unique Identifiers" on page 374, below.)

Relationships (Associations)

A relationship is called an "association" in the object-oriented world. Rather than using graphic symbols, all the information on a UML association is conveyed by characters.

Cardinality/Optionality

Both cardinality and optionality are conveyed by characters in the form:

<lower limit>
..
<upper limit>

where the <lower limit> denotes the optionality (nearly always 0 or 1, although conceivably it could be something else), and the <upper limit> denotes the cardinality. The <upper limit> may be an asterisk (*) for the generic "more than one", or it may be an explicit number, a set of numbers, or a range.

For example, "0..*" means "may be one or more" (zero, one, or more), and "1..1" means "must be exactly one".

Since they are most common, "0..*" may be abbreviated "*", and "1..1" may be abbreviated "1".

In Figure B.8, for example, the fact that each Party may be a vendor in one or more purchase orders is shown by the string "0..*" next to Purchase Order. The "0" makes it optional ("may be"), and the * means that it can be any number. Similarly, the fact that each Purchase Order must be to one and only one Party is shown by the string "1..1" next to Party. The first 1 means that the relationship is mandatory ("must be"), and the second means that the purchase order may be to no more than one Party.

Names
There are two primary ways to name associations. A simple verb phrase may name the association in its entirety. A triangle next to the name tells which way to read it. Alternatively, "roles" can be defined at each end to describe the part played by the class in the association. The concept of role is very close to the relationship names used in the Barker notation, so that convention could be applied here, as was done in Figure B.8.

"Part of/composed of"
Extra symbols represent the particular association where each object in one class is *composed of* one or more objects in the other class. (Each object in the second class must be *part of* one and only one object in the first class.) The association acquires a diamond symbol next to the parent ("composed of") class. If the association is mandatory and the referential integrity rule is "cascade delete"—that is, deletion of the parent deletes all the children—this is called "composition" and the diamond is solid. This is shown for the PurchaseOrder/LineItem association in Figure B.8. If the association is optional to the parent (and therefore has the referential integrity rule "nullify delete")—that is, a parent can be deleted without affecting the children—then the diamond is open and is called "aggregation". The notation does not address the "restricted" rule, in which deletion of a parent is not permitted if children exist. Nor does it address referential integrity rules for any other kind of association.

Unique Identifiers
Unique identifiers are rarely referred to in the object-oriented world. When the behavior of objects in a class requires locating a particular occurrence of another class, however, the attribute used for locating that occurrence is shown in a box next to the entity type needing it. For example, in Figure B.8, "PO number" is required from the point of view of Party to locate a particular Purchase Order. This reflects the programming that will be required to navigate from Party to Purchase Order when the classes are implemented, but it is not meaningful in an analysis model.

Alternatively, stereotypes can be used to designate attributes and relationships that constitute unique identifiers, in a structure very similar to that of the Barker notation. These are shown as «ident» in Figure B.8.

Sub-types

The UML shows sub-types as separate entity-type boxes, each removed from its super-type and connected to it by an "isa" relationship. (Each occurrence of a sub-type "is a[n]" occurrence of the super-type.)

Note in Figure B.8 that the sub-type structure is labeled {disjoint, complete}. This is equivalent to the rule in other notations that each occurrence of the super-type must be a member of one of the sub-types (*complete*), and an occurrence may not be a member of more than one sub-type (*disjoint*). In UML, this constraint is not required. The sub-type structure could be {*overlapping, incomplete*} or any other permutations of the two.

Constraints between Relationships

Constraints between relationships are shown as dashed lines between pairs of associations. Such a line is called a *constraint*. If it is annotated {xor} or simply {or}, it is an *exclusive or*. In Figure B.8, a constraint says that each occurrence of LineItem must be (or may be) *either* for an occurrence of Product *or* for an occurrence of Service, *but not both*. If it were {ior}, however, it would be an *inclusive or*. (Each occurrence of the base entity type must be (or may be) related to *either* an occurrence of one entity type, *or* to an occurrence of the other, *or both*.) Indeed, the dashed line can represent any relationship desired between two associations.

Comments

UML has a number of advantages over its predecessors:

1. A constraints between relationships in the Barker notation is replaced by a simple line between two associations that can be annotated to describe any relationship between two associations. The Barker constraints between relationships is represented in the UML by the word "xor", but other interassociation relationships may be represented that the Barker notation cannot represent. This is useful for introducing many kinds of business rules.

2. For business rules that are not simple relationships between two associations, the UML introduces a small flag that can include text describing any business rule.

3. Attributes can be described in more detail than in other notations.

4. The UML approach to optionality and cardinality makes it possible to express more complex upper limits, as in "each <entity type 1> may be related to zero, 3, 6–7, or 9 occurrences of <entity type 2>".

5. Overlapping and incomplete configurations of sub-types are allowed.

6. Multiple inheritance and multiple type hierarchies are permitted.

These are valuable concepts. The first three could easily be added to other notations, with good effect. The fourth cannot, but it is rare that such a construct is needed, so its omission in other notations is not a serious practical problem. Such specific upper limits tend to be derived from business rules that might change, so it is not a good idea to include them in a conceptual data model. In the fifth case, the requirement that subtypes be complete and disjoint turns out to be a very useful discipline that produces much more rigorous models than if the restriction were relaxed. The final case describes a point which is controversial even in the object-oriented world. In your author's experience, nearly all examples that appear to require multiple-inheritance or multiple-type hierarchies can be solved by attacking the model from a different direction.

All of these may be valuable, however, if the model is being used to support design.

Other aspects of UML, however, are problematic if the models are to be presented to the public for requirements analysis.

First of all, in UML, cardinality and optionality are represented by numbers instead of graphic symbols. Yes, this has the advantage of permitting any kind of cardinality, such as 1, 4–6, 7, but requirements for such a statement are rare. It has the disadvantage, however, of making it an intellectual exercise to decode the symbols—instead of a visual processing one. You no longer "see" the relationship. You must "understand" it. The left side of the brain is used instead of the right. With information engineering or with Mr. Barker's notation, the entire process of decoding how many participants there are in a relationship is a visual one—and this makes the models much easier to read for those untutored in the notation.

The shorthand of using an asterisk for "may be one or more" and a one for "must be one and only one" in one sense simplifies the UML model, since these are the most common cardinalities and optionalities. On the other hand, it destroys the systematic semantic structure in which you automatically know both the upper and lower limits.

Second, the UML has added unnecessary symbols for specific kinds of relationships. The concepts of composition and aggregation are handled in entity-type/relationship diagrams by simply labeling a relationship *part of* and *composed of*. Having special symbols for two of the many possible kinds of relationships unnecessarily complicates the model.

More significantly, these additional symbols are incomplete. They represent the *cascade delete* and *nullify delete* rules for "composed of/part of" relationships, but what about the *restricted delete* rule? (You may not delete the parent at all if children exist.) And what about showing these rules for other relationships? Adding "C", "R", or "N" to an e/r diagram uniformly describes whether deletion of the parent is permitted and whether it calls for deletion of the children—regardless of the relationship. In addition, Entity-Type Life Histories more completely describe how entity-type occurrences may be created and under what circumstances they can be deleted (see Chapter 7, pages 262–282).

The justification for these symbols turns out to be that there are physical design implications for the aggregation and composition concepts. In an object-oriented implementation, it is possible for one object to be physically inside another object. Showing the diamonds on a UML design model provides information to the programmers. This is, however, both distracting and unnecessary in the conceptual model used for requirements analysis.

As stated previously, while it does permit showing multiple-inheritance and multiple-type hierarchies, the multi-box approach to sub-types takes up a lot of room on the drawing, limiting the number of other entity types that can be placed on it. Moreover, it does not clearly convey the fact that an occurrence of a sub-type *is* an occurrence of a super-type.

There are two other shortcomings of the UML, but these can be addressed, either through the use of stereotypes or by imposing discipline on the way the UML is used.

In the first case, the UML could be significantly improved by increased discipline in the use of relationship names. Most commonly a relationship name in the UML is a single verb that describes it in one direction. Were this the only option, it would be unacceptable. It is, however, possible to add "roles" to each end of the relationship. This provides the ability to portray how an entity type is viewed from the perspective of another entity type. Given this structure, it would be valuable if these role names were constrained to follow the Barker naming convention.

Second, the UML deals only partially with unique identifiers. The philosophy behind object orientation is that it isn't necessary explicitly to show unique identifiers. But then it turns out that, from the point of view of a parent entity type, it is often necessary to identify occurrences of a child entity type. So "qualified associations" allow this to be expressed. But you are allowed to identify an occurrence only to a parent entity type. You are not allowed to identify it to the world at large.

This means that, instead of a simple symbol attached to a relationship or attribute to indicate a unique identifier universally, you have to add a whole new box whose meaning is constrained and confusing at best.[3]

Note that this can be addressed using stereotypes as described above. In Figure B.8, "«ident»" was added to several attributes and a relationship to show their participation in unique identifiers.

---

3. As a measurement of how confusing this is, different authors themselves cannot agree on how to present it. Martin Fowler shows the qualifying attribute as presented here attached to the parent entity [Fowler 2000, p. 96]. Paul Harmon and Mark Watson, on the other hand, show the attribute next to the child entity [Harmon and Watson 1997, p. 172].

This doesn't mean that the UML shouldn't be used for the physical design model. To the contrary, the additional expressiveness described here makes it eminently suitable for that purpose. (And designers are not the least bit bothered by the aesthetic objections raised above.) But the UML is fundamentally that—a design tool.

Extensible Markup Language (XML)

The last technique presented here isn't really a data-modeling language at all. Rather is a way of representing data structure in text, using specially defined "tags" or labels to describe the structure of text. The data being described could be either from an entity-type/relationship model or from a database design.

The Extensible Markup Language (XML) is similar to the Hypertext Markup Language (HTML) that is used to describe pages to the World Wide Web. XML and HTML are both subsets of something called "Standard Generalized Markup Language", or SGML. This is a sophisticated tag language, which, "due to [its] complexity, and the complexity of the tools required," as the Object Management Group has so delicately put it, "has not achieved widespread uptake" [OMG, 1997].

In each case, a set of "tags" are inserted into a body of text. In the case of HTML, the tags are predefined to be interpreted by a standard piece of software called a browser. The browser uses the tags to determine how various parts of the document should be displayed.

XML, on the other hand, allows tags to be defined by users and is not concerned with display at all. Rather, the tags can be defined to describe a data structure, and data can be transmitted over the Internet in that structure.

Because tags are defined by users, no existing software will automatically understand the tags. Software can read the definitions of tags and insure that data transmitted using them follows them, but it cannot provide more interpretation to the structure unless it is specifically written to do so.

This means that XML is most useful when within a community that defines the semantics of a set of tags in common for its purpose. For example, the chemical industry has set up an XML-based *Chemical Markup Language*, and astronomers, mathematicians and the like have similarly defined sets of tags for describing things in their respective fields.

What Is It?

Figure B.9 shows an example of XML used to describe a data record that might be presented in a document.

```
<?XML version="1.0"?>
<!-- **** Purchasing **** -->
<PURCHASE_ORDER>
  <ISSUED_TO_PARTY>
        <party_id>234553</party_id>
        <name>Acme Sporting Goods</name>
        <party_type>Organization</party_type>
        <surname></surname>
        <corporate_mission>Get America
        moving</corporate_mission>
  </ISSUED_TO_PARTY>
  <po_number>743453</po_number>
  <order_date>12 November, 1999</order_date>
  <LINE_ITEM>
        <line_number>1</line_number>
        <quantity>12</quantity>
        <price>64.75</price>
        <product_service_indicator>
            product
        </product_service_indicator>
        <PRODUCT>
            <product_code>X-23</product_code>
            <description>Nike sneakers</description>
            <unit price>75.00</unit_price>
        </PRODUCT>
  </LINE_ITEM>
  <LINE_ITEM>
        <line_number>2</line_number>
        <quantity>12</quantity>
        <price>64.75</price>
        <product_service_indicator>
          service
        </product_service_indicator>
        <SERVICE>
            <service_id>x-87</product_code>
            <description>Walking the dog</description>
            <rate_per_hour>12.00</rate_per_hour>
        </SERVICE>
  </LINE_ITEM>
  <LINE_ITEM/>
</PURCHASE_ORDER>
```

FIGURE B.9 An XML Document.

Note a few interesting things about this example.

First, as with HTML, each tag is surrounded by less-than and greater-than brackets (<>) and is usually followed by text. The text is in turn followed by an end tag, in the form </...>.   A tag may have no content, in which case either the end tag follows immediately upon the tag (as in <surname></surname>), or the tag itself ends with a forward slash (as in `<LINE_ITEM/>`). Unlike with HTML, however, the end tag is *always* required in one of those two forms.

A second thing to note is that, in this case, following the tag for `<PURCHASE_ORDER>`, a set of *related* tags follow, describing characteristics (columns and relationships from data models, in this case) of `<PURCHASE_ORDER>`. In this particular case, the tag `<PURCHASE_ORDER>` has been defined such that it must be followed by exactly one tag for `<ISSUED_TO_PARTY>`, one for `<po_number>`, and so forth. You can't see this from the example, but the tag `<corporate_mission>` is optional. In addition, the tag for line_item is also optional, and there may be *one or more* occurrences of it.

Although it is optional, all XML documents should begin with `<?XML version="1.0"?>` (or whatever version number is appropriate.)

Note that the structure is hierarchical, so that an element can be under only one other element, and there can be only one hierarchy in a document. In the example, therefore, party was only defined as `<ISSUED_TO_PARTY>` under `<PURCHASE ORDER>`. If it were related to something else in the model, the description would have to be repeated.

Comments are in the form `<!-- . . . -->` Note that the double hyphens must be part of the comment. Note also that, unlike HTML, XML lets you use a comment to surround lines of code that you want to disable.

The meaning of a tag is defined in a *document type declaration* (DTD). This is a body of code that defines tags through a set of *elements*. It is the DTD that allows you to specify a data structure. While an XML document contains data, the DTD contains the model of those data.

It is the DTD that is the analogy to the modeling techniques we have seen in this appendix.

Entity Types and Attributes

The DTD for the above example is shown in Figure B.10.

```
<!DOCTYPE PURCHASE_ORDER [
   <!ELEMENT PURCHASE_ORDER (ISSUED_TO_PARTY, po_number,
   order_date, LINE_ITEM*)>
          <!ELEMENT ISSUED_TO_PARTY (party_id, name,
          party_type, surname?, corporate_mission?)>
                 <!ELEMENT party_id (#PCDATA)>
                 <!ELEMENT name (#PCDATA)>
                 <!ELEMENT party_type (#PCDATA)>
                 <!ELEMENT surname (#PCDATA)>
                 <!ELEMENT corporate_mission (#PCDATA)>
          <!ELEMENT po_number (#PCDATA)>
          <!ELEMENT order_date (#PCDATA)>
          <!ELEMENT LINE_ITEM (line_number, quantity,
price,
                 product_service_indicator, PRODUCT?,
                 SERVICE?)>
          <!ELEMENT line_number (#PCDATA)>
          <!ELEMENT quantity (#PCDATA)>
          <!ELEMENT price (#PCDATA)>
          <!ELEMENT product_service_indicator
(#PCDATA)>
          <!ELEMENT PRODUCT (product_code,
          description,
                 unit_price)>
                 <!ELEMENT product_code (#PCDATA)>
                 <!ELEMENT description (#PCDATA)>
          <!ELEMENT unit_price (#PCDATA)>
          <!ELEMENT SERVICE (service_id, description,
          rate_per_hour)>
                 <!ELEMENT service_id (#PCDATA)>
                 <!ELEMENT description (#PCDATA)>
                 <!ELEMENT rate_per_hour (#PCDATA)>
]
```

FIGURE B.10 An XML Data-Type Definition.

The DTD for an XML document can be either part of the document or in an external file. If it is external, the DOCTYPE statement still occurs in the document, with the argument "SYSTEM -filename-", where "-filename-" is the name of the file containing the DTD. For example, if the above DTD were in an external file called "xxx.dtd", the DOCTYPE statement would read:

```
<!DOCTYPE PURCHASE_ORDER SYSTEM xxx.dtd>
```

The same line would then also appear as the first line in the file xxx.dtd.

Note that the name specified in the DOCTYPE statement must be the same as the name of the highest-level ELEMENT.

Each element in the specification refers to a piece of information. An XML element is defined in terms of one or more *predicates,* where a predicate is simply a piece of information about an element. This may be either an attribute or an entity type in your data model. In the example above, `<PURCHASE_ORDER>` has as predicates `<ISSUED_TO_PARTY>`, `<po_number>`, `<order_date>`, and `<LINE_ITEM>`. `<ISSUED_TO_PARTY>` and `<LINE ITEM>` are relationships to the parent entity type in the data model that this was based on. `<Po_number>`, and `<order_date>` are attributes from that model.

Cardinality/Optionality

Relationships are represented by the attachment of predicates to elements. In the absence of any special characters, this means that there must be exactly one occurrence of each predicate for each occurrence of parent element. If the predicate is followed by a "?", then the predicate is not required. If it is followed by a "*", it is not required, but if it occurs, it may have more than one occurrence. If it is followed by a "+", at least one occurrence is required, and it may have more than one.

In the example in Figure B.10, each purchase_order must have an `<ISSUED_TO_PARTY>`, a `<po_number>` and an `<order_date>`. In addition, a `<PURCHASE_ORDER>` may or may not have any `<LINE_ITEMS>`s, but it could have more than one.

Each predicate is then itself an element defined in turn by its predicates that follow. At the bottom of the tree in each case, "#PCDATA" means that the element will contain text that can be parsed by browsing software.

Names

Names in XML may not have spaces. XML *is* case sensitive. XML keywords are in all upper case. The case of a tag name in an element definition must be the same as was used if the element appeared as a predicate, and the case of an element used an XML document must be the same as in its DTD definition.

Note that there is nothing in XML to prevent you from specifying multivalued attributes, but in the interest of coherence for the data structure, following the rules of normalization is strongly recommended. By convention in the above example, elements that would be entity types in an entity/relationship model appear in upper case. Elements that would appear in that model as attributes are in lower case. Your naming conventions may be different.

Unique Identifiers

XML has no way to recognize unique identifiers.

Sub-types

XML has no way to recognize sub-types and super-types. Note, in the example above, that the attributes of `<ISSUED_TO_PARTY>` had to include both attributes of person and attributes of organization from our other models. The attribute `<product-service-indicator>` was included in `<LINE_ITEM>` to determine which case was involved. Similarly, `<Party_type>` determined which kind of `<ISSUED_TO_PARTY>` a record referred to. Software would be required to enforce this.

Constraints between Relationships

XML has no way to describe constraints between relationships.

Comments

As noted above, XML isn't really a data-modeling language. It is not very sophisticated in its ability to represent the finer points of data structure. It shares the limitations of a relational database, for example, with no ability to recognize sub-types or constraints. It is being recognized, however, as a very powerful way to describe the essence of data structures for use as a template for transmitting data from one place to another.

While the tag structure does seem to be a good vehicle for describing and communicating database structure, the requirement for discipline in the way we organize data is more present than ever. XML doesn't care if we have repeating groups, monstrous data structures, or whatever. If we are to use XML to express a data structure, it is incumbent upon us to do as good a job with the tool as we can. (This is, of course, true of any modeling technique.)

In recognizing that XML is a good vehicle for describing database structure, the most obvious issue is that this will put greater responsibility on data administrators to define data correctly. XML will not do that. XML will only record whatever data design (good or bad) human beings come up with.

As Clive Finkelstein has said, the advent of XML is going to make data modelers and designers even more important than they are now. "After fifteen years of obscurity, data modelers can finally become overnight successes" [Finkelstein, 1999].

Recommendations

Because the orientation and purposes of data modeling are very different when supporting analysis than when supporting design, no one modeling technique currently available is appropriate for both. Those with the best aesthetics don't describe as many aspects of the issue as others, which are much less accessible.

The one exception to this is object role modeling, which is both rich in detail and relatively easy to read. It differs radically from the other modeling approaches, so it has therefore been less successful in gaining acceptance.

Among those using the more common entity-type/relationship view of the world, Richard Barker's notation is clearly superior as a vehicle for discussing models with prospective system users, and the UML has advantages in supporting design—particularly object-oriented design.

For Analysis—Richard Barker's Notation

There are several arguments in favor of Mr. Barker's data-modeling syntax for use in requirements analysis:

Aesthetic simplicity

This notation is the easiest to present to a user audience. It is the simplest and clearest among those that are as complete. By using fewer kinds of symbols, Barker's technique keeps drawings relatively uncluttered, and fewer kinds of elements have to be understood. Simpler, less cluttered diagrams are more accessible to nontechnical managers and other end users.

It uses a line in two parts, each of which may be dashed or solid, to convey the entire set of optional or mandatory aspects of the relationship pair. The presence or absence of a crow's foot is all that is necessary to represent the upper limit of a relationship. The single symbol of a split line which is either solid or dotted, plus the presence or absence of a crow's foot, is aesthetically simpler than, say, information engineering, which requires combinations of four separate symbols to convey the same information.

In Barker's notation, the "dashedness" or solidness of a line (its most visible aesthetic quality) represents the optionality of the relationship, which is its most important characteristic to most users. IDEF1X, on the other hand, uses "dashedness" to represent the extent to which a relationship is in a unique identifier.

Other systems of notation add symbols unnecessarily: Chen's notation uses different symbols for objects that are implementations of relationships and objects that are tangible entity types; Chen also uses separate symbols for each attribute; IDEF1X also distinguishes between "dependent" entity types and "independent" ones. IDEF1X also uses different symbols at the different ends of relationships. The UML designates certain kinds of relationships ("part of" and "member of") by either of two special symbols, depending on the referential integrity constraint in effect.

In each case, the additional symbols merely add to the complexity of a diagram and make it more impenetrable, without communicating anything that is not already contained in the simpler notation and names of Barker's notation.

James Martin's version of information engineering is the only one other than Barker's notation that represents sub-types *inside* super-types, thereby reinforcing the fact that it is a subset, and saving diagram space in the process.

Also, other techniques introduce extra complexity by allowing relationship lines to meander all over the diagram. Barker's notation calls for a specific approach to layout which keeps relationship lines short and straight.

Completeness

Most of the techniques show the same things that Barker's notation technique does, although some are more complete than others. Each of them lacks something that Barker's notation has.

Information engineering does not show attributes; IDEF1X does not show constraints; only Mr. Martin's version of information engineering shows sub-types within super-types. Mr. Chen's notation, information engineering, and UML do not show unique identifiers. Only ORM has all of the same features that the Barker method has, but with its external attributes and sub-types it uses way too much space on the diagram.

In fairness, some of the techniques do things that Barker's does not. IDEF1X, ORM, and the UML show nonexhaustive sub-types, where the sub-types do not represent all occurrences of the super-type. (Barker's technique deals with this only indirectly—by defining a sub-type called "OTHER..."). The UML also shows nonexclusive sub-types, where an occurrence of the super-type can be an occurrence of more than one sub-type. Information engineering and the UML also show nonexclusive constraints between relationships, not available in Barker's technique.

These are all useful things.

The addition of processing logic to data models in the manner of object-modeling techniques (including behavior in the model) is also a very powerful idea. Clearly provision for describing the behavior of an entity type is something that could be added to Barker's notation. Whether it is more appropriate to extend this notation, in the manner of the UML, or to use separate models, such as entity-type life histories and state/transition diagrams, remains to be seen.

Language

Barker's notation requires the analyst to describe relationships succinctly and in clear, grammatically sound, easy-to-understand English. As mentioned above, where all the other techniques use verbs and verb phrases as relationship names, Barker's notation uses prepositional phrases. This is more appropriate, since the preposition is the part of speech that describes relationships. Verbs describe not relationships but actions, which makes them more appropriate for function models than data models. To use a verb to describe a relationship is to say that the relationship is defined by actions taken on the two entity types. It is better simply to describe the nature of the relationship itself.

Using verbs makes it impossible to construct a clean, natural English sentence that completely describes the relationship. "Each party *sells in* zero, one, or more purchase orders" is not a sentence one would normally use in conversation.

Moreover, finding the right prepositional phase to capture the precise meaning of the relationship is often more difficult than finding a verb that approximately gets the idea across. The requirement to use prepositions then adds a level of discipline to the analyst's assignment. The analyst must understand the relationship very well to come up with exactly the right name for it. Correctly naming relationships often reveals that in fact there is more than one.

This requirement for well-built relationship sentences, then, improves the precision of the resulting model. In each modeling technique, Mr. Barker's naming conventions could be used, but analysts are not encouraged to do so.

For Object-Oriented Design—The UML

While Mr. Barker's notation is preferred as a requirements analysis tool, UML is more complete and detailed and therefore the most suited to support design—particularly object-oriented design.

The method for annotating optionality and cardinality is much more expressive of different circumstances than any of the other techniques. It can specifically say that an occurrence of an entity type is related to 1, 7–9, or 10 occurrences of another entity type.

The UML can describe many more constraints between relationships than can other notations. With proper annotation, it can describe both exclusive and inclusive or relationships, or any other that can be named.

For business rules that are not simple relationships between two associations, UML introduces a small flag that can include text describing any business rule.

Attributes can be described in more detail than in other notations.

Overlapping and incomplete configurations of sub-types are allowed.

"Multiple inheritance", where a sub-type may be one of more than one super-types, is permitted, as are multiple type hierarchies. While these may not be desirable in analysis models, they could be useful as solutions to particular design problems.

In an object-oriented environment, the extra symbols address specific object-oriented situations.

For Relational Design—IDEF1X

For the reasons described above, it is not advisable to use IDEF1X in an analysis project, since the notation is far too complex to present to a non-technical audience. This complexity, however, is exactly what makes it a good tool for representing relational database design. Its notation highlights the existence of foreign keys, and these are documented explicitly. The differences in annotating optionality and cardinality reflect the different way these could be implemented.

Summary

The ideal CASE tool, then, will be one which supports Mr. Barker's techniques for doing requirements analysis, then has the facilities for converting entity-type definitions into either (1) table definitions or (2) class definitions that can be used by C++ or a similar language. It would then have the ability to represent these design artifacts in IDEF1X or the UML for further refinement.

C

The Business Rules Group Motivation Model

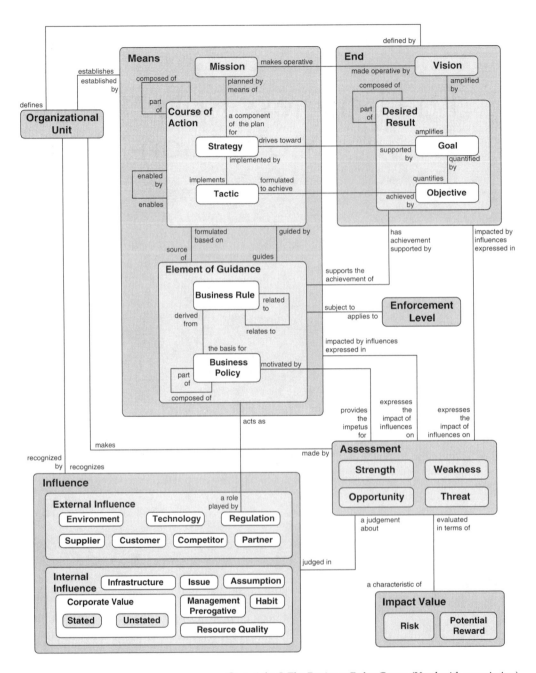

Copyright © The Business Rules Group (Used with permission)

D
The Business Rules Group and
David C. Hay Modified Motivation Model

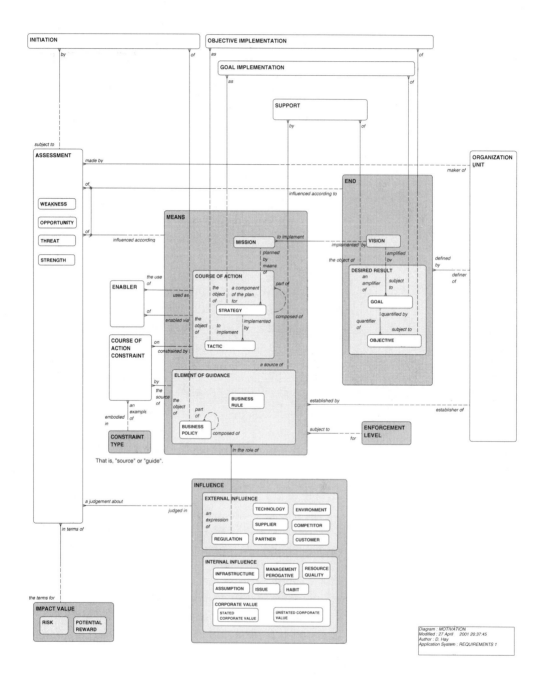

Glossary

Term	Definition	Chapter
accepted environment	[cybernetics] in Stafford Beer's <u>viable system</u>, the part of the environment that <u>Systems One</u> already address.	5
action	[activity modeling] "an executable atomic computation that results in a change in the state of the model or the return of a value" [Rumbaugh et al., 1999, p. 122]. (See <u>elementary business function</u>.)	4
action assertion	[business rules] (See <u>constraint</u>.)	8
action diagram	[activity modeling] the presentation of <u>structured natural language</u> or <u>pseudo-code</u> in graphic form.	4
action-enabler rule	[business rules] a kind of <u>business rule</u>: a statement that tests a condition, and upon finding it true, initiates another <u>business rule</u>, a <u>message</u>, or an <u>activity</u>.	8
activities column (Architecture Framework Column Two)	[architecture framework] the portion of the <u>Architecture Framework</u> that is concerned with what the enterprise *does* to support itself. This is its <u>mission</u> in the scope row, the business processes used to carry out that mission in Row Two, and the underlying <u>functions</u> the strategies and tactics implement in Row Three. In Row Four it concerns program functions, and the Row Five perspective is of the specifics of programming languages implementing the program functions.	1, 4

activity	[activity modeling] a general term to describe something that is done, used when a more specific definition is not available. It is represented by a round-cornered rectangle or a circle on a <u>data flow diagram</u>, <u>UML activity diagram</u>, or <u>dependency diagram</u>. It is represented by a square-cornered rectangle in an <u>IDEF0 Diagram</u> and a line in a <u>UML interaction diagram</u>	4
activity fragment	[activity modeling] Messrs. McMenamin and Palmer's term for the lowest-level <u>activity</u> in an exploded <u>data flow diagram</u>. Some of these will be <u>essential activities</u>, and some will be physical <u>mechanisms</u>.	4
activity model	[activity modeling] a representation of the <u>processes</u> and <u>functions</u> of an organization. Depending on the row involved, it is more focused either on business processes or on technical processes. This is an artifact of Column Two of the <u>Architecture Framework</u>.	2, 4
actor	1) [people and organization modeling] in a <u>use case</u> a person, organization, or computer system that is interacting with a <u>system</u>. This is equivalent to an <u>external entity</u> in a <u>data flow diagram</u>. 2) [activity modeling] in a <u>UML activity model</u> or <u>business process diagram</u>, the person, organization, or computer system that performs a set of activities.	4
acyclic ring constraint	[data modeling] in ORM, prohibition of an <u>occurrence</u> of an <u>entity type</u> to be related to a second occurrence of the entity type that in turn is related to a third entity type, and so on, with the last occurrence then related back to the first occurrence of the entity type. <u>Asymmetric ring constraint</u> is a special case of the <u>acyclic ring constraint</u>. Allowance of such an occurrence is a <u>cyclic ring constraint</u>.	8
adjuster organizer	[cybernetics] a mechanism for modifying a basic <u>feedback loop's</u> <u>set points</u> and other structures. This enables the loop to handle a new situation. This outer loop adjusts the <u>feedback</u> process itself, to respond to things that the inner loop could not.	5

agricultural age	[knowledge management] the era before the nineteenth Century in which the economy was dominated by agriculture. Manufacturing was characterized by individuals making products one at a time.	5
analysis	[project management] the second phase of a system development life cycle. See requirements analysis. This is done from the architect's view (Row Three)	
amplifier	[cybernetics] in a communications channel, something which increases the amount of variety perceived on the receiving end of the channel.	5
anchor	[business rules] in Ronald Ross's business-rule modeling notation, an entity, attribute, or relationship in a business rule whose value will be affected by implementation of a business rule. (This is also called a constrained object.)	8
application approach to systems development	[project management] approaching the task of developing information systems by emphasizing the programs to be written and the functions to be performed. This is as opposed to the database approach to systems development.	3
applications software	[project management] one or more computer programs to perform a business function, as opposed to a system maintenance process.	2
architect's view (Framework Row Three)	[architecture framework] a perspective represented by Row Three in the Architecture Framework (called the "information system designer's view" in the Zachman Framework). This is a view of the underlying structures of the enterprise.	Introduction, 1
Architecture Framework	[architecture framework] a modification of the Zachman Framework that is presented in this book. This modifies the terms used to describe three of the rows.	Introduction, 1
arity	[data modeling] in a particular data modeling notation, the number of entity types permitted to participate in a relationship. A relationship among three entity types has an arity of 3. Relationships in most data-modeling techniques have an arity of 2.	3, 8

artificial knowledge management	[knowledge management] knowledge management that is concerned with information processing using technological tools. This is the concern of our operational systems and our data warehouses. (This is as opposed to natural knowledge management.)	5
assessment	[*business rules*] in the Business Rules Group's Motivation Model, a measure of the effect an influence has on either a means or an end.	8
association (object)	[data modeling] as with a data model relationship, in an object model this is a connection between two (object) classes. In analysis a relationship and association mean the same thing—a structural relationship between two entity types. In relational design, however, relationships are usually implemented by means of a foreign key, while object-oriented design is via programs that navigate from one class to another.	3
associative entity type	[data modeling] (See intersect entity type.)	3
asymmetric ring constraint	[data modeling] in ORM, prohibition of an occurrence of an entity type to be related to another occurrence that in turn is related to the first occurrence. This is a special case of the acyclic ring constraint. (Allowance of this is called a symmetric ring constraint.)	8
attenuator	[cybernetics] in a communications channel, something which decreases the amount of variety perceived on the receiving end. (This is also called a filter.)	5
attribute	[data modeling] a discrete, atomic piece of information that identifies, describes, classifies, or measures an entity type.	3, 8
availability requirement	[project management] a non-functional requirement that data must be made easily accessible to the people who need them. This is subject to requirements for procedures to prevent the loss of data, as well as design of security procedures so that authorized users are not inhibited from using the data.	2

behavior	[object orientation] in object-oriented design, the actions taken by an <u>object</u> in response to a trigger or <u>message</u> from another object.	3
behavioral response-time requirement	[project management] concerns the interaction of a <u>system</u> with a <u>user</u>. In general, no matter what they are doing, users expect the computer to respond to an <u>input</u> within a few seconds. That response may not be delivery of an <u>output</u>, but it is at least an acknowledgement of the input. It is essential that, no matter what the application is, entry into the computer be immediately responded to in one way or another.	2
bill of materials	[manufacturing] a list of component assemblies and parts that comprise a manufactured product.	3
binary relationship	[data modeling] a <u>relationship</u> between exactly two <u>entity types</u>. This is a <u>relationship</u> with an <u>arity</u> of 2.	3
Boyce/Codd Normal Form	[relational theory] a refinement of <u>third normal form</u>: No part of a primary key may be dependent on another part of that primary key.	3
briefing	[project management] in general, a short presentation. In the context of the <u>system development life cycle</u>, this is a meeting at the beginning of a project where analysts introduce themselves and their approach to the project.	2
builder's view (Framework Row Five)	[architecture framework] 1) a perspective represented by Row Five in the <u>Architecture Framework</u> (called either the <u>out-of-context</u>, <u>detailed representation</u> or <u>subcontractor's view</u> in the <u>Zachman Framework</u>). This is the view of the one who is constructing the system, and who is presumably immersed in the technology being used. 2) in John Zachman's <u>Zachman Framework</u>, his name for Row Four.	Introduction, 1
business data model	[data modeling] (See <u>data model—business</u>.)	3
business event	[time modeling] an <u>external event</u> that invokes one or more business <u>activities</u>.	7

business object	[data modeling] a tangible thing seen by people in the enterprise or an intangible thing commonly understood by people in the enterprise. This is equivalent to an occurrence of an <u>entity type</u>.	3
business owner's view (Framework Row Two)	[architecture framework] a perspective represented by Row Two in the <u>Architecture Framework</u>. This is the view of the people who run the business, with their particular jargon and technology.	Introduction, 1
business policy	[*business rules*] in the Business Rules Group's <u>Motivation Model</u>, an <u>element of guidance</u> that is a statement (or set of statements) whose purpose is to guide the enterprise.	8
business-process diagram	[activity modeling] a variation on a <u>physical data flow diagram</u> organized according to participants. Its purpose is specifically to discuss collections of activities with business people, so its notation may be extended to include specialized symbols to represent different kinds of <u>activities</u>. The purpose of a <u>business-process diagram</u> is to upgrade the workings of the processes of an enterprise, not necessarily to implement them with technology.	2, 4
business-process re-engineering	[activity modeling] the process of evaluating and changing an enterprise's activities and communications for the purpose of improving their overall effectiveness.	4
business rule	[business rules] in the Business Rules Group's <u>Motivation Model</u>, a directive, intended to influence or guide business behavior, *derived from* (in support of) a <u>business policy</u>. Business rules are the <u>constraints</u> that determine the everyday workings of business.	8
cardinality constraint	1) [data modeling] The assertion that an occurrence of an <u>entity type</u> may be related to no more than a specified number of occurrences of another <u>entity type</u>. 2) [data modeling] in ORM, the assertion that an occurrence of an <u>entity type</u> may participate in a <u>role</u> no more than a specified number of times. (See also <u>uniqueness constraint</u>.)	3, 8

cascade delete	[referential integrity] a rule attached to a <u>relationship</u> asserting that if the parent is deleted, all children will be deleted as well.	3, 8 Appendix B
case	[activity modeling] a structure in <u>pseudo-code</u> or <u>structured natural language</u> that is a complex condition, wherein several alternatives are possible. Usually this is in the form IF <condition 1> THEN <action 1> ELSE IF <condition 2> THEN <action 2> ELSE IF . . . END IF.	4
CASE	[project management] (See <u>Computer-Aided Systems Engineering</u>.)	2
channel	[*cybernetics*] a means of communication between two business elements. A <u>channel</u> has a specific capacity in terms of the amount of information it can carry.	5
class (object)	[data modeling] [object orientation] the definition of a collection of <u>objects</u> that have the same attributes. If an <u>object</u> is perceived by people running an enterprise, its class is equivalent to an <u>entity type</u>.	3
column	1) [data modeling] a structural component of a table or relation. 2) [architecture framework] a dimension of the information captured in an <u>Architecture Framework</u>.	3
commercial off-the-shelf package	[project management] a software package that was purchased rather than built in-house. (This is also called <u>COTS</u>.)	
comparative evaluator	[business rules] in Ronald Ross's business-rule modeling notation, a category of <u>business rule</u> that defines comparisons (less than, equal to, etc.) between the attributes of two occurrences of the same or different <u>entity types</u>.	8
complete (sub-types)	[data modeling] a data modeling rule asserting that any occurrence of a <u>super-type</u> must be an occurrence of at least one <u>sub-type</u>. (Also <u>exhaustive</u>)	3, 8, Appendix B
computer-aided system engineering	[project management] A collection of automated tools for managing all the artifacts (models and documentation) for a system-development project.	

conceptual data model	[3-schema architecture] [data modeling] (See <u>data model—conceptual</u>.)	3
conceptual join path	[data modeling] in ORM, a connection between two <u>relationships</u> suggesting that they are in fact related to each other.	8
conceptual schema	[3-schema architecture] an organization of data where each <u>datum</u> is defined only once for the enterprise, and its <u>relationship</u> to all other data is clearly and uniquely defined as well. Each <u>external schema</u> consists of a selection of the data in the conceptual schema. The underlying definitions from the conceptual schema apply to all external schemata as well and are consistent across them all. The architect's view of data is of the conceptual schema.	3
condition	1) [business rules] in Ronald Ross's business-rule modeling notation, something that determines whether a subsequent rule or action is invoked. It may evaluate to either true or false. Depending on the condition, other constraints may apply. Alternatively, this is an assertion that may be made true by another constraint. 2) [data modeling] a structure in <u>pseudo-code</u> or <u>structured natural language</u> that is the application of a test ("if") to determine which step should be taken. This is depicted by using the key words IF, THEN, and ELSE. That is, the structure is IF <condition> THEN <action 1> ELSE <action 2> ENDIF.	8, 4
confidentiality requirement	[project management] a <u>non-functional</u> <u>security requirement</u> that only authorized people may see a particular data element. What security is required to prevent unauthorized use of data? How important is it to keep the data out of the hands of unauthorized users? This will determine the amount of money and effort that must be spent as the system is developed.	2
constrained object	[business rules] in Ronald Ross's business-rule modeling notation, an <u>entity</u>, <u>attribute</u>, or <u>relationship</u> in a business rule whose value will be affected by implementation of a <u>business rule</u>. (This is also called <u>anchor</u>.)	8

constraining object	[business rules] in Ronald Ross's business-rule modeling notation, an <u>entity</u>, <u>attribute</u>, or <u>relationship</u> in a business rule whose value affects the outcome of a business rule. (This is also called <u>correspondent</u>.)	8
constraint	[business rules] any restriction applied to <u>data</u>. This is referred to in the first Business Rules Group paper as an <u>action assertion</u>. A constraint affects values that can be assigned to <u>attributes</u>, or indeed even occurrences of <u>entity types</u> that can be created in the first place.	8
construction	[project management] the fourth phase of a <u>systems-development life cycle</u>. Here you build the new system. The <u>builder's view</u> (Row Five) is operative here.	2
context diagram	[activity modeling] a top-level <u>data flow diagram</u> or <u>IDEF0 diagram</u> representing an entire operation as a single <u>process</u>, with all of the principal <u>external entities</u> affecting that <u>process</u> shown.	4
control	[activity modeling] in an <u>IDEF0 diagram</u>, the data that affect the processing of an <u>activity</u>. This is the same as a <u>message (data flow)</u> in a <u>data flow diagram</u>, but in an <u>IDEF0 diagram</u> it is identified as such explicitly.	4
controller	[*cybernetics*] an agent which controls a <u>process</u> in a <u>feedback loop</u>.	5
convergent data model	[data modeling] a data model that brings different concepts together into single entity types. A generalized model. (as opposed to a <u>divergent data model</u>.)	3
correspondent	[business rules] in Ronald Ross's business-rule modeling notation, an <u>entity</u>, <u>attribute</u>, or <u>relationship</u> in a business rule whose value affects the outcome of a business rule. (This is also called <u>constraining object</u>.)	8
COTS	[project management] (See <u>customized off-the-shelf package</u>.)	2

course of action	[*business rules*] in the Business Rules Group's Motivation Model, a means that is an approach or plan for configuring some aspect of the enterprise, involving things, processes, locations, people, timing, or motivation undertaken to achieve ends. It must be either a strategy or a tactic.	8
crow's foot rule	[data modeling] a positional data-modeling convention which dictates that entity types be arranged so that the "many" end of a relationship points either to the left or to the top of the diagram. In Richard Barker's ("dead crow") data-modeling notation, this means that the toes of the crows point to the left or the top of the diagram. This has the effect of clustering independent entity types (usually reference entity types) toward the lower right and dependent entity types (usually transaction entity types) toward the upper left.	3
CRUD matrix	[data modeling] [activity modeling] a matrix showing, for each business function, which entity types and attributes are (C)reated, (R)etrieved, (U)pdated, or (D)eleted. This is also called a function/entity-type matrix.	2, 3, 4, 6
custodial activity	[activity modeling] an essential activity that establishes and maintains the system's essential memory by acquiring and storing the information needed by the fundamental activities.	4
customer capital	[knowledge management] the value of the company's franchise and its ongoing relationships with its customers (and vendors).	5
cybernetics	[cybernetics] the science of communication and control. Developed during World War Two, this is concerned with the mechanisms of control, especially variations on feedback loops.	5

cyclic ring constraint	[data modeling] in ORM, allowance of an <u>occurrence</u> of an <u>entity type</u> to be related to a second occurrence of the entity type that in turn is related to the occurrence of a third entity type, and so on, with the last occurrence then being related back to the first occurrence of the entity type. The <u>symmetric ring constraint</u> is a special case of the <u>cyclic ring constraint</u>. (Prohibition of these relationships is called an <u>acyclic ring constraint</u>.)	8
data	[data modeling] the plural of <u>datum</u>.	5
data administrator	[project management] the person responsible for the integrity of data. The <u>data administrator</u> is responsible for data models and for the quality of the data captured.	3
data column (Architecture Framework Column One)	[architecture framework] the portion of the <u>Architecture Framework</u> that is about understanding and dealing with the things of significance to an enterprise, about which information is to be held. In the <u>scope</u> row, this is about the most significant objects dealt with by the enterprise. In Row Two, it is about the language used to describe in detail the things of significance to the enterprise, and it may include a model of that language. In Row Three it is about specifically defined <u>entity types</u> and their <u>relationships</u> to each other. In Row Four it concerns the representation of data by computer software and <u>database management systems</u>. This may be in terms of <u>tables</u> and columns, <u>(object) classes,</u> and the like. In Row Five it is about the way data are physically stored on the computer, in terms of tablespaces, disk drives, and so forth.	1
data conversion	[project management] during the <u>transition</u> phase of the <u>system development life cycle,</u> moving data from existing systems into a new system, converting existing representations of data structure into new ones.	2
data dictionary	[data modeling] a compilation of file layouts, including field definitions.	2, 3

data flow	[activity modeling] on a <u>data flow diagram</u> a communication <u>channel</u> between one <u>process</u> and another, represented by an arrowed line.	4
data flow diagram	[activity modeling] a drawing of the flows of <u>data</u> though an enterprise. It includes a box or circle describing each physical <u>process</u> and lines showing the communications <u>channels</u> between processes. It also includes representations of <u>data stores</u> which are the holding of data over time.	4
data flow diagram— physical	[activity modeling] a <u>data flow diagram</u> that represents the physical <u>mechanisms</u> used for processing <u>data</u> in an enterprise. This includes <u>mechanisms</u> for processing as well as for transmitting <u>data</u> (telephone, fax, physical movement of forms, etc.).	2, 4
data mart	[data warehousing] a subset of <u>data</u> from a <u>data warehouse</u> specifically organized according to someone's <u>external schema</u>. That is, a <u>data mart</u> is organized to optimize the particular kinds of queries that person is likely to require.	3
data model	[data modeling] a representation of the things of significance to an enterprise, and the relationships among them. Kinds of data model include the <u>entity/relationship model</u> and the <u>object (class) model</u>. A diagram of the model consists of boxes, each representing an <u>entity type</u> which defines classes of those things. Documentation of a <u>data model</u> includes definitions of all <u>entity types</u> and descriptions of their <u>attributes</u>. A <u>data model</u> is a collection of <u>entity types</u> and <u>relationships</u>. A data-model *diagram* is a representation of some of the <u>entity types</u> in a <u>data model</u>. This is an artifact of Column One of the <u>Architecture Framework</u>. Sometimes the term "data model" is erroneously applied to database design.	2, 3

data model— business

[data modeling] a Row Two <u>data model</u> describing   2, 3
the objects seen by the people who carry out the
business. This tends to consist of tangible entity
types representing the things people see (<u>reference
entity types</u>), as well as the transactions they use to
carry out their business (<u>transaction entity types</u>).
Relationships may be multivariate, involving more
than two entity types (an <u>arity</u> of more than 2), and
they may be "many-to-many". There is no
requirement for the models to be subject to
<u>normalization</u>.

data model— conceptual

[data modeling] a Row Three <u>data model</u> of the   2, 3
fundamental things the business is concerned with.
First of all, this means that certain modeling
constraints are applied: If Richard Barker's entity/
relationship modeling technique is used, for
example, all relationships are binary and all
<u>relationships</u> are "one-to-many", following the rules
of <u>normalization</u>. It also means that the <u>entity types</u>
themselves are defined to be relatively abstract, so
that they represent the more generic things, of which
the things viewed by the business are often
examples.

data-model diagram

[data modeling] a physical representation of a   3
portion of a <u>data model</u>. The model itself is a
conceptual structure, typically stored in a <u>meta-data
repository</u>. A data-model diagram shows only some
<u>entity types</u> and <u>relationships</u>.

data-model pattern

[data modeling] a generic <u>data model</u>, representing a   3
typical situation in an enterprise. (See <u>semantic data-
model convention</u>.)

data steward

[project management] a person from the business   2, 3
community who is responsible for the integrity of a
particular body of <u>data</u>. (The person holding this
role probably began as a <u>subject-matter expert</u>.)

data store

[activity modeling] on a Sarson and Gane <u>data flow   4
diagram,</u> the occurrence of storing data temporarily
on its way from one <u>process</u> to another. Called
simply a <u>file</u> on a DeMarco <u>data flow diagram</u>.

data warehouse [data warehousing]   3
1) a configuration consisting of a central, normalized, database fed by operational systems in the enterprise and supporting subsidiary databases (data marts) organized according to likely query structures.

2) the central database described for configuration 1. This database is organized around the conceptual schema and is intended to maintain the bulk of an enterprise's data for future reference. The data here can be retrieved without interfering with the activities of the operational system, and because the database is not involved with day-to-day operations, data can be kept in a more summarized form. Data are more static in a data warehouse than in an operational system. (See also operational data store.)

database administrator [project management] a person responsible for maintenance of database management system software.   2, 3

database approach to systems development [project management] approaching the task of developing systems by emphasizing the structure of the data to be managed. This is as opposed to the applications approach to systems development.   3

database management system [project management] [data management] a computer program that allows a user to specify data structures, enter data into those structures and retrieve data from them, without having to program these transactions. Traditional programs tended to have a lot of code concerned with reading from and writing to files. A database management system is specifically equipped to read from and write to the database using standard components.   2, 3

datum [data modeling] (plural: data) a set of letters or characters that contain meaning. (The meaning itself is information.)   5

decision table	[activity modeling] a table representing a sequence of decisions to be taken in a particular evaluation. A set of conditions is shown on the left, with one row for each permutation of values for the decisions. A column on the right shows each resulting decision, based on the particular permutations in the decision's row.	4
decision tree	[activity modeling] a set of lines drawn to show the possible paths that may be taken in a particular evaluation, depending on various tests of values. The graphic allows you to represent each alternative value for a variable and map of what is to be done, depending on that value.	4
definition	[business rules] the specification of a meaning for a <u>term</u> as it is used. By defining it, we recognize that it is a term of importance, and we specify exactly what it means.	2, 3, 8
dependent entity type	[data modeling] an <u>entity type</u> whose occurrences cannot be created without relating them to another <u>entity type</u>.	
dependency diagram	[activity modeling] a diagram showing <u>activities</u> and how they depend on each other. That is, one activity cannot be carried out until another activity has been completed.	4
derivation	[business rules] the creation of new information from existing information. This may be an <u>inference</u>, which is the drawing of logical conclusions from <u>facts</u>. (For example, if the scheduled "delivery date" has passed and the material hasn't been delivered, this implies that the shipment is "late".) It may be a <u>mathematical derivation</u>, which is a mathematical calculation. (For example, "Age" is equal to the "System Date" minus the "Birth Date".)	8
design	[project management] the third phase of a <u>systems-development life cycle</u>. Here you determine the technologies to address the <u>requirements</u> derived in the first two phases and define the specific configurations of those technologies. This is done from the <u>designer's view</u> (Row Four) of the <u>Architecture Framework</u>.	2

designer's view (Framework Row Four)	[architecture framework] a perspective represented by Row Four in the <u>Architecture Framework,</u> (called the "builder's view" in the <u>Zachman Framework</u>). This view encompasses the technology that will be used to build a new system. The designer constructs the structures of the new system.	Introduction, 1
desired result	[*business rules*] a state or target that the enterprise intends to attain or maintain.	8
detailed representation	[architecture framework] (See <u>builder's view</u>.)	1
dimension	[data warehousing] an aspect of a data <u>fact</u> useful for retrieving it. For example, the <u>fact</u> of a "sale" may have the <u>dimensions</u> "time", "region", "customer category", and so forth.	3
disjoint (sub-types)	[data modeling] a rule asserting that no occurrence of a <u>super-type</u> may be an occurrence of more than one <u>sub-type</u>. (This is also called <u>exclusive</u>.)	3, Appendix B
divergent data model	[data modeling] a data model representing all the things described in data collection interviews, without any attempt to derive general categories. (As opposed to <u>convergent data model</u>.)	3
document type definition	[XML] a file which contains the definitions of the <u>tags</u> that will be used in XML documents.	Appendix B
domain	[data modeling] a set of characteristics that can be applied to validate one or more <u>attributes</u>. This could include a list of legal values, a range of values, a format, or an expression,	8
education	[project management] during the <u>transition</u> phase of the <u>systems-development life cycle,</u> explaining to an entire organization what we are doing and why we are doing it. (This is as compared to <u>training</u>.)	2
element	[XML] a component of an XML statement, referring to a piece of data.	Appendix B

element of guidance	[*business rules*] in the Business Rules Group's <u>Motivation Model</u>, either a <u>business rule</u> or a <u>business policy</u> that is a declarative statement (or set of such statements) defining or constraining some aspect of an enterprise. It is intended to assert business structure or to control or influence the behavior of an enterprise.	8
elementary business function	[activity modeling] in a <u>function hierarchy</u> or a <u>data flow diagram</u>, an <u>activity</u> that "when triggered must either be completed successfully, or, if for some reason it cannot be completed successfully, must 'undo' any effects that it had up to the point of failure" [Barker and Longman, 1992, p. 40]. This is called an <u>action</u> in a <u>UML activity diagram</u>.	4
elementary fact	[data modeling] in ORM, a <u>relationship</u> that has a minimum number of roles, which cannot be broken into component relationships.	8
end	[*business rules*] in the Business Rules Group's <u>Motivation Model</u>, a statement about what the business seeks to accomplish. The important thing to remember about an end is that it does not include any indication of how it will be achieved.	8
enforcement level	[*business rules*] a value that specifies the severity of action imposed in order to put or keep a business rule or business policy in force.	8
entity	[data modeling] an <u>occurrence</u> of an <u>entity type</u>.	3
entity/ relationship model	[data modeling] a kind of <u>data model</u> that is expressed in terms of <u>entity types</u> and their <u>relationships</u> to each other.	2, 3
entity life history	[event modeling] a technique for diagramming the set of events that affect an <u>entity type</u> and the <u>activities</u> carried out in response to them.	3, 7
entity type	[data modeling] the definition of something of significance to an organization, such as "person", "product", or "activity". An <u>entity type</u> has as predicates <u>attributes</u> and <u>relationships</u> with other <u>entity types</u>.	3, 8
equality constraint	[data modeling] in ORM, a constrainst asserting that the populations of two roles must be equal.	8

essential activity	[activity modeling] [event modeling] the complete response to an <u>external event</u>. This is either a <u>fundamental activity</u> that performs a task that is part of the enterprise's stated <u>mission</u>, or a <u>custodial activity</u> that establishes and maintains the system's <u>essential memory</u> by acquiring and storing the information needed by the fundamental activities [McMenamin and Palmer, 1984, pp. 17–20]. This may be part of an <u>essential data flow diagram</u> or a level on a <u>function hierarchy</u>.	4
essential data flow diagram	[activity modeling] [event modeling] a <u>data flow diagram</u> which is a description of the <u>activities</u> required to carry out the business of the enterprise. Unlike <u>physical data flow diagrams</u>, these activities are described not as physical <u>activities</u>, but in terms of the underlying <u>functions</u> being performed. For example, instead of "Fill out purchase order", you have "Order products". In addition, activities that are simply there to accommodate inadequate systems but do not add value to the organization are not included. In other words, the only activities presented are those which add value to the enterprise's efforts, plus those that directly support these activities.	2, 4, 7
essential memory	[activity modeling] the total of all data used by an enterprise's <u>essential activities</u>.	4, 7
ETL program	[data warehousing] (See <u>extraction, transformation, and load program</u>.)	3
event	[activity modeling] [event modeling] something which happens in the world, requiring a response (in this case, from an enterprise).	4, 7
event and timing model	[activity modeling] [event modeling] a representation of how time affects an operation—in terms both of corporate schedules and of the <u>events</u> that cause things to happen in the company. This is an artifact of Column Five of the <u>Architecture Framework</u>.	2, 4, 7

exclusion constraint	[data modeling] in ORM, a constraint asserting that if an entity type participates in one relationship, it cannot participate in another. This is the ORM version of the <u>exclusive</u> or constraint in entity/relationship modeling.	8
exclusive (sub-types)	[data modeling] the rule that any occurrence of a <u>super-type</u> may be an occurrence of only one <u>sub-type</u>. (Also <u>disjoint</u>.)	3, Appendix B
exclusive or (relationships)	[data modeling] the assertion that an <u>entity type</u> must (or may) be related *either* to one <u>entity type</u> *or* to another <u>entity type</u> but *not both*.	3, Appendix B
exhaustive (sub-types)	[data modeling] the rule that any occurrence of a <u>super-type</u> *must be* an occurrence of at least one <u>sub-type</u>. (Also <u>complete</u>.)	3, Appendix B
exploding a process	[activity modeling] in a <u>data flow diagram</u> the depiction of components of a <u>process</u> as a separate <u>data flow diagram</u>.	4
external entity	[activity modeling] a person, organization, or external system that is either a source of or the ultimate destination of data in a <u>data flow diagram</u>. All <u>data</u> portrayed on the diagram must originate in one or more <u>external entities</u> and they must ultimately be deposited with one or more <u>external entities</u>. This is equivalent to an <u>actor</u> in a <u>use case</u>.	4
external event	[activity modeling] [event modeling] an <u>event</u> which occurs outside the part of the enterprise being studied.	7
external influence	[*business rules*] in the Business Rules Group's <u>Motivation Model</u>, an influence from outside the organization, such as technology, a supplier or vendor, or a regulation.	8

external schema	[3-schema architecture] an organization of <u>data</u> according to terms appropriate for the job being done by an individual person or group of people. Since different people have different views of data, each <u>external schema</u> in an enterprise may be different, but they may overlap. They may be using the same terms of reference, although even these may be defined differently. The <u>business owner's view</u> of data is fundamentally of <u>external schemata</u>.	3
external uniqueness identifier	[data modeling] in ORM, the fact that two or more <u>roles</u> that are not in the same relationship combine to form a unique identifier for an <u>entity type</u> or an <u>objectified relationship</u>.	8
extraction, transformation, and load program	[data warehousing] a software product to ease the mechanical task of copying <u>data</u> from one file to another. Also known as an <u>ETL program</u>.	3
facility	[location modeling] (See <u>site</u>.)	6
fact	1) [business rules] the linking of <u>terms</u> to produce useful concepts. <u>Facts</u> are what are presented in <u>data models</u>, when <u>entity types</u> are related to each other, when <u>attributes</u> apply to entity types, and when <u>sub-types</u> are defined. 2) [data modeling] in ORM, an object's playing a role. 3) [data warehouse] a numerical measurement about the enterprise's operations. For example, this could be a sale or a purchase.	8
feedback	[cybernetics] information sent to a <u>controller</u> from a <u>process</u>.	5
feedback loop	[cybernetics] a structure consisting of an environment, an ongoing <u>process</u>, and a <u>controller</u>. If the value of a specified <u>variable</u> reported from the <u>process</u> goes above or below (depending on its purpose) the value of a <u>set point</u>, the controller takes action to modify the <u>process</u>.	5

Fifth Normal Form	[relational theory] the fifth of Dr. Codd's constraints on a relational design: A three-way (or more) relationship is redundant if all its occurrences may be derived from combinations of two-way occurrences.	3
file	[activity modeling] in a de Marco <u>data flow diagram</u>, the occurrence of storing data temporarily as it makes its way from one <u>process</u> to another. (See <u>data store</u>.)	4
filter	[cybernetics] (See <u>attenuator</u>.)	5
First Normal Form	[relational theory] the first of Dr. Codd's constraints on a relational design: Every <u>row</u> may have only one value for an <u>attribute</u> in a <u>relation</u>.	3
First Principle of Organization	[cybernetics] a principle of <u>cybernetics</u> articulated by Stafford Beer about how an organizational system should be constructed: "Managerial, operational and environmental varieties, diffusing through an institutional system, tend to equate; they should be *designed* to do so with minimal damage to people and to cost" [Beer, 1979, p. 97].	5
Fourth Normal Form	[relational theory] the fourth of Dr. Codd's constraints on a relational design: There may be no independent sets of dependencies within a <u>primary key</u>.	3
freedom	[cybernetics] in Stafford Beer's <u>viable system</u> the concept that a <u>System One</u> has an optimal amount of guidance and interference from its <u>meta-management</u>. In principle, it is "a computable function of systematic purpose as perceived" [Beer, 1979, p. 158].	5
function	[activity modeling] an activity that carries out an <u>objective</u> of the enterprise. It is described solely in terms of what it is to accomplish, without regard for the technology used to carry it out. It is described without reference to time. An example of a <u>function</u> is "order material". <u>Functions</u> are used to describe the business in Row Three terms, but they are usually accessible to business owners as well. This is represented on a <u>function hierarchy</u>.	4

function decomposition diagram	[activity modeling] (See <u>function hierarchy</u>.)	2, 4
function hierarchy	[activity modeling] a hierarchical representation of the <u>functions</u> of the enterprise. At the top of the hierarchy is the company's <u>mission</u>, broken into the five, six, or seven primary functions that contribute to that mission. Each of these is broken out in turn. (This is also called a <u>function decomposition diagram</u>.)	2, 4
function/entity-type matrix	[data modeling] [activity modeling] (See <u>CRUD matrix</u>.)	3, 4, 7
functional dependence	[data modeling] A <u>column</u> is "functionally dependent" on another column, if, given a value of the second column, you will always have the same value for the first column.	3
functional requirement	[project management] "the things the product [system] must do—an action that the product must take if it is to provide useful functionality for its user. <u>Functional requirements</u> arise from the fundamental reason for the product's existence" [Robertson, 1999, p. 104].	2
functional verifier	[business rules] in Ronald Ross's business-rule modeling notation, a rule about an occurrence of an <u>entity type</u>, relative to other occurrences in the entity. For example, the "Unique" rule might address whether occurrences of an entity type must have unique "Effective Dates".	8
functioning system (Framework Row Six)	[architecture framework] the perspective represented by Row Six in the <u>Architecture Framework</u>. This is the view of a new functioning system.	1
fundamental activity	[activity modeling] a kind of <u>essential activity</u> that performs a task that is part of the enterprise's stated <u>mission</u>,	4
glossary	[data modeling] [business rules] a catalogue of <u>terms</u> of interest to the enterprise or a part of it. You are looking at an example.	3, 8

goal	[*business rules*] in the Business Rules Group's <u>Motivation Model</u>, a statement about a desired general state or condition of the enterprise, to be brought about or sustained over time through appropriate <u>means</u>.	8
guideline	[*business rules*] a <u>constraint</u> that is not rigorously enforced.	2, 8
human capital	[knowledge management] the value of the knowledge held by a company's employees.	5
IDEF0 Diagram	[activity modeling] similar to a <u>data flow diagram</u>, except that it merges the elements represented on both physical and essential data flow diagrams. In addition to the data flowing into or out of an <u>activity</u>, an <u>IDEF0 diagram</u> also shows which <u>activities</u> *control* it, and what <u>mechanisms</u> may be used to perform it. It doesn't show <u>external entities</u> or <u>data stores</u> explicitly, but it does provide a much more sophisticated approach to <u>exploding</u> an <u>activity</u> into its component <u>activities</u>. Some companies may prefer to use this technique over the <u>data flow diagram</u>.	2, 4
impact value	[*business rules*] in the Business Rules Group's <u>Motivation Model</u>, an evaluation that quantifies or qualifies an assessment in specific terms, types, or dimensions. This may be either a <u>risk</u> or a <u>potential reward</u>.	8
inclusive or (relationships)	[data modeling] a constraint on two relationships such that an entity type must (or may) be related to *either* one entity type, *or* another entity type, *or both*.	3, 8, Appendix B
incomplete (sub-types)	[data modeling] a rule asserting that an occurrence of a super-type does *not* have to be an occurrence of any sub-type. (This is as opposed to <u>exhaustive</u> or <u>complete</u>.)	3, 8, Appendix B
independent entity type	[data modeling] an <u>entity type</u> that has no mandatory relationships to other <u>entity types</u>.	3
industrial age	[knowledge management] the era of the nineteenth and twentieth centuries whose economics was characterized by mass production.	5

inference	[business rules] the drawing of logical conclusions from <u>facts</u>. (For example, if the scheduled "delivery date" has passed and the material hasn't been delivered, this implies that the shipment is "late".)	8
influence	[*business rules*] in the Business Rules Group's <u>Motivation Model</u>, the act, process, or power of producing an effect without apparent exertion of tangible force or direct exercise of command, and often without deliberate effort or intent.	8
information	1) [knowledge management] the meaning contained in <u>data</u>. 2) [data modeling] on a <u>data flow diagram</u>, a data flow that carries data from one <u>process</u> to another for processing. This is an <u>input</u> in an <u>IDEF0 diagram</u>. An <u>information (data flow)</u> is different from a <u>message (data flow)</u>, which communicates instructions to the <u>process</u>, but this distinction is not shown on a <u>data flow diagram</u>. 3) [information theory] the quantity of variety in a communication.	5
information age	[knowledge management] the current era, when the economy is dominated by the use of information to reduce physical effort.	5
information engineering	[data modeling] [project management] 1) a comprehensive approach to the whole process of system development, organized around a <u>system-development life cycle</u> and making use of the <u>database approach</u> to systems development. 2) a particular notation for creating a <u>conceptual data model</u>.	3
information resource manager (IRM)	[project management] [data modeling] (See <u>data administrator</u>.)	2, 3
inheritance	[data modeling] the principle that a <u>sub-type</u> "inherits" all the attributes of its <u>super-type</u>. It also inherits all relationships attached to the <u>super-type</u>.	3

Term	Definition	Chapter
input	1) [project management] data entered into a computer system. 2) [activity modeling] in an IDEF0 diagram, the data that are used by an activity. This is the same as an information (data flow) in a data flow diagram, but in an IDEF0 diagram it is identified as such explicitly. (See also control.)	4
instance verifier	[business rules] in Ronald Ross's business-rule modeling notation, a category of business rule that requires—or tests for—an occurrence of an object to be present at the creation of, during the life of, and so on, an occurrence of another object.	8
integrity	[project management] a security requirement that all data received from an adjacent system be recorded accurately. It should not be possible to change data except under controlled circumstances. It should be difficult to misuse data (the toughest requirement of all). If there is a major disruption, such as a power failure, it must be possible to determine whether any data were corrupted and to recover from the failure.	2
integrity constraint	[business rules] in Ronald Ross's business-rule modeling notation, something that *must be true* about an entity type, relationship, or attribute, by definition.	8
internal event	[time modeling] an event which occurs inside the part of the enterprise being studied.	7
internal influence	[business rules] in the Business Rules Group's Motivation Model, an influence from inside the organization, such as the company's infrastructure, resource quality, or corporate culture.	8
internal schema	[3-schema architecture] an organization of data according to the technology being used to record it. This includes—for a particular database management system—the external terms of reference ("tables", "segments", "object classes", etc.) and the internal terms of reference ("tablespaces", etc.). It also includes terms for the physical storage of data on the computer ("cylinder", "track", etc.). (See also logical schema.)	3

intersect entity type	[data modeling] an <u>entity type</u> whose sole purpose for existing is to relate other entity types to one another.	3
intransitive ring constraint	[data modeling] in ORM, a <u>ring constraint</u> that prohibits an <u>occurrence</u> of an <u>entity type</u> both to be related to a second occurrence of the entity type that in turn is related to a third occurrence of the entity type—and to be related to the third occurrence directly as well. Allowance of these occurrences is called a <u>transitive ring constraint</u>.	8
irreflexive ring constraint	[data modeling] in ORM, a <u>ring constraint</u> that prohibits an <u>occurrence</u> of an <u>entity type</u> to be related to itself. (Allowance of such an occurrence is called a <u>reflexive ring constraint</u>.)	8
iteration	1) [activity modeling] a structure in <u>pseudo-code</u> or <u>structured natural language</u> that is the specification of one or more steps to be repeated one or more times. This may be either <u>repeat while</u> or <u>repeat until</u>. 2) [activity modeling] [event modeling] in an <u>entity life history</u>, an annotation that an event may occur one or more times, or not at all. This is shown by an asterisk (*) in the upper right corner of the event box.	4, 7
join	[relational theory] the linking of two <u>relations</u> together, based on an attribute in common to both that means the same thing and is in the same domain.	
joint application-development (JAD) session	[project management] a meeting of a small group of <u>subject matter experts</u> to examine an application area in detail. Often this involves creating one or more models of the enterprise in front of the experts and getting their agreement at that time.	2
key performance indicator	[knowledge management] a measurement defined in <u>strategic planning</u> to determine success or failure in carrying out the enterprise's mission. <u>Key performance indicators</u> may also be specified in the course of an enterprise's operation to evaluate success against goals and objectives as well.	2, 5

knowledge	[knowledge management] the application of information to useful ends. If data are letters and numbers, and information is the meaning given to those numbers, then knowledge is the application of that meaning to achieve objectives.	5
knowledge age	[knowledge management] the later years of the information age, when emphasis has been placed more on the usefulness of information manipulated by people than on the information itself.	5
knowledge management	[knowledge management] the management of an enterprise's capabilities with an emphasis on the knowledge content of the work being done. Knowledge management is about employing the knowledge held in an organization effectively.	5
label	[data modeling] in ORM, a value type that identifies occurrences of an entity type.	3, 8, Appendix B
law of requisite variety, the	[cybernetics] one of Ross Ashby's natural laws of cybernetics: "only variety absorbs variety" [Ashby, 1956].	5
legacy system	[data warehousing] a computer system that existed prior to a particular systems-development effort. The term is most often used in the context of an effort to build a data warehouse. Typically, its scope is relatively small (or at least smaller than the entire enterprise).	3
location	[location modeling] a place on the earth, such as "New York City", "Section 3, township 5 of Kern County, California", or "the Southeastern Marketing District". (This is as compared with site.)	6
location column (Architecture Framework Column Three)	[architecture framework] the portion of the Architecture Framework that is about the effects of location on the enterprise. Row One is concerned with the places where the enterprise is located. Row Two is about the specific offices and other facilities in those places. Row Three is about the communications required between those offices. Row Four is about the design of the technology to make possible those communications, and Row Five is about the specific technological parameters involved.	1, 6

location model	[location modeling] a representation of an enterprise's distribution of functions in geographical terms. This is an artifact of Column Three of the <u>Architecture Framework</u>.	2, 6
logical schema	[3-schema architecture] 1) a kind of <u>internal schema</u> that describes how data would be represented in a particular database management system. 2) commonly and incorrectly used as a synonym for the <u>conceptual schema</u>.	3
look and feel requirements	[project management] specification of operational standards for a proposed system, as well as its overall aesthetic.	2
mandatory constraint	[business rules] a <u>constraint</u> that is rigorously enforced. This is different from a <u>guideline</u>, which is only a suggestion.	2, 8
mapping	[data warehousing] the definition of the conversion of data from one structure to another. In the <u>data warehouse</u> environment, this is either from a <u>legacy system</u> to the warehouse, or from the warehouse to a <u>data mart</u>.	3
material flow	[activity modeling] the movement of physical material from one <u>activity</u> to another. This is usually not portrayed in a <u>data flow diagram</u>, although a special kind of line may be used in a Sarson and Gane version. It may be shown in an <u>IDEF0 diagram</u>.	4
mathematical derivation	[data modeling] [business rules] a mathematical calculation of an attribute. (For example, "Age" is equal to the "System Date" minus the "Birth Date".)	3, 8
mathematical evaluator	[business rules] in Ronald Ross's business-rule modeling notation, a category of business rule that derives values from other values.	8
means	[business rules] in the Business Rules Group's <u>Motivation Model</u>, a device, capability, regime, technique, restriction, agency, instrument, or method that may be called upon, activated, or enforced to achieve one or more ends.	8

mechanism	[activity modeling] the physical means by which an activity or a communication is carried out. This may be a computer system, a form, or the telephone, for example. These may be shown in a <u>physical data flow diagram</u> or in an <u>IDEF0 diagram</u>, but not on a <u>function hierarchy</u> or an <u>essential data flow diagram</u>.	4
message	1) [object orientation] in object-oriented programming, a communication from one <u>object</u> to another, usually triggering an action by the second <u>object</u>. 2) [activity modeling] on a <u>data flow diagram</u>, a <u>data flow</u> that carries instructions from one <u>process</u> to another, controlling the latter's processing. This is as opposed to an <u>information (data flow)</u>, which simply conveys data. (This distinction is not actually represented on the diagram.) This is equivalent to a <u>control flow</u> on an IDEF0 diagram.	3, 4
meta-data	[data modeling] [data warehousing] <u>data</u> that describe the <u>entity types</u>, <u>attributes</u>, <u>tables</u>, <u>columns</u>, and all other elements that constitute a modern information system.	3
meta-data repository	[data warehousing] a database containing the <u>meta-data</u> for a <u>data warehouse</u>.	3
meta-management	[cybernetics] a <u>controller</u> at one level of recursion that is responsible for managing a set of systems at the next level of <u>recursion</u> down.	5
mission	[business rules] in the Business Rules Group's <u>Motivation Model</u>, the means to achieve one <u>vision</u>. It defines the ongoing operational activity of an enterprise.	8
model of fundamental concepts	[architecture framework] (See <u>architect's view</u>.)	1
model of the business	[architecture framework] (See <u>owner's view</u>.)	1

motivation column (Architecture Framework Column Six)	[architecture framework] the portion of the Architecture Framework that is concerned with what causes an enterprise to do what it does. As Mr. Zachman originally described this column, it concerned the translation of business goals and strategies into specific ends and means. This has since been expanded to include the entire set of constraints (business policy and business rules) that apply to an enterprise's efforts. Row One is concerned with the enterprise's vision and mission. Row Two addresses its Goals, Objectives, Strategy, and Tactics, as they are translated into business policies and business rules. Row Three addresses the specific articulation of business rules in terms of their effects on data. Row Four is about the design of the programs that will implement those effects, and Row Five is about the construction of those programs.	1
motivation model	[business rules] a metamodel, developed by The Business Rules Group, describing the concepts of mission, means, and ends, specifically as they relate to business policy and business rules.	2, 8
multi-valued column	[data modeling] a column which can take more than one value for an occurrence of its corresponding table or relation. This violates First Normal Form. (See also repeating group.)	3
n-ary relationship	[data modeling] a relationship between more than two entity types. That is, it is a relationship whose arity is more than 2.	3
natural knowledge management	[knowledge management] knowledge management that is concerned with the way people learn and communicate with each other. In the past, it has not been concerned with technology, but this is slowly changing. (This is as opposed to artificial knowledge management.)	5
navigation path	[object-oriented design] the use of an association between two (object) classes to move from the processing (behavior) for one to the processing for the other.	3

network column (Framework Column Three)	[architecture framework] (See <u>location column</u>.)	1
non-functional requirement	[project management] "properties, or qualities, that the product [system] must have. In some cases the <u>nonfunctional requirements</u> are critical to the product's success" [Robertson, 1999, p. 112]. These are properties such as <u>security requirements</u> that do not directly contribute to the purpose of the proposed system.	2
nullify delete	[referential integrity] a rule attached to a <u>relationship</u> asserting that if the parent is deleted, the relationship occurrences to all children will be deleted as well, leaving the children without references to a parent.	3, Appendix B
object	1) [object orientation] [data modeling] a thing of interest—an occurrence of an <u>(object) class</u>. This may be a <u>business object</u>—something dealt with in the enterprise's operations—or a technical object, manipulated by a computer program. 2) [business rules] in Ron Ross's business-rules notation, an <u>entity type</u>, an <u>attribute</u>, or a <u>relationship</u>. 3) [data modeling] in ORM, an <u>entity type</u> or a <u>value type</u>.	3
object cardinality constraint	[data modeling] in ORM, (See <u>cardinality constraint</u>.)	8
object identifier	[data modeling] Term used in the object-oriented world for a system-generated attribute whose sole purpose is to identify occurrences of an <u>(object) class</u>. (See <u>surrogate identifier</u>.)	3
object model	[data modeling] a <u>data model</u> expressed in terms of (object) <u>classes</u>. If used for analysis of business objects, this is equivalent to an <u>entity/relationship model</u>. If used for design, it describes the objects to be manipulated by a computer program.	3
object model (business)	[object orientation] for <u>requirements analysis</u>, a kind of <u>data model</u>.	2, 3

objectified relationship	[data modeling] in ORM, the assertion that a relationship in fact behaves like an object. This permits it in turn to have <u>roles</u> in other relationships.	8
objective	[business rules] in the Business Rules Group's <u>Motivation Model</u>, a statement of a specific time-targeted, measurable, attainable target that an enterprise seeks to meet in order to achieve its <u>goals</u>. It quantifies a <u>goal</u>.	8
object-oriented analysis	[data modeling] requirements analysis carried out under the auspices of a project specifically to develop an object-oriented application. To do this violates the principles of requirements analysis, since, by definition, it is to identify *what* is required without specifying *how* it will be supplied.	3
object-oriented design	[data modeling] [activity modeling] an approach to designing computer programs that focuses on the things being addressed before focusing on the processes used to address them. In conventional program design, the approach is to describe a series of computer processes and attach data to these processes. In <u>object-oriented design</u>, the approach is to describe a series of things being manipulated and then to describe the processes for manipulating each one.	3
occurrence	[data modeling] an entity—an instance of an <u>entity type</u>.	3
ongoing event	[data modeling] a kind of <u>temporal event</u> that is the cyclical passage of the beginning of a day, the first day of a month, the first day of a year, and the like.	7
ODS	[data warehousing] (See <u>operational data store</u>.)	
operational data store	[data warehousing] a database used as the basis for an operational application area, such as manufacturing. It is organized according to the <u>conceptual schema,</u> but it processes operational transactions directly. This is as opposed to a <u>data warehouse,</u> which may have the same organization but is used primarily for retrievals.	3

operational response-time requirement	[project management] the requirement for the overall timing of results from a system. If this system is replacing a manual one that required a week to produce results, and if it now takes an hour to do the same thing, this is a net benefit. It is important, in evaluating response time, that the response time required to perform a function be honestly evaluated. How soon are results required, in order to achieve the function being addressed? This is different from <u>behavioral response time</u>, which is always required to be instantaneous.	2
opportunity	[business rules] in the Business Rules Group's <u>Motivation Model</u>, an <u>assessment</u> asserting that an <u>influence</u> (in this case, something in the environment) can have a favorable impact on the organization's employment of a <u>means</u> or achievement of an <u>end</u>.	8
optionality constraint	[data modeling] The assertion that an occurrence of one <u>entity type</u> must be related to at least one occurrence of another <u>entity type</u>.	3, 8
organization	1) [data modeling] a collection of people to achieve a purpose. 2) [activity modeling] in a <u>function decomposition model</u>, one of the ways a <u>function</u> may be "exploded" into other functions: Here the parent function or process is broken into the organizational units that carry out parts of it. This is clearly not a good idea, since the objective of the model is to determine what is done, not how it is done or who does it. This does not reveal the true nature of the function itself.	4
out-of-context view	[framework] John Zachman's name for the <u>builder's view</u> in Row Five of his Framework.	
output	1) [project management] data obtained from a computer system. 2) [IDEF0] the data that are produced by an <u>activity</u>.	4

overlapping (sub-types) [data modeling] a rule asserting that an occurrence of one sub-type may be an occurrence of another sub-type. (This is permitted in UML.) (This is as opposed to exclusive or disjoint sub-types.) — 3, 8, Appendix B

people and organization column (Architecture Framework Column Four) [architecture framework] the portion of the Architecture Framework that is about who is involved in the business and in the introduction of new technology. The planner's row addresses the enterprise's attitudes and philosophy concerning the management of human resources. The business owner's row is concerned specifically with the positions people hold and how they are related to each other. The architect's row addresses the fundamental nature of human organizations. This includes the interactions between people and functions. The designer's row is concerned with the design of man-machine interfaces, while the builder's row, in conjunction with the activities column, is concerned with the programming of those interfaces. — 1

people and organization model [architecture framework] a representation of an enterprise's organization and how people both work together and work with prospective systems. This is an artifact of Column Four of the Architecture Framework. — 2, 5

performance requirement [project management] a non-functional requirement that is "the actual accuracy, timing, and other measures with which a system performs its required capabilities" [Hatley et al., 2000, p. 41]. — 2

phase [project management] a major division in the system-development life cycle for the development of a system. In this book, the phases described are "Strategy", "Analysis", "Design", "Construction", "Transition", and "Production". — 2

physical data flow diagram [activity modeling] (See data flow diagram—physical.) — 2, 4

planner's view	[architecture framework] a perspective represented by Row One in the <u>Architecture Framework</u>. This is the view of the enterprise as a whole. It also defines the boundaries of specific projects to be undertaken and the relationships among them.	
position verifier	[business rules] in Ronald Ross's business-rule modeling notation, a category of business rule that requires—or tests for—occurrences of <u>entity types</u> to be created in a particular order.	8
positional data-modeling convention	[data-modeling] a convention governing the way a <u>data-model</u> diagram is organized on the page.	3
potential reward	[*business rules*] in the Business Rules Group's <u>Motivation Model</u>, an <u>impact value</u> that indicates the possibility of a gain. As with <u>risk</u> (the other kind of <u>impact value</u>), a <u>potential reward</u> may be expressed as a probability or as an absolute number.	8
predicate	1) [data modeling] a characteristic of an <u>entity type</u>. This may be either an <u>attribute</u> or a <u>relationship</u>. 2) [<u>XML</u>] piece of information about an <u>element</u>. Another <u>element</u> subordinate to this one.	3, Appendix B
primary key	1) [database design] in a relational database, the <u>unique identifier</u> of a <u>relation</u>. 2) [relational theory] the unique identifier of a <u>relation.</u>	3
priority	[strategic planning] an element of an enterprise's strategy that is something of prime importance to be achieved.	2, 8
problem space	[project management] the environment being analyzed. This includes the data, processes, organizations, and so on, of the enterprise that are the object of the analysis project. (Compare with <u>solution space</u>.)	Introduction
problematic environment	[cybernetics] in Stafford Beer's <u>viable system</u>, the environment not seen by Systems One.	5

process

[activity modeling] [cybernetics] an <u>activity</u>   4, 5
performed by an enterprise to produce a specific
<u>output</u> or achieve a <u>goal</u>. It may or may not be
described in terms of the <u>mechanisms</u> used.
<u>Processes</u> are usually represented in terms of their
timing relative to each other—either in sequence or
in parallel—and they also are usually described in
terms of their inputs and outputs. An example of a
process is "issue purchase order". Row Two
descriptions of activities are typically in terms of
processes, although processes may also be terms for
Row Three descriptions. A <u>process</u> is represented by
a round-cornered rectangle or a circle on a <u>data flow
diagram</u>.

production

[project management] the sixth phase of a <u>systems-   2
development life cycle</u>. This is an ongoing phase,
where you maintain the system, ensuring that it
continues to meet requirements. This involves fixing
bugs and adding enhancements. This is a view of the
production system (Row Six).

project manager

1) [project management] a person with   5
responsibility for successfully completing a system-
development project.
2) [knowledge management] a career category for
those who buy or lease resources from resource
providers, negotiating a budget and getting people
assigned to the project and putting them to work to
achieve a particular objective [Stewart, 1997, p. 204].

projection controller

[business rules] in Ronald Ross's business-rule   8
modeling notation, a category of <u>business rule</u> that
causes things to happen under specified
circumstances.

prototype approach

[project management] a way of developing systems   2
that involves building a small portion, trying it out,
and then improving and expanding upon it.

pseudo-code

[activity modeling] a kind of formal language for   4
describing a process. It uses key words derived from
programming and is similar in many ways to
programming languages such as Pascal or C.

recursion
1) [linguistics] (See recursion.) 5
2) [cybernetics] the concept that each system is entirely contained within a larger system.
3) [data modeling] a data-model pattern in which one occurrence of an entity type is related to another occurrence of the same entity type.

reference entity type
[data modeling] an entity type that usually refers to something tangible in the enterprise, such as PRODUCT. It may also refer to a quality (like COLOR) that is used to describe another entity type, or to a classification for other entity types, such as ACTIVITY TYPE or CONTRACT TYPE. Usually, a reference entity type is also an independent entity type. 3

referential integrity
[business rules] the constraints on a relationship that control one's ability to delete an occurrence of a parent entity (the "one" side) in a one-to-many relationship. The three rules are:
Cascade delete – deletion of parent also deletes all of that parent's children.
Restricted – deletion of parent is prohibited if that parent has children.
Nullify – deletion of parent causes the values of the join attribute (or the occurrences of the relationship implemented by that join column) for all children to be set to "null". (Allowed only if that column is optional.)

reflexive ring constraint
[data modeling] in ORM, allowance of an occurrence of an entity type to be related to itself. Prohibition of such an occurrence is called an irreflexive ring constraint. 8

relation
[relational theory] a two-dimensional array of data, consisting of rows (called tuples) and columns (called attributes). These are unique and their order is not meaningful. This is the basis for relational theory. A relation is analogous to an entity type and is usually implemented as a table with columns. 3

relational theory
[relational theory] an approach to organizing data originally proposed by Dr. E. F. Codd in 1970, which involves defining simple two-dimensional tables ("relations") and relating them explicitly to each other via common columns. 3

relationship	[data modeling] 1) a structural association between two <u>entity types</u>. (See also <u>association</u>.) 2) in ORM, two or more <u>entity types</u> playing roles with respect to each other.	3, 8, Appendix B
repeat until	[activity modeling] a kind of <u>iteration</u> in <u>pseudo-</u> <u>code</u> or <u>structured natural language</u> in which a set of operations is continued until a condition exists. The condition is tested *after* each iteration. Key words may be FOR, DO UNTIL, REPEAT UNTIL, or LOOP UNTIL. For example, a structure might be DO UNTIL amount received is greater than or equal to 1000, THEN receive shipment END DO UNTIL. In this case, the shipment of 200 units that takes the total to 1100 would be accepted, since the check is not done until after it is received.	4
repeat while	[activity modeling] a kind of <u>iteration</u> in <u>pseudo-</u> <u>code</u> or <u>structured natural language</u> in which operations are continued as long as a condition exists. The condition is tested *before* each iteration. Key words may be DO WHILE, REPEAT WHILE or LOOP WHILE. For example, a structure might be DO WHILE amount received is less than 1000, THEN receive shipment END DO WHILE. Any shipment that would take the total over 1000 would not be accepted.	4
repeating groups	[data modeling] a set of <u>attributes</u> that can take multiple values for a given <u>occurrence</u> of an <u>entity</u> <u>type</u>. This is not permitted for a relational structure in <u>First Normal Form</u>. (See also <u>multi-valued</u> <u>column</u>.)	3
required capability (for a system)	[project management] something a system must deliver. This may be either a <u>functional requirement</u> or a <u>nonfunctional requirement</u>.	2
requirement constraint (for a system)	[project management] limits the design choices available to meet one or more required capabilities. That is, you may want a system to take orders over the Internet, but there are <u>requirement constraints</u> that limit how you can go about that. These include hardware platforms available, budgetary limits, and architectural decisions previously made.	2

requirements analysis	1) [project management] the conversion of <u>business owners' views</u> of an organization to an <u>architect's view</u>, in order to determine how automation would improve the operation of the enterprise. 2) [cybernetics] the examination of an organization to determine the most effective <u>amplifiers</u> and <u>attenuators</u> to build. What is needed? How are those now in place ineffective or counterproductive? What should they look like, given the purpose and organization of the enterprise?	Introduction, 1, 2, 5
resource provider	[knowledge management] a career category for those who develop and supply talent, money, and other resources; they are the chief financial officers and chief information officers, human resource managers, temporary services firms, or heads of traditionally functioning departments like engineering and marketing [Stewart, 1997, p. 204].	5
response-time requirement	[project management] the time required for a system to react to an input and produce an output. This may be either a <u>behavioral response-time requirement</u> or an <u>operational response-time requirement</u>	2
restricted delete	[referential integrity] a rule attached to a <u>relationship</u> asserting that a parent cannot be deleted if children exist.	3, 8, Appendix B
ring constraint	[data modeling] in ORM, a constraint on the available links between occurrences of a single entity type	8
risk	[*business rules*] in the Business Rules Group's <u>Motivation Model</u>, an <u>impact value</u> that indicates the possibility of a loss. This loss could be expressed either as a probability (e.g., "5% probability of a project's failing") or as an absolute number (e.g., "There is a <u>risk</u> that we will lose $500,000 on this venture").	8
role	[data modeling] in ORM, the half of a <u>relationship</u> reading in one direction. In other words, <u>entity type</u> 1 plays a <u>role</u> with respect to entity type 2. Entity type 2 plays a complementary role with respect to entity type 1.	3

rolename	[data modeling] in ORM, a name assigned to a <u>role</u> in a <u>relationship</u>, for use in calculations using the role.	8
rule pattern	[business rules] 1) a matrix, with one row per <u>business rule</u> and columns describing a rule identifier, one or more conditions, and the effect of the rule [von Halle, 2002, pp. 316–325]. 2) a rule structure described in natural language, used to classify other business rules [Brenner et al 2002].	8
scheduled event	[time modeling] [event modeling] [activity modeling] a kind of <u>temporal event</u> that occurs at specified dates and times.	7
scope view (Framework Row One)	[architecture framework] a perspective represented by Row One in the <u>Architecture Framework</u>. This is the view of the enterprise as a whole. It also defines the boundaries of specific projects to be undertaken and the relationships among them.	Introduction, 1
Second Normal Form	[relational theory] the second of Dr. Codd's constraints on a relational design: Each attribute must be dependent on the *entire* <u>primary key</u>.	3
Second Principle of Organization	[cybernetics] a principle articulated by Stafford Beer about how an organizational system should be constructed: The four directional <u>channels</u> carrying information between the management unit, the operation, and the environment must each have a higher capacity to transmit a given amount of information relevant to variety selection in a given time than the originating subsystem has to generate it in that time [Beer, 1979, p. 99].	5
security requirement	[project management] the <u>non-functional</u> requirement that the integrity of a computer system's data and access to them be controlled. This is expressed in terms of the data's <u>confidentiality</u>, <u>availability</u>, and <u>integrity</u>.	2

selection	[event modeling] [activity modeling] in an <u>entity life</u> <u>history</u> an annotation on a set of events indicating that only one of the events in the set may occur for each occurrence of the event above. This is shown by a small circle in the upper right corner of the event box. 7
semantic data-modeling convention	[data modeling] a convention describing standard ways to represent standard business situations. (See <u>data-model pattern</u>.) 3
sequence	1) [activity modeling] a structure in <u>pseudo-code</u> or <u>structured natural language</u> that is a series of steps, one following after the other. No key words are involved. A step may be either an information-processing or a physical step. 4 2) [event modeling] in an <u>entity life history</u> an annotation that the events on a row must be encountered in the sequence shown. This is the case if there are no special markings. 3) [activity modeling] one of the ways a function may be "exploded" into other functions: This conveys the sense that <u>processes</u> are carried out as sequential steps to accomplish the parent function or process. Even if they are kept technologically neutral, there is a strong sense of the means by which the parent function is carried out.
set constraint	[data modeling] in ORM, the assertion that one relationship constrains another in some way. Includes <u>subset</u>, <u>exclusion</u>, and <u>equality constraints</u>. 8
set point	[cybernetics] a target value of a <u>variable</u> in a <u>feedback loop</u> against which values from a system are compared. If a value or a <u>variable</u> exceeds (or goes below, depending on the purpose of the set point) the set point's value, remedial action is taken. 5
single-valued attribute	[data modeling] an attribute which can take only one value for an occurrence of its corresponding <u>entity type</u>. Thus <u>single-valued attributes</u> obey the constraint of <u>First Normal Form</u>. (This is as opposed to a <u>multi-valued attribute</u>.) 3

site	[location modeling] a place on earth with a purpose, such as a home, an office, a warehouse, or an architectural dig. (This is as compared to a <u>location</u>.)	6
solution space	[project management] the set of technologies available for solving the problems identified during <u>requirements analysis</u>.	Introduction
split by type (function decomposition)	[activity modeling] one of the ways a <u>function</u> may be "exploded" into other functions: This is the case where a <u>function</u> or <u>process</u> may be carried out in more than one way. For example, the function "Fabricate product" may be done differently in each of ten different work centers. Each of these work centers is then broken out in its own right, revealing its component functions or processes. In a <u>function hierarchy</u> this is acceptable, but it is not quite the same kind of thing as a true <u>functional decomposition</u>.	4
stakeholder	[project management] someone who has a vested interest in the behavior of a system.	5
state	a condition or stage in the physical being of something.	
state/transition diagram	[time modeling] a diagram representing the set of <u>states</u> that a particular <u>entity type</u> (or part of the business, for that matter) can assume. It consists of a set of circles or round-cornered rectangles that each represent one state of the entity type. Arrows then describe the transition from one state to another. Each arrow is labeled with the <u>event</u> that causes the transition.	2, 7
strategic planning	[project management] the first phase of a <u>system-development life cycle</u>. In this phase, you lay out the vision and mission of the enterprise, along with its <u>objectives</u>, <u>priorities</u>, and <u>constraints</u>. Determine the projects that will follow. From this, you define a set of projects, carefully setting the boundaries among them so as to make the whole coherent. These boundaries then define the scope of each project. This phase is carried out from the perspective of the scope row (Row One) of the Architecture Framework.	2

strategy	1) [project management] the first phase of a systems-development life cycle. Here you do strategic planning for a system development effort. This includes defining specific projects and setting the boundaries between them. This is done from the planner's view (Row One) of the Architecture Framework. 2) [*business rules*] in the Business Rules Group's Motivation Model, a resource, skill, or competency that the enterprise can call upon—accepted by the enterprise as the *right* approach to achieve its goals, given the environmental constraints and risks.	8
strength	[*business rules*] in the Business Rules Group's Motivation Model, an assessment that asserts that an influence (an advantage or area of excellence, for example) exists within an enterprise that can have a positive impact on its employment of a means or achievement of an end.	8
structural capital	[knowledge management] the physical means by which knowledge and experience can be shared.	5
structured English	[activity modeling] your author's version of structured natural language.	
structured natural language	[activity modeling] a kind of formal language for describing a process. It is similar to pseudo-code in that it uses key words from programming but relaxes the syntax to make it more readable by the casual user.	4
sub-contractor's view	[framework] John Zachman's name for the builder's view in Row Five of his Framework.	
subject-matter expert	[project management] someone who will be interviewed during a requirements analysis project, attend modeling sessions, and so forth. This person will be the final arbiter of whether the resulting system performs its intended functions. Ideally, subject-matter experts should be high enough in the organization to provide perspective, but not so high that they are ignorant of the detailed business processes.	2

subset constraint	[data modeling] in ORM, a constraint asserting that occurrences of one relationship must be a subset of the occurrences of another relationship.	8
sub-type	[data modeling] an entity type whose occurrences are also occurrences of a more general entity type (its super-type).	3
super-type	[data modeling] an entity type whose occurrences must be in one or another of at least two other entity types (its sub-types). For example, PARTY is a super-type of PERSON and ORGANIZATION. PERSON is a sub-type of PARTY, as is ORGANIZATION. "Charlie" is a PARTY and a PERSON. "AT&T" is a PARTY and an ORGANIZATION.	3
surrogate identifier	[data modeling] an attribute whose sole function is to uniquely identify occurrences of an entity type. It is normally generated by the computer, and it has no intrinsic meaning. Usually it is never viewed by the users of a system.	3
swim lane	[activity modeling] a vertical (in a UML activity model) or horizontal (in a business-process flow diagram) portion of an activity diagram that collects the activities performed by a single person, organization, or system.	4
SWOT	[business rules] in the Business Rules Group's Motivation Model, an assessment of an influence to determine if it is a (s)trength, (w)eakness, (o)pportunity, or (t)hreat.	
symmetric ring constraint	[data modeling] in ORM, allowance of an occurrence of an entity type to be related to another occurrence that in turn is related to the first occurrence. This is a special case of the cyclic ring constraint. (Prohibition of this is an asymmetric ring constraint.)	8
synergy	[cybernetics] an increased output for a set of components, even if it means that one or more of them is less than fully productive.	5
syntactic data-modeling convention	[data modeling] a convention governing the symbols used to create a data-model diagram.	3

system	1) [project management] a collection of computer components. 2) [cybernetics] an arrangement of components *that is self-perpetuating* [Beer 1979]. This includes everything from corporations and governments to the human body.	2,5
system development life cycle	[project management] a predefined approach to developing systems, beginning with strategic planning and carrying through requirements analysis, physical design, construction, transition, and production. The specific phases vary from methodology to methodology, but the overall concept is the same: plan carefully before executing the plan.	Introduction, 2
system-development plan	[project management] a comprehensive statement of the enterprise's intended projects and their purposes, showing scope, sequence, manning, and performance criteria.	2
System Five	[cybernetics] a component of Stafford Beer's viable system that resolves differences in point of view between System Four and System Five, based on its understanding of the *identity* of the viable system. It is part of the meta-management.	5
System Four	[cybernetics] a component of Stafford Beer's viable system that communicates not with other parts of the system but with the *environment*. Note that there are really two domains in the environment that System Four must deal with. The first is the accepted environment, which is the environment already dealt with by the Systems One. The second, more important part is the problematic environment. It is in the second environment—the one not seen by Systems One—that System Four has the ability to identify the true opportunities (and risks) to the business. This is part of the meta-management	5
System One	[cybernetics] a component of Stafford Beer's viable system that is a process and a controller operating in a particular environment.	5

System Three	[cybernetics] a component of Stafford Beer's <u>viable system</u> that manages the set of Systems One to direct them to one or more corporate (metalevel) goals. Its objective is to achieve *synergy*. This is a component of <u>meta-management</u>.	5
System Two	[cybernetics] a component of Stafford Beer's <u>viable system</u> that controls oscillation between pairs of <u>Systems One</u>.	5
table	[relational theory] implementation of a <u>relation</u> or of an <u>entity type</u> in a relational <u>database management system</u>.	3
tactic	[*business rules*] in the Business Rules Group's <u>Motivation Model</u>, an <u>activity</u> or set of activities to fulfill a strategy.	8
tag	[XML] a word or phrase used to identify a portion of XML data. Identified by greater than (<) and less than (>) symbols. The tag has a definition that must be shared between the sender and the receiver of the data being transmitted.	Appendix B
talent	[knowledge management] a career category for the chemists, finance personnel, salespeople, bakers, candlestick makers (and presumably the odd system developer or two), and so forth, who actually carry out the work of the enterprise. [Stewart, 1997, p. 204].	5
technologically neutral	[project management] [activity modeling] an aspect of an operation that is true, regardless of the technology that may be employed to implement it.	2, 4
technology model	[architecture framework] (See <u>designer's view</u>.)	1
temporal event	[event modeling] [activity modeling] an <u>event</u> which is brought about by the passing of time, such as "the first day of the month", "the end of the quarter", "each morning", and so on.	7
term	[business rules] a word used in the business. Its meaning is specified in a <u>definition</u>.	8
Third Normal Form	[relational theory] the third of Dr. Codd's constraints on a relational design: Each attribute must be dependent *only* on the primary key.	3

third principle of organization	[cybernetics] a principle articulated by Stafford Beer about how an organizational system should be constructed: "Wherever the <u>information</u> carried on a <u>channel</u> (capable of distinguishing when a given variety crosses a boundary), it undergoes <u>transduction</u>; and the variety of the transducer must be at least equivalent to the variety of the channel" [Beer, 1979, p. 101].	5
threat	[*business rules*] in the Business Rules Group's <u>Motivation Model</u>, an <u>assessment</u> asserting that an influence (also something in the environment) can have an unfavorable impact on the organization's employment of a means or the achievement of an end.	8
timing column (Architecture Framework Column Five)	[architecture framework] the portion of the <u>Architecture Framework</u> that is about the effects of time on the enterprise. It is difficult to describe or address this column in isolation from the others, especially Column Two. This includes annual planning at the *scope* level, business <u>events</u> at Row Two, and data-related *events* at Row Three. Row Four translates the data-related *events* into system triggers. Row Five is concerned with the implementation of those triggers.	1, 7
training	[project management] during the <u>transition</u> phase of the system development life cycle, explaining to specific people how a new system will work. Which button do you push to do a specific action? (This is as compared with *education*.)	2
transaction entity type	[data modeling] an <u>entity type</u> whose occurrences represent events or activities in the business. These nearly always include date references as attributes. They are always <u>dependent entity types</u>.	3
transduction	[cybernetics] the translation of information as it passes to the recipient of a message.	

transition	[project management] the fifth phase of a <u>systems-development life cycle</u>. This is the establishment of a new system as part of the infrastructure of the enterprise. It involves <u>education</u>, <u>training</u>, implementation of software, and data conversion. It addresses the conversion of a set of existing <u>business owners' views</u> to a new set of <u>business owners' views</u>.	2
transitive ring constraint	[data modeling] in ORM, allowance of an <u>occurrence</u> of an <u>entity type</u> both to be related to a second occurrence of the <u>entity type</u> that in turn is related to a third occurrence of the <u>entity type</u>—and to be related to the third occurrence directly as well. (Prohibition of these occurrences is an <u>intransitive ring constraint</u>.)	8
type verifier	[business rules] in Ronald Ross's business-rule modeling notation, a category of <u>business rule</u> that requires—or tests for—occurrences of <u>entity types</u> to be mutually exclusive, mutually dependent, and the like.	8
tuple	[relational theory] Dr. Codd's name for a row in a <u>relation</u>.	
UML activity diagram	[activity modeling] A <u>data flow diagram</u> organized in terms of the actors performing the <u>activities</u>.	4
UML collaboration diagram	[activity modeling] a kind of <u>UML interaction diagram</u> that is similar to a <u>data flow diagram</u> but shows, instead of communication between <u>activities</u>, communication between objects.	4
UML interaction diagram	[activity modeling] A diagram showing the interactions between <u>activities</u> and <u>object classes</u>.	4
UML interaction diagram	[activity modeling] a representation of the interaction and communication among objects. This may be either a <u>UML sequence diagram</u> or a <u>UML collaboration diagram</u>. (Both of these diagrams are important for <u>object-oriented design</u>, but it is not clear how effective they are for analysis.)	4
UML process diagram	[activity modeling] a variation on a <u>physical data flow diagram</u> in which <u>activities</u> are organized according to the participants who perform them.	2, 4

UML sequence diagram	[activity modeling] a kind of <u>UML interaction diagram </u>that portrays a set of objects across the top of a page, showing the communications among them as a set of parallel lines.	4
UML, the	[data modeling] (See <u>Unified Modeling Language</u>)	3, 4, 8, Appendix B
Unified Modeling Language, the	[data modeling] a modeling approach comprised of several notations for representing <u>class</u> structures, <u>activities</u>, object-interactions, and <u>use cases</u>.	3, 4, 8, Appendix B
unique identifier	[data modeling] a combination of <u>relationships</u> and <u>attributes</u> whose values uniquely identify an <u>occurrence</u> of the <u>entity type</u>.	3
uniqueness constraint	[data modeling] in ORM, the assertion that an occurrence of an <u>entity type</u> may participate in a <u>role</u> no more than once. (See also <u>cardinality constraint</u>.)	
universe of discourse	[project management] the environment being analyzed. This includes the <u>data</u>, <u>activities</u>, organizations, and so on of the enterprise that are the object of the <u>requirements analysis</u> project.	Introduction
use case	[people and organization modeling] "a functional description of a system and its major processes. It also provides a graphic description of who will use the system and what kinds of interactions they can expect to have with the system" [Harmon and Watson, 1998, p. 112]. This can be a graphic model, showing an <u>activity </u>(embodied in a system) and one or more <u>actors</u>. There may be considerable documentation in addition to the drawing, however, describing the details of the interactions.	4
user	[project management] a person who operates or interacts with a computer system directly.	2, 4, 5
value constraint	[data modeling] in ORM, a list of available values for an entity type or value type.	8
value type	[data modeling] in ORM, a domain. A value type describes a kind of data, such as "date" or "amount", and can be related to entity types just like to other entity types. In fact an "attribute" of an entity type is simply a relationship to a value type.	3

variety	[cybernetics] a term from <u>cybernetics</u> that means the number of states that a situation can have. This turns out to be very good way to measure the degree of complexity of the situation. In information theory, this is also the technical definition of <u>information.</u>	5
viable system	[cybernetics] Stafford Beer's vision of a system which can sustain itself by virtue of its being in conformance with the natural laws of <u>cybernetics</u>.	5
variable	[cybernetics] [business rules] a term of reference describing something that may be given a value.	5
view	[relational theory] a relation (not necessarily following the rules of normalization) which is derived from one or more other relations.	3
vision	[business rules] in the Business Rules Group's <u>Motivation Model</u>, a statement about the future state of the enterprise, without regard to how it is to be achieved.	8
weakness	[business rules] in the Business Rules Group's <u>Motivation Model</u>, an assessment asserting that an influence (such as an area of inadequacy) exists within the enterprise that can have a negative impact on its employment of a <u>means</u> or achievement of an <u>end</u>.	8
Zachman Framework	[architecture framework] an organization of the body of systems knowledge originally developed by John Zachman. It is a matrix consisting of six rows representing different points of view held by different kinds of participants, and six columns representing the six kinds of <u>knowledge</u> held by those six sets of people.	Introduction, 1

Bibliography

Allee, V. 1997. *The Knowledge Evolution: Expanding Organizational Intelligence*. Boston: Butterworth-Heinemann, pp. 67–68.

American National Standards Institute. 1975. "ANSI/X3/SPARC Study Group on Data Base Management Systems; Interim Report." *FDT (Bulletin of ACM SIGMOD) 7:2*.

Ashby, W. R. 1956. *An Introduction to Cybernetics*. New York: John Wiley & Sons (Science Editions).

Adams, D. 1982. *The Restaurant at the End of the Universe*. New York: Pocket Books, pp. 37–38.

Ambler, S. 1999. "Mapping Objects to Relational Databases" (An Amblysoft White Paper). Newmarket, Ontario: Amblysoft, Inc.

Barker, R. 1990. *CASE*Method: Entity Relationship Modeling*. Wokingham, England: Addison-Wesley.

_____. 1989. *CASE*Method: Tasks and Deliverables*. Wokingham, England: Addison-Wesley.

_____, and Cliff Longman. 1992. *CASE Method: Function and Process Models*. Wokingham, England: Addison-Wesley.

Beer, S. 1979. *The Heart of Enterprise*. Chichester, UK: John Wiley & Sons.

Berkshire Hathaway. 1998. *Annual Report*.

Booch, G., James Rumbaugh, and Ivar Jacobson. 1999. *The Unified Modeling Language User Guide*. Reading, MA: Addison-Wesley.

Brenner, P., E. Campbell, and D. Wendelken. 2002. "Implementing Business Rules in a Java J2II and XML Environment," *Conference Proceedings, Oracle Development Tools User Group 2002 Conference*.

Brown, R. G. 1993. "Data Modeling Methodologies—Contrasts in Style." *Handbook of Data Management*. Boston: Auerbach.

Bruce, T. 1992. *Designing Quality Databases with IDEF1X Information Models*. New York: Dorset House.

Business Rules Group. 1995. "Business Rules: What Are They Really?" Available at http://www.businessrulesgroup.org

_____. 2000. "Organizing Business Plans: The Standard Model for Business Rule Motivation." Available at http://www.businessrulesgroup.org

Carlis, J., and Joseph Maguire. 2001. *Mastering Data Modeling*. Boston: Addison-Wesley.

Chen, P. 1976. "The Entity-Relationship Approach to Logical Data Base Design." *The Q.E.D. Monograph Series: Data Management*. Wellesley, MA: Q.E.D. Information Sciences, Inc. This is based on his article, "The Entity-Relationship Model: Towards a Unified View of Data," *ACM Transactions on Database Systems*, 1:1 (March 1976), 9–36.

_____ . 1977. "The Entity-Relationship Model: A Basis for the Enterprise View of Data," AFIPS Conference Proceedings, 46 (1977 National Computer Conference), 77-84. AFIPS Press, New Jersey.

Coad, P., and Edward Yourdon. 1990. *Object-Oriented Analysis*. Englewood Cliffs, NJ: Yourdon Press.

Cockburn, A. 2000. *Writing Effective Use Cases*. Reading, MA: Addison-Wesley.

Codd, E. F. 1970. "A Relational Model of Data for Large Shared Data Banks," *Communications of the ACM*, 13:6 (June).

Constantine, L. L., and Lucy A. D. Lockwood. 1999. *Software for Use*. New York: Addison-Wesley/ACM Press.

Date, C. J., 1986. *An Introduction to Database Systems*, Fourth Edition. Reading, MA: Addison-Wesley.

DeMarco, T. 1978. *Structured Analysis and System Specification*. Englewood Cliffs, NJ: Prentice Hall.

Downs, E., P. Clare, and I. Coe. 1988. *Structured Systems Analysis and Design Method*. London: Prentice-Hall.

The Economist, "When the Bull Turned." March 20, 1993.

_____, "All Fall Down," March 20, 1993.

Embley, D. W., Barry D. Kurtz, and Scott N. Woodfield. 1992. *Object-Oriented Systems Analysis: A Model-Driven Approach*. Englewood Cliffs, NJ: Yourdon Press.

English, L. P. 1999. *Improving Data Warehouse and Business Information Quality*. New York: John Wiley & Sons, Inc.

Eva, M. 1994. *SSADM Version 4: A User's Guide*, 2d ed. London: McGraw-Hill International.

Federal Information Processing Standard (FIPS). 1993. *IDEF1X Federal Information Processing Standard*. FIPS pub. 184. Dec, 1993.

Feldmann, C. G. 1998. *The Practical Guide to Business Process Reengineering Using IDEF0*. New York: Dorset House.

Finkelstein, C. 1989. *An Introduction to Information Engineering: From Strategic Planning to Information Systems*. Sydney: Addison-Wesley.

_____. 1992. Strategic Systems Development. Sydney: Addison-Wesley.

_____. 1999. Lecture. *Data Resource Management Association*, Seattle, Washington, May 1999.

Fowler, M. 1997. *Analysis Patterns*. Reading, MA: Addison-Wesley.

_____. 1999. "Is There Such a Thing as Object-Oriented Analysis?", *Distributed Computing*, October 1999. (Available at http://martinfowler.com/articles/analysis.pdf)

_____. 2000. *UML Distilled*, 2d ed. Reading, MA: Addison-Wesley.

Gane, C., and Trish Sarson. 1979. *Structured Systems Analysis: Tools and Techniques*. Englewood Cliffs, NJ: Prentice Hall.

Halpin, T. 1995. *Conceptual Schema & Relational Database Design*, 2d ed. Sydney: Prentice Hall.

_____. 2001. *Information Modeling and Relational Databases*. San Francisco: Morgan Kaufman Publishers.

Hatley, D., Peter Hruschka, and Imtiaz Pirbhai. 2000. *Process for System Architecture and Requirements Engineering*. New York: Dorset House.

Harmon, P., and Mark Watson. 1998. *Understanding UML: The Developer's Guide*. San Francisco: Morgan Kaufmann Publishers, Inc.

Hay, D. C. 1996. *Data Model Patterns: Conventions of Thought*. New York: Dorset House.

_____. Winter, 1998. "Making Data Models Readable," *Information Systems Management,* 15(1), Boca Raton, FL: CRC Press, pp. 21–33. (This article may also be found at http://www.essentialstrategies.com/publications/modeling/-makingrd.htm)

_____. 1996. "What Data Models Can't Do." Various Conferences. (Available at http://www.essentialstrategies.com/publications/businessrules/brules.htm)

Inmon, W.H., John A. Zachman, and Jonathon G. Geiger. 1997. *Data Stores, Data Warehousing and the Zachman Framework: Managing Enterprise Knowledge*. New York: McGraw-Hill.

Jacobson, I. 1992. *Object-Oriented Software Engineering: A Use Case Driven Approach*. Harlow, England: Addison-Wesley/ACM Press.

_____. 1994. *The Object Advantage: Business Process Reengineering with Object Technology.* Wokingham, England: Addison-Wesley.

_____, Grady Booch, and James Rumbaugh. 1999. *The Unified Software Development Process.* Reading, MA: Addison-Wesley.

Jackson, M. 1983. *System Development.* Englewood Cliffs, NJ: Prentice-Hall.

Kelly, K. 1998. *New Rules for the New Economy.* Harmondswoth, Middlesex: Viking.

Kersner, H. 2001. *Project Management: A Systems Approach to Planning, Scheduling, and Controlling*, 7th ed. New York: John Wiley & Sons.

Larman, C. 1998. *Applying UML and Patterns: An Introduction to Object-Oriented Analysis and Design.* Upper Saddle River, NJ: Prentice Hall PTR.

Landale, E. 2001. Letter to the author.

McMenamin, S., and John Palmer. 1984. *Essential Systems Analysis.* Englewood Cliffs, NJ: Yourdon Press.

Martin, J., and Carma McClure. 1985. *Diagramming Techniques for Analysts and Programmers.* Englewood Cliffs, NJ: Prentice Hall.

Martin, J. and Clive Finkelstein. November 1981. "Information Engineering," *Technical Report*, 2 vols. Lancs, UK: Savant Institute, Carnforth.

Merriam Webster Collegiate Dictionary. 1998. http://www.m-w.com

Microsoft Corporation. 1999. *Microsoft Windows User Experience.* Redmond, WA: Microsoft Press.

Miller, G. A. 1956. "The Magical Number Seven, Plus or Minus Two: Some Limits on Our Capacity for Processing Information," *The Psychological Review*, 63:2 (March 1956), 81–97.

Norman, D. A. 1988. *The Psychology of Everyday Things.* New York: Basic Books.

Object Management Group (OMG). 1997. "XML Metadata Interchange (XMI) Proposal to the OMG OA&DTF RFP3: Stream-based Model Interchange Format." Framingham, MA: Object Management Group, p. 4–33.

_____. 1998. "Unified Modeling Language Specification." Framingham, MA: Object Management Group. (More recent versions may be found at http://www.rational.com); (Note that UML is still being developed and new versions are often available. For the latest version, see http://www.omg.org)

Oracle Corporation. 1986. "Strategic Planning Course," SQL*Development Method. Belmont, CA.

Oracle Corporation. *Custom Development Method*, 1996.   Redwood Shores, CA: Oracle Corporation.

POSC 2000. Petrochemical Open Software Corporation data model. http://www.posc.org

Rational Software Corporation. 1997. *Unified Modeling Language Notation Guide*. Santa Clara, CA: Rational Software Corporation.

Ridderstråle, J., and Kjell Nordsröm. 2000. *Funky Business*. Harlow, UK: Pearson Education Limited.

Raiffa, H. 1968. *Decision Analysis*. Reading, MA: Addison-Wesley.

Robertson, S., and James. 1999. *Mastering the Requirements Process*. Harlow, UK: Addison-Wesley.

Robinson K., and J. Hall. 1991. *Logical Data Modeling and Process Specification*. Stamford, CT: Model Systems Consultants, Inc.

Ross, Ronald G. 1987. *Entity Modeling: Techniques and Applications*. Boston: Database Research Group.

——————. 1994. *The Business Rule Book: Classifying, Defining, and Modeling Rules*, 1st ed. Boston: Database Research Group.

——————. 1997. *The Business Rule Book: Classifying, Defining, and Modeling Rules*, 2d ed. Boston: Database Research Group.

Rumbaugh, J., Michael Blaha, William Premerlani, Frederick Eddy, and William Lorensen. 1991. *Object-Oriented Modeling and Design*. Englewood Cliffs, NJ: Prentice Hall.

Rumbaugh, J., Ivar Jacobson, and Grady Booch. 1999. *The Unified Modeling Language Reference Manual*. Reading, MA: Addison-Wesley.

Schmidt, R. 1999. *Data Modeling for Information Professionals*. Upper Saddle River, NJ: Prentice Hall PTR.

Sharp, J. 1998. "Where is the 'Engineering' in 'Information Engineering'?", *The Journal of Conceptual Modeling*, October 1998.

——————. 2000. "Natural Language Modeling Creates Precise Requirements," 12th International DAMA Conference.

Shlaer, S., and Stephen Mellor. 1988. *Object-Oriented Systems Analysis: Modeling the World in Data*. Englewood Cliffs, NJ: Prentice Hall/Yourdon Press.

Shugart, A. 1997. *Business Week*, August 25, 1997.

Simsion, G. 1994. *Data Modeling Essentials: Analysis, Design, and Innovation*. Boston: International Thomson Computer Press.

Sowa, J. F., and John A. Zachman. 1992. "Extending and Formalizing the Framework for Information Systems Architecture," *IBM Systems Journal*, 31:3. IBM Publication G321-5488.

Spewak, S. 1992. *Enterprise Architecture Planning*. New York: John Wiley & Sons, Inc.

Stewart, T. A. 1997. *Intellectual Capital*. New York: Doubleday/Currency.

Tsichritzis, D.a.D., and A.C. Klug. 1978. "The ANSI/X3/SPARC DBMS Framework Report of the Study Group on Database Management Systems." *Information Systems*. 3(3): p. 176-191.

Tufte, E. R. 1983. *The Visual Display of Quantitative Information*. Cheshire, CT: Graphics Press.

——————————. 1990. *Envisioning Information*. Cheshire, CT: Graphics Press.

——————————. 1997. *Visual Explanations*. Cheshire, CT: Graphics Press.

Von Halle, B., and David Kull, eds. 1993. *Handbook of Data Management*. Boston: Auerbach.

Von Halle, B. 1994. *Database Programming and Design* articles: "Back to the Business Rule Basics," October 1994, "Living by the Rules," November 1994, "Lessons to Learn from Tee-ball," December 1994.

——————————. 2002. *Business Rules Applied*. New York: John Wiley & Sons, Inc.

Warmer, J., and Anneke Kleppe. 1999. *The Object Constraint Language: Precise Modeling with UML*. Reading, MA: Addison-Wesley.

Wendelken, D. 2001, "Building a Business Rules Playbook," Conference Proceedings, Oracle Development Tools User Group 2001 Conference.

Wiegers, K. 1996. *Creating a Software Engineering Culture*. New York: Dorset House.

Wight, O. 1974. *Production and Inventory Management in the Computer Age*. Boston: Cahners Publishing Company, Inc.

Williams, Simon. 2000. *The Associative Model of Data*. London: Lazy Software.

Yourdon, E., and Larry L. Constantine. 1979. *Structured Design: Fundamentals of a Discipline of Computer Program and Systems Design*. Englewood Cliffs, NJ: Prentice Hall.

Zachman, J. 1987. "A Framework for Information Systems Architecture," *IBM Systems Journal*, 26:3 (IBM Publication G321-5298).

——————————. 1999. "A Revolution in Concepts," ZIFA 1999 Annual Forum, August 23–25, 1999.

Index

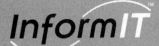

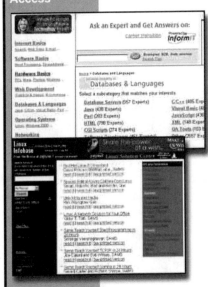